Delivery as Dispossession

Delivery as Dispossession

Land Occupation and Eviction in the Postapartheid City

ZACHARY LEVENSON

OXFORD

UNIVERSITY PRESS

OXFORD
UNIVERSITY PRESS

Oxford University Press is a department of the University of Oxford. It furthers
the University's objective of excellence in research, scholarship, and education
by publishing worldwide. Oxford is a registered trade mark of Oxford University
Press in the UK and certain other countries.

Published in the United States of America by Oxford University Press
198 Madison Avenue, New York, NY 10016, United States of America.

© Oxford University Press 2022

CIP data is on file at the Library of Congress

ISBN 978-0-19-762925-3 (pbk.)
ISBN 978-0-19-762924-6 (hbk.)

DOI: 10.1093/oso/9780197629246.001.0001

In memory of Michael Blake (1954–2017),
who knew well that laughter is
inseparable from struggle

South Africa as a concrete totality is an entity whose diverse populations are bound together against their wills, in such a way that any one of them considered separately is an abstraction. It is not an aggregate sum of its parts. The urban-industrial areas provide an empirical confirmation of this assertion.

—Bernard Makhosezwe Magubane

If every State tends to create and maintain a certain type of civilisation and of citizen (and hence of collective life and of individual relations), and to eliminate certain customs and attitudes and to disseminate others, then the Law will be its instrument for this purpose.

—Antonio Gramsci

Contents

Contents

Figures

Preface

Dispossession: under apartheid, 3.5 million Black South Africans were forcibly removed from their places of residence, relegated either to distant rural areas or to remote townships on the outskirts of the city. *Delivery*: since the end of apartheid in 1994, South Africa's first democratic government has delivered roughly four million houses to those in need. Unfortunately, this neat periodization does not do us any analytic favors. The government's housing delivery program began under apartheid, and it was only in building new housing on the periphery that dispossession was able to proceed unabated. And today, the postapartheid government regularly evicts both individuals and, more commonly, entire settlements—typically in the name of protecting its housing delivery program from those who refuse to wait their turn. Both under apartheid and since, delivery and dispossession have gone hand in hand, the one enabling the other. The trick is not to map them onto mutually distinct historical epochs but to understand how the two concepts work together in novel ways in each period.

Delivery as Dispossession makes three interrelated arguments along these lines. First, it tries to understand why a government that stakes its very legitimacy on reversing the damage wrought by centuries of apartheid, segregation, and colonialism evicts new land occupations and dispossesses residents on a regular basis. This book argues that it does so because, by labeling land occupations as disorderly and distinct from other residents who wait patiently, housing officials believe that dispossession enables delivery. This first argument, then, is about how government actors see residents. Most of the literature on mass evictions focuses on land grabs, development projects, and real estate profits,[1] but the logic of evictions in postapartheid South Africa is notably different: rather than economic, it is political. Under apartheid, the government built many hundreds of thousands of houses to which it could forcibly relocate Black residents living in cities. In other words, *delivery enabled dispossession*.

After apartheid, the relationship between these two state-initiated processes was reversed: today, housing officials believe that *dispossession enables delivery*. However, dispossession does not ultimately enable delivery, but instead reproduces the problem anew, driving residents lacking alternative options to occupy land yet again. The crucial point here is that housing officials *think* that dispossession enables delivery, and this is the primary rationale for evictions today. The postapartheid government has provided millions of homes to needy residents since 1994, registering countless others on a waiting list. However, the scale of this need vastly outstripped the state's capacity to deliver, and the housing backlog—those in need of housing— remained constant or actually increased in most major municipalities. This meant that residents had to provide for themselves in the meantime, and they did: by occupying land. But rather than a consequence of the state's failure to deliver, these new occupations tend to be read by housing officials as its cause. They are evicted, paradoxically, in the name of protecting delivery, even if these evictions accomplish no such thing.

Ultimately, housing officials frame occupations as inherently disorderly, making the case to judges that housing delivery requires residents who wait patiently rather than "jumping the queue" and seizing housing on the spot. But not all occupations are evicted. Under which conditions, then, do they tend to be read as disorderly? This brings me to the second argument advanced in this book, which moves us from how state actors see residents to how residents see the state.[2] How they see the state impacts how organizers articulate the project of occupation, which shapes the organizational form assumed by its participants. This organizational form, in turn, affects how the state sees them. When, for example, initiators frame an occupation as if it were a social movement, they may do so for a variety of reasons. In one of the cases considered in this book called Siqalo, organizers united residents under a single leadership because they had a history of clashing with government actors, whom they viewed as an obstacle to their project of attaining housing, and they saw unity as essential to resisting state violence.

But in a second case considered here called Kapteinsklip, organizers framed their occupation quite differently: as the legitimate distribution of plots to needy residents. In this case, participants comported themselves as atomized recipients of housing. They participated in the occupation simultaneously, but they did not do so collectively, and their leadership quickly fragmented into competing factions. This contrast is crucial to making sense of eviction outcomes. We might expect a wary municipality to view the collective actors, rather than the atomized squatters, as the more substantial threat. But this book demonstrates that the opposite tends to be the case. Interacting with housing officials, lawyers, police, and judges through the mediation of an agreed-upon leadership makes the occupation appear orderly; while fragmenting into competing factions makes the occupation appear disorderly and, therefore, a threat to the order required for delivery. Siqalo was tolerated, but Kapteinsklip was evicted.

This is not to suggest some one-to-one correspondence between organizational form and eviction outcome. After all, we do need to understand the conditions under which one organizational form prevails over another. If this form is shaped by the way organizers articulate their collective project, we need to ask how these articulations come into being in the first place. This book argues that leaders' social visions are informed by their respective understandings of the state. In the case of Siqalo, leaders articulated an occupation as a collective action because they viewed the state as an antagonist and mobilized accordingly. In Kapteinsklip, participants viewed the state as a partner in delivery rather than an agent of dispossession. In both cases, how residents saw the state affected how they mobilized, which shaped how they were seen by the state. States may "see" populations, but residents can shape how they themselves are "seen." Yet their ability does not exist in a vacuum; it is itself informed by how organizers "see" the state. As should be evident, the state's vision, much like residents' vision, emerges through complex engagements, interactions, and struggles with antagonists. How the state sees populations, in other words, should not be our constant point of departure, but an outcome in its own right.

The law is the primary terrain upon which these struggles play out. South Africa's 1996 constitution was among the first in the world to guarantee "access to adequate housing" and freedom from "arbitrary evictions."[3] But in practice, this is incorrect: the constitution only guarantees access to housing insofar as the state can "achieve the progressive realisation of this right" by "tak[ing] reasonable ... measures, within its available resources." While this might seem like splitting hairs, it is an enormously consequential point. The determination as to when the local state has the responsibility to provide housing, as well as when it can legally evict people, is made in the courtroom, and often province-level High Court judges have the final say: each eviction requires "an order of court ... after considering all the relevant circumstances." This means that how occupiers collectively appear in the courtroom shapes judges' decision-making. As the later chapters of this book demonstrate, when an occupation appears orderly, with a functioning self-government and little to no visible factionalism, judges are more likely to view it as a deserving population in need of housing. But when an occupation appears fractured into contending factions, judges are more likely to read its participants as greedy opportunists undeserving of toleration.

This connection is not straightforward to occupiers, whose collective appearances are not generated intentionally. Rather, they are unintended consequences of strategies designed for very different ends. In neither case did occupiers mobilize to communicate with government actors; in both, they hoped to fly below the state's radar. But regardless, both occupations quickly found themselves in dialogue with the state, and more precisely, with legal representatives on the floor of the courtroom. This is the book's third argument: while certainly progressive in guaranteeing socioeconomic rights, the constitutional guarantee to housing nevertheless forces occupiers onto the government's terrain. This is a textbook instance of hegemony, "the process by means of which social forces are integrated into the political power of an existing state":[4] occupiers' interest in securing official toleration is integrated into property's interest in adjudicating all land disputes in the courts. Of course, when occupations begin, participants are rarely concerned with toleration as such; they are typically far more interested in eluding the state altogether and straightforwardly taking the land that they need. Nevertheless, in nearly every case, residents find themselves arguing for their moral legitimacy in a courtroom.

As the historian Barbara Fields succinctly puts it, "Exercising rule means being able to shape the terrain."[5] And shaping the terrain is precisely what the 1996 constitution did: it turns out that both the right to delivery and freedom from dispossession are qualified, and it is up to the courts to adjudicate. All housing struggles therefore inevitably find themselves squabbling over this or that policy through legal intermediaries rather than straightforwardly appropriating land and defending it directly. Constitutional rights then are a double-edged sword. Surely the right to housing is progressive, but it absolutely, to borrow the Comaroffs' turn of phrase, "judicializes" politics,[6] shifting all substantive debates onto a terrain shaped and controlled by government actors. And this terrain is, ultimately, about language:[7] "Forms and languages of protest or resistance," the late anthropologist William Roseberry insisted, "*must* adopt the forms and languages of domination in order to be registered or heard."[8] But as soon as they translate their demands into this obligatory idiom, they find themselves no longer in protest or resistance, but in dialogue.

"Lastly," to quote the late South African revolutionary Neville Alexander, "it is perhaps also necessary to comment on the use of inverted commas around words denoting groups of people."[9] Throughout this book, racial categories appear in scare quotes, especially the apartheid holdovers "Colored" and "African." This may be awkward, but it is far less awkward than qualifying these descriptors upon their every occurrence. Many of the people appearing throughout this book, for example, would regularly refer to themselves as "*so-called* Colored," or else simply as "Black," but as will become clear, there is a real analytical need to disaggregate this catch-all, which tends to include all nonwhite South Africans. As Alexander shows, this racial schema has its origins in a very specific brand of Afrikaner sectionalism, itself emerging against the backdrop of British imperial expansion into Africa. Hence our predicament: how to describe these distinct conceptual categories, which absolutely inform people's thoughts, desires, and actions, without further entrenching this pernicious classificatory scheme designed to aid imperial expansion? Unfortunately, this is the predicament of discussing race itself in any context. If the scare quotes appear awkward and even tedious, good: that is their intended function.

The relational theory of the state developed in this book is transportable far beyond South Africa, or even cases of housing delivery. It is a theory that insists that the state is not an airtight institutional space with the power to rule, but rather a site of ongoing contestation. On the one hand, this means that mass pressure impacts policy outcomes, and we therefore need to move beyond the notion that the state is fully autonomous, or that the actions of marginalized people do not impact governmental decisions. On the other, it means that popular struggles are often absorbed into the state, containing them in the process. Those who find themselves in dialogue with government actors often never meant to engage on this terrain. This is precisely what hegemony entails.

Acknowledgments

When I arrived in Cape Town for the first time just over a decade ago, I encountered someone who transformed my understanding of housing struggles. This was Michael Blake, then a researcher at the International Labour Research and Information Group (ILRIG), an NGO that emerged from the anti-apartheid union movement of the 1980s. Mike was himself a leader in a number of groups at the time, not least among them the Cape Areas Housing Action Committee (CAHAC), one of the first organizations active in the United Democratic Front (UDF), the most effective alliance in the subsequent defeat of apartheid. Once the ancien régime fell, many of Mike's erstwhile comrades hung up their red T-shirts, whereas he decided he would be buried in his. A decade after the transition, he played a key role in Cape Town's Anti-Eviction Campaign, and once that group deteriorated, he worked tirelessly to build the Housing Assembly, which remains active today. Mike was an organizer's organizer, more interested in facilitating self-organization than imparting this or that correct position to an impossibly passive crowd. I last saw him in early August 2017 when we spent hours on his couch debating the #FeesMustFall movement then multiplying across South Africa's campuses. The next day, I flew back to California, where I was completing my dissertation. Just over a month later, he unexpectedly passed away from a heart attack, not yet sixty-five. Mike's impact on this project cannot be overstated. It is to him that I dedicate this book.

There are, of course, countless others without whom this project would be inconceivable. I owe a debt of gratitude to all of the pseudonymous participants in both land occupations, as well as to those whom I can name here: Faeza Meyer and Ebrahiem Fourie. It is unfortunately rare for organic intellectuals to be both of and for the class, but Faeza and Ebrahiem are undoubtedly both. I love you and your kids (and now grandkids!) like family. I also want to thank members of the Housing Assembly, including Kashiefa Achmat, Yolanda Anderson, Fuad Arnold, Meagan Biggs, Joann Cupido, Stephane Frederiks, Evelyn Greeves, Eleanor Hoedemaker (RIP), Bevel Lucas, Amanda Makolwa (RIP), Xolile Masoqoza, Kenneth Matlawe, Thembelani Maqwazima, Eve Muller, Charney Paulse, Sharol van Reenen, and many others who taught me about the landscape of housing struggle in Cape Town.

Back in Berkeley, where this book began as a dissertation, there are two people who played an outsized role in its development. Michael Burawoy taught me what it means to be a social theorist and an ethnographer at the same time, without needing to sacrifice one for the other. He makes me proud to call myself a sociologist, and his influence should be apparent throughout this book. The feedback I received in Michael's dissertation group made those bimonthly gatherings easily the best experience of my graduate school career, and I am thankful to all its participants over the years: Andy Chang, Julia Chuang, Siri Colom, Herbert Docena, Fidan Elcioglu, Aya Fabros, Elise Herrala, Shannon Ikebe, Andrew Jaeger, Thomas Peng, Josh Seim, Ben Shestakofsky, and Shelly Steward. The second person at Berkeley who shaped this book until the very end was Gillian Hart, who taught me everything I know about thinking relationally. If it was Michael's job to make sure I developed coherent concepts, it was Gill's job to explode every last one of them. In writing this book, whether they know it or not, I consistently filtered my thinking through the dialectic of Michael and Gill. Both are not only model scholars, but exemplary pedagogues, cothinkers, and friends.

Many others at Berkeley shaped my thinking. Dylan Riley taught me most of what I know about rigor, and it was at Michael Watts's suggestion that I began working on South Africa. Cihan Tuğal took my political sociology mold and smashed it to bits. I also owe thanks to Sharad Chari, Laura Enriquez, Peter Evans, Tom Gold, Jean Lave, John Lie, Mara Loveman, Raka Ray, Nancy Scheper-Hughes, Ann Swidler, and Loïc Wacquant for feedback and advice along the way. Mostly, though, it was my fellow graduate students who made Berkeley such a formative experience for me. I cannot imagine surviving the program without the friendship of Edwin Ackerman, Katy Fox-Hodess, Elise Herrala, Kate Maich, Fithawee Tzeggai, and Gowri Vijayakumar. And in addition to those who were a part of Michael's dissertation group, I want to thank Amanda Armstrong-Price, Nina Aron, Diego Arrocha, Laleh Behbehanian, Shane Boyle, Ryan Calder, Julia Chang, Erin Collins, Sanders Creasy, Alex Dubilet, Barry Eidlin, Eli Friedman, Chris Herring, Gabriel Hetland, Graham Hill, Jessie Hock, Daniel Immerwahr, Carter Koppelman, Mike Levien, Allison Logan, Geo Maher, Jordanna Matlon, Patricia Munro, Dan Nemser, Shaun Ossei-Owusu, Tianna Paschel, Gretchen Purser, Manuel Rosaldo, John Stehlin, Becky Tarlau, Erin

Torkelson, and Josh Williams. And a special shout goes to Marcel Paret, who remains my go-to interlocutor when it comes to South African politics.

I am incredibly lucky to teach at an institution with such a vibrant crop of junior professors. While I am thankful to all my colleagues at the University of North Carolina, Greensboro, who have been incredibly supportive, I particularly want to thank Şahan Karataşli, Şefika Kumral, and Tad Skotnicki for feedback on portions of this manuscript, and Sarah Daynes and Dave Kauzlarich for encouragement along the way. In addition to Michael, who miraculously found the time to read a draft during finals week, only one other person heroically read my manuscript in its entirety: Tad. He was so generous with his criticism, in fact, that I nearly wrote a second book typing it all up. I also want to thank Edwin Ackerman, Mathieu Desan, Gillian Hart, Elise Herrala, and Gowri Vijayakumar for commenting on assorted chapters. My series editor Javier Auyero and Oxford editors James Cook and Emily Benitez have made the publishing process remarkably painless, and I am grateful for their support. I also received helpful comments from anonymous reviewers, one of whom has since revealed herself to me as María José Álvarez Rivadulla. Thank you.

In Cape Town, I owe special thanks to my ILRIG family, the NGO where Mike worked. While I was never formally affiliated, a number of ILRIG researchers allowed me to plunder their library, use their offices, and attend their events over the past decade. In addition to Mike, I am especially grateful to Koni Benson, Judy Kennedy, and Anele Selekwa. Elsewhere in Cape Town, as well as in Durban and Johannesburg, I want to thank interlocutors at various stages of this project: Kate Alexander, Richard Ballard, Patrick Bond, Liza Cirolia, Owen Crankshaw, Des D'sa, Mashumi Figlan, Ben Fogel, Faizal Garba, Disha Govender, Lunga Guza, Martin Jansen, Mazibuko Jara, Steve Kahanowitz, Bridget Kenny, Martin Legassick (RIP), Charlotte Lemanski, Mike Louw (RIP), Thembi Luckett, Andre Marais, Bandile Mdlalose, Nate Millington, Mark Misselhorn, Adrian Murray, Prishani Naidoo, Mnikelo Ndabankulu, Trevor Ngwane, Lungisile Ntsebeza, Mazwi Nzimande, Mosa Phadi, Leo Podlashuc, Max Rambau, Niall Reddy, Carin Runciman, Jared Sacks, Melanie Samson, Suraya Scheba, Luke Sinwell, Kate Tissington, Steve Topham, Erin Torkelson, and Ahmed Veriava. There are also two figures who deserve special mention: Marie Huchzermeyer, whose writing influenced this project more than she probably realizes, and Sophie Oldfield, who reminds me by example of what an engaged researcher should be. And finally, I am grateful to the librarians staffing the African Studies Book Collection at the University of Cape Town, who always knew where to find whatever it is I was looking for, and to the staff at Clarke's Bookshop, in which I spent more hours than I care to admit.

For additional engagement, I want to thank Jenn Bair, Franco Barchiesi, Robert Brenner, Merlin Chowkwanyun, Loren Goldner, Kate Doyle Griffiths, Kevan Harris, Phil Hough, Ricado Jacobs, Sean Jacobs, Heinz Klug, Richard Lachmann (RIP), Anne-Maria Makhulu, Nick Mitchell, Sylvia Pasquetti, Giovanni Picker, Maddy Rolka, Gay Seidman, David Stein, Thea Tagle, Nantina Vgontzas, Lise Vogel, Shannon Walsh, and Suzi Weissman. I also owe special acknowledgment to Gerald Sanders in Oakland, who first introduced me to the Ravan Press back catalog sometime in 2010. Gerald was a key organizer of the International Longshore and Warehouse Union's 1985 Bay Area port shutdown against apartheid, and I learned as much debating around his kitchen table a few nights per week as I did in any seminar room. And finally, thanks go to my coeditors at *Spectre* for sharpening my political thinking over the past couple of years: Amanda Armstrong-Price, Cinzia Arruzza, Tithi Bhattacharya, Kate Doyle Griffiths, Aaron Jaffe, Holly Lewis, David McNally, Charlie Post, Ashley Smith, and Vanessa Wills.

I owe more than they probably think I do to my parents, Jim and Janet, my sisters Carly and Zoe, my brother-in-law Joe, my sister-out-of-law Emma, and my nephew Isaac for putting up with my mishegoss over the last decade and a half. And to Astrid, who cannot possibly understand what she means to me: I promised I would calm down as soon as this book was out; now I finally can.

Abbreviations

AEC	Anti-Eviction Campaign
ALIU	Anti-Land Invasion Unit
ANC	African National Congress
BRICS	Brazil, Russia, India, China, South Africa
CAHAC	Cape Areas Housing Action Committee
DA	Democratic Alliance
DHS	Department of Human Settlements
EFF	Economic Freedom Fighters
GIS	Geographic Information System
IEC	Independent Electoral Commission
ILRIG	International Labour Research and Information Group
KZN	KwaZulu-Natal
LHR	Lawyers for Human Rights
LRC	Legal Resources Centre
MDM	Mass Democratic Movement
MK	uMkhonto weSizwe ["Spear of the Nation"]
MPBDA	Mitchells Plain Backyard Dwellers' Association
MPHA	Mitchells Plain Housing Association
NGO	nongovernmental organization
NHF	National Housing Forum
NP	National Party
PAC	Pan Africanist Congress of Azania
PIE	Prevention of Illegal Eviction from and Unlawful Occupation of Land Act of 1998
PISA	Prevention of Illegal Squatting Act
PRASA	Passenger Rail Agency of South Africa
PT	Partido dos Trabalhadores ["Workers' Party"] (Brazil)
RDP	Reconstruction and Development Programme
SACP	South African Communist Party
SANCO	South African National Civil Organization
SANZAF	South African National Zakáh Fund
SAPS	South African Police Service
SCA	Supreme Court of Appeal
SERI	Socio-Economic Rights Institute
SMS	short message service
SPRM	Ses'khona People's Rights Movement

TRA	temporary relocation area
TRU	Tafelsig Residents United
UDF	United Democratic Front
UN	United Nations
ZAWCHC	Western Cape High Court

1

Two Occupations, One Eviction

Faeza sat on her sleeping bag on the floor of her structure—calling it a shack would be generous. It was more of an improvised tent really. Every morning, just after dawn, she and her husband Ebrahiem would disassemble the thing, pulling off the plastic tarp, breaking down the wooden scaffolding, and gathering their few belongings for storage behind some nearby bushes. But the evenings were her brief respite; no cops, no government officials, just her and Ebrahiem lounging in bed. Granted, it was not much: the police had long since repossessed their best building materials, and they were only left with scraps. But it was something.

Faeza had not yet changed out of her sweatshirt and jeans for the night—she was too eager to begin recording the day's events. It was only recently that she began keeping a diary, and now it was an obsession. She nervously flicked her false upper teeth in and out with her tongue as she tightened the bright red scarf wrapped around her hair. Ebrahiem shot her a smile, his bearded underbite filling in his own missing upper teeth, as he took a drag from the joint he had just rolled in a page from the phone book. He loved watching her deep in thought. Faeza began to write:

> They arrived at 10:30 am. Taking all our wood and plastic, leaving only the small tent. Once again, no name tags, no response when we asked for names either. Last night someone from Law Enforcement came around and told us to break down our structures before 7 am and he promised nothing will be taken.
>
> Yet today, they still come and take our things. Our people are being pushed into a corner and not allowed to move freely on the field while they move around us like we are ghosts.
>
> It's sad when they leave. It feels like we have been robbed once again. 26 days for us to go to court. That means another 26 days of being robbed.
>
> We have no shelter. No food. No water. And soon, no hope. They even took the wood we use for fire. What's even more depressing is that they

Delivery as Dispossession. Zachary Levenson, Oxford University Press. © Oxford University Press 2022.
DOI: 10.1093/oso/9780197629246.003.0001

threw the holes our people live in closed with sand—not even giving us the opportunity to remove our clothes and our other belongings.[1]

Faeza and Ebrahiem were among the more fortunate residents occupying the field. Their neighbors, Victor and Kayla, lived with their toddler son quite literally as Faeza described it: "the holes our people live in" (see figure 1.1). Having lost all their building materials, save for a couple of wooden planks, they dug a cave into the sandy earth of the field and used their remaining boards as a roof of sorts. But even this was too much. Every morning, the police would return and confiscate anything they could before kicking piles of freshly dug sand back into the holes. They seemed to relish the agitation it would cause, Victor pleading as he anxiously shook his cropped dreadlocks, Kayla trying to keep him calm.

All of them had been on the field for nearly two months by that point. Every morning it was the same drill: break down their structures and hide their belongings before the cops arrived. In less than a month, they would finally have their day in court, along with 150 or so other occupiers. But until

Figure 1.1 One of "the holes our people live in," Kapteinsklip occupation, 2011.
Credit line: Still from camcorder footage shot by Ebrahiem Fourie.

then, there was not much they could do. Even if police were illegally stealing their few possessions or plainly harassing them, what legal recourse did they have?

Kapteinsklip

The occupation took place on a field called Kapteinsklip, located in a township called Mitchells Plain, about twenty-five kilometers from downtown Cape Town (see figure 1.2). Cape Town is South Africa's second largest city, and the majority of its residents live on the sandy plains of the Cape Flats, which includes Mitchells Plain. As in most cities in South Africa, "outskirts" tend to be *townships*: urban areas reserved for any population defined as "nonwhite" under apartheid. While apartheid has of course been over for more than a quarter century, racial segregation persists,[2] albeit unevenly,[3] and is particularly egregious in this city[4]—surpassed only by Durban and Port Elizabeth[5] in degree. When South Africans use the term "township" today, they are referring to these highly segregated areas, which rarely contain a significant number of white residents, if any at all.

Townships also tend to be primarily inhabited by members of a single racial group, of which there were officially four under apartheid: white, "Asian," "Colored," and "African." Mitchells Plain remains the largest "Colored" township in the country, and it is Cape Town's second largest township overall, with a population of over 625,000. It is on the eastern border of Mitchells Plain that the Kapteinsklip occupation took place. In the immediate vicinity of this field, there is not much in the way of middle-class housing. There are a few working-class homes constructed by the late apartheid state a few minutes' walk from the field and quite a few more another couple hundred meters away, but it would be a stretch to claim that Kapteinsklip abuts a sizable residential area. Plus, the homes that are nearby are located in the poorest section of the poorest ward in the entire township.

Kapteinsklip is also fairly out of sight (see figure 1.3). The final mile on the way there is flanked by overgrown fields on both sides. These serve as buffers between a nature reserve along the southern coast and the residential area above the road, but it could hardly be construed as a major thoroughfare. The only reason there is a road at all is so that taxis can pick up passengers returning on the Metrorail, Cape Town's commuter railway. Kapteinsklip was the final stop on Metrorail's Mitchells Plain line. The train

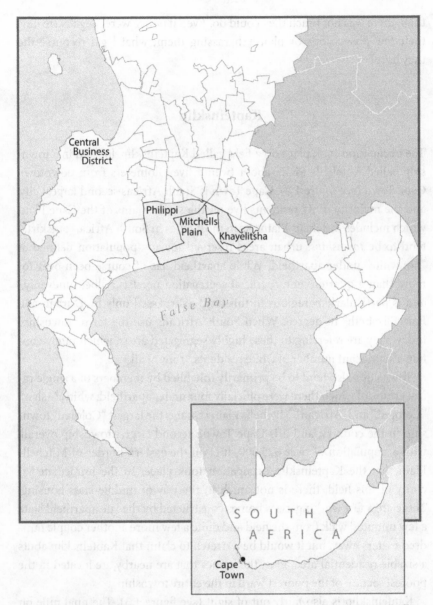

Figure 1.2 Map of the city of Cape Town. Note the distance between Mitchells Plain and the central business district.

Credit line: By Alicia Cowart.

Figure 1.3 Satellite photograph of Kapteinsklip, December 2012. Note the location of the field in relation to the Metrorail station and its distance from any major roads.
Credit line: City Maps, City of Cape Town.

was constantly late, if not entirely out of service. A recent headline captured it quite aptly: "Metrorail's Own Stats Show How Bad Its Service Is."[6] These were certainly not commuters who were going to complain if the adjacent field was not properly maintained.

And so it should come as no surprise that there was no immediate outcry when a thousand squatters moved onto the Kapteinsklip plot in the early hours of a chilly autumn morning. None of the structures that they erected impeded the railroad tracks, nor did they come particularly close to doing so: there was a good distance between their shacks and the station. Their neighbors in the formal houses a few hundred meters away did not seem to mind either. They certainly did not demand their removal in any case.

Faeza and her husband Ebrahiem were among this group of squatters. He was just a few years older than she was, and like her, he grew up in a formal house in Mitchells Plain. They wound up in this township after each spending their respective childhoods in a neighborhood called District Six. Adjacent to Cape Town's central business district, it was once the cultural heart of "Colored" life.[7] But in 1966, the neighborhood was declared an exclusively white zone in accordance with the 1950 Group Areas Act.[8] Apartheid was the project of the National Party, which had just come to power two years earlier. The 1950 act was the first of three major laws that would comprehensively remake South Africa's urban landscape. Black[9] residents were forcibly expelled to townships, with the most developed and centrally located land reclaimed exclusively for white use. This included District Six, and nearly every one of its residents was forcibly relocated to newly constructed townships on the Cape Flats. Between 1968 and 1982, sixty thousand "Colored" residents were evicted from this neighborhood and resettled in townships, Mitchells Plain the largest among them. Today, nearly two-thirds of Capetonians live on the Flats.

Their parents' homes quickly grew overcrowded as Faeza and her siblings started families of their own, but without any subsidized housing comparable to what their parents received. In theory they were eligible for the government's formal housing distribution program, but they had all been on the waiting list for many years. They could only wait so long.[10] Frustrated with the lack of space, Faeza and Ebrahiem obtained a plywood structure from a friend and set it up in Faeza's parents' backyard—a space just large enough to park three small cars. But this arrangement quickly grew overcrowded as well, and besides, neither of them wanted to live in someone else's yard. It made them feel dependent. "We wanted a home," Faeza later explained to me. "We didn't want to be by my ma and pa any longer. We wanted *our* place." Their motivation was dignity. Of course, Faeza's participation in the Kapteinsklip occupation meant that her housing would become more precarious for the year, but this was not the point. She wanted a place of her own to demonstrate her worthiness as a parent.

When they joined the Kapteinsklip occupation, they were part of an overwhelmingly "Colored" group of backyarders trying to secure new homes—or at least land upon which to build informal housing. The bulk of them came from backyards in the surrounding area, or else in Faeza and Ebrahiem's neighborhood, both of which were mostly "Colored." Of course, there was no legal ban on "African"[11] residents moving into a predominantly "Colored" area, but there was quite a bit of anti-"African" sentiment in these areas. But the Kapteinsklip occupation remained overwhelmingly "Colored," and no one protested the occupation. Formally housed residents did not even voice a demand for eviction in class terms, namely, as homeowners protecting their property value.

Nor did residents articulate their opposition in partisan terms. In Cape Town, the overwhelming majority of "Colored" voters support the Democratic Alliance (DA), the African National Congress's chief rival. While the ANC has retained power over the national government since the transition to democracy in 1994, it began to lose municipalities in the 2000s. Cape Town was the first major municipality to fall, with the DA ruling in coalition in 2006 and with a clear majority by 2009. Also by 2009, the party had gained control of the Western Cape government, the province in which Cape Town is located. And after the 2016 local elections, the DA came to power in four of the nation's six largest municipalities. More generally, the ANC's share of the national vote slipped below 60 percent for the first time, so tensions run high.[12]

Sometimes land occupations are an attempt to gerrymander in reverse, shifting populations instead of ward boundaries. Political operatives try to transfer their voters into another party's territory to affect election outcomes. If a large number of "African" squatters were to suddenly move onto the Kapteinsklip field, for example, DA party operatives might assume that an ANC front group had convinced a group of potential supporters to accept land in exchange for votes. DA-affiliated ward councilors and other local officials might then try to mobilize their supporters against the occupiers, excoriating them as ANC voters. More than 80 percent of the population of the ward in which Kapteinsklip is located voted for the DA in the last election; this was firmly DA territory. While many of the Kapteinsklip occupiers were less firm in their support for one party or another than those living in formal homes, no one would mistake a field full of "Colored" residents born and raised in this township for ANC supporters. There was little reason to believe that they posed some sort of political threat, at least in partisan terms.

The combination of all these factors makes Kapteinsklip an unlikely candidate for eviction, or so we would assume. It was hardly visible to passersby, and in any case the land was municipally owned; no homeowners mobilized against the squatters; the occupiers were predominantly "Colored" in a "Colored" area; and there was no reason to suspect that they were not DA supporters moving around within DA territory. But early on the second morning of the occupation, a sheriff arrived on the field in a police truck. "You are here illegally!" he barked through his vehicle's bullhorn, addressing the thousand squatters living under makeshift structures. "Everyone has five minutes to vacate the land!" As he read out the eviction order, armored vehicles began to surround the settlement, both from the city's Anti-Land Invasion Unit (ALIU) and the South African Police Service.

A month into the occupation, there were only 150 or so residents left on the field, but they were resolute: they were not going anywhere. One appeal after another meant that court dates were perpetually delayed, and residents began to squabble over access to their lawyer and other resources. The unity that Faeza described in the face of police violence soon dissipated.

At the same time, this atomization was there from the outset. The group that organized the occupation had framed the thing as land distribution rather than some kind of collective action. "They didn't use those words, 'land invasion,'" Faeza explained. "They told us we were going to get plots." The group took down everyone's name and identification number, providing them with an official-looking piece of paper with a number on it corresponding to a plot. The occupiers did not understand themselves as active organizers but as passive recipients. In a perverse way, even an illegal occupation like Kapteinsklip emulated the formal rationality of the government waiting list, with participants receiving land rather than taking it. Sure, they occupied the land together, but in the way people wait in line for a bus together: "The mode of life occasions *isolated behaviour* in everyone."[13]

And this is how the municipal government's chief lawyer framed the occupiers, though he invoked a less neutral term: opportunists. He repeatedly dismissed them as "queue jumpers," suggesting that they were not patiently waiting their turn for housing. Each municipality ran a housing waiting list, and if residents just waited long enough, he suggested, they would eventually gain access to formal homes. They participated in a land occupation not because they lacked other options, but because they were attempting to force the municipal government to include them in a new formal housing project. Of course, none of the Kapteinsklip squatters framed it to me in this way. Most of them legitimately appeared to want the city to leave them be. They were not asking for formal housing, but simply wanted access to land upon which they could erect their shacks. Yet by constituting themselves in multiple contending factions, the municipality and, ultimately, three different High Court judges dismissed them as disorderly obstacles to the realization of the city's housing program. They were evicted from the field. Faeza, Ebrahiem, and their 150 neighbors had to evacuate Kapteinsklip immediately, lest they face arrest.

Siqalo

As far as land occupations go, Kapteinsklip was not a likely candidate for eviction. It was far flung, out of sight, and located on public land, and the composition of its residents posed no threat to the established social order in the neighborhood. No one in the immediate vicinity demanded their removal, and there was no indication that their encroachment changed political dynamics in their ward. But maybe judges authorize the evictions of all new land occupations in South African cities?

Far from it: sometimes occupations are tolerated and gain the right to stay put. This was the case in Siqalo. Within a year of Kapteinsklip occupation, a second group of squatters set up shop less than a mile westward in the same township (see figure 1.4). Unlike Kapteinsklip, which was on public land, the Siqalo occupation straddled two different plots of private property: one was held by an absentee landlord, and the other was used by a sand-mining company to dump waste. Kapteinsklip was peripheral and out of sight, but this

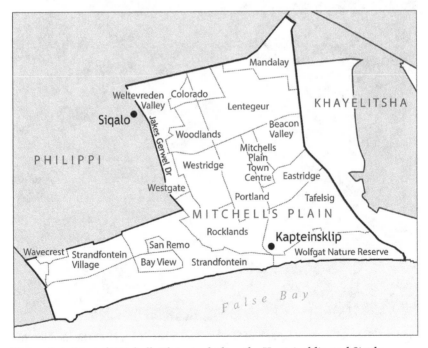

Figure 1.4 Map of Mitchells Plain, including the Kapteinsklip and Siqalo occupations.

Credit line: By Alicia Cowart.

new piece of land, Siqalo, was located along the major thoroughfare connecting Mitchells Plain to the city center (see figure 1.5). It was not a poor area either. In fact, across the street from the occupation was the closest thing the township had to a middle-class neighborhood. While it would probably be read as a working-class area in a US context, its residents were almost entirely formally housed, with relatively few backyarders in the vicinity. The neighborhood in which Kapteinsklip was located (Tafelsig) had three times as many people living in shacks as the area around Siqalo did, and the average household income here was nearly double that in Tafelsig.[14] People actually had green lawns, a rarity in most other parts of Mitchells Plain, especially in drought-stricken Cape Town. And there was a vibrant residents' association in the area. This was not the sort of neighborhood where one would expect the municipality to tolerate a land occupation.

Figure 1.5 Satellite photograph of Siqalo, December 2011. Note the location of the field in relation to the main road and the middle-class neighborhood across the street.
Credit line: City Maps, City of Cape Town.

This is especially the case given the social composition of the Siqalo occupation. It is rare in South African cities to find multiracial settlements, but this one was initially about three-quarters isiXhosa-speaking "African" and a quarter Afrikaans-speaking "Colored." Regardless, it was perceived by the residents across the road as "African" and immediately stigmatized as such. Were these ANC foot soldiers being unwittingly channeled into DA territory? Or were they active supporters of the then recently founded Economic Freedom Fighters (EFF), a Black nationalist party that is now the third largest in Parliament? And would they bring more crime to the area? The township was already plagued by numerous gang wars. Did they really need another potential source of violence?

"Colored" homeowners immediately began to mobilize, holding public meetings with municipal officials in community centers and even organizing marches. "Hoot if you want them relocated!" read one local resident's placard, as he marched down the major road separating the occupation from the houses, imploring passersby to honk in approval. A woman stood behind him with a large piece of posterboard, simply stating, "Move Siqalo!" Residents were clear: they wanted the squatters out of their neighborhood. And if they were insufficiently direct in their signage, they certainly did not mince words at the community meetings. When Siqalo residents tried to attend, police had to hold angry homeowners back, who proceeded to lob a series of South Africa–specific racial slurs at the occupiers. They did not just view them as squatters then, but as *African* squatters who had no place in their neighborhood. They wanted them gone.

With all of this in mind, Siqalo appears to be an obvious case: it was on private property, highly visible along a main road, adjacent to a mobilized middle-class neighborhood, an instance of "African" squatters in "Colored" space, and a potential case of the ANC or EFF trying to make inroads into DA territory. And whereas Kapteinsklip began with a thousand squatters and pretty quickly tapered off, Siqalo began with a few dozen, and within days there were hundreds of residents, and soon thousands. By the time their case was heard in court, there were over six thousand people living on the field.

After Faeza and Ebrahiem were evicted from Kapteinsklip, they decided to try their luck at Siqalo. I asked them how many structures were there when they moved in. It was still the very beginning. "There were fifty shacks," Faeza recalled.

Ebrahiem interjected: "But every day—that's *every* day—you could literally see that there's more shacks."

Faeza agreed with him. "People were building," she added. Yet despite the rapid pace of expansion, Siqalo was ultimately tolerated by the courts. Even though both the city government and the private landowners wanted the squatters gone—not to mention their neighbors—the judge would not grant them an eviction interdict. Why? What made Siqalo different from Kapteinsklip, which was fully evicted within a year?

A first major clue is the way participants in the Siqalo occupation organized themselves from the outset. In Kapteinsklip, occupiers saw themselves as recipients of land, as homeowners in the making. But in Siqalo, the occupation was understood to be a collective political project of realizing their constitutionally[15] guaranteed right to housing. No one was going to simply give them land; they had to obtain it through their own self-activity. There were no mutually exclusive units involved. Many of its chief organizers cut their teeth in the anti-apartheid movement. Moreover, the first wave of occupiers came not from isolated backyards, but from large informal settlements where they were already having to organize collectively. This was immediately evident to Faeza:

> We drove past Jakes Gerwel Drive and saw a new occupation a while ago. Law enforcement was standing on the road. We knew there has been a group of rastas living there for a while, a few shacks and then more and then something like 80 shacks. And what is different is that there is a mixture of people: Xhosa, Coloured, and foreigners. We went back and met Bonginkosi, who was the chairperson of the very newly formed informal settlement. What is different is that they are allowing more and more people to come, [as] opposed to how people are in Tafelsig and the boundaries and split groups trying to keep people away and calling the cops.

Each occupation, then, was carried out by people who had two very different respective readings of their constitutional right to housing. In one case, they thought they were realizing this right themselves; in the other, they understood themselves to be part of a process of housing distribution. Different understandings of this right led to different modes of organizing: a cohesive group with a clear leadership in one case, atomized "homeowners" in the other. In Kapteinsklip, occupiers defended their individual plots, emulating the logic of private property. In practice, this meant that they assumed an exclusivist orientation. Small alliances formed and attempted to secure material benefits and access to information for its members, but at the expense of other squatters in competing blocs. The entire occupation was fragmented into these contending factions. This was starkly different from Siqalo, whose leadership actively tried to expand its ranks and draw in as many people as possible. This was closer, in other words, to the model of a social movement.

> Within days there were a thousand shacks and serious people, and unlike our occupation, which is all I have known, where we ended up there accidentally, these people are clear—they need houses and they are taking the land. This new group with new energy is doing what it has felt impossible to do in Kapteinsklip.

It was easy enough to idealize them from the outside, especially from the vantage point of Kapteinsklip. But this was not quite a social movement—probably closer to what sociologist Asef Bayat calls social *non*movements. They were not taking land "to put pressure on authorities to meet their demands[;] in nonmovements actors directly practice what they claim, despite government sanctions. Thus, theirs is not a politics of protest, but of practice, of redress through direct and disparate actions."[16] This was a politics of necessity. Siqalo occupiers did not win the right to stay put because they applied political leverage on the government, nor was it their collective capacity to inflict violence. The only reason they were not forcibly removed from the field was their constitutional protection from eviction, which could only proceed if authorized by a court.[17] It was therefore up to a judge to decide which occupations to tolerate and which to evict.

This, then, brings us to a second major clue. When the judge issued his Kapteinsklip ruling, he adopted the prosecution's formulation, namely, that occupiers were "opportunists" in search of a handout. He explicitly pointed to the group that had organized the occupation, chastising them as "deceivers." And he repeatedly remarked upon the disorderly behavior of the occupiers in court that day, who he accused of infighting (*geklappery*), and instructed them, "If you want to work to satisfy your rights, it begins with discipline, and this starts with yourself and then your organizations and your community." And this was not a stretch: by the time of his verdict, opposing factions were regularly throwing burning rags into rivals' shacks, beating up antagonists, and so forth.

Making Sense of Evictions after Apartheid

Forced removals were central to the project of apartheid, which lasted from 1948 until 1994. During this period, more than 3.5 million Black South Africans were forcibly displaced.[18] Of course, racialized dispossession long preceded the ascension of the National Party in 1948, dating from the seventeenth-century arrival of Dutch colonists, who drove much of the indigenous population out of the Cape. By the mid-nineteenth century, land dispossession and segregation were systematized in legislation, culminating in the passage of the notorious Natives Land Act in 1913, which prohibited "Africans" from owning land in 93 percent of the country.[19] A series of subsequent laws restricted Indian ownership, illegalized squatting, and further regulated Black residents in urban space.[20] But with the exception of the Natives Land Act, the bulk of these laws applied to one section of the country or another. It was only with the passage of the Group Areas Act in 1950 that these were systematized and implemented on a nationwide basis.

Against this backdrop of centuries of racialized dispossession, postapartheid democratization is often articulated as a project of remedying the injustices wrought by white supremacist rule. One of the key means for realizing this aim was housing delivery. Nelson Mandela's first minister of housing, Joe Slovo, made it clear right off the bat that the "April election—in itself a miracle—did not deliver liberation; it has only provided us with a launching pad to build a liberated South Africa." And how to bring that about? "Housing is not a privilege; it is a fundamental human right. To live in an environment of degradation," he argued, "is to produce a degraded people. We have striven endlessly for freedom and liberation. Now is the time to deliver."[21]

Delivery: this was seen to be a primary technology for realizing liberation. The leadership of the liberation struggle now controlled the newly democratic state apparatus. This was a necessarily zero-sum game: the government monopolized the legitimate means of realization, thereby stripping civil society of these means. Mandela famously urged anti-apartheid militants to toss their weapons into the sea.[22] But the early ANC regime also actively sought the demobilization of social movements, cautioning against what Mandela called a "culture of entitlement."[23] It sought instead to incorporate civil society actors into more formal democratic institutions, which could safeguard democracy (or at least the limited capacity of an indebted state to *realize* this democracy) from being overwhelmed by frivolous demands.

By assuming a technocratic guise, democracy could be regulated, with "deserving" recipients of goods and services determined unilaterally by the state.[24] It was a select group of experts, in other words, who were expected to order the population in such a way as to make housing delivery feasible given the state's finite capacity. Only so many homes could be distributed each year, meaning that the entire backlog could not be housed right away. Rather, in this view, citizens needed to wait patiently. They had no other option than to provide for themselves in the meantime. And this meant occupying land. For where else where they to go?

But as new land occupations proliferated, they were not understood as temporary self-provisioning. By and large, housing officials viewed them as a problem to be remedied: on paper, they undid the gains won through delivery.[25] Indeed, the entire project of housing delivery was reduced to a technocratic scheme of organization from on high. Officials were to classify residents into discrete populations and order them in terms of seemingly rational criteria: time on the waiting list, age, family size, immediate need, and so forth. But being less in need is not the same as *not* being in need, and besides, one of the country's leading experts on the waiting list recently estimated that Cape Town's average waiting period is roughly sixty years.[26] What other option did people have than to take matters into their own hands, occupying land? But since officials saw these occupations as signs of their own failure—the failure to deliver—they tended to target them for eviction, as they continue to do today.

Eviction orders can be hard to secure, however, given the constitution's explicit prohibition of arbitrary removal. Many housing officials resent the broad constitutional guarantee to housing, which was a constant point of reference in my interviews with Cape Town's Department of Human Settlements (DHS) employees. For example, Marlize Odendal, who coordinated the acquisition of new land for government housing for DHS, explained to me:

> If I take your car, I'm guilty of theft, and the court doesn't expect the government to give me your car back. But our legislation at the moment says that, if we apply to evict people from a private landowner trying to protect his land. The court would say yes, but what alternative can the city or the government or the state offer? So what I'm saying to you is that we are rewarding criminality purely because in our constitution it's written that it's a basic right. So I think what we're doing is actually encouraging, through our very liberal legislation, we are encouraging people to act illegally. And

I don't subscribe to that. I think it's wrong, and I think it calls forth a lot of resentment.[27]

Like Odendal, many officials reduce land occupations to criminal behavior, describing them as intentional rather than inevitable. More broadly, they tend to view the persistence of informality as emblematic of the state's failure to deliver. They therefore want these occupations cleared immediately. But given the difficulty of securing eviction interdicts, not to mention the lengthy timelines that such cases can entail, they sometimes search for other ways to relocate them. One of the most common is offering squatters spots in new government housing developments.[28] While this might be an efficacious means of relocation, it also means that in practice, officials are bumping occupiers to the top of the waiting list. This directly contravenes the logic of that list's formal rationality, which should be calculable, based on written rules, and above all, impersonal.[29] Word soon gets around, and residents grow furious.

They have been waiting patiently for however many years, and suddenly so-and-so obtains a house before they do? How can housing officials explain this to those on the list? How can they possibly uphold the illusion of impartiality?

In a bout of self-imposed irony, housing officials try to justify their disdain for new occupations by claiming that impatient residents are refusing to wait their turn. They are said to occupy land, in other words, to force the government's hand. By irritating officials, they hope to be bumped to the top of the list, bypassing the interminable waiting period. For this reason, housing officials frequently refer to land occupiers as "queue jumpers," attributing to squatters housing officials' own decision to move them up the list. But it is government officials who *produce* queue jumpers in the first place, misrecognizing land occupations as a cause, rather than a consequence, of the state's failure to deliver. I have yet to encounter an occupier who took land because they hoped to hail the state and be bumped to the top of the list. If anything, they tried to evade the gaze of the state,[30] flying under its radar. In the bulk of cases, occupations are need-based: people simply hope to secure land.

On the other hand, this framing is hardly surprising. Imputing motivations to abstract populations is par for the course when it comes to technocratic democracy. Rather than engaging with populations as they actually exist, understanding their concrete impetuses for occupation, they are imagined as having the same rationale as all other occupiers: queue jumping. Yet as we have already seen, officials do not treat all occupations equally: some are evicted, while others are tolerated. How then do they choose among them? This is where our two clues come in handy. The first clue pointed to the way each occupation was organized. In Kapteinsklip, residents were relatively atomized, whereas in Siqalo they were constituted self-consciously as a group. Of course, this only begs the question. How can we explain why the Kapteinsklip occupiers were fragmented while in Siqalo they were united? As I argue in chapters 3 and 4, this was shaped by how occupiers saw the state. By this, I mean that in each occupation, residents had very different conceptions of what they were doing and how it related to the state's project of housing delivery.

In Kapteinsklip, residents attended meetings convened by an organization that they assumed was working with the city government. This organization instructed participants to sign up on a list, telling them that at a specified date and time, they would distribute plots to those in need. For this reason, when the Kapteinsklip occupation began, residents comported themselves much like individuals on the housing waiting list: as homeowners in the making. As they saw their situation, they were legally and legitimately receiving housing opportunities from the government. As with most recipients and customers, there was no obvious benefit to organizing themselves into a collective unit; rather, they remained relatively atomized, only entering into tiny alliances when they thought doing so would help them defend their "property."

In Siqalo, the occupiers saw the state quite differently. For them, the state was not facilitating delivery but inhibiting it. More specifically, it was at odds with their constitutionally mandated right to housing: they sought to shift the struggle to judicial terrain, realizing the Bill of Rights' intent through their own agency, despite the obstacles raised by the city's housing department, its ALIU, and its police. They largely came to this view of the state through participation in prior occupations during which they had faced sustained repression and surveillance. By contrast, this was not the experience of the Kapteinsklip occupiers, most of whom came to the field from backyards,[31] where they enjoyed relative security vis-à-vis the state's repressive forces. The Siqalo occupiers knew, then, that the state was not a partner but an antagonist in this process, and that they would need to mobilize collectively and maintain organizational unity. They could not, however, use existing political institutions to pull this off, as their local representatives remained hostile to their very presence. Without access to these formal institutions, the occupiers created informal institutions in their place.

If the first clue involves how occupiers see the state, the second clue captures how the state sees occupiers. The judge in the Kapteinsklip case was quick to invoke the prosecution's moralistic framing, dismissing the occupiers as "opportunists" and "queue jumpers" before ordering them to vacate the field. Like the DHS and ALIU, he saw them as troublesome elements, fragmented into contending factions and only in it for the free land. In stark contrast, the judge in the Siqalo case granted the occupiers the right to stay put, describing them as homeless people without any other viable options. He condemned the prosecution for failing to provide alternative accommodations for those facing eviction. Rather than criminalizing the squatters, he invoked the rhetoric of human rights, focusing not on whether or not they had broken the law, but instead on how the eviction would affect their actual lives.

But why did these two judges view their respective cases so differently? This book argues that how state actors see populations is inseparable from how populations see the state. By this, I mean that the way occupiers viewed the role of the state in relation to their right to housing affected how they organized themselves: as a collective force in Siqalo, but as contending proprietors in Kapteinsklip. And this, in turn, impacted how they were seen by the state. Where they represented themselves as mutually cooperative and as a cohesive population, they were recognized as such. But where they split into multiple opposed factions, it was not apparent to the judge that their lawyer spoke for all of them. Clearly something was going on, and he was quick to lecture them about their counterproductive behavior.

These examples reveal that as much as housing officials like to think of themselves as purely technocratic, projecting policies devised in a vacuum onto populations below, this is not how such policies are implemented in practice. This location of decision-making—often called "political society"[32] by social theorists—turns out not to be a vacuum at all, but a site permeated by those about whom decisions are made: civil society. It is at the level of civil society that residents' associational forms, political experiences, and collective self-understandings affect how they are seen, analyzed, and assessed by housing officials, judges, police, and other government actors. Their form of collective self-organization, experienced as civil society, is articulated as political society to government actors. Even if it is not occupiers' intention to be read as making appeals to the state, this is indeed how they are perceived. "Political society" is not an airtight institutional space that hovers above "civil society," formulating a coherent will of its own accord and projecting it upon a civil society fragmented into "populations" below. Rather, government actors are in constant dialogue with residents' organizations on the ground. They do not encounter a civil society already divided into discrete "populations" vying with one another for access to "the state." These populations are not pregiven but are instead the outcome of the organizational struggles traversing civil society. It was only through the coordination of an occupation, and all of the organizing work that this entails, that residents become intelligible populations. And since their approach to organizing was shaped so heavily by how they imagined the state, civil society struggles are never fully separable from those of political society.

The inverse is also true: how government actors recognize these populations, how they are seen by the state, is powerfully shaped by the ways residents collectively organize themselves. I hesitate to suggest that they represent themselves *to* the state because this is not necessarily their intention; their wish is often for the state to let them be, to evade its gaze. But being exclusively articulated on the terrain of civil society is not an option; all civil society articulations are also political society articulations. That's the thing about bourgeois hegemony: in producing the terrain upon which people organize themselves, the very conceptual repertoire with which they articulate their demands and desires, there is no "purely" autonomous action, no sanctified space of the "from below." Whether or not residents want to be perceived by government actors is beside the point; they are perceived regardless. Even intentionally autonomous actions, attempts to sidestep the state altogether, still end up in communication with local government officials, police, judges, and the like. Neither government activity nor that of occupiers should be understood as an ultimate "cause" of an eviction outcome; rather, these are co-constitutive elements in an ongoing process. Even self-organization, which is sometimes associated with an approach "from below," must be treated with care: the "self" in this context should never be reduced to a theory of "pure" agency. As I argue in chapters 3 and 4, occupiers' variable approaches to self-organization are as much cause as outcome; they are shaped by people's living situations, engagement with state repression, interface with local political intermediaries, and so forth. This means that we need to examine how occupiers see the state, how this in turn shapes how the state sees them, and how this further modifies residents' vision of the state—a continuous feedback loop of political articulation.

This book explains how these collective struggles for land, organized beyond the purview of the state, still wind up as struggles with—and in—the
state. Under apartheid, an authoritarian state could simply shift populations
at will without having to worry about the fallout. But the postapartheid state
is democratic, meaning it can no longer ignore discontent. It must reproduce
a basic level of legitimacy, actively breaking with apartheid modes of population management. To do so, it tends to channel decisions regarding land dispossession through its judicial system, perceived as impartially adjudicating
people's constitutional rights. In examining the sociological bases of these
legal determinations, we can begin to understand how postcolonial democracies balance these two needs: they manage their surplus populations, controlling their location in urban space, but they do so without impinging upon
their status as nascent democracies. What then are these social bases? How
are these decisions made?

Beyond the Autonomous State Paradigm

I began this project with an autonomist[33] bias: I conceived of the municipal
state as a coherent entity that acted "upon" populations. This state was an
instrument—a tool—available to anyone who came to control it. Adapting
models of growth coalitions[34] to a South African context, I assumed that
postapartheid evictions were part of a strategy of invisibilizing poverty so as
to entice capital to invest in urban redevelopment. The beginning of South
Africa's long economic crisis[35] in the 1970s and 1980s maps nicely onto the
shift David Harvey[36] identified as the urbanization of capital, with declining
profitability in manufacturing prompting capital to shift investment into its
secondary circuit: consumption goods and the built environment. Inspired
by the work of geographer Neil Smith[37] on gentrification frontiers, I would
obtain eviction data from municipalities and use geographic information
system (GIS) software to map them over time and discern patterns, or what
I assumed would take the form of "eviction frontiers." And following both
Smith and Harvey, I suspected that securing maximum returns on investment would explain the patterns I observed.

My email inbox was constantly inundated with press releases from
housing-related social movements in Durban, Cape Town, and Johannesburg
suggesting that this was precisely what was going on in postapartheid cities.
"Rich capitalists have been evicting people without even following proper

procedures and have used their power to remove the poor to the outskirts of the City," read one statement distributed by the Cape Town–based Anti-Eviction Campaign.[38] This view accorded nicely with the literature on gentrification and world-class city making, with a good deal written about Cape Town.[39]

Increasingly, however, I began to notice that evictions and informal settlement eradication were being fitted into the narrative of gentrification, or at the very least, a story in which the municipal government acts on behalf of real estate speculators. The role of the state in this formulation, then, is one in which the government straightforwardly attempts to foster investment—above all, through "revitalization" campaigns, clearing unsightly shack settlements in the process. The existing literature on evictions in informal settlements, however sparse, accorded with this narrative as well: it was these neighborhoods' visibility that made them likely candidates for eradication.[40]

Of course, in Smith's pathbreaking account, he largely avoids the problem of the autonomous state. His key actors are developers, and he goes out of his way to refute explanations for gentrification rooted in intentionality. Rather than attributing the process to the consumption choices of yuppies or a creative class,[41] the reclaiming of the city center by these actors is an effect of reinvestment rather than its cause. Smith's entire explanation is predicated upon a theory of the rent gap in which developers buy when cheap and therefore act to facilitate this cheapening. This is the moment of devalorization. Once real estate loses its value, developers buy properties by the dozen, coordinating a massive marketing campaign in order to rebrand the city center as amenable to middle-class lifestyles. This is the moment of revalorization. The difference between actual and potential capitalization—the rent gap—governs the geography of investment and divestment. Certainly city governments partner with developers in order to expand their tax base, but there is little in the way of a state-initiated gentrification scheme in Smith's account.

After Smith, however, gentrification research took a state-centered turn, heralding the rise of a "global, state-led process of gentrification via the promotion of social or tenure 'mixing' (or 'social diversity' or 'social balance') in formerly disinvested neighbourhoods populated by working-class and/or low-income tenants."[42] Initially analysts focused on increasingly frequent public-private partnerships, coalitions in which "local governmental powers . . . try and attract external sources of funding" for development projects,[43] or in some cases, provide partial funding themselves "to offset risks posed to real estate capital."[44] This could take the form of jointly financing a megaproject in a central business district under the banner of "revitalization," or it might assume less visible forms, such as increased state involvement in gentrification[45] or strategic stigmatization of properties targeted for redevelopment.[46] In the case of the latter, local capital helps finance the renovation or even demolition of areas that the municipality actively constructs as "blight," whether public housing,[47] buildings occupied by stigmatized groups,[48] or public parks serving the houseless.[49] Even the penal wing of the state makes an appearance, "quash[ing] opposition and mak[ing] the streets safe for gentrification."[50] In sum, these researchers argued that the promotion of economic development, whether through publicly financed public relations campaigns or the rebranding of "revitalized" neighborhoods, is increasingly being seen as the responsibility of municipal governments rather than independent developers.[51]

Given some of the claims made by gentrification researchers about its global applicability,[52] tying it to a larger process of neoliberalization, it was only a matter of time before state-initiated development frameworks were brought to bear upon southern cities. An initial wave of ethnographic literature[53] on urban informality in cities of the South emphasized the agency of squatters, frequently elevating self-provisioning to the status of resistance. But unlike the collective mobilization underpinning the occupations discussed here, many of these works describe individualized survival strategies, leading geographer Michael Watts[54] to ask, "Is this really about a 'collective system' or a desperate search for human agency (improvisation, incessant convertibility) in the face of a neoliberal grand slam?"

On the other hand, attempts to explain the global proliferation of informal housing since the 1970s, situating it in its proper political economic context, were often far too sweeping. No work is more representative of this tendency than Mike Davis's *Planet of Slums*.[55] To his credit, Davis identifies this sudden burst of informal urbanization as a consequence of the World Bank's structural adjustment programs against a backdrop of deindustrialization across the global South. This is a crucial move, as it allows us to actually explain the return of survivalism rather than simply redescribing it, let alone reducing it to a form of ingenuity. To be clear, of course these strategies demonstrate incredible resilience and resourcefulness in the face of extreme adversity. But the celebration of self-provisioning as a valorized form of autonomy lacks nuance: surely surviving on an open field requires inventiveness, but this hardly qualifies as an ideal solution. It is in writing against these patronizing tendencies that Davis is at his best. But as numerous critics have pointed out,[56] he bends the stick too far, deploying apocalyptic natural metaphors to describe the growth of so-called "slums," a moralizing rather than a technical or analytic term. The consequence, his detractors claimed, is that Davis's account is hardly distinguishable from the UN-Habitat report[57] with which his critical analysis is in dialogue. In reducing informal settlements to a scourge, policymakers are encouraged to eradicate them without providing adequate alternative accommodations. And this they did, with national governments often reinterpreting the Cities Alliance's "cities without slums" initiative as a mandate for mass clearances—including the government of South Africa.[58]

In the wake of these debates, scholars[59] have attempted to navigate between the Scylla of a decontextualized descriptivism and the Charybdis of a God's-eye view, considering survival strategies in relation to broader state rationales for informal settlement eradication drives, above all in the crisis-ridden BRICS countries. While these works represent a major advance over the unreconstructed transposition of a northern gentrification framework to southern cities,[60] many of them still retain a theory of the autonomous state. National and municipal governments raze shack settlements in the name of world-class city making, with evictions on the ground read as consequences of national- and provincial-level policy. Sometimes the rationale is humanitarian, purportedly complying with the UN's Millennium Development Goals and its attendant program of "cities without slums." Or else attracting foreign capital might be stated up front as a development strategy or even tied to a megaevent, as in recent World Cup competitions in South Africa and Brazil.[61]

In South Africa, the literature on such clearances remains sparse, despite the pervasiveness of land occupations and their frequent evictions. Much more substantial is the literature on social movements fighting these evictions.[62] The most comprehensive work[63] providing an overview of clearances themselves identifies a calculated project of world-class city making, a totalizing scheme in which shack eradication is tied to the image of the city. Sometimes this is linked to the tourism industry,[64] or else to attracting foreign investment.[65] In both cases, the key variable determining which settlements will be targeted is visibility:[66] those settlements most visible from major highways are the first to go.

The state in this telling, whether municipal or national, is described as intentionally targeting shacks as part of a comprehensive accumulation strategy. But in most accounts along these lines, empirical support is thin beyond national-level DHS statements and press releases. South African

municipalities do publish citywide and submunicipal redevelopment strategies, but these have yet to be concretely linked to a systematic program of
dispossession. In Cape Town, for example, many of the sites allegedly cleared
to create a cordon sanitaire in the run-up to the 2010 World Cup were actually targeted years earlier, often as part of national upgrading projects. The
point is that these autonomist narratives only arise after the fact. There is no
question that the peripheralization of urban surplus populations perpetuates
apartheid-era geographies of relegation, but this is quite distinct from the
claim that most urban dispossession in South African cities is tied to an identifiably state-led accumulation strategy.

And this is how evictions tend to be discussed in the literature: as part of a
broader program of spatial dislocation. A local state decides what it wants to
do, and then it does it, projecting its decisions onto populations below. But in
practice, this is not how evictions proceed, and this formulation does little to
advance our understanding of divergent outcomes *within* a city. Why would
one land occupation be evicted while another was tolerated? The obvious
explanation would be its visibility—say, from a major road, or to wealthier
residents or visitors—but the cases I have described suggest that this framework is inadequate. The Kapteinsklip occupation was relatively out of sight;
and in any case, it was far less visible than Siqalo. Yet it was the latter settlement that was ultimately tolerated and remains standing to this day.

In addition to being more visible, Siqalo is located on privately owned
land. It actually sprawled across two contiguous plots with two different corporate owners. By contrast, Kapteinsklip took place on public land owned by
the city. According to the gentrification literature and, above all, followers
of Neil Smith, we would expect governments to facilitate evictions where
occupations interfered with the cultivation of privately held real estate. Yet
here too, we observe a counterintuitive outcome: the Siqalo occupation was
tolerated, but the Kapteinsklip occupation was eradicated. Cape Town's government did not appear to be straightforwardly facilitating private development. Instead, something else was at work. As I argue in subsequent chapters,
being located on private property had unexpected consequences. In the next
chapter, I discuss the legal framework underlying evictions. While the government can legally evict occupiers from municipal land if it acts quickly, it
can only evict people from private property once the landowners have filed
for an eviction order. But when they fail to do so promptly, as in the case of
Siqalo, waiting many months before approaching the court, the ALIU cannot
remove them in the meantime. This buys participants many months during

which they can establish representative organizations. It also means that police cannot repossess their building materials during this period, allowing them to function in less of a state of siege than we would see in an occupation like Kapteinsklip, where residents faced ALIU agents and police daily.

Like property type, none of the other standard explanatory factors get us very far. Siqalo brought "Africans" into "Colored" space, which inflamed the middle-class residents living across the road. Their wealthier neighbors regularly held demonstrations demanding Siqalo's relocation. They organized massive neighborhood association meetings that even featured a speech from the mayor. I thought that the municipal government might evict this occupation to reduce the potential for interracial violence—but of course it was tolerated. Or else the city government, controlled by the DA, "Colored" voters' preferred party, would assume "African" residents were supporters of rival parties. It would therefore be strategic to keep them out of DA strongholds. Kapteinsklip, meanwhile, was overwhelmingly "Colored," and none of their neighbors sought their removal. The bulk of them would be assumed to be DA supporters. Yet it was the Kapteinsklip occupation that was evicted. How then to make sense of this counterintuitive outcome?

Toward the Integral City-State

This book leaves sweeping theorizations at the door. It suggests that rather than thinking about the state as an actor making rational calculations in a vacuum, these decisions are always made in the context of ongoing political struggles. States do not simply "see" ready-made populations,[67] nor is this status of "population" straightforwardly imposed from on high. What the state "sees" are groups of residents collectively attempting to forge settlements. But they are not trying to be seen by this state; their collective action, we might say, is organized in *civil society*. But use of that term requires some clarification.

As it is typically understood, civil society is the private sphere beyond the purview of the state, or "political society," in which people begin to organize themselves. This might take the form of voluntary associations, trade unions, or even the family. This opposition between civil and political societies is characteristic of both liberal political theorists and scholars claiming to work in the Gramscian tradition, though as I demonstrate in this section, this is precisely the opposition *against* which Gramsci was writing in his

Prison Notebooks. He introduces an expanded understanding of the state that encompasses both moments in the political process. How, for example, is patriotism fostered by those in power? On the one hand, we might envision coercive means, where legal categories like "sedition," "alien," and even "terrorist" function as a pretext for state violence. Those who subvert patriotic norms may be subject to arrest and incarceration, or even beatings or death. On the other, we might contend that these violent outbursts are exceptional. In most cases, patriotism is quietly reproduced in schools, families, the media, popular culture, and so forth—and people actively desire to participate. They are not being deceived; they willingly show up to a sporting event on their own time, place a hand over their heart, and belt out their country's national anthem, actually enjoying the collective effervescence that results. Or they might even watch their country bombing another on television at home with their families or with friends in a bar, spontaneously bursting into patriotic chants until the whole room is shouting in unison.

As this example illustrates, identifying which processes belong to the state and which are beyond its reach is a tricky endeavor. When uniformed agents storm into a compound and arrest a given individual, the insignia on their clothing leaves no doubt: they are acting on behalf of the state. And those lawmakers, judges, and bureaucrats who created the laws being enforced by the state's repressive apparatus? They too clearly comprise a formal institutional apparatus that we typically designate "the state" in everyday discourse. But what about the more quotidian ways that allegiance is secured? Schools operate under government authority, so they are not too much of a stretch. But what about the family or popular culture? What would it mean to think about these as sites of reproduction for state power? And what about the violence of social sanction, through which spontaneous crowds might enforce a set of norms through coercion?

Land occupations are an ideal test case in that they are about as far from intentionally direct engagement with the state's institutional apparatus as possible. Social movements typically issue some sort of demand, thereby hailing the state. But occupations are not asking for anything other than to be left alone; what they want, in other words, is what they have already taken and provisioned for themselves. This is the sense in which they are akin to Asef Bayat's *non*movements. Writing about occupiers illegally appropriating electricity and water connections, he points out that "they do not steal urban services in order to express their defiance vis-à-vis the authorities. Rather, they do it because they find no other way to acquire them."[68] But as he is quick to acknowledge, even if they are not trying to engage the state—and indeed, they are actively trying to evade its gaze—they ultimately come into conflict with government agents as their nonmovement grows. When a dozen or so squatters lived secretly behind a few bushes at Siqalo, no one seemed to mind. But when dozens of shacks went up overnight, they were easily spotted by the ALIU and police, and neighbors began to complain to their ward councilor. In response, the occupiers needed to strategize defensively, and so they began to organize. Eventually they would march to Cape Town's Civic Centre and deliver a memorandum to the mayor demanding that their shacks gain official recognition. They elected leaders, held regular meetings, and even began to talk about the most effective political strategies. In short, the government forced a nonmovement to become a social movement.

To put the same point in a Gramscian idiom, we can say that the occupation was organized on the terrain of civil society with no attempt to communicate via political society. But their intentions were irrelevant, and their civil society movements had immediate reverberations at the level of political society. They were regularly visited by police, DHS officials, national level politicians, the mayor, the ALIU, and so forth, and whether or not they wanted their representatives to communicate to municipal government agents, their statements were interpreted as such. Even the most extrastatal (non)movement imaginable—a land occupation—involved prolonged entanglement with the state's legal apparatus, not to mention its coercive arm. This process—self-organization being articulated simultaneously at the levels of civil and political society—is the subject of this book, detailed ethnographically in chapters 3 through 6.

But what is novel about this approach? Typically, this is not how Gramsci has been received in an Anglophone context. In Perry Anderson's influential reading,[69] for example, which introduced many English-language readers to the *Prison Notebooks* for the first time, civil society and political society are mutually distinct institutional locations—the latter in "the state," the former beyond its formal institutional purview. This neat distinction is thereby "reproduced in spatial terms, with each being assigned its respective sovereign zone within any given social formation."[70] But this was not Gramsci's intention when he opposed civil to political society. In fact, he cautioned against ossifying this distinction between civil and political society into an "antinomy," to borrow Anderson's framing, which represents the opposition "as an organic one, whereas in fact it is merely methodological."[71] As Gramsci goes to great pains to emphasize, "civil society and State are one and the same,"[72] by which he means two moments—civil society and political society—that exist in a single empirical location, which he terms the *integral state*.

This concept is key to understanding Gramsci's theory of the state, though it remains sorely underutilized in most social science applications of his work. The integral state is an expanded understanding of the state as a terrain of struggle, distinct from the set of administrators and buildings captured by the term in mainstream political science. Gramsci wanted to understand what was novel about the capitalist state. A unified Italian government had only emerged a half century before his imprisonment and within a matter of decades had consolidated into a Fascist regime. Accordingly, we might expect Gramsci to emphasize the authoritarian aspects of this novel state form, yet if anything, he bends the stick in the opposite direction, demonstrating Fascism's basis in civil society.[73] For Gramsci, what is novel about the capitalist state is its ability to appear as an abstraction that both subordinates and organizes civil society.[74] Here he was translating into strategic terms Marx's insight that "the abstraction of the state as such belongs only to modern times."[75] "Political life in the modern sense is the Scholasticism of popular life," Marx writes, by which he means that we typically only understand actions as properly "political" when they follow a formal set of procedures that connect them to the state as such. We imagine this state as a "thing" with which we might interact— what Poulantzas[76] called the "Thing-State."

For Gramsci, it is precisely this ability to appear as an abstraction hovering above civil society that is the source of the capitalist state's power. But, following Marx, he roots the actual state—as opposed to the apparent state—in civil society. Hegemony then—the concept most widely associated with Gramsci—does not straightforwardly play out on the "terrain" of civil society, as Anderson argues. Against this understanding, Peter Thomas[77] argues that Gramsci's project was instead to explain how

> bourgeois hegemony has traversed the boundaries between civil society and political society, simultaneously a form of both "civil" and "political" organization and leadership. It is the social relation of coordination and direction through which the bourgeois class project made the transition from a merely (economic) corporative to a properly hegemonic or political phase, successfully positing its own particular interests—above all, the form of private property as valid for the society as a whole.

Hegemony, in other words, does not take place "in" civil society, as if this were some spatially discrete entity, mutually exclusive from political society. Instead, what makes hegemony effective is its ability to represent every seemingly independent and autonomous collective action as necessarily in dialogue with political society. Every civil society action is also articulated as political society action. Even "the collective practices and ingenuity of the subaltern masses in struggle"—say, as in a land occupation—assume a "reciprocal relation" with political society.[78]

Hence the involuntary movement in Bayat from nonmovement evading the state to increasingly movement-like formation actively engaging the state might be described in Gramscian terms as a case of bourgeois hegemony. Even a most deliberately extrastatal form of collective organization like a land occupation is absorbed into the formal-legal apparatus of government. This goes beyond what the Comaroffs[79] have called the "judicialization of politics," the shifting of all social struggles onto the legal terrain, which they identify as characteristic of late decolonizers. Rather, for Gramsci this is characteristic of *all* bourgeois states. Following Thomas's reading, hegemony entails not just organizing civil society but equally ensuring that the political society articulation of a collective struggle safeguards a class project. Hegemony is therefore "a practice 'traversing' the boundaries between" civil society and political society; these are not distinct locations "in a spatial but [rather] a functional sense."[80]

This is not an arcane political theory formulation, but one that allows us to understand how a capitalist democracy like South Africa can maintain order despite hundreds of thousands of residents participating in land occupations every year. Even when residents organize into mass formations and militantly defy the rule of property by taking land rather than asking for it, their actions are read as in communication with government employees, judges, and elected officials. In other words, their civil society actions necessarily have political society articulations. As I explain in the next chapter, this is particularly ironic given that the primary reason residents participate in land occupations is because they have abandoned faith in the government, tired of waiting for state-provisioned housing that never seems to arrive.

In order to understand the process by which civil society formations are simultaneously articulated as political society formations, I turn to a detailed comparative analysis of the occupations in Siqalo and Kapteinsklip. The eviction of the latter but not the former was not overdetermined by any variety of factors, nor was it decided in a vacuum by an omniscient state. Rather, the form of struggle adopted by each set of occupiers produced distinct, albeit unintended, political society articulations, which impacted how their struggle leaped from civil to political society, or at the very least, traversed these two moments. To differentiate these forms, I draw on Jean-Paul Sartre's opposition of the "series" to the "fused group," two possible trajectories of group formation. In *Critique of Dialectical Reason*,[81] he is concerned with how oppositional collectivities form, typically in relation to some object. Sartre famously describes the banal situation in which people are waiting in line for a bus. This is inherently a situation defined by scarcity:[82] they queue precisely because there are a limited number of seats, and it is their line that creates a legitimate sense of order in how seats are distributed—first come, first served. Their isolation is reciprocal, meaning that no division of political labor emerges; they work simultaneously but not together as such. The bus, seemingly just an object, "takes on a structure which overflows its pure inert existence."[83] It is no longer an object sui generis, but one that mediates among all the various individuals waiting for it. They are united in the "structure of their practico-inert being, and it unites them from the outside," but they are only "united" by an "abstract unity": their waiting for the bus at the same time and in the same place. This situation, Sartre argues, is characteristic of seriality: they are members of a *series*—fragmented, isolated, and acting in simultaneity rather than in common.

He contrasts this series to the *fused group*. Here too, a mass of people relates to an object, but in this case, they do so collectively, together. Seriality for Sartre is actually characteristic of capitalist subjectivity—fused groups are the exception. Much like reification in Lukács or hegemony in Gramsci, serialization explains how collective life in relation to commodities—to objects under capitalism really—yields passivity. But in certain key moments, people are able to break through this veil of passivity; in such moments, "The passive activity of the gathering [is] taken from it in its passivity and inert seriality reappear[s] on the other side of the process of alterity as *a united group which had performed a concerted action*."[84] This is a patently phenomenological account of struggle, one that attempts to identify the experiential conditions under which people are able to act in concert, collectively, and self-consciously rather than merely simultaneously. In a celebrated passage, Sartre explains how formerly serialized workers were able to shed their docility and join forces as they stormed the Bastille during the French Revolution. Why were they able to do so? Sartre locates his explanation in what he calls the field of praxis: "*The people of Paris armed themselves against the king*."[85] As the government unleashed repression against those in the streets, "The political *praxis* of the government alienated the passive reactions of seriality to its own practical freedom." The status of the object in relation to which people act has shifted: no longer is the object a bus or a sandwich or a house to be delivered by the state; it became a symbolic object, not one to use as such, but one against which everyone collectively defined their practical action. Here, in other words, collaboration would benefit all, and scarcity was no longer an objective constraint. Participants were not pitted against each other in competition, as in the series, but were united into a singular political force that actually benefited from cooperation: the fused group.

In this book, I argue that the Kapteinsklip occupation was characterized by its seriality, while the Siqalo occupation assumed the form of a fused group. As in Sartre, the object was everything. In Kapteinsklip, this object—housing—was experienced much as Sartre's bus. For their entire adult lives, many of the participants were waiting with countless others for housing; but the "with" here must be qualified. They were not doing so collectively or collaboratively, but simply simultaneously. And they were alienated by the process, bitter that they had to wait decades for housing and were not provided with decent alternative options in the meantime. During this waiting period, they were largely living in backyard shacks scattered around Mitchells Plain in various homeowners' backyards. Their spatial fragmentation perfectly encapsulates the idea of seriality. When an organization appeared on the scene and promised to deliver "houses" to each of them, they did not have to adapt their passive seriality to a new situation; once again, they understood themselves to be patients of the state,[86] waiting for an external organization to distribute plots of land as if they were seats on a bus.

Siqalo was quite different. There most participants did not come from backyards, but from informal settlements elsewhere in Cape Town. Many of them had experienced conflict with the state—the ALIU, police, and so forth—and viewed it not as a partner in delivery, but as an obstacle to realizing homeownership. As such, they related to this object collectively and cooperatively, protecting one another from arrest, building shacks together, and actively trying to expand the settlement. They formed something closer to the model of a social movement, albeit with one major difference: they did not make any demands on the state and actively sought to be left alone. But "the state" is not a discrete object upon which one issues demands. Whether or not they sought to engage the municipal government, they soon found themselves in dialogue with DHS officials, lawyers, and judges, marching for housing, their signs clearly addressed to the municipal government. Their civil society articulation as a fused group, in other words, already had an articulation at the level of political society, whether or not they wanted to communicate with state officials. Their organizational form was never powerful because it granted them some collective leverage over the state; it was powerful because it represented them as a "deserving" poor—not jockeying with each other for a handout but working together to realize their constitutionally guaranteed right to housing.

The political society articulation of the Kapteinsklip occupation was quite different. This was ironic, as the Siqalo occupiers were far more dismissive of the state, whereas the Kapteinsklip occupiers perceived the organization distributing housing *as* the state—even if, as we will see in chapter 3, it was not. They constituted themselves as a series, "passive" in Sartre's sense: they were waiting in relation to an object (housing) that would presumably be distributed to each of them. But there were a finite number of plots, or so they were led to believe, yielding a situation of artificial scarcity as in the *Critique*. And so they acted simultaneously but never collectively. If anything, they understood themselves to be in direct competition with one another, mobilizing to keep newcomers out and forming constantly shifting factions that were often violently in conflict with one another. Even if they did not seek to relate to municipal officials, they soon found themselves having to do so, read by DHS officials and judges as an "undeserving" poor who were self-interested and refused to work as a community.

Both of these cases exemplify hegemony in the sense previously described. This was not something that was forged on the terrain of civil society alone, but one that traversed the boundaries between civil society and political society. Even when occupiers sought to evade the state altogether, organizing independently and attempting to withdraw themselves from the government's delivery apparatus, they found this to be an impossible task. They were soon facing proliferating court dates and had to secure legal representation, and they were issuing memoranda to the municipal government in marches and rallies. Even when they sought to disarticulate themselves from political society, acting "solely" on civil society, it turned out to be an impossible task under conditions of bourgeois hegemony. Private property and the legal order its defense requires were represented as if they were in the interest of all, as opposed to the class of property owners who actually benefited from such an arrangement. This was hegemony at work.

Methods

Theoretically this makes sense.[87] Each collective action has both an intended civil society articulation and an often unintended political society articulation. But how to study these double articulations as they occur concretely in the social world? This is where I turned to ethnography paired with a number of supplementary methods. The detailed narratives presented for both occupations are not common knowledge, nor were these occupations covered in any detail in mainstream newspapers. Occupations occur with sufficient regularity in Cape Town that even thousands of people seizing a plot of land is not typically deemed newsworthy. Or even when it is, most Capetonians living beyond Mitchells Plain, and even many of those living in that township, would be oblivious to it. So my primary task was to systematically reconstruct the narrative in both locations, Kapteinsklip and Siqalo.

To do this, I conducted twenty months of fieldwork between 2011 and 2019, spanning a period that includes the entirety of the Kapteinsklip occupation and the first seven years of the Siqalo occupation. I visited both settlements frequently, but I also had to remain cautious, remaining as much of an absent presence as possible. The incursion of outside actors into an occupation can facilitate distrust among contending groupings, even helping to catalyze their formation into well-developed factions. As I demonstrate in chapters 3 through 6, this was actually fairly common: outside actors, understood as bearers of resources, functioned much like Sartre's bus. And if anyone were to be read as a bearer of resources, it would be me, a white American visiting "African" and "Colored" occupations in an area in which I rarely saw white people at all—and when I did, they tended to be police. This is how I would be read by most of the occupiers, if not by most residents in Mitchells Plain: as an officer, or else as a representative of the government or a charity or an NGO. If one of the occupiers were to shepherd me into their shack and then I were to leave, the consequences could be disastrous.

One elected settlement committee leader in Siqalo, Karen, told me that if people thought she was the one bringing me to the occupation, they would demand that she distribute to everyone the blankets and food that I gave her. Of course, I never gave Karen a thing, but she explained the hypothetical situation. It would not matter if I had not given her anything; people would still assume that I was a charity worker distributing essential goods to my contacts. Then when she denied having received anything, she might be accused of corruption, and this is when her neighbors could confront her with violence. So I had to tread very lightly. This meant that rather than standard fly-on-the-wall ethnography, I had to combine multiple data sources to tri-angulate and make sense of political processes in each occupation, all while minimizing my own impact on settlement-level politics. I had originally planned to stay in one or two close contacts' shacks, but I risked being the "object" in relation to which group formation takes place. Both ethically and scientifically, there were good reasons to minimize my impact upon both occupations.

As an alternative, I frequently met with individual members of the oc-cupation outside of the settlement, often at a fast-food restaurant down the road, or else in neighbors' shacks in nearby backyards. When the occupa-tion would hold settlement-level report-backs, I was able to attend in a way that did not imply allegiance to any particular faction. As in any social sit-uation, I became closer to some participants than others. Sometimes this was a function of perceived reliability. I secured a number of contacts whom I assessed to be dependable, both in terms of the information I received and in terms of my personal safety. I was deliberately reflexive about this convenience sampling: as long as I understood a source to be a represen-tative, a bearer, of a certain politics, I could map the political field in both occupations. From there I secured introductions to additional occupiers, but it was essential that my primary contacts conveyed my own trustworthi-ness. Otherwise, I would receive whatever information participants thought would be most likely to secure them material resources. To be clear, as in any instance of an obvious outsider suddenly appearing in a tightly knit com-munity, plenty of the information I collected turned out to be worthless—either deliberately so, or else by virtue of misremembering. But even after Kapteinsklip was evicted—for years afterward, in fact—I would regularly interview participants about the events, verifying them against as many ad-ditional sources as I could.

I therefore paired this ethnography-at-a-distance with a number of other data sources. In Kapteinsklip, a few participants filmed over eleven hours of footage on a borrowed camcorder. The participant who had the tapes allowed me full access, and I digitalized the footage for him. After the oc-cupation was evicted, I regularly rewatched this footage with a number of the original participants and paused frequently so that they could discuss what had happened. In addition, Faeza, introduced previously, lived in both occupations, and she granted me access to the detailed daily diary she kept over the entire duration. While the original draft was fragmentary and incomplete, she collaborated with a friend[88] to type up the entire thing in chronological order. She provided me with a full copy.

I also created an archive of media coverage over the period 2011–17, including every mention of either occupation in both major community newspapers[89] in the township. These were not available digitally at the time, and I thumbed through hard copies of every issue released during this period in these publications' offices in the city center. I photocopied every page that mentioned either occupation or dealt with housing politics in the vicinity, pairing these with digitally available local and national newspapers that covered the occupations—though such coverage was predictably scarce. I also reviewed relevant court records and interviewed some of the lawyers involved in the cases, as well as lawyers and legal scholars with experience in eviction law. Finally, I copied many hundreds of pages of planning documents related to the construction of Mitchells Plain by the apartheid government in the 1970s and 1980s. The majority of these were accessed in the African Studies Special Collection at the University of Cape Town, while the remainder were borrowed from the Jagger Library, which was unfortunately partially destroyed in a major fire in April 2021.

In addition to this ethnographic and archival research, I conducted lengthy interviews with as many relevant housing officials as I could, as well as other key players in the housing policy world. The bulk of these were DHS employees, at both municipal and provincial levels, interviewed in Cape Town and the Western Cape respectively. I also interviewed a handful of DHS employees in Johannesburg and Durban to gain a sense of differences across municipalities, and I talked with private sector consultants and other contractors who worked on DHS policy. I subsequently interviewed housing policy and legal experts at think tanks and NGOs in Cape Town and Johannesburg, comparing information I received from them with the account I got from DHS employees. And whenever possible, I attended housing policy workshops, typically attended by NGO workers, DHS employees, and academics.

Finally, I spent as much time as possible with residents who had either been evicted from Kapteinsklip or forced out of Siqalo, asking them to recount everything in detail as we sat in their backyard shacks. I am sure they grew irritated over the course of multiple years, as I made them tell and retell their stories. As I gained new information from one, I would interrogate another about these developments. In the end, I reconstructed the narratives of these struggles in both their civil society and political society articulations—stories not recounted anywhere else. While both occupations were certainly mentioned occasionally in local media coverage, this was largely either to examine the plight of the houseless or else to scold squatters for alleged freeloading. Nowhere was the story of these occupations told. My task then was to reconstruct these narratives in both occupations to explain how it was that the occupation I expected to be evicted, Siqalo, was ultimately tolerated, whereas the one I expected to be tolerated, Kapteinsklip, was cleared altogether.

Overview of the Book

Why would a country that delivers millions of free homes and guarantees the right to housing evict thousands of squatters waiting for homes? How can delivery and dispossession coexist in a single regime? This is how this book characterizes South Africa after apartheid: rather than a complete shift from dispossession to delivery, it argues that democratization entailed a new relationship between the two. Under apartheid, delivery was used to facilitate dispossession; but afterward, dispossession became a strategy of enabling delivery. Following the transition in 1994, the new government staked its legitimacy on realizing access to housing for the millions of Black South Africans who had been forcibly relocated under apartheid. And this it did. Since 1994, roughly four million homes have been delivered—enough to house 20 percent of the current population. Yet over this same period, people in need of housing have continued to build shacks for themselves. New land occupations have proliferated at an unprecedented rate, and these typically face eviction. But why would a democratic government guaranteeing housing evict on such a regular basis?

We might suppose that this is a function of a municipal growth machine trying to secure its tax base, or else through collusion with private developers, an attempt to reclaim profitable real estate. Or perhaps it was not about the land but the people on it: evictions might be a way for a political party in power to discipline unruly protesters or punish partisan rivals. But this book provides a completely different sort of explanation: government officials order evictions to keep housing delivery functioning. Dispossession, in other words, is not *opposed* to delivery; it is a tool officials use to *protect* delivery.

Chapter 2 considers delivery and dispossession as linked governmental technologies of managing surplus populations. It begins with an account of their articulation under apartheid, or what I call *dispossession through delivery*. It was only through the construction of new townships, I argue, that forced removals were able to proceed effectively. But after apartheid, this relationship was inverted and remains so today: *delivery through dispossession*. The government's promise to remedy apartheid-era removals quickly became an end in itself, something housing officials defended at all costs. But when delivery failed to reduce the housing backlog, they identified land occupations as a cause, rather than a consequence, of this failure. And how are delivery and dispossession linked in practice? I suggest that this articulation is concretized in law, from the 1996 constitution to a series of more recent Constitutional Court rulings. While the constitution is quite generous, comparatively speaking, in guaranteeing the right to housing, it winds up shifting politics onto the judicial register, rendering political decision-making technocratic. This results in the demobilization of organized resistance and is central to my Gramscian argument about the legal dimension of hegemony. Whenever land occupiers self-organize, they intentionally produce a civil society articulation of their politics; but they also always unintentionally produce a political society articulation. It is through the latter that they enter the judicial stage. These twin articulations, civil and political, are the basis of bourgeois hegemony in contemporary South African land politics: even when occupiers think they are evading the state's gaze, they still end up engaging the state on its own terrain. The chapter ends by drawing on interviews with housing officials to demonstrate how they link dispossession to delivery in their everyday practice.

In chapters 3 and 4, I argue that these political society articulations were unintended consequences of participants' organization at the level of civil society. These chapters provide an ethnographic account of civil society articulation in both occupations. Chapter 3 chronicles the beginning of the Kapteinsklip occupation, in which residents constituted themselves as a series. The organization that mobilized them represented the project of land occupation as legal, suggesting that each participant would receive a small plot of land. They therefore viewed the state as a partner in realizing the dream of distributive democracy. Rather than forming a unified front against an antagonistic state, each household instead passively received plots from the organization on an atomized basis. When they were subsequently confronted by armed police, they organized defensively into factions to secure access to their own plots, rather than as a collective defending the entire occupation.

Chapter 4 provides a contrasting account of civil society articulation in Siqalo. In that occupation, participants viewed the municipal state as their enemy from the outset—not as a partner, as in Kapteinsklip. This was for two reasons. First, most of the occupiers had faced regular police violence in their former living arrangements, with their tenure rights being called into question. And second, they had come from established informal settlements—communities—rather than atomized backyard shacks as in Kapteinsklip. In practice this meant that they mobilized collectively, electing a single leadership to represent the entirety of the occupation. In each of the two cases, participants' prior views of the state shaped the organizational form they used to mobilize, or what this book calls civil society articulation.

Chapters 5 and 6 demonstrate how the civil society articulations described in chapters 3 and 4 translated into political society articulations in both occupations. Chapter 5 shows how the seriality characterizing Kapteinsklip translated into factionalism, which was in turn exacerbated once residents gained access to a lawyer. Without an elected representative, each grouping competed with one another for information from their counsel. In the process, what were previously loose groupings congealed into formally defined factions. After months of delays and appeals, the Kapteinsklip occupiers finally had their day in court. Judges read factionalists as opportunists squabbling over handouts and ordered residents off the field within a month.

Chapter 6 traces the same process in Siqalo, where a fused group translated into an elected representative committee. As residents expanded this committee, their lawyer came to deal exclusively with their elected leadership, which publicly reported back to the rest of the community. As in Kapteinsklip, their case was perpetually delayed. But ultimately, when they had their day in court, judges viewed them as houseless people in immediate need of shelter. Of course, this was objectively true in both cases, but only in Siqalo were residents actually read as such. This pair of chapters contends that occupiers were legible to judges, housing officials, and other government employees as political society articulations, even if these were unintended consequences of their articulation in civil society. Following Gramsci, I argue that these are two aspects of a single process rather than discrete spatial locations or temporal moments. Every collective project has both civil society and political society articulations.

Chapter 7 concludes the book by emphasizing the ongoing nature of these struggles. Political society articulations are inextricable from movements in civil society, and as the latter come into new configurations, the former change as a result, which has ramifications for the fate of the occupation. This conception of the state—as an *integral* state—means that how residents organize themselves on the ground can impact how they are "seen" by the state. The chapter concludes with four theses on the applicability of this framework to other postcolonial democracies, putting South African evictions in conversation with those in Brazil and India. In these contexts more generally, postcolonial democracies tend to face a dilemma: as colonial mobility controls are lifted, they tend to experience rapid urbanization, which, given the limited capacity of the postcolonial state to deliver housing, tends to be *informal* urbanization. This overwhelms the state, producing a stable backlog of those in need, but only a limited annual supply of housing and services to close the gap. It means that the collective struggle to articulate one's occupation as a "population" assumes a competitive dimension. Each occupation then vies with all others for the attention of its respective local government. These struggles are the subject of this book.

2

Dynamics of Delivery and Dispossession

Delivery and dispossession are usually understood to be necessarily antithetical. If dispossession is the separation of people from land, housing, and essential services, typically by force, then delivery is assumed to remedy this condition. When the postapartheid government rolled out housing and service delivery programs in the early 1990s, it did so in the name of reversing the wrongs wrought by centuries of dispossession under colonialism, segregation, and apartheid. The former program, housing delivery, is the subject of this chapter, but I want to treat it in a very particular way. Delivery, I argue, is inseparable from dispossession. Rather than map each concept onto a bounded period—for example, dispossession under apartheid and delivery under democracy—I want to explore how the two are articulated in novel configurations in different historical conjunctures.

After all, housing delivery in South Africa was an invention of the apartheid state, and today's housing waiting list has its origins under National Party rule. Conversely, mass evictions are hardly a thing of the past, with both individuals and mass occupations facing removal on a regular basis today, that is, in the *post*apartheid period. But why did the apartheid government distribute housing on a mass basis to its racialized subjects of dispossession? Or today, why would a democratically elected government, one that stakes its very legitimacy on the success of remedying apartheid removals, risk that legitimacy by evicting those most desperately in need of housing? This is only a puzzle if we think about the state as *either* repressive or consensual. But as Gramsci argued, every state is both: rather than select one or the other, the question is which predominates in the couplet he called the integral state. Rather than writing force out of the postapartheid story altogether, obscuring it from view, this chapter wants to understand the actually existing violence of ongoing evictions as a constitutive part of the state's delivery apparatus. Delivery and dispossession are not always antithetical, in other words; sometimes dispossession can work *in the service of* delivery.

But what would this look like in empirical terms? In what sense can evictions be said to *enable* delivery? The central argument of this chapter

Delivery as Dispossession. Zachary Levenson, Oxford University Press. © Oxford University Press 2022.
DOI: 10.1093/oso/9780197629246.003.0002

is that the postapartheid government articulated—and continues to articulate—democracy as a remedial project, a state-led restoration of access to
land and housing in the face of centuries of dispossession. The growth of
new shack settlements, meanwhile, appears as a sign of governmental failure.
Where eviction is not an option, housing officials frequently attempt to bump
squatters to the top of the waiting list in order to clear these occupations. But
as I explain later in this chapter, this inverts the causality of the sequence.
Residents do not typically occupy land in order to reduce their time on the
waiting list; they do so out of sheer necessity, because they have no alternative
in the meantime. It is housing officials who link occupations to "jumping the
queue," even where no explicit request for housing is made. As the number
of exceptions becomes substantial, subsequent occupiers are disparaged as
unruly "queue jumpers" and "opportunists," earning the disdain of government officials and being targeted for eviction. All of this is justified in the
name of preserving the formal rationality of the waiting list—and therefore
democracy.[1]

It is in this way that during the process of democratization, dispossession enables delivery. But before turning to an extended analysis of the
postapartheid articulation of delivery and dispossession, I examine how
they were linked in a very different configuration during the final decades
of apartheid. If, after apartheid, dispossession proceeded in the name of delivery, during apartheid, delivery enabled dispossession. The next section
provides an account of this novel combination. It was only through the construction of new townships, I argue, that forced removals were able to proceed effectively. While the standard narrative emphasizes the moment of
dispossession, there is remarkably little scholarship on the construction of
relocation sites constituting the moment of delivery. I then proceed to intro-
duce delivery through dispossession after the arrival of democracy in 1994.
The ANC promised housing delivery as a means of counteracting apartheid-
era dispossession. But as delivery became an end in itself, housing officials
sought to protect it at all costs. Unable to reduce the housing backlog, they
identified land occupations as a *cause* of this failure, rather than its logical
outcome.

In a third section, I describe how delivery and dispossession are linked
by law, examining how housing distribution and eviction are tied together
in both the postapartheid constitution and a series of twenty-first-century
Constitutional Court rulings. The fourth section explains how despite good
intentions, the articulation of the right to housing in law winds up shifting

politics onto the judicial register, rendering political decision-making technocratic. This results in the demobilization of organized resistance; to borrow the Comaroffs' expression, class struggle is transformed into class action. Lawyers mediate between residents' assertion that squatters are the logical outcome of the lack of postapartheid land reform, and officials' claim that they are not the consequence but the cause of insufficient housing. Drawing on interviews with DHS officials in Cape Town, the final section emphasizes the moralism inherent in the bureaucratic gaze, with eviction deployed, paradoxically, in order to allegedly protect the very squatters who face it. Dispossession, in other words, proceeds in the name of delivery. But first, we must examine delivery enabling dispossession under apartheid.

Dispossession through Delivery

Very little has been written about the role of housing delivery in relation to dispossession under apartheid.[2] To be clear, there is a vast literature on apartheid-era removals, during which well over 3.5 million Black South Africans were forcibly relocated.[3] But there is very little written about the de novo construction of peripheral townships to which urban evictees were relocated. In other words, this moment of construction, and therefore delivery, is rarely directly connected to the moment of destruction: dispossession.

In this section, I elaborate on the linkage between the two concepts in a specific context, explaining how it was that new township construction facilitated evictions beginning in the period of high apartheid, roughly spanning from the late 1960s to the demise of the regime. In some sense, removals are linked to relocation by definition, and even before the rise of the apartheid regime in 1948, there are some prominent cases. For example, Cape Town's first "African" township, Langa, was constructed in 1927 following the passage of the Native (Urban Areas) Act four years earlier, after residents were forcibly relocated from Ndabeni, a stone's throw to the west.[4] This 1923 law was the first to formally segregate urban space, defining "Africans" as migrant workers and requiring them to carry passbooks.[5] But it also required the government to provide accommodation for relocated "natives." This was hardly limited to Cape Town. In 1931, for example, "Africans" were forcibly removed from Johannesburg to the newly constructed township of Orlando to the southwest—what would become the first neighborhood in the South

Western Townships, popularly known as Soweto, which remains by far the largest "African" township in South Africa today. Even earlier, "African" residents of Korsten in Port Elizabeth were removed to the newbuild township of New Brighton.[6]

Once the National Party came to power in 1948, mass relocations picked up pace and so too, therefore, did the construction of new housing for racialized populations. The "African" cultural hub of Sophiatown in Johannesburg was forcibly displaced in 1955, with the majority of residents relocated to additional neighborhoods constructed in Soweto.[7] This reclaimed white group area was renamed Triomf in Afrikaans, which was only changed back to Sophiatown in 2006. Because the Immorality Amendment Act had illegalized multiple "races" residing in the same area, Sophiatown's "Colored" population was pushed to Eldorado Park and its Indian population to Lenasia, both of which remain sizable townships today. Similar removals occurred in all major South African cities. In Durban, tens of thousands were purged from Cato Manor. "African" residents were "deported" to the "homeland" of KwaMashu, about twenty kilometers north of their old homes. Meanwhile, Indian residents were relocated to the newly constructed townships of Chatsworth and Phoenix.

Cape Town was unique in that there were initially only a couple of "African" townships established within city limits. The bulk of "Africans" there were initially relocated to areas designated amaXhosa Bantustans nearly a thousand kilometers eastward in the Eastern Cape. In 1955, the apartheid government's notorious Secretary of Native Affairs W. W. Eiselen pushed through the 1955 Coloured Labour Preference Policy, which effectively declared parts of Cape Town to be the "Colored" "homeland." "Africans" were mostly endorsed out of the city entirely, while Cape Town's center of "Colored" cultural life, District Six, was razed to the ground. In 1966, in accordance with the Group Areas Act, the neighborhood was designated a white group area, and demolition began immediately. Residents were relocated to newly constructed townships on the Cape Flats, far from the city center, with the largest of them, Mitchells Plain, built in the mid-1970s. By 1982, more than sixty thousand "Colored" residents had been dispossessed, with a white university and a handful of churches arising from the ruins of the former residential and commercial district. Meanwhile, city engineers were busy designing forty thousand new units in Mitchells Plain for a projected quarter million[8] relocatees during precisely the period in which District Six was leveled. Similar processes were at work elsewhere in the city. "African" residents living in informal housing, most notoriously in Crossroads, were designated "squatters" by the government.[9] Despite earlier promises to move them into adjacent formal housing, in 1983, Minister of Cooperation and Development Piet Koornhoof announced that they would be moved to Khayelitsha, isiXhosa for "new home." Construction commenced that same year, and today Khayelitsha is the largest township in Cape Town. Delivery, in other words, facilitated dispossession.

The late historian Bill Freund calls this process "pseudo-suburbaniza- tion."[10] If the erection of suburbs in, say, the United States was only pos- sible because residents owned their own vehicles, the same was not true in South Africa. These new townships were intentionally designed to be sat- ellite cities, self-enclosed and, above all, separate and far away from white neighborhoods—what the sociologist Ivan Evans calls "manufactured frag- mentation."[11] They were largely designed along classic modernist lines, and if one were to examine some of the architectural plans, one might notice the influence of Ebenezer Howard's "garden city" ideals.[12] But as Saul Dubow points out, these "green belts or 'park strips' in beautifully drawn architec- tural plans could easily become military buffer zones surrounding bleak featureless fields of barrack-like housing."[13] Anyone who has spent time in a South African township will immediately recognize Dubow's characteri- zation: countless sprawling fields, typically barren, and the drab concrete of paved-over sections painting the landscape a monotonous taupe.

But why did the apartheid government invest so much energy in empha- sizing the delivery side of the equation? According to the Surplus People Project, in what is easily the most comprehensive analysis of relocations under apartheid, the government feared bad publicity, and conditions began to improve in the late 1960s and early 1970s.[14] Especially after the English- born Franciscan priest Cosmas Desmond published his popular exposé *The Discarded People*[15] in 1971, criticism of existing relocation schemes increased, with the lack of essential services and subpar housing structures widely condemned. In the face of domestic criticism, a rising chorus of inter- national condemnation, and a revived Black militancy in all major cities, the government shifted "away from the direct use of force and towards a greater reliance on indirect methods of coercion to pressurise people to move voluntarily."[16]

The activist researchers of the Surplus People Project were hardly alone in characterizing this as a strategic consideration on the part of the state. Evans suggests that this shift "diminished the need for state cadres to activate *continually* the means of coercion," depoliticizing evictees through the spatial regimentation of their everyday lives.[17] Others go further, arguing that beyond straightforward depoliticization, the provision of housing was intended to serve as a buy-in for those whose homes had been demolished. "However searing as the destruction of District Six in Cape Town or Sophiatown in Johannesburg was," Freund points out, "it should not obscure the significance of the massive construction directly by the state of new townships at first with family housing."[18]

And what was this significance? As numerous scholars have suggested, delivery was frequently a material enticement sufficient to overshadow the loss of community resulting from dispossession. "Matchbox houses and waterborne sewerage," Dubow argues, "represented a material gain, whatever the ensuing loss of freedom and community."[19] He also points out that working-class recipients of subsidized rent-to-own homes were enthusiastic about the opportunity to pay rent to municipal authorities instead of private landlords.[20] Evans goes so far as to call state-provisioned housing and services a "silver lining, for it meant an end to the immediate squalor and high rents that prevailed" in more informal living situations.[21] Sometimes apartheid planners worked to cultivate an attachment to new places, drawing on nostalgia for old neighborhoods. In the case of District Six, for example, the historian Vivian Bickford-Smith points out that two of Cape Town's newly constructed relocation townships, Hanover Park and Lavender Hill, were named after prominent streets in the old neighborhood.[22]

When it came to Mitchells Plain, the largest of the relocation townships associated with District Six, these considerations were central to the project. Above all, planners hoped to nurture the emergence of a home-owning "Colored" middle class. Cape Town's assistant city engineer for housing at the time remarked, "The impact of home ownership in an amenable environment can be seen in the lack of violence and the strong sense of neighbourhood-identity amongst the inhabitants."[23] Of course, in practice things played out quite differently. Very low crime rates in District Six, which was retrospectively stigmatized as dangerous by the government, actually increased tenfold following removal. Without romanticizing conditions in District Six, we can still safely say that the existing community was fragmented, and evictees were "moved out individually to buildings where they knew nobody."[24]

Still, planners and administrators wholeheartedly believed that fostering homeownership would split Black opposition to the regime, with elements of the "African" and "Colored" petty bourgeoisie realigning with a state that guaranteed their access to housing and services, as against the Black working class. In addition, as Dan O'Meara[25] observes, in the face of a recession in the early 1970s, the government saw shoring up Black demand as central to rescuing the economy. The provision of affordable housing was central to this neo-Keynesian project of subsidizing consumption. The chief planner overseeing the construction of Mitchells Plain rationalized the project along exactly these lines at the time. City Engineer J. G. Brand argued, "Social stability and improvement must lead to economic improvement and an increase in productivity. Mitchells Plain cannot but act as a considerable stimulus to Cape Town's economic base."[26] He proposed that a path to homeownership would get the urban poor to "pull themselves up 'by their own bootstraps.'"[27] Summarizing the rationale for the project, Brand suggested,

> As far as the new town of Mitchells Plain was concerned one of the first objectives was to shed the image of "low-cost" housing and to plan a town which could materially promote social stability, security, privacy and personal satisfaction by creating an environment which would encourage upward social mobility and assist in the formation of social groups and community interest.[28]

The formation of a Black middle class was central to the apartheid project of delivery starting in the early 1970s, which ultimately, served two general purposes. First, as I have argued in this section, without delivery, dispossession would not have been physically possible. The project of delivery entailed the establishment of self-contained satellite cities far removed from the white central business district and surrounding suburbs. It provided relocation sites for the majority of urban forced removals. It also provided an incentive, however bleak, to those in informal or especially exploitative housing situations. Receiving formal housing and access to essential services was a real, material enticement.

Second, delivery was part of a larger strategy of stratifying Black populations as a preemptive form of counterinsurgency. Planners consciously created different class environments within each township, reserving the best-located and best-constructed housing for what was deemed the "economic" population—as opposed to "subeconomic" and "sub-subeconomic," both of which required subsidies. Thus even within each relocation township, class divisions assumed spatial form. The idea was that distinct "African," "Colored," and Indian middle classes would emerge and align themselves with fractions of the white bourgeoisie and petty bourgeoisie. As Neville Alexander[29] has argued, this would allow the apartheid government to reconfigure itself as a fully bourgeois state, no longer dependent upon its compact with white workers. Of course, as Deborah Posel[30] has warned, we must be cautious about representing the apartheid state as a monolith with a coherent set of aims. We might do better to instead return to O'Meara's[31] account of various contending fractions within the ruling class and think about this policy as a compromise between intransigent Verwoerdians on the one hand, and incipient neoliberals on the other. Delivery enabled dispossession for the former while developing a class of Black entrepreneurs for the latter.

But delivery was not particularly successful as a means of containing burgeoning unrest. By the mid-1980s, anti-apartheid struggles reached their peak, particularly on the Cape Flats. A neighborhood in Mitchells Plain was home to the decade's most iconic struggle organization, the United Democratic Front (UDF).[32] While the UDF and other organizations campaigned against apartheid rule, other Cape Flats residents had to wage a more immediate struggle: against evictions. Black urbanization was finally legalized during this period, culminating in the abrogation of influx controls in 1986.[33] Apartheid urban policy often oscillated between extreme repression and bursts of toleration, but even during its more lenient moments, violence was a constant. Black squatters were criminalized and arrested, their homes were demolished, and they were left to fend for themselves. Compounding the problem, struggles with the apartheid state were often refracted through competing factions on the ground. In one of the larger Black townships of the time, for example, the UDF-affiliated settlement leadership became embroiled in a civil war with a Black vigilante group called the *witdoeke* ("white cloths"), named for the strips of white cloth they used to identify themselves.[34] They worked with the apartheid police and helped facilitate the demolition of UDF-aligned shacks. Yet despite this ever-present violence faced by squatters, both from the government and from contending factions, the final years of apartheid saw Black residents returning to cities in large numbers. Soon the newly constructed homes were overcrowded, and new land occupations quietly began to emerge in the interstices.

Delivery through Dispossession

Land occupations proliferated rapidly during the transition. In Cape Town, these included both "Africans" who had been expelled from the city altogether under apartheid, and "Coloreds" living in overcrowded homes on the Flats. It would be no exaggeration to claim that dispossession remains at the heart of what it has meant historically to be Black in South Africa. It should come as no surprise then that the first democratically elected government in South African history, elected in 1994, framed democratization as a remedial project, attempting to reverse patterns of dispossession so that Black South Africans could return to cities—not as precarious squatters on the urban fringe, but as residents with rights to both the city and adequate housing. Access to decent housing was not a new demand at this stage but occupied a significant place in the African National Congress's (ANC) program for at least forty years. Most notably, it was a key component in the party's 1955 Freedom Charter,[35] a document that signaled a break with the ANC's strategic orientation since its founding in 1912. Rather than demanding civil and political rights in an unequal society, the Freedom Charter defined full citizenship as inseparable from the securing of certain socioeconomic rights. When it came to housing, for example, the Charter proclaimed, "All people shall have the right to live where they choose, to be decently housed, and to bring up their families in comfort and security. Unused housing space [should] be made available to the people." Along with housing, the Charter demanded the full-scale redistribution of the country's material wealth, with land to be apportioned to "those who work it" and education, healthcare, and food to be guaranteed to all. These socioeconomic rights provide a material basis for the realization of the formal civil and political rights enumerated in the same document—speech, assembly, free trial, and so forth. The ANC then articulated its conception of democracy as markedly *distributive*: formal political rights only become meaningful when citizens can access the material means for realizing their citizenship.

This formulation of democracy, so central to the Freedom Charter, was subsequently incorporated into the postapartheid constitution, ratified in 1996. In contrast to late eighteenth- and early nineteenth-century constitutions, which tended to limit their guarantees to political rights, many late twentieth-century postcolonial constitutions explicitly protected socioeconomic rights as well.[36] The South African constitution guarantees "the right to have access to adequate housing" and insists that the state must "take reasonable legislative and other measures, within its available resources, to achieve the progressive realisation of this right."[37] It also prohibits arbitrary evictions, associated in the collective memory with the forced removals of apartheid: "No one may be evicted from their home, or have their home demolished, without an order of court made after considering all the relevant circumstances. No legislation may permit arbitrary evictions." In general, these provisions constitute an attempt to facilitate spatial transformation by establishing a legal framework for the redistribution of land and housing.[38] But more specifically, they should be understood as a concrete attempt to reverse a set of policy tools that were central to apartheid's spatial project of ethnoracial compartmentalization. In addition to the Group Areas Act (1950), as discussed in chapter 1—a law that redefined the best-located land as "white group areas," thereby legitimizing the expulsion of Black residents—the National Party passed a second major law one year later: the Prevention of Illegal Squatting Act (PISA), which effectively authorized the forced relocation of any Black residents the state deemed illegal. In a play on this name, the postapartheid Parliament passed the Prevention of Illegal Eviction (PIE) Act in 1998, which, in conjunction with a series of subsequent Constitutional Court cases,[39] requires the government to provide alternative accommodation when eviction is unavoidable. This means that no one is supposed to be evicted before the government offers them another housing option.[40]

The postapartheid government then explicitly articulated its project of democratization as one of remedying the inequalities wrought by apartheid, and it sought to do this in distributive terms. In so doing, it staked its very legitimacy on its ability to realize these socioeconomic rights, including the right to housing. This was the project of delivery, provisioning formal housing to those in need. In addition to getting structures to inadequately housed residents, the government used housing delivery to manage the rapid urbanization of un(der)employed Black South Africans. Whether they came to cities from rural hinterlands, peri-urban settlements, or overcrowded apartheid-era houses, delivery facilitated the relocation of these surplus populations to formal neighborhoods typically located on the outskirts of cities, in effect rendering the racial geography of apartheid permanent. But it did so in a way that allowed the government to proclaim the achievement of distributive democracy. Housing delivery, in other words, was not just about getting houses to people in need of them; it was (and remains) about managing the distribution of populations in urban space.

Paradoxically, however, delivery was facilitated through dispossession. Municipalities could not possibly deliver fast enough to meet the overwhelming demand for new housing following the relaxation of influx controls, and so new land occupations were inevitable. The proliferation of shacks since the demise of apartheid was a visible symbol of the state's failure to realize distributive democracy.[41] For this reason, municipal governments have tended to disperse new occupations, either incorporating them into the delivery process, or else further peripheralizing them in urban space through eviction. But despite this threat of removal, urbanization proceeded at an unprecedented rate.[42] Johannesburg more than doubled in population between the first postapartheid census (1996) and the most recent social survey (2016), and two nearby cities (Pretoria and Ekhuruleni) came close to doing so. Cape Town, which was roughly the size of Johannesburg at the time of the transition, is today South Africa's second largest city, with a population of four million, having overtaken Durban.

A similar trend characterizes informal housing over the same period. The government's official count[43] for shacks nationwide has nearly doubled since the transition, to 2 million. Of these, 1.3 million are in informal settlements and 700,000 are in backyards. By one measure, this is still an improvement, as informal housing as a percentage of total households declined from 16 percent in the 1996 census to 13 percent in the most recent social survey (2016), despite a brief uptick in the early 2000s. On the other hand, using a different measure, the results are not as clear. In addition to debates about substantial undercounting in the 2011 census,[44] we can examine figures on what the Department of Human Settlements— South Africa's housing ministry—calls the housing backlog: those officially in need of formal housing. The national backlog stood at 1.4 million at the time of the transition and within seven years had risen to nearly 2.5 million.[45] It dipped below 2 million in the early 2000s, but by 2005 it was back to 2.5 million, and today it hovers between 2.1 and 2.7 million.[46] In the Western Cape, where Cape Town makes up the bulk of the backlog, an even more pronounced trend is observable over the first decade of democratization: just over 165,000 in 1996, up to 230,000 the following year, and leveling off in the low 200,000s until about 2005.[47] Then in 2006, the figure nearly doubles to more than 400,000 as new Capetonians are formally included in the housing program.[48] Today it fluctuates between 300,000 and 400,000—more than a doubling of the backlog since the moment of transition.

In the early 1990s, debates over how to manage the sudden urbanization of racialized surplus populations occupied a central place in transitional talks.[49] In 1992, the ANC worked with apartheid-era opposition leaders, policy analysts, and private sector consultants to form the National Housing Forum (NHF) to discuss policy options for addressing this emergent crisis of informal urbanization.[50] But the NHF was quickly dominated by a neoliberal think tank called the Urban Foundation,[51] which effectively kept public housing off the table. The group produced the Housing White Paper in 1994, which contains the postapartheid government's plan to build one million formal houses within the first five years of democracy. This was in line with the ANC's inaugural social spending plan, the Reconstruction and Development Program (RDP),[52] although in the first seven years of democracy most housing was actually constructed by private developers.[53]

After 2001, however, new housing projects were primarily driven by public sector investment. Today more than four million subsidies have been released for RDP houses.[54] According to official data on how many homes have been distributed, at the end of fiscal year 2016–17, nearly 3.1 million formal ("RDP") houses had been delivered since 1994, as well as more than a million additional "housing opportunities." A "housing opportunity," language popularized in DHS documents in the early 2000s, describes the provision of a partial top-structure and a plot on a greenfield site, although how much these structures resemble housing has been gradually reduced over time, with the current iteration of "housing opportunity" closer to the old site-and-services approach—accent on the "opportunity" rather than the housing itself.

The annual figures reveal a few major trends. First, if the ANC promised a million houses in its first five years, we see it scrambling to meet this promise in 1998–99, followed by a drop-off and leveling out to between 130,000 and 170,000 formal homes annually. Second, an increased reliance on site-and-services from the early 2000s led the government to combine total figures (RDP houses and "housing opportunities") to exceed all but the exceptional period 1997–99. Third, a steady decline began in 2010–11, with recent drop-offs marking a downward trend, or potentially even skepticism about the financial sustainability of the program altogether. Human Settlements Minister Lindiwe Sisulu notoriously associated housing delivery with freeloading, insisting, "I don't know of a country that gives free houses to young people. Free housing in a few years will be something of the past."[55] She was distinguishing between those dispossessed under apartheid, whose sociospatial relegation the RDP housing program was designed to aid; and those born after 1994, who, she insisted, do not qualify as victims of apartheid.

Tokyo Sexwale, who succeeded Sisulu as Minister of Human Settlements, made a similar statement in 2011: "The solution will come not from free housing. There has to be a cut-off date for discussing that."[56] Of course, he added the qualifier, "But we can't cut off the poor right now, particularly in the current national economic environment," revealing Sexwale's hesitation to wind down the housing program.

When confronted about remarks Sisulu made at the Habitat III conference in Quito in 2016 about the limits of housing delivery, she responded, "The Department of Human Settlements will continue creating housing opportunities for all needy South Africans as part of living up to our ethos of respecting human rights and our people's dignity."[57] Whether these scattered remarks represent an impending phaseout of the housing program remains to be seen, but according to my interviews with provincial and municipal officials in Cape Town, Durban, and Johannesburg, this is not currently being discussed.

In any case, these figures demonstrate that South Africa has distributed more free, formal homes than any other democratic government in the modern period.[58] Yet despite this impressive scale of delivery, supply is continuously outstripped by demand. Municipalities cannot reduce their housing backlogs, most of which have grown since 1994. The number of shacks in the country has doubled since the transition, with informal settlements proliferating widely after the end of apartheid. While municipalities reluctantly recognize this fact, the national government refuses to acknowledge it and recalibrate policies accordingly. As Sisulu proudly declared at the ANC's Policy Conference in 2017, "We've done exceedingly well, when you look at the latest stats from Stats SA in the delivery of formal housing whether by the government or the individuals themselves. . . . We stand at something like 79 percent of people in this country are in formal housing," she beamed.[59] But this represents no improvement from 1994!

Managing Surplus Populations

When the government first conceived of housing distribution in its 1994 Housing White Paper, it emphasized the impartiality of its program. Against the backdrop of "the specter of Zimbabwe"[60] just next door, a case of redistribution rife with nepotism, not to mention the contentious debates[61] over land reform during the transition at home, the transitional team tried to reduce the risk of local politicians using free homes as a means of securing political loyalty. While such cases are not unknown,[62] control over distribution was centralized in provincial and municipal governments through the development of what is popularly known as the "waiting list." In its current iteration, registering on the waiting list requires the completion of a form at a local branch office of the DHS. Residents can typically find these offices in their own neighborhoods. Applicants must produce a government-issued identification card and provide basic personal information. The receipt they receive, called a "C-Form," contains the date of registration, the key datum for ordering registrants. When a registrant is selected, the DHS releases a subsidy in their name to the contractor assigned to the given RDP housing project. The municipality advertises tenders in local newspapers, and through a public procurement process, applicants (both public and private sector) are selected to construct RDP developments with municipal subsidies.

But this program is far from seamless. My fieldwork revealed numerous residents in Cape Flats townships who had documentation proving to me that they had been on the waiting list for over thirty years, meaning that they registered with the old apartheid system.[63] Some would wait for decades, while others would receive homes in a few years, contributing to perceptions of corruption, or else the conclusion that no waiting list actually exists.[64] A leading expert on housing law told a group of squatters in Cape Town that he estimates the current waiting period there at about sixty years[65]—assuming, of course, that no one else registers for housing. In addition to these interminable waiting periods, municipalities sometimes make exceptions, incorporating squatters they view as potentially problematic into new housing developments—even when they are not next in line.[66] While DHS officials tend to balk at these exceptions, they are typically requested by elected politicians for reasons of political expediency. Perhaps they made a direct promise to squatter constituents from another party and hope to win them over,[67] or else a group of formally housed residents or a private developer saw an adjacent informal settlement as a threat; or maybe a new occupation impeded a government development project, and transferring residents to state-provisioned housing was the most expedient route to getting them out of the way.

All of this produces substantial skepticism about the waiting list. Even those residents who are confident that the list both exists and functions impartially rarely wait the decades required for a home. Some are relatively recent returnees from the Eastern Cape, having been expelled to Bantustans as "Africans" under apartheid; others grew up in houses delivered by the apartheid state, but without anywhere to expand their families. Housing delivery was an initial attempt to manage these migrants, both rural-urban and intraurban, though it was hardly sufficient. As demand overwhelmed supply, self-provisioning became residents' only viable alternative in the meantime. And this took the form of land occupations: the typically collective (though occasionally individual) autoconstruction of housing on a plot of land to which residents do not have legal title.

An enormous literature characterizes the postapartheid state as "neoliberal," whether in terms of social policy retrenchment, liberalizing capital controls, indiscriminate privatization, industrial restructuring, or some combination.[68] But if the South African state were ideal-typically neoliberal, it would tolerate (and even encourage) self-provisioning when this did not impede ongoing development projects, affect labor force dynamics, or lead to the depreciation of nearby real estate values.[69] In the cases I observed in Cape Town over the course of this study, a different dynamic was in play. In the case of Kapteinsklip, for example, a thousand residents built homes on municipally owned land that was out of sight, uncontested by neighbors, and conformed to the general racial and political demographics of the vicinity. In short, it would seem to be an ideal solution for a neoliberal state shifting from formal housing distribution to provision of serviced greenfield sites ("housing opportunities"). But the city government still used its Anti-Land Invasion Unit (ALIU) to monitor the occupation, issue legal threats, and encourage the squatters to leave, while the South African Police Service regularly confiscated building materials and threatened arrest of residents pending a court interdict allowing them to do so. After a year of legal battles, all residents were evicted and the occupation was eradicated—but why?

If we think about the clearance of land occupations as an instance of managing surplus populations in the context of a crisis of rapid urbanization, we need to ask why a government might devote so much energy to regulating the social geography of poverty on the Cape Flats. Housing delivery and dispossession work in tandem as a technology of spatial regulation, controlling the distribution of populations in urban space. In this context, I understand dispossession to mean the physical separation of residents from their homes, land, and social networks. Eviction and relocation constitute a moment of dispossession insofar as residents' new homes are divorced from established networks, lack access to expected services, and are further from employment opportunities. In its classical Marxian iteration, dispossession was theorized as coerced separation from the means of production.[70] But this limited definition does not do much for us here, as its analytic power is trained upon the creation or reproduction of a formally free wage labor force. But in our case, all of the occupiers were already formally free. In the neighborhood in which Kapteinsklip was located, the real unemployment rate approached 60 percent. A functionalist conception of evictions as necessary for continual proletarianization, or even simply reproducing a wage labor force, does not make sense in a context in which an enormous percentage of the population is actively searching for work. In other words, a sizable surplus population already exists without requiring evictions to call them into being.

Another rationale for dispossession does not so much concern the people removed from the land as the land itself. Residents are removed so that land can be "developed" in order for its potential capitalization to be realized. This is what sociologist Michael Levien[71] describes in an Indian context as dispossession driven by land speculation. And while certainly this is in line with much of what the recent "land grab" literature identifies as a shift in development strategy from labor to land,[72] it does not accurately capture what is happening in postapartheid cities. The Siqalo occupation was officially tolerated even though it was highly visible, clearly growing, and across the road from a well-organized, middle-class neighborhood that wanted the squatters removed. And Kapteinsklip, which unlike Siqalo was not located on private property, was evicted in 2012, but nothing has been done with the land since, and no plans are in place for its private use. Far from an anomalous case, this is a fairly regular outcome. An occupation four times the size of Kapteinsklip was organized just a kilometer down the road in the same week. It too was located on public land and did not threaten any neighbors. After all four thousand occupiers were evicted in 2012, it lay vacant for years—and remains so today.

These evictions then were not sanctioned to recover valuable real estate, nor to create more labor power. Instead they were part of a larger pattern of state-driven dispossession that involved managing the rapid urbanization of surplus populations following the demise of apartheid. Rapid urbanization during and after the waning of authoritarian rule occurs in many (if not most) postcolonial contexts. In South Africa, the envisioned solution of market liberalization came with a corollary: the liberalization of labor and, therefore, of movement. And so the postapartheid state needed to deal with this crisis of sudden urbanization, but it could no longer simply shift residents around at will. It was a democratic state, after all.

Without any economic resolution of the question of unemployment, dispossession becomes the postapartheid state's primary strategy of containment—a holding pattern, so to speak. This does not mean we need to adopt a formulation in which state actors are involved in some strategy of counterinsurgency. Wishful characterizations of South Africa's surplus populations notwithstanding,[73] they do not currently pose a credible threat to the ruling party. If anything, their frustration with the ANC (and in Cape Town, with the DA) manifests in declining electoral support, but evicting these populations would make them even less likely to support the ruling party in their respective municipalities. Clearing land occupations is less a conscious strategy on the part of an autonomous state than an attempt by desperate bureaucrats to implement stopgap measures in the face of embarrassment. In South Africa, this means dispersing disorganized squatters, who are viewed by housing officials as impediments to realizing the goals of social policy. Whether this is the distribution of free or affordable housing, the provision of healthcare, or the coordination of labor markets, state projects of distribution require order. The local state demands formal rational order, and so disorganized residents remain illegible to the delivery apparatus. It cannot see them as its potential beneficiaries, for only organized populations qualify for this status. Instead, disorganized squatters are perceived as a threat to the very functioning of this apparatus, and they are dealt with accordingly. Eviction, then, is a means of dispersing these potential threats to the realization of distributive democracy in the only way local states know how: legally justified coercion.

After apartheid, dispossession became the sine qua non of delivery. New land occupations produce "queue jumpers," who upset the order of the waiting list, which undermines the capacity of the state to deliver, thereby threatening the realization of distributive democracy. Of course, this is to invert the causal sequence. In making this argument, officials are claiming that squatters undermine the state's capacity to deliver rather than acknowledging the obvious fact that squatters exist in the first place *because* of this limited capacity. And squatters allegedly do this because they lack proper morals. This recalls Gareth Stedman Jones's account of Victorian London, in which he observes that officials lacked an understanding of structural poverty, instead viewing unemployment "through the distorting lens of . . . 'demoralization.'"[74] Comparable moralizing is at work in postapartheid Cape Town in the specter of the opportunistic "queue jumper."

But not every occupation is targeted for eviction. Under what conditions do housing officials read an occupation as opportunistic? While every case is ultimately unique, removal is most likely when officials, lawyers, and judges are more readily able to represent occupiers as opportunists. And this is easiest to execute whenever factionalism prevails in an occupation, with small groupings of squatters jockeying with one another for access to lawyers, journalists, and material goods and services. This is not to isolate factionalism as a discrete cause, for we also need to understand the sources of factionalism itself. This book therefore takes a relational view of politics, thinking about how interactions with the state shape settlement-level strategies, and conversely, how squatters' mobilization impacts governmental decision-making. In other words, these are two moments in a mutually co-constitutive process through which residents and government actors shape each other's politics, which in turn comes to structure their own politics.

So, for example, in Siqalo, many of the earliest residents had either been active in the anti-apartheid movement or, more likely, had come from informal settlements in which ALIU patrolmen and police had harassed them on a regular basis. They therefore viewed state actors with great suspicion and sought to unify residents against this chief antagonist. They did not ultimately unite so that a judge would read them as a population worthy of the right to stay put; they did so to increase their associational power. But as it turned out, this power did not particularly threaten the state. In the Gramscian terms of my argument, they may have sought to challenge state power by organizing at the level of civil society, but intentionally or otherwise, their organization also produced a political society articulation: a unified population, which was ultimately deemed to be deserving of toleration.

By contrast, many participants in the Kapteinsklip occupation were far less skeptical of the state. The majority had come from backyard shacks. Even if they were exploited by landlords, they often had little to no prior contact with the ALIU or, at least in the context of housing rights, police. Nor were community leaders or politicians calling for their removal in the way that they often did for land occupations. When the community organization that first orchestrated the occupation represented it not as collective land expropriation, but as the delivery of plots, most participants assumed that their actions were perfectly legal and that the state was a partner in delivery. Their history of interaction with state representatives then shaped their organizational approach. Unlike the fused group in Siqalo, they comported themselves as members of a series: as atomized, interchangeable units rather than a singular body. Once police announced that the occupation was illegal, they quickly formed factions and scrambled to gain access to limited resources for their immediate allies. But even if their approach to civil society organization was not intended to challenge the state, their political society articulation—factionalism—was associated by both housing officials and judges with opportunism.

To think about a form of mobilization, then, as the ultimate determinant of an eviction is to arbitrarily freeze a given sociopolitical context into a synchronic moment, a static cross-section of an otherwise dynamic process. Civil society articulations are never autonomous "causes," but are rather themselves the outcome of engagement with the state. How residents see the state affects how they organize, which in turn affects how they are seen by the state. In the case that they are evicted and later try their luck in another occupation, their previous eviction experience undoubtedly shapes their subsequent organizational approach. This is important because it means that thinking dialectically in this way, situating each strategy in its proper context, can help us understand the dynamics of occupation and eviction. The alternative approach—isolating a strategy as a proximate cause—is not particularly useful in a context in which many occupiers, especially those without histories of conflict with state agents, may not think about strategy so deliberately and reflexively. In any case, most of them are not looking for strategic advice from movement intellectuals or academics; their strategies are shaped through experience. I therefore suggest that it is far more useful to understand the complex of state-society relations, making sense of eviction outcomes against this backdrop, than it is to abstract an organizational form from its social context and hold it up as a ticket to toleration.

Everyday entanglements with the state,[75] therefore, crucially shape residents' strategic decision-making. But what about governmental processes of decision-making? How does the self-organization of land occupiers in turn affect eviction outcomes? In order to fully explain this relationship, I first need to take a brief detour and explain why in the postapartheid context, struggles over housing are typically waged on the judicial terrain—whether or not this is the intention of land occupiers. In the following section, I consider the "judicialization of politics" in South Africa, explaining why social struggles, including those that attempt to evade the gaze of the state, still typically play out in the courts. In a follow-up section on the "judicialization of resistance," I explain how the constitutionally mandated right to housing shifts struggles over land and shelter onto the judicial terrain. I end the chapter by considering the role of housing officials in this arena. This entails an analysis of their moralizing discourse, which I analyze based on extensive interviews and situate in relation to distributive democracy: it is in the name of a "deserving poor" that an "undeserving poor" must be evicted. But of course, this governmental standpoint does not translate directly into policy from above. I conclude with a word on the relational nature of these struggles, which, I argue, allows us to trace the ongoing processes through which evictions result—or do not. Following Nicos Poulantzas,[76] I examine how policy outcomes, eviction among them, are shaped by struggles that themselves constitute the terrain we recognize as "the state": "Class contradictions are the very stuff of the State: they are present in its material framework and pattern its organization; while the State's policy is the result of their functioning within the State." This is the sense in which I argue for a relational conception of the state, thinking about it not as a preformed entity, but as a constantly shifting balance of forces characterized by contradictions, tensions, and even cracks.

From Class Struggle to Class Action

The state may be the "condensation of a relationship of forces between classes and class fractions,"[77] but we still need to specify the institutional forms in and through which these struggles materialize. In South Africa, struggles over accessing socioeconomic rights guaranteed by the constitution, housing among them, are usually ultimately resolved in the courts. The Bill of Rights mandates that the government refrain from arbitrary evictions and provide alternative accommodation in cases where eviction is deemed to be necessary. But laws as written rarely translate into laws as realized, just as government policies as formulated typically diverge from policies as actually implemented. Rather, legal outcomes are the product of drawn-out contestation over access to housing, and the courts have become the primary site in which these struggles translate into concrete decision-making.

The centrality of the judicial terrain to these struggles is actually quite characteristic of states that decolonized after the 1970s. The first round of postwar decolonization yielded constitutions that stressed the autonomy of the state, placing the onus of decision-making on elected officials in the legislative and executive branches. But since the early 1980s, postcolonial constitutions have shifted toward "the rule of law and the primacy of rights," facilitating what anthropologists John and Jean Comaroff call the "judicialization of politics," through which "class struggles seem to have metamorphosed into class actions."[78] Nowhere is this truer than in postapartheid South Africa, whose constitution was among the first to enumerate socioeconomic rights as justiciable and therefore enforceable.[79]

As conceived during the transition, South Africa's Constitutional Court was to be the highest appellate court for all questions pertaining to constitutionality. But in 2013, it became the highest court in the land.[80] This court has clarified what it would mean in practice for the government to guarantee socioeconomic rights over a series of rulings in the early years of the new century. The first of these landmark cases was the *Government of the Republic of South Africa v. Grootboom*,[81] in which nine hundred residents were evicted from their shacks just beyond Cape Town's municipal border, about thirty kilometers northeast of the Kapteinsklip occupation. The municipal government had plans to use the land to build a social housing complex, and paradoxically, it evicted the current occupants in the name of beneficiaries yet to come.[82]

When the evictees challenged the local government's policy, they won the first in a series of Constitutional Court rulings upholding (and giving practical specificity to) Section 26 of the Bill of Rights, which is the second chapter of the constitution. Section 26 includes three provisions:[83]

(1) Everyone has the right to have access to adequate housing.
(2) The state must take reasonable legislative and other measures within its available resources, to achieve the progressive realisation of this right.
(3) No one may be evicted from their home, or have their home demolished, without an order of court made after considering all the relevant circumstances. No legislation may permit arbitrary evictions.

The first is the most amorphous of the three,[84] declaring adequate housing a right without specifying how it is to be achieved. This is only truly given teeth by the two subsequent guarantees that enumerate the state's positive and negative obligations toward residents.[85] We might read these next two lines as standardizing delivery and protecting against dispossession, respectively.

In the case of the former, *Grootboom* and subsequent Constitutional Court cases have interpreted this line as imposing an obligation on the government to meet basic housing needs. Yet it simultaneously limits the scope of these obligations, citing the availability of resources and issues of capacity to delivery. The concept of progressive realization, derived from the first postapartheid housing minister Joe Slovo's "incremental approach,"[86] is then "both a sword and a shield": it requires the government to work toward meeting its socioeconomic obligations as specified in the Bill of Rights, but it provides it with a "degree of temporal latitude in its achievement of this goal."[87] How this balance actually plays out is then the prerogative of the courts.

If the first two sections regulate delivery, the third governs dispossession, limiting the conditions under which residents can legally be evicted. The blanket prohibition of arbitrary evictions is an attempt to break with urban governance under apartheid,[88] which relied so heavily on forced removals to regulate marginalized populations in urban space. A subsequent law, the Prevention of Illegal Eviction from and Unlawful Occupation of Land Act of 1998, usually referenced as the PIE Act, rendered this provision a bit more concrete. It was explicitly envisioned as a counterpoint to the apartheid-era Prevention of Illegal Squatting Act of 1951,[89] which authorized the destruction of informal settlements. Its replacement with the PIE Act meant that unprocedural evictions were criminalized for the first time in South African history.[90] In cases in which occupiers have been on the land for less than six months, it only authorizes evictions when they can be reasonably construed as "just and equitable."[91] Once squatters have been on the land for longer than six months, the PIE Act obligates "a municipality or other organ of the state or another land owner" to make additional land "available . . . for the relocation of the unlawful occupier."[92]

And what constitutes "just and equitable" removals "after considering all the relevant circumstances"? This is up to the discretion of the courts. Building on the foundation of the PIE Act,[93] the *Grootboom* ruling entrenched the requirement that the government provide "alternative accommodation" in cases of evictions. Increasingly, municipalities are standardizing these options by building "temporary relocation areas" (TRAs), as they are called in Cape Town,[94] comparable to Durban's "transit camps"[95] and Johannesburg's "decant camps."[96] Most of these were initially intended to last for roughly six months as a stopgap measure in emergency situations, as the names imply: temporary, transit, decant. But few TRA structures have served this transitional function in practice. Instead, they have become regular features of the South African urban housing landscape, functioning as state-provisioned housing even in nonemergency situations and lasting for well over a decade. This produces a peculiar state of precarity that I have elsewhere termed "permanent temporariness."[97] Despite the emergence of TRAs on a case-by-case basis rather than a citywide program, they have been unified after the fact under the policy umbrella of the Emergency Housing Programme.[98]

In Cape Town, TRAs tend to be stigmatized and unpopular among residents—as they are in most South African cities. They are poorly located, with the majority in the apartheid-era belt of "African" townships above Mitchells Plain. After being relocated, residents lose their community support networks and often find themselves in unfamiliar gang terrain.[99] They reinforce the spatial mismatch wrought by apartheid, with Black populations moved further from the city center, increasing their transport costs while decreasing their likelihood of employment.[100] They are also often far from social and municipal services. As a result, when offered a spot in a TRA, squatters often refuse it. This is what happened in the case of Kapteinsklip, as well as at a simultaneous occupation just down the road. The occupiers were shown housing in Symphony Way TRA, popularly known as "Blikkiesdorp" (Afrikaans for "tin can town"), but most turned it down after a visit. A half dozen residents did accept, but the rest could subsequently be evicted, as the Blikkiesdorp option met the legal requirement for alternative accommodation.

The Judicialization of Resistance

In order for eviction proceedings to begin, they must be initiated by either the municipality, in cases of public land, or the landowner, in instances of private property. Such cases can either originate at a local magistrate's court, or else in the provincial-level High Court. Both of the cases I examine in this book began at the Western Cape High Court, located just off Long Street in the city center. One housing lawyer[101] explained to me that complainants often initiate proceedings in the High Court because this requires potential evictees to enlist the services of an advocate. In South Africa, these are specialist litigators who argue cases before the High Court. This, she told me, increases the barrier for land occupiers, as they typically lack immediate access to an advocate. And besides, occupations are usually located quite a distance from the High Court. By contrast, magistrate's courts are scattered across the Cape Flats and are therefore much more accessible to squatters on short notice.

These cases are usually drawn out over a prolonged period. The Kapteinsklip occupation was tied up in the High Court for a year, and the Siqalo case for even longer. The process begins when a complainant brings an ex parte application to the court and asks for permission to serve papers to squatters. Typically these papers must be served to identified and named respondents (as well as unnamed occupiers, who can be added at a later date), meaning that eviction interdicts are physically attached to shack doors. When papers are not served in person, the applicant needs both an ex parte application and a Section 4(2) notice. This is a reference to Section 4(2) of the PIE Act: "At least 14 days before the hearing of the proceedings contemplated in subsection 50(1), the court must serve written and effective notice of the proceedings on the unlawful occupier and the municipality having jurisdiction."[102] The respondent is then given a specified time period in which they must respond, which, according to the PIE Act, is no fewer than forty days.

Next, the complainant must bring a notice of motion, which includes their attorneys, what they seek, the case number, and the dates by which squatters must respond. In order to do this they must draft a founding affidavit, which establishes why the applicant has standing to evict, which in most cases means establishing themselves as an owner or the person in charge of the land, as well as why they think that the occupation is unlawful and how the eviction will comply with the "just and equitable" provision of the PIE Act. If the people facing eviction want to contest these facts, they are within their rights to respond to the founding affidavit.

Once the eviction interdict is issued, the case is assigned a number. If land occupiers ignore it, they are typically evicted. But when they do comply, the case goes to trial, as happened for both the Kapteinsklip and Siqalo occupations. The judge sets a date for arguments, which rarely finish in a single day. Sometimes they can be delayed for months. And if potential evictees appeal the case, as they can to the High Court in cases originating in the magistrate's court, or to the Supreme Court of Appeal or Constitutional Court in cases originating in the High Court (depending upon the nature of the appeal), it can drag on even longer.

And how do residents contest evictions? Building upon the Comaroffs,[103] Gautam Bhan[104] calls this process in an Indian context the "judicialization of resistance." He points out that "multiple strategies of resistance are further complicated when the object of resistance is the Court rather than the Executive."[105] While she does not deploy the same term, Marie Huchzermeyer[106] observes a similar phenomenon in her analysis of one South African social movement's challenge to the Slums Act in KwaZulu-Natal: a once militant squatters' movement that has historically disavowed engagement with the government finds itself reorienting its strategy toward the courtroom. One critic of this tendency argues that this shift has "neutralizing results" for its politics, which necessarily adapts to "liberalizing discourse."[107] But Huchzermeyer[108] maintains that this shift does not necessarily come at the expense of more militant direct action, which can often complement legal strategies, and in any case, she insists, the two have grown in tandem in recent years; they do not exist in zero-sum relation.

Whatever the case, with the shifting of class struggle onto the judicial register, we can observe a major strategic reorientation. This is not a case of collective actors applying some form of pressure on the state, whether through direct action, violence, or a combination of both; something else is at work here. While certainly violent tactics can be a regular feature of land occupations, force is typically reserved for minor outbursts against representatives of the state, whom residents recognize as agents of their eviction. Such targets are often marginal, if not irrelevant, to the eviction process. For example, when the Independent Electoral Commission set up a tent to register voters on the road next to Siqalo, residents set it on fire. This was most likely because participants understood it as a symbol of the municipal state—the same state that was trying to have them evicted. But these occupiers never attempted to collectively pressure the state, and in the occupations considered here, it was never their intention to do so. The significance of collective representation in these cases lies not in the combined power it bestows upon the squatters, but instead in the recognition it gives them in the face of the law. Intentions are beside the point. Occupiers may understand their own self-organization as autonomous, beyond any engagement with the state, and therefore solely on the terrain of civil society. But as I argue in this book, every civil society articulation is also a political society articulation, and the consequences of one are often quite distinct from the consequences of the other—and they may even be in conflict. So, for example, when the Siqalo occupiers elected a unified committee, they were not particularly concerned with how doing so might appear to housing officials or a judge; they were instead dealing with logistical questions of the occupation. Regardless, the political society articulation of this form of organization rendered them legible to the judge as houseless people in need, as opposed to, say, opportunists scrambling for handouts, or else unruly obstacles to the project of delivery. The key point here is that land occupations do not directly pressure the state, and the most consequential effect of their organization is often unintentional.[109]

A political society articulation, then, is not about an occupation collectively projecting itself as legible and legitimate to judges as some autonomous, self-enclosed force. The process of articulation is also shaped by engagement with "the state," whether representatives of the DHS, their legal team, their police enforcers, or in some cases, private landholders as well (as in Siqalo). As residents undertake the narrative work of representation via their lawyers, the government's legal team always presents an opposing account. The court then adjudicates between these two competing narratives, deciding whether residents are houseless people in need or opportunistic queue jumpers.[110] This process of negotiation is comparable to what Julie-Anne Boudreau describes as the informalization of the state. Rules are always negotiable, she argues: "Law is seen as open, flexible, subject to multiple interpretations as inscribed in a changing relation between the legal/illegal, legitimate/illegitimate, authorized/unauthorized."[111] Laws, much like the state, are always relational processes rather than inflexible monoliths determined in advance.[112]

It may be the case that without concretely specified guidelines as to which occupations may stay put and which may be subject to eviction, the subjective decision of the judge remains the ultimate determinant of squatters' fates. Yet this is not a unilateral decision, but rather one in which squatters' civil society articulation can shape their political society articulation; that is, how they self-organize can impact how they are recognized. But this is not necessarily "agency" in a sense that should be valorized; rather, it approximates the " 'spontaneous' consent given by the great masses of the population to the general direction imposed on social life by the dominant fundamental group," or what Gramsci[113] described as hegemony. As much as the law remains a site of contestation, it is also a decidedly hostile terrain that provides the grammar with which occupiers must communicate their project. As soon as they adopt this grammar, they accept the legitimacy of the very legal system that orders their removal. Even when they feel as if they are part of a social movement, this is not how their project is articulated on the terrain of political society. They are not challenging state power so much as communicating

via an organizational form, hoping to be read as "deserving" of the right remain on the land. In other words, their class struggle becomes class action,
and their fates are determined in enemy territory.

Seeing Like a Housing Official

If the courts adjudicate between two competing visions, with residents
asserting their moral worth and housing officials challenging it, we need to
flesh out each of these narratives. We will see how residents construct their
own narratives, articulating civil society projects, in the following chapters.
But how do housing officials understand land occupations? In this section,
I draw on interviews with officials in Cape Town and attempt to reconstruct
this vision. Broadly construed, their aversion to new occupations is articulated in the language of moralism: occupiers are seen as constituting an
undeserving poor whose refusal to wait their turn impedes compliant citizens from receiving housing. Eviction, then, is understood as a means of
preserving the impartiality of the waiting list, prohibiting "queue jumping"
altogether; dispossession is seen to enable delivery. Since the waiting list is
framed as a key component of distributive democracy, the "opportunism" of
squatters is understood to pose a barrier to democratization itself. Occupiers
are therefore misrecognized as cause, rather than consequence, of the insufficient pace of delivery. Eviction then, paradoxically, is wielded in the name of
the very squatters who face it.

We know how officials view occupiers, but what about their counter-
part: ideal citizens from the vantage point of bureaucracy? I sat down with
the Cape Town Department of Human Settlements' head of public housing,
who was clear right from the outset: the housing waiting list includes "those
who expressed a need and actually came forward to register like a good citizen should."[114] Those who both register and wait patiently are "good citizens," she rationalized, whereas those who are later to register or else remain
skeptical of the delivery system are delinquents. "We [are] paying for people,"
she complained. "You can imagine how they abuse the system. They will benefit from a house [when] they sell it or they rent it out, and they go and sit in
an informal settlement." She was suggesting that recipients of RDP houses
often refuse to live in their newly constructed homes, either renting them out
or selling them illegally for a small sum. While this is of course a real phenomenon, this has more to do with location than anything approximating

opportunism. When residents receive houses that are further from their workplace, this increases their transport costs. Without thinking about housing delivery holistically, tying its location to employment, transportation, education, healthcare, and so forth, many residents have no choice but to abandon their homes. Left without any other option, why would they not try to sell them off?

Two other officials,[115] who oversee new housing developments for the city's DHS, attributed occupations to those residents who do not believe that the waiting list actually functions as described. "There's a lot of mistrust against the system," one of them told me. "You've probably picked it up. People out there are not necessarily convinced that the correct people got the houses." This was true. I encountered countless residents during my fieldwork who alleged fraud, or else who could not understand the logic of the waiting list. They knew some residents who registered and received homes within a few years; but they also knew people who had been on the waiting list since the apartheid period.

"There's always allegations that, yes, there's someone that came from the outside that was very fairly new on the list, that he or she got a job or a house because they slept with this one or they paid that one or the whatever. So there's always that allegations. . . . But besides one or two single incidents, we have never been able to—what's the word?—obtain evidence to the effect that there was corruption or any foul play in any of those allocations." Residents made claims all the time, officials argued, but these were based solely on rumors. In proper bureaucratic form, corroboration requires written documentation. As one of them nodded, the other added, "People come with allegations. It's easy to make an allegation. But as soon as you must provide evidence, written evidence, then they are, well, 'I don't know.' Where's the letter you sent? '*Ja*, I can't find the letter now.' You know, this story."

This approach to delivery can be characterized as technocratic, with democracy administered from above by representatives of the state. These experts claim a monopoly over potential solutions to housing scarcity, dismissing self-provisioning as a nonstarter. They express hostility toward occupations because they view them as undermining these solutions, forgetting that delivery and self-provisioning are two very different sorts of solutions. Delivery is an ultimate solution, resolving the problem of houselessness once and for all. By contrast, squatting is an intermediate solution. The very existence of a waiting list means that waiting is inevitable: so where are residents supposed to live in the meantime? But when residents pursue such a stopgap measure, they are misrecognized by the government as hailing its agents and demanding regularization, or at least incorporation into the state's own regulatory framework. If residents try to fly under the government's radar, officials perceive them as trying to initiate a dialogue with the state. They are read as demanding consideration on a personalized basis, which is at odds with the impersonal treatment that is supposed to define a classic bureaucracy.[116] The waiting list represents the latter, and occupations represent the former.

In practice, I rarely encountered someone who occupied land to secure a formal house. And in cases where occupiers were moved into houses, it was only framed by DHS officials as intentional queue jumping in retrospect. Sometimes members of the city council, or even the mayor, would promise formal housing to a manageable constituency in the name of securing political loyalty.[117] Or else it was seen to be the most effective means of quickly clearing a small occupation that might otherwise grow in size. This is what happened, for example, in a small occupation in another of Cape Town's "Colored" townships called Zille Raine Heights. The "Zille" in its name comes from Cape Town's mayor at the time, Helen Zille, who authorized their occupation.[118] After sixty-three families occupied an initial plot of land, police tried to force them off, "arguing on behalf of the city that land 'invasions' cannot be permitted as this allows anyone to 'jump the queue for people on the waiting list for state-provided homes.'"[119] Zille intervened, facilitating the relocation of the occupation to a nearby plot, which was named in her honor: Zille Raine Heights, with the "Raine" short for Lorraine Heunis, a community activist instrumental in the settlement's founding. Nearby backyarders raised objections, claiming that these occupiers were given land before they were, and threatened violence. Zille's successor as mayor, Dan Plato, resolved the situation by offering them spots in a newly constructed formal housing development. The occupiers had never asked for formal housing, yet they were unilaterally moved to the front of the queue by the local state. I conducted interviews in Zille Raine Heights just before the relocation, and a number of residents confirmed to me that some of their neighbors were working for Zille's and Plato's political party, the Democratic Alliance.[120] This was also corroborated by two DHS employees, who scoffed when I brought up the incident, attributing it to "political favors."[121] While this is certainly a case of personalized treatment in violation of the Weberian ideal type, it was not the occupiers' premeditated aim. Rather, municipal officials gave them the option of "jumping the queue," only blaming them for accepting after the fact.

The retrospective application of this epithet—"queue jumpers"—suggests that the entire point of living in a shack is to bypass the waiting list. By contrast, officials see their proper place as objective data in a formally rational calculus of housing distribution. Of course, this does not solve the problem of where people are supposed to live in the meantime. But housing officials unequivocally demonize anyone they perceive as out of place, frequently likening them to thieves. I interviewed the city's head of land acquisition, which entails purchasing land for relocating squatters.[122] "If I take your car," she explained to me, "I'm guilty of theft, and the court doesn't expect the government to give me another car before I give your car back. But our legislation at the moment, we apply to evict people [on behalf of] a private landowner trying to protect his land. The court would say yes, but what alternative accommodation can the city or the government or the state offer?"

She was quite critical of the requirement that municipal governments offer alternative accommodation in cases of eviction and, more broadly, of the blanket prohibition of arbitrary evictions enshrined in the constitution. "So what I'm saying to you," she continued, "is that we are rewarding criminality purely because in our constitution it's written that it's a basic right." Her use of "criminality" was revealing, a concept she deployed not in its legal sense—as violation of the law—but as a moral concept. Even when occupations are lawful, the act of seizing land is wrong by definition in her formulation. Rather than viewing occupations through a historical lens, in which centuries of dispossession have rendered a racially stigmatized population houseless, she reduced squatting to a matter of personal choice: "If I'm sick and tired of actually staying in your backyard because I pay you a monthly rent or something, and there's a piece of vacant land, I will just steal it. It's not different from that. It is basically, to me, an unauthorized occupation."

But if not out of desperation, why would someone choose to live under constant threat of eviction in a shack on an open field in one of the most dangerous neighborhoods in the country? "From my perspective," she explained, "I think a lot of what is happening is need-driven, by all means. I understand that." But she added a caveat: "Having said that, urbanization alone is a reality that we need to cope with, but I think a lot of it is politically motivated and purely aimed at embarrassing and/or just jumping queue. I mean, this is really the issue." In her telling, the growth of new land occupations is not a function of the government's failure to close the housing backlog over the quarter

century since apartheid's demise. Rather, she reasoned, each occupier is individually attempting to undermine the government's redistributive project for
one of two reasons. Her "politically motivated" rationale suggests that Black
land occupiers resent the DA's consolidation of rule in Cape Town, and that
new occupations are an attempt by the DA's chief rivals—namely the ANC
and the Economic Freedom Fighters (EFF)[123]—to create chaos, reviving the
old "ungovernability" strategy of the anti-apartheid movement.[124] A second
rationale—her "just jumping queue"—frames occupiers as posing an exis-
tential threat to the government's housing delivery program. Once again, we
see occupations articulated as threats to distributive democracy.

Now we can see why housing officials are so intensely averse to urban informality, and above all, to land occupations. They view them as direct threats
to the ordering project of housing delivery. The waiting list must be bureaucratic in Weber's sense,[125] ordered in terms of written files with generalizable
criteria for inclusion. Accordingly, it should be calculable and meritocratic,
with time on the list determining access to formal housing. This Weberian
project of bureaucratizing the delivery apparatus is tied to a Foucauldian
one of disciplining unruly subjects.[126] In incorporating squatters onto the
waiting list, not only does the formal expand its reach, but the informal is
eliminated—the dream of any bureaucrat. Land occupiers become "patients,"
passively submitting to state logics of modernization and control. This would
seem to corroborate Bourdieu's[127] argument that "waiting implies submission." Javier Auyero[128] develops this line of argument, demonstrating empirically how welfare states can produce subjectivities of submission and
compliance. "The urban poor," he writes,

> in their frequent encounters with politicians, bureaucrats, and officials,
> learn to be patients of the state. In recurrently being forced to accommo-
> date and yield to the state's dictates, the urban poor thereby receive a subtle,
> and usually not explicit, daily lesson in political subordination. This has the
> effect of "mold[ing] a particular submissive set of dispositions among the
> urban poor."

These sorts of bureaucracies are particularly emergent in postcolonial
democracies like South Africa. As the transition to democracy facilitates
rapid urbanization, state capacity is overwhelmed, and delivery targets are
perpetually deferred to the future. Elaborate lists, registries, and backlogs
are then created to manage populations in the meanwhile, rendering them

formal in that they are legible to the government, but not-yet-formal in that they remain in shacks. As they wait in backyards and informal settlements, they become compliant subjects in Bourdieu's and Auyero's sense. The waiting necessitated by delivery[129] "modifies the behavior of the person who 'hangs,' as we say, on the awaited decision."[130] This project of behavioral modification, akin to what Foucault[131] describes as the "conduct of conduct," is particularly evident in government officials' attitudes toward new land occupations, and even informal settlements more generally. As I have demonstrated, they articulate a disdain for informality that focuses less on the structures themselves than on condemning what they believe to be immoral behavior.

But these attitudes do not simply translate into policy as implemented, or else we would see the indiscriminate clearance of occupations. Instead, some settlements like Kapteinsklip are cleared, whereas others like Siqalo are tolerated. This is where we need to get away from Bourdieu's top-down conception of power and turn instead to a Foucauldian analysis of bureaucratic incorporation. Domination cannot be reduced to the production of docility alone. Power is relational, Foucault[132] teaches us, meaning that every new mode of its exercise alters forms of resistance as well. Working in this vein, Sophie Oldfield and Saskia Greyling[133] point out that people waiting for houses often learn to "work the system" in order to secure exactly the sorts of exceptions we saw on display in the Zille Raine Heights occupation. Rather than patients in waiting, they observe residents learning the rules of the game and acting accordingly. Or else they extricate themselves from the housing bureaucracy altogether, as Richard Ballard argues, "tak[ing] charge by dodging, resisting, defying, commandeering, diverting, building homes, earning incomes and attempting in many other banal and spectacular ways to improve their lives."[134] More concretely, this is akin to what Asef Bayat[135] calls the "quiet encroachment of the ordinary": "noncollective but prolonged direct actions of dispersed individuals and families to acquire the basic necessities of their lives . . . in a quiet and unassuming illegal fashion." Tatiana Adeline Thieme[136] describes a similar phenomenon as "hustling," by which she means "a potentially progressive politics of adaptation and experimentation." This is not to suggest that we should idealize squatters as militants or insurgents. Most typically, they are not. But it does mean that we should avoid seeing them as governmental actors tend to: namely, as passive material to be manipulated from above.

Conclusion

It should be clear by this point that I am trying to break with two sorts of accounts of urban informality. In this chapter, I presented how housing officials "see" occupations and construct moralizing narratives about their participants in order to justify their eviction. But if in Victorian London this outlook translated directly into slum clearances,[137] in postapartheid Cape Town it is mediated by the judiciary. This means that squatters have an opportunity to represent themselves as deserving of the right to stay put. Unlike housing officials, however, they rarely do so consciously. Rather, how they are ultimately perceived is shaped by their self-organization. And how they self-organize, in turn, depends upon how they "see" the state. This should put paid to any "top-down" conceptions of state action. If how the state sees residents depends upon how residents see the state, which in turn revolves around how they think the state sees them, we can only understand legal struggles over eviction through a relational lens.

By the same token, I do not see it as helpful to understand land occupations as urban planning "from below." While certainly such settlements are autonomously constructed without governmental authorization, they do require sanction after the fact. Valorizing survival strategies, however brilliant they may be, does not bring us any closer to understanding why some occupations are successful whereas others are not. This instead requires us to think about how these strategies—and more broadly, social dynamics at the level of the settlement—impact decision-making on the terrain of political society. How residents see the state matters, but not only in terms of how it shapes their actions; these actions also affect how the state sees them. Civil society articulations within the occupation are simultaneously political society articulations, the latter being how occupiers are seen by various state agents ranging from judges and housing officials to the mayor, police, and ALIU.

Divorcing civil society struggles from their location in a real, material context obscures any assessment of strategic outcomes. By the same token, abstracting political society from its social context limits politics to the formal institutions of government. It therefore fails to account for how social struggles impact processes of political decision-making. Rather than select a perspective "from above" or "from below," I suggest we refuse this choice, maintaining civil society and political society in relation to one another. This is what Gramsci[138] meant when he argued against thinking about the state as limited to formal political institutions. While we might separate civil and political societies in thought as a methodological move, we should never consider them in mutual isolation or as "organically" distinct, as he puts it. As an alternative, his notion of the integral state enables us to trace the processes through which political decisions actually come into being.

Struggles within each occupation can sometimes appear oppositional, with residents organizing autonomous governing bodies that coordinate their actions. These operate beyond the zone of legality, functioning to decommodify land and refuse the process of government-directed housing delivery. Yet they simultaneously incorporate unruly residents into formal legal dialogue with the municipality, requiring them to either consent to leave their occupations, or else gain governmental sanction for their settlements. Hegemony operates in relation to state power in this way, establishing the very conceptual terrain upon which struggles must be waged. As Stuart Hall[139] explains, this arrangement "precisely allows for the space in which subordinate and excluded people develop political practices and social spaces of their own. Hegemony does not mean that they have to be driven out of existence or brutalised into acquiescence. They can maintain their own space as long as they are contained within the horizon of political practices and ideological systems of representation which place them always in the subordinate position."

In the following chapters, I show what this type of hegemony looks like in practice. The first pair of chapters details how occupiers in both Kapteinsklip and Siqalo developed discrete visions of the state. As should now be clear, these were not developed in isolation, but only in the context of constant interface with the formal political institutions of government. In a second pair of chapters, I explain how these visions of the state affected how each occupation was seen by the state, which in turn impacted eviction rulings. I follow Gramsci in this regard: while I may separate civil and political societies for methodological purposes, this is an artificial separation that can never actually be achieved. The first pair of chapters unfolds through the lens of civil society, whereas the second pair unfolds through the lens of political society. But these are simply lenses; I will not try to completely abstract one from the other, which would be a futile enterprise. Instead, my examination of emergent civil society formations will remain mindful of how these are simultaneously operative on the terrain of political society, just as deliberate entrée into political society is also always articulated in civil society.[140] We begin, then, with an account of how residents saw the state in Kapteinsklip, the subject of the next chapter.

3

Civil Society I

Kapteinsklip and the Politics of Seriality

The occupation of Kapteinsklip began as a coordinated incursion. On a brisk autumn morning, just before dawn, over a thousand squatters moved onto a field owned by the city. Most participants were backyarders from nearby sections of Mitchells Plain. They sought to leave behind the dependency inherent in backyarding, constantly having to beg for water or access to a toilet, let alone having to pay rent that they could not afford. For most of them, the goal was autonomy. This chapter recounts their various rationales for participation in the first section below. But how did these markedly individualist aspirations translate into a collective project of occupation, which required coordination and planning? In the second section, it shows how an ANC front group called the Mitchells Plain Housing Association (MPHA) appeared on the scene and mobilized individuals in advance. But it mobilized them in a very particular way: rather than organizing occupiers into a social movement with a collective interest, the MPHA addressed[1] each participant as an aspiring homeowner. In the language advanced in chapter 1, occupiers were hailed as members of a series rather than a group. The process may have been collective insofar as occupiers acted in simultaneity, but it was not collective in terms of their perceived interests. To paraphrase Sartre,[2] from whom this pair of concepts is adopted, they existed in a relationship of seriality, having nothing more in common than what they were concurrently doing.

But how and why did the MPHA address the occupiers as members of a series? As this chapter demonstrates in the second section, the MPHA represented itself as an arm of the municipal government, or at the very least, as its officially sanctioned partner. Residents[3] did not anticipate a major battle with police or the Anti-Land Invasion Unit; rather, they understood the process to be a component of delivery. The MPHA articulated its project as in line with the constitutional right to housing, as if it were helping residents to realize this right for themselves. Given the government's recent

Delivery as Dispossession. Zachary Levenson, Oxford University Press. © Oxford University Press 2022.
DOI: 10.1093/oso/9780197629246.003.0003

shift from actual homes to so-called housing opportunities (greenfield sites and building materials), this would not seem particularly far-fetched to participants. This understanding, however, altered their very political subjectivity. It affected how they saw the state: as a partner in delivery. This in turn molded the collectivity into a series. Individual occupiers understood themselves to be homeowners in the making. In articulating the project as one of delivery, the MPHA facilitated the development of a series of petty proprietors. Instead of banding together, they tended to protect their own plots, or else they formed small alliances with their neighbors. But in general, their outlook was exclusive.[4] Rather than mediating a collective will through an elected leadership, they issued more immediate and individualized demands, which ultimately coalesced into contending factions. It was not, of course, the MPHA's intention to facilitate such factionalism; but it was the real effect of their articulation of the occupation as an extension of delivery.

In a third section, this chapter explicates how the MPHA's organizational approach yielded a series rather than a coherent group with shared interests. This was just the first stage of serialization, which was only formalized into factions through the mediation of outside actors. In a final section, it introduces some of these external players and charts the beginnings of factionalism in the occupation. Chapter 5 will recount how the search for legal representation set this factionalism into overdrive. Without an elected intermediary body, as in Siqalo, interactions with lawyers exacerbate seriality into a seemingly irreversible factionalism. This has far-reaching consequences for how occupiers are seen by the state, the subject of a later chapter. But first, this chapter will explain why backyarders in Mitchells Plain found the Kapteinsklip occupation appealing in the first place.

Leaving Backyards

It seemed to me that Faeza and Ebrahiem had it made, relatively speaking. Certainly a formal home would have been preferable to the deteriorating wendy house[5] situated between the driveway and the doghouse in Faeza's parents' backyard, but the thing was not so bad. It was relatively sturdy, unlike the haphazard structures cobbled together from scraps of wood and metal that I observed in nearby informal settlements. And it was in the backyard of a formal home, surrounded on three sides by concrete walls, with a wrought-iron gate between the shack and the driveway, meaning that it was fairly secure. Their section of Mitchells Plain was plagued by gang violence and a *tik* (crystal meth) epidemic, meaning that armed robberies were frequent; a backyard shack proved far more secure than an informal settlement on an open field. While we occasionally heard gunfire when I stayed with them in their backyard shack, the only threat of robbery we ever faced came from Faeza's brother, who would sometimes steal from her and her children to fund his *tik* addiction.

Security was not the only apparent benefit of backyarding. Faeza's parents granted them access to the bathroom and the kitchen faucet, only locking them out after they would go to sleep. While this arrangement was particularly fortunate, it is common for backyarders to work out arrangements with homeowners for potable water access, especially if they are friends or family of the owner. But this is not always the case. Faeza and Ebrahiem's neighbor Kathy, also a participant in the Kapteinsklip occupation, lived in a backyard shack with her twin infants a few blocks away. Each morning, she would push a stroller down the road, loaded with two large pails and her children. She would go door to door, asking neighbors if she could fill her buckets to obtain enough water to make it through the day. Ever since the installation of prepaid water meters in her neighborhood, Kathy's daily quest had grown more arduous.[6] Residents would purchase a certain daily quota of water, and the tap would automatically switch off when the limit was reached. As one Cape Town housing official[7] told me, "As soon as you've used up your limit, it goes on drip. So you won't die of thirst—don't listen to that myth either. You will have drip water until tomorrow morning, when they open it up again. That's the only way we can control the water flow or the usage." While homeowners and renters may not perish, the limited daily supply of water did mean that they were less likely to provide it to beggars like Kathy.

Still, backyards afford residents with a certain amount of security and are therefore relatively appealing in Cape Town. Indeed, backyarding is a more common mode of dwelling in Cape Town than in any other major municipality in South Africa.[8] While nearly twice as many households live in informal settlements as in backyard shacks in the Western Cape,[9] these numbers are shifting over time. The recorded number of shacks in informal settlements in the province has slightly declined since 2001, whereas the number of backyard shacks has increased substantially over the same period, from just over 450,000 in 2001 to more than 710,000 by the time I began my fieldwork in 2011.

By contrast, participating in a land occupation comes with a number of inherent risks, including unfamiliar territory and inevitable conflict with the police. Why then would anyone move from a backyard to a land occupation? Sometimes individual circumstances precipitated this decision. I heard tale after tale of conflict with acquaintances or relatives who owned the house and wanted the backyarders out. Others were bitter about paying rent. "Once we got married," Faeza wrote in her diary, "we moved into the backyard of my sister's husband's aunt. We paid 500 rand[10] a month and 80 rand a month for electricity and 100 towards the water every third month if we had. They were very understanding people. It was just one lady with her daughters living there."

But the most common explanation I encountered was the feeling of a backyard shack as temporary or derivative rather than a home of one's own. Participation in a land occupation, then, is primarily a quest for dignity and autonomy. I asked Faeza why she and Ebrahiem decided to leave their backyard shack and join the Kapteinsklip occupation. "Desperation," she told me. I asked her to elaborate. "We were living in a backyard in a shack that's probably one by two—one meter by two meters." She could not help but chuckle at the absurdity of the situation. "And we literally had nowhere to go and were living there, struggling to survive, so—I mean, we had both families that we wanted to, at the end of the day, we wanted to settle down with them and whether we going to rent a house, whether we going to do whatever, the point was that we going to make supervision for our children to be able to make provision. So that our children can at the end of the day come to us, you know, and visit us. Not visit us; come and *live* with us."

This resonates with Faeza's explanation quoted in the first chapter: "We wanted a home. We didn't want to be by my ma and pa any longer. We wanted *our* place." This is not far off from anthropologist Anne-Maria Makhulu's[11] insistence that we view occupations as a strategy of "making freedom," a demand for recognition beyond the sphere of formal organization. "The everydayness of politics," she argues, "drew strength from an organic and ever-evolving set of needs and demands on the part of ordinary people in the course of daily life."[12] This is precisely what I observed in Mitchells Plain. While formal organizations sometimes emerged amid (and from) occupations, and they sometimes catalyzed participation in these occupations, it would be erroneous to claim that they organized them. The organizations and the political space in which they act are mutually inseparable. In order to understand the politics of land occupations, then, we would do well to interrogate formally organized politics in relation to the processes Asef Bayat[13] calls "the quiet encroachment of the ordinary," assigning a key role to quotidian desires and demands.

Individuals, Together

While the motivations for participating in a land occupation are inherently individualistic, rooted in personal aspirations and desires, the act of taking land typically (and paradoxically) begins as a collective effort. Certainly additional squatters filter in once an occupation is well established, even when it lacks legal sanction, but the initial phase of settlement is decidedly coordinated, organized, and collective. How then do individual desires translate into collective action? This is where formal political organizations enter the picture. In the case of Kapteinsklip, a group called the MPHA[14] began to hold meetings in the neighborhoods surrounding the field. "The first time we heard about them was mid April," Faeza wrote in her diary. "They had a meeting at the sports field," just around the corner from Kapteinsklip. "They were talking about the land that is going to be made available and how people need to pay the registration fee. A shoebox was going around for people to put money into. At first I thought this will be another one of those projects I could not afford." She assumed that participation would require a hefty start-up fee. "But I spoke to one of the people who seemed to be in charge but also seemed to be part of the crowd and he said no you can still register. Then one of the leaders said we are going to issue out land on the 13th of May, but that we must be there on the 12th."

The MPHA was not formally a part of the ANC, but it did function as a front group[15] of sorts. None of its members would admit as much, but they worked with the local branch of the South African National Civic Organization (SANCO)[16] and regularly featured ANC politicians at their mass meetings. Together with another ANC-affiliated group in the "African" township immediately to Mitchells Plain's east, the MPHA claimed it was helping to develop a plot of land straddling the two townships. The land was previously owned by the parastatal munitions producer Denel, but in 2003, the neighboring high school had to be evacuated following a tear gas leak. The factory was subsequently shuttered due to its proximity to one of the most densely populated sections of the township. After Denel abandoned the building, local ward councilors began to promise residents that the land would be used for new housing developments. The plot was strategically located between Mitchells Plain, overwhelmingly "Colored" (91 percent) and Cape Town's second largest township, and Khayelitsha, which is nearly entirely "African" (99 percent), isiXhosa-speaking, and the city's largest township. This mattered because Khayelitsha is the ANC's key support base in Cape Town, whereas Mitchells Plain consistently goes for the DA. ANC politicians working in Khayelitsha attempted to recruit organizers in Mitchells Plain, who could hope for some degree of political capital. Rarely was this capital forthcoming, however. While the MPHA continues to hold meetings to this day, it has not developed much of a base. The same can be said for the local SANCO branch, which remains anemic and operates out of a rented room above a nearby gas station.

And who were these operatives? The MPHA, like the Mitchells Plain SANCO branch, was largely made up of backyarders and other precariously housed individuals from the area. One of the MPHA leaders, for example, Rahim, would regularly resort to physical violence against people who questioned his authority, and he was notorious for his *tik*-fueled antics in the occupation, ranging from reselling food and blanket donations to outright robbery. Ivy, by contrast, was far less confrontational and was fluent enough in policy jargon to convince a room full of backyarders that she was a serious player in township housing politics. As the chairperson of the MPHA, she would regular speak calmly in community centers and schools around the neighborhood. When I listened to her speak to a group of backyarders in 2013,[17] she told them that the MPHA "formed because people need homes in line with their rights as citizens." She cited Section 26 of the constitution, repeating the line, "Everyone has the right to have access to adequate housing." This was enough for those in the crowd who were precariously housed, many of whom seemed to read this as a sign of her ability to work with the city government.

There were a half dozen figures associated with the MPHA's leadership, though it was a revolving cast and often appeared to function more like a social clique than a political organization. Most of the other members fit somewhere on this spectrum from Rahim to Ivy, and the same was true for their allied members in the local SANCO branch. I collectively interviewed[18] its top three figures. Its chairperson, Martin, worked as an ANC organizer for a few years in an informal settlement up the road from the Kapteinsklip occupation before joining SANCO. Like Ivy, his self-presentation was quite professional, though he was all form and no content. He opened by telling me that Mitchells Plain has a population of 2.8 million people excluding children, which would mean that two-thirds of all Capetonians live in the township. Jenny, the organization's spokesperson, was much more like Rahim. She was intensely religious, lived in a tent behind a nearby church, and could not seem to focus. She kept switching topics, regaling me with stories of her time in Spain and how she met a German prophet there, or how she was related to a number of ANC bigwigs. "The ANC runs deep in my blood!" she insisted. I certainly could not imagine her as a spokesperson for a political organization. She repeatedly referenced an ANC ward councilor from Khayelitsha,[19] suggesting that he was feeding them talking points. In return, she had access to an office, a title, and potentially even petty cash for lunch and transport expenses.

But backyarders in this part of Mitchells Plain did not seem to notice if these people were not seasoned political operatives. Many of them did not have other options and so had nothing to lose. Besides, in a South African context, framing the politics of land occupations in the language of "rights" and making occasional references to Section 26 of the constitution gave the MPHA an air of legitimacy. The government was left deeply vulnerable to collective demands for land and housing following the transition to democracy. It had staked its very legitimacy on claims to be a remedial force capable of reversing the material wrongs of racialized dispossession, but in practice its redistributive programs were slowly implemented, underfunded, and technocratic by design. This meant that those residents waiting for access to urban housing could occupy tracts of vacant land, especially those already owned by municipalities, but also plots held by absentee landlords, and they could claim to be enacting the same program of decolonization and national liberation that the ANC asserted as part of its "national democratic revolution."[20]

On 11 May 2011, the MPHA implemented its plan on two municipally owned plots of land. In practice, this amounted to having as many people as possible gather on each field in the earliest hours of the morning. The turnout was stunning. At Kapteinsklip, adjacent to the Metrorail stop, a thousand squatters set up camp. And on a sports field about three kilometers east, four thousand residents began to erect shacks. Both plots are toward the Khayelitsha side of Mitchells Plain: the sports field immediately bordering that ANC stronghold, and Kapteinsklip along the township's southern border, sandwiched between the train station and a coastal nature reserve.

Both occupations immediately drew the South African Police Service (SAPS) and the Anti-Land Invasion Unit (ALIU), with a particularly prolonged and violent battle on the sports field and lesser (though still notably violent) clashes at Kapteinsklip. The most intense fighting followed the first few days of the occupation of the sports field, with the police chasing down occupiers with Casspirs, pummeling them with purple-dyed water cannon, and firing at them with rubber bullets. The use of armored vehicles and, above all, the purple dye, reminded participants of the apartheid state confronting squatters in the 1980s. Casspirs came into general use during the last decade of apartheid, and purple-dyed water cannon were used during the same period. The 1989 Purple Rain Protest saw thousands of Mass Democratic Movement (MDM)[21] members doused with dyed water in downtown Cape Town, marking protesters for subsequent arrest. It gained such notoriety that "the purple shall govern" soon became an MDM slogan. Many people living in Mitchells Plain, birthplace of the UDF, would be intimately familiar with that episode, and in Kapteinsklip, it actually inspired a moment of solidarity among the squatters, though this would soon prove ephemeral.

But on the sports field, the confrontation escalated quickly given the sheer size of the occupation, and police tried to clear the squatters as quickly as possible. Live ammunition was allegedly fired by two of the squatters, but more commonly, they lobbed bricks at police vehicles and armored officers running toward residents. Some of the occupiers set tires alight, and "Whe shal [sic] not be moved" was spray-painted on the wall bordering the field, an image that accompanied most of the media coverage the following day. Police tore down hundreds of the structures that residents had erected under the cover of the night. By the next morning, fourteen residents were in jail, eighteen in the hospital, and most importantly for our purposes, only five structures remained. These half dozen residents were, in accordance with legal protocol, offered alternative accommodation in a peripherally located temporary relocation area.

Police successfully cleared the sports field, but given the lesser intensity of the battles at Kapteinsklip, a couple hundred squatters remained there by the end of the week. Without an eviction order, there was nothing the city could legally do other than to apply for one in the High Court. Officials did pursue this route, but it was a long, drawn-out process that would take more than a year. This was an ironic outcome, given what one of the occupiers told me[22] more than two years after she was evicted from Kapteinsklip: "According to me and what we figured out or found out afterwards, even from the MPHA, which is the organization that was in the forefront of organizing this thing, even they told us that Kapteinsklip was only supposed to be a—what's that word again?—decoy. So Kapteinsklip was never supposed to be an actual occupation. It was just to distract the police. But they never informed people about stuff like that."

According to a number of participants in the initial stage of the Kapteinsklip occupation, they were duped into occupying a field in order to draw as many police as possible, allowing the majority of occupiers to set up on the sports field. But this was a gross miscalculation. As it turned out, SAPS and ALIU were far more concerned with clearing the "real" occupation—not because they perceived it as "real," but because the field was in use and was surrounded by formal housing. Perhaps MPHA organizers assumed the police would care more about an occupation that could potentially interfere with the functioning of the commuter rail line, but this is not how things turned out. And so the "decoy" lasted for over a year, whereas the "real" occupation did not make it to the end of the week.

The Politics of Seriality

The violent police response actually caught residents off guard in both occupations. The MPHA never represented the collective action as akin to a social movement, and it certainly never invoked the rhetoric of radicalism or decommodification. Rather, it portrayed the occupations as the realization of the constitution's promise of land and housing. If the government could not help people realize their rights as South Africans, they would have to do it themselves. This was not framed as an oppositional struggle then, but as the devolution of government responsibility onto citizens.

When Faeza described the origins of the Kapteinsklip occupation in her diary, she claimed that the MPHA "told us about this land invasion that was going to take place. They didn't use those works: 'land invasion.' They told us we were going to get plots. They gave out numbers, little numbers, with their stamp on it and charged people 10 rand[23] for registering with them and gave us a plot. They had a book where they put your name and ID number, which they said would then secure your plot. They said we will get the plots that Friday—Friday the 13th of May, 2011."

Mimicking the formal rationality of the municipality's waiting list, the MPHA represented itself as acting legitimately as a sanctified partner of the local government. "When we got there on Friday," Faeza continued, "we took all our stuff from where we were living—our self-built structure like a wendy house. Myself and my husband and my four kids: we moved onto the land, and they told us that the plot size was supposed to be 6 × 4 meters. The structures were up, people were starting to move in. People were happy. On our field, Kapteinsklip, there were plus or minus 1000 people. The sports field next to us had about 4000 people. They were under the impression that they were going to get houses here." Faeza's use of the passive voice is striking: housing, or at least plots, would be *distributed* by the MPHA. "That Saturday the atmosphere was wonderful, a happy environment. Everyone who used to live in backyards, and some homeless, everyone was going to get houses. Everyone felt free."

As Faeza's entry makes clear, the formal order imposed by the MPHA made the initial process appear less like a land occupation than yet another means of obtaining access to housing. At the occupation's inception, residents perceived this as a typical instantiation of registration and delivery—not too far removed from the waiting list. They would register with an administrative body, in this case the MPHA, and then they would subsequently receive the equivalent of title deeds: the moral authority to lay claim to a given parcel of land. Even if the DHS and the High Court would later frame the occupation as an "invasion," it was understood by residents in its first stages as legitimate engagement with a government realizing distributive democracy—even if this "state" turned out to be a self-appointed committee with ambiguous ties to the ANC. What the city would represent as disorderly "queue jumping" was experienced by the occupation's participants quite differently: as orderly, regimented, and, ultimately, state sanctioned. This is the chief limit of the government's moralizing categories. While officials understand participants in occupations as simple opportunists, in the case of Kapteinsklip they clearly understood themselves as homeowners in the making. Their very participation was rooted in the aim of becoming a homeowner—or at least having one's *own* home. The goal was to break with the image of dependence and marginality tied to backyarding and become autonomous, rights-bearing citizens.

It was not only this formal order that gave residents the impression that they were in compliance with the law. In addition, the MPHA frequently represented itself as working with city officials to get the "project" off the ground. Given that sanctioned site-and-service projects are quite common in South African cities and residents typically did not know the difference between these and land occupations, their confusion should not come as a surprise. Another Kapteinsklip participant named Myra[24] told me, "[The Kapteinsklip occupiers] think it's that this organization is working with the city and has the right. They give people lot numbers and like registration fees and—"

I cut her off. "The MPHA? They give people registration numbers to stay on the field?"

"Yes, plot numbers," she replied.

"And they presented it as completely legal?"

"Yes, they were supposedly walking around speaking to the mayor on the phone, which was all lies. But we only figured that out after awhile." In addition to simply mimicking the formal rationality of the state then, MPHA organizers consistently represented themselves in proximity to city officials. Sometimes this would mean speeches from ANC ward councilors at their preliminary meetings, but sometimes it would be sheer deception.

Faeza confirmed in her journal that the MPHA insisted the mayor was involved. "People were standing there with no hope—hoping the Association [MPHA] will sort it out because they even pretended to speak to [former Cape Town mayor and Western Cape premier] Helen Zille on the phone and say that these guys had no right to do what they were doing and that she would sort it out." This was not so far-fetched given that many of the occupiers knew of Zille's role in securing residents housing in the Zille Raine Heights occupation a couple of years earlier, as described in chapter 2.

Faeza went on to suggest that the MPHA even presented confrontational tactics as officially sanctioned: "They left a committee of marshals, and the marshals told us we must put tires on the road and the [railway] station, and they wanted us to burn the road and the station. We refused because we knew what was happening at [the sports field, i.e., the violent confrontations with police] and we didn't want the same violence, and so we said no." The Kapteinsklip occupiers had neighbors involved in the sports field occupation and communicated with them in real time via WhatsApp. The MPHA then clearly tried to normalize even these sorts of confrontational tactics as state sanctioned. The group worked tirelessly to normalize the occupation more generally, rendering it a routine means of housing distribution even when it was patently unsanctioned and illegal.

But in framing the occupation as a project of housing distribution, the MPHA successfully sutured moralizing discourses of aspiring homeownership to a politics of necessity.[25] In practice this meant that people without anywhere else to go were persuaded that participating in a land occupation was a viable option. The MPHA appealed to them through their desire to become homeowners, which in government discourses amounted to becoming rights-bearing citizens. This sense of viability was actively legitimized through discourses of ordered individual restitution. The distribution of ersatz property to hopeful residents by an ersatz government organization mimicked the logic of the government's housing program, obscuring the fact that it was just as illegal as a disorderly land occupation without any intermediary body governing "distribution." And the consequence was that rather than participating in a collective project akin to a social movement, the collectivity was closer to Sartre's series: squatters shared the simultaneous experience of making a home, but nothing more. They certainly did not act in a coordinated manner in their campaign to hold onto the Kapteinsklip field in the months that followed the initial skirmishes with police, nor did they maintain any sort of collective solidarity. Instead, the MPHA's framing of the occupation as the distribution of plots produced a politics of small property-holders—a politics of seriality. Residents saw themselves as homeowners-in-the-making, and, as such, they protected their plots at all costs.

This began as early as the first day of the occupation. When residents arrived, the MPHA had begun to mark out individual plots with wooden stakes. Residents wrapped twine around these poles in order to indicate boundaries, often shifting them to enlarge plots, which of course produced disputes with their neighbors. The seeds of Kapteinsklip's factional politics were thus already sown. The factions that emerged in subsequent squabbles over governing the settlement did not reflect preexisting divisions but were instead forged in the process of occupation. They were overdetermined by the politics of seriality, which ultimately amounted to exclusivism: residents defended their land not as a total occupation, but as an assemblage of plots. This meant that alliances were often fleeting, and that rather than attempting to use outside actors (charity workers, lawyers, party operatives, and the like) as a means toward achieving collective recognition, residents vied with one another for access to these actors. They treated these connections as a limited set of goods, meaning that they competed with one another for access. And so as outside actors began to interact with the occupation, the politics of seriality shaped the form of residents' appeals: factionalism.

The Consolidation of Factionalism

Seriality is a necessary but insufficient condition for factionalism. Its basis in civil society—how collectivities are articulated—does not automatically translate into a corresponding articulation at the level of political society, that is, in the formal organizational domain. In Kapteinsklip, factions only emerged in relation to concrete struggles over competing interests. At the most basic level, this means that as outside actors, ranging from MPHA organizers to charity workers, began to interact with the occupation, temporary alliances formed around these characters. Residents were primarily concerned with securing their plots, as well as access to means of subsistence, such as blankets, food, building materials, and the like. Because the occupation was not constituted as a group but as a series marked by direct competition among participants, residents made little attempt to seek collective mediation between themselves and the formal institutions of the state. Or in Gramscian language, the occupation's civil society articulation (seriality) mitigated against a unified political society articulation. Instead, small groups of residents aligned themselves with outside representatives rather than representing themselves, seeking a shortcut to acknowledgment by governmental actors. This would have disastrous implications for the way occupiers were seen by the state, as detailed in chapter 5.

But to reiterate, there was no guarantee[26] that factionalism would prevail; the outcome was uncertain in the first weeks of the occupation. The persistently violent confrontations initiated by police continued for weeks. "Law enforcement came every day," Faeza wrote in her diary. "The Monday. The Tuesday. Most people were left with little bits of plastic to sleep under." Police and ALIU confiscated their building materials, and people were desperate for shelter, as this was both late autumn and the beginning of the rainy season. People initially shared their improvised shelter with one another. Friends and relatives would drop off new building materials, though these too were confiscated by police. Whoever had covering would allow others "to share accommodation. I think at the time that was the best thing that could happen to us, because it drew everyone closer. It formed unity. We got to know everyone and their situation—why they were there and why they couldn't go back. We started to form unity."

But at this point, residents were still working under the assumption that the occupation was legal, or at least that the MPHA had some kind of privileged relationship with the DHS. It actually took a few days for participants to accept that they had committed an illegal act.

> On Tuesday 17th May the sheriff of the court said over an intercom that we were there illegally and we were not allowed to be there. They gave us an interdict and gave us 5 minutes to vacate the land. Once again they removed whatever we had. People lost their IDs, their papers, their dentures. There was a lot of things people lost while law enforcement and land invasion units [ALIU] removed our structures. That was when we realized that this is illegal, we were not going to get anything. Nobody was going to be able to help us with this. We had been manipulated into the situation we are in now. People started to retreat—the lucky ones who could go back to where they were at. The rest that stayed behind, about 120 people, had nowhere to go. Yes, we all tried to go back, but either there was someone else now living where we were living before or the people didn't want us back [in their backyards], or people had no structure to put up in someone's yard [because it was confiscated by the police], so they just stayed with us on the field.

Those who remained at Kapteinsklip truly had nowhere else to turn. In a matter of days, the occupation was down to an eighth of its initial size.

With their standard building materials broken or seized, occupiers had to improvise (see figure 3.1). Residents began to search for shopping carts, as there were a couple of malls a few kilometers away. They would use overturned carts to support tarps and shield them from the rain. But even this proved too much for the ALIU. "They say even if you live under a trolley [shopping cart] with a blanket over top of it, it is a structure," Faeza wrote. "They say anywhere you are living is considered a structure, so they can take it. Interim interdict [from the High Court] says that both parties stand apart till the next court date. Our lawyers say they can remove structures, but not us. Are they working towards our death?" she wondered.

Even a month later, police and ALIU returned to the site to destroy structures. A number of residents had dug deep burrows into the sand, constructing makeshift roofs out of anything they could (see figure 3.2). When the police arrived on the scene, they kicked dirt into the holes, attempting to fill them up again, but before they allowed residents to remove their possessions. They even seized what Faeza described as "the roof structure."

Figure 3.1 Improvised housing in Kapteinsklip after most building materials were seized.

Credit line: Still from camcorder footage shot by Ebrahiem Fourie.

These visits proved traumatic to children on the field. Even after all semipermanent structures were destroyed, an ALIU agent removed tents occupied by children and drove a pickup truck through the occupation, "swearing and threatening to lock us up. [He] broke the small tent our mother and baby sleeps in. They referred to us as animals. The driver told one of our elders that he is going to remove his uniform and *moer* [beat] him and kick him in the *poes* ["pussy," a common insult in Afrikaans]. When we reported the situation to what appeared to be the senior officer among them he reckoned we had no witnesses. Then they left."

Clinton, one of the remaining squatters, was a "Colored" man in his midforties. He told me that the officers all covered their name tags with electrical tape, though residents began to recognize their faces. When residents asked for identification, officers cursed at the occupiers. "*Hou jou bek!*" they would shout. "Shut your mouth!"

Faeza confirmed Clinton's account in her journal. "They take our things once again. I don't know if what these people are doing is legal. If it is legal,

Figure 3.2 When occupiers lacked additional building materials, they lived in burrows dug into the sand.
Credit line: Still from camcorder footage shot by Ebrahiem Fourie.

why are their identities hidden?" Another time the police showed up in the middle of the night. "They had everyone get out of their beds because the police claimed they had a complaint about us selling *dagga* [marijuana]. They never searched for the *dagga* but they had us get out of our beds and did a move and touch fingerprinting to check for criminal records. They found no *dagga* or criminals among us."

After a month, these sorts of violent confrontations with police became relatively routinized. Partly residents became familiar with the ALIU and SAPS officers visiting the field, and partly they began to grow accustomed to experiencing this sort of violence on a daily basis. Once the initial shock of these encounters wore off, any unity that existed in the settlement, largely constituted against the police,[27] began to dissipate. As occupiers realized they would have to figure out how to subsist amid scarcity, they began to look to outside operators for help.

They also engaged these sorts of actors to gain legitimacy in the eyes of the government, including judges, police, and housing officials. But the politics that characterized most residents' approach to the occupation meant that their search for recognition was largely articulated on a serialized basis. Residents did not view defense of the entire occupation as their primary goal as in Siqalo but instead focused on defending their individual plots. They were homeowners in the making, after all, and this newly cultivated subjectivity led them to form localized alliances rooted in the defense of their (and their allies') homes, typically to the exclusion of other occupiers. Not only was there no sense of solidarity among groupings, but they often coalesced into hardened factions that competed with one another over finite resources, ranging from blankets and bread donations to access to legal services.

It was at this juncture that residents began to look in earnest to outside organizations for advice and material support. Faeza began to describe a new character in her journal around this time: "Everyone arrives including Mrs. M from the 'Cape Party,' with the MPHA. Mrs. M is also a community worker, and came with some other sponsors who brought us some soup and party packets for the kids. SANZAF [South African National Zakáh Fund, a Muslim charity] delivered 50 blankets and promises to bring us food. Land invasion [ALIU] and Law Enforcement just drove by. They didn't remove our things like they normally do. We think it's because we had too much people visiting us." In addition to "Mrs. M," an evicted resident from the sports field urged residents to unite behind Lawyers for Human Rights (LHR), a group offering pro bono legal support. While residents would work with LHR, they never successfully united; instead, factions jockeyed for access to lawyers—a process described in detail in chapter 5. And a representative of the Pan-Africanist Congress of Azania (PAC),[28] a Black nationalist political party, showed up as well. He had offered advice to residents prior to the local elections held in mid-May, but he refused to disclose his name or party in an effort to convince occupiers that he was not helping them score cheap political capital. They remained suspicious of him regardless.

"Mrs. M" was Marina Laurova, the director and seemingly sole employee of Cape Care Charity, an organization that purports to highlight "the plight of the Cape Coloreds"[29] and distributes food and basic necessities to poor "Colored" neighborhoods around Cape Town. Her son is a founding member of the Cape Party, an insignificant political party that advocates for the Western Cape and two adjacent provinces to secede from South Africa and form the "Cape Republic." After the 2009 presidential elections, its deputy leader called President Jacob Zuma an "illegitimate colonial occupier of the Cape."[30] When the party was criticized for propagating thinly veiled white supremacist politics, it formally responded that the Cape is diverse and that the party does not discriminate, but that it wants independence for the Cape from the rest of the country: "The Cape is the true 'Rainbow Nation' and we deserve once and for all to govern ourselves free from the grasp of totalitarian racist governments,"[31] by which they meant the ANC regime.

This politics also characterized Marina's involvement in the Kapteinsklip occupation. "She started an organization on the field called 'First People[32] First,'" Faeza wrote. "I think the Cape Party has this idea that if people of the Eastern Cape go home, there will be more jobs, and more houses." These were of course isiXhosa-speaking "Africans." "I said if you want people to leave, you leave. You are also not from the Cape." Marina's parents were themselves immigrants, making her a curious candidate for the invocation of claims to indigeneity, but she proceeded to advocate a politics congruent with the Cape Party's: whites and "Coloreds" would unite against "African" residents, redefining the latter as migrants.

"So if you want them to go, you go," Faeza continued. "It doesn't matter if we have people from the Eastern Cape or from China here, we will still have the same problems—it is government and capitalism causing our problems, not people who come here. . . . They argue for black (Xhosa) people to go back to the Bantustans. And the field is so full of people now, but for every black person who comes to the field and asks to put up a shack"—she was referring to a tiny number of squatters who tried to join the occupation after it was already established—"they [Marina's faction] will call the cops. They only focus on people on the field, but their chair does not live on the field and their secretary is a white lady that lives in Newlands[33] somewhere in a very nice house. Her son is in the Cape Party. And what is strange is the people on the field were arguing saying they want nothing to do with political parties." In the first days of the occupation, many participants were wary of affiliating with party operatives. Since the occupation occurred in the run-up to the 2011 municipal elections,[34] residents knew that the DA-run city would accuse them of working with the ANC or EFF—yet another iteration of the moralistic charge of opportunism. They hoped to avoid this at all costs. But once the initial luster of the first days began to wear off and residents had to deal with more mundane issues like obtaining food and securing their plots, they began to entertain outside actors.

While the involvement of a charity like Cape Care might seem trivial, the distribution of items like old bread and blankets sowed divisions on the field. It began when Marina accused other outside organizations of stealing money from occupiers. But she was herself collecting money: "She is also collecting money from the 16 respondents on the courts list, I am not even on that list, and she went to find out how much grant money they each get. So she is taking money from them so that she can save up and buy them wendy houses. She is only collecting from the 16, so how much division do you think that is going to cause?!" I tried to interview Marina to make sense of this patently divisive strategy, but she stood me up twice. Whenever she would subsequently respond to my emails, she would attach newspaper articles about her work and images of "Colored" children she told me she was mentoring.

By late June, Marina and members of the MPHA had entered into alignment. At an occupation-wide meeting on the thirtieth, residents raised concerns about the MPHA's role in the occupation, fearful that it was protecting some occupiers but at the expense of others. They began to call attention to the dangers of factionalism. "At that meeting," Faeza wrote, "we saw their corruption in their committee. They had collected donations in our name, in the name of people living in the field and we never got money or food that Multi-Score and Winners shops [grocery chains] gave to them." A settlement-wide committee was established that would include both MPHA representatives and residents skeptical of the MPHA. During this entire period, SAPS and ALIU continued to appear on the field, seizing building materials and even firewood. Ebrahiem later told me that the situation was so dire at this point that they had to venture into the surrounding neighborhoods—homes that were not immediately adjacent to the occupation—to beg for water.

By early July, Faeza, Ebrahiem, Clinton, and other residents skeptical of the MPHA figures formed a rival organization on the field: Tafelsig Residents Unite (TRU). Tafelsig—Afrikaans for "Table View," a reference to Cape Town's iconic Table Mountain—is the poorest and most violent neighborhood in Mitchells Plain, with a real unemployment rate well above 50 percent, and it was home to both Kapteinsklip and the sports field. The idea was to build an inclusive and expansive organization in stark contrast to the politics of seriality that characterized the MPHA and its affiliation with outside NGOs and charities. Indeed, it was hard for MPHA affiliates to conceive of such a politics, and rumors quickly spread that TRU leaders were engaging in the same kind of donation hoarding. Faeza told me that a local organizer, notorious in activist circles for his demagogic tendencies, was spreading rumors about her, telling other Kapteinsklip residents that she was taking money from a local advocacy campaign[35] and failing to tell the others.

A few weeks later, TRU officially launched, attempting to break with the possessive politics of the MPHA-aligned faction. Even the organization's name captures this tendency: rather than naming itself after the field (Kapteinsklip), the organizers named themselves after the wider neighborhood. Nine people were elected to the TRU committee: four from the field, four backyarders in the immediate vicinity, and a homeowner whose house was overcrowded. The idea was to build a united front of all those affected by the postapartheid housing crisis, in all of its iterations. Whereas most existing housing-related activist groups tended to be organized sectionally—backyarders, squatters, informal settlement residents, homeowners, renters, and the like—TRU attempted to unite all of these subject positions under a single rubric,[36] namely, that of a generalized housing crisis. Faeza was elected its first chairperson.

The day after the first TRU meeting, the land occupation physically split into two camps. Members of both factions had threatened their adversaries with violence, and in some cases, altercations broke out. A year later, months after the eviction, we sat on Faeza and Ebrahiem's bed in yet another backyard shack. Candy, a mother in her midtwenties, and her four-year-old daughter occupied the field at Kapteinsklip as well. They would frequently stay in Faeza and Ebrahiem's backyard shack, as their own post-Kapteinsklip living situation was precarious. Candy described to me how an affiliate of the MPHA would repeatedly kick the door of her shack late at night, sometimes even explicitly threatening to rape her. One night, she decided she had enough. She chased the man, who was drug-addled and quite emaciated, to the edge of the field, where she repeatedly punched him until he was lying on the grass bloody and barely conscious. Ebrahiem beamed, "Candy doesn't take their *kak* [shit]!"

The tensions were hardly subterranean. By early September, a community newspaper carried the headline, "Squatters Squabble over Eviction Order." "[M]embers of the [MPHA] committee—which claims to have a membership of 5000 people renting in backyards across Mitchells Plain, accused the [Kapteinsklip] train station group of being 'backbiters.'"[37] In interviews with local reporters, MPHA leaders continued to represent the organization as expansive and inclusive, pointing out that it formed in late 2010 when the Tafelsig People's Association and the Mitchells Plain Backyard and Residents' Association combined forces. The MPHA chairperson at this point, a

"Colored" man in his fifties named Samuel, insisted that the organization had a mandate from all residents in Mitchells Plain, though tensions between TRU and the MPHA factions on the Kapteinsklip field demonstrated otherwise. Likewise, he insisted that participants were not charged a fee to join the organization, a prerequisite for participating in the land occupation. All occupiers with whom I spoke at both the sports field and Kapteinsklip either paid the fee or else were asked to but refused.

By the end of the year, the struggle against eviction had largely shifted to the courts. MPHA representatives publicly claimed that TRU activity was jeopardizing their case, whereas TRU members insisted that the MPHA was acting in an exclusionary manner and that their lawyer refused to represent anyone who MPHA leaders did not favor. In response, Faeza told the *Plainsman*, a community newspaper, "They never had a lawyer. How can we have done anything for them to lose when they never had a case in the first place?"[38] She was questioning that they even *had* a strategy.

Conclusion

In this chapter, I showed how a politics of seriality gets articulated on the terrain of civil society. More concretely, I explained how individuals, who have distinct interests and motivations for participating in a land occupation, were organized collectively by the MPHA. It is tempting to reduce seriality to a mere collection of individuals, but there is a key distinction to be made. While living in backyards, participants were already individuals as such. But the MPHA hailed them by deploying a very particular articulation of the constitutional right to housing; and in hailing them, it transformed them from individuals into a series. In posing as a legitimate arm of the government, however ambiguous its language may have been, the MPHA convinced residents that by moving onto the field, they were not jumping the queue, but actually realizing their right to delivery. If the state is the chief agent of distributive democracy but is incapable of realizing this aim, it becomes incumbent upon residents to realize it for themselves. This was, in any case, the rationality enacted by the Kapteinsklip occupiers. And it was the articulation of the project as in line with the state project of delivery that serialized civil society.

But following Gramsci, the organization of civil society is inseparable from that of political society. These should be understood not as distinct spatial or institutional locations, but as two moments in a single process of politici-zation.[39] If the production of a series is the form that civil society takes in Kapteinsklip, then factionalism is the form that political society takes in this case. These are related but distinct articulations of politics: one is about the consolidation of social forces, while the other is about "condensing them into political power on a mass basis,"[40] or translating them into terms operative on the formal, institutional terrain of government. A more concrete analysis of this process of factionalization in Kapteinsklip is the subject of chapter 5. But first, the following chapter charts an alternative trajectory of civil society organization in the case of Siqalo. Rather than a series, squatters formed a fused group.

4

Civil Society II

Siqalo and the Politics of Fusion

The Siqalo occupation began slowly at first. For its first few weeks, residents trickled in, though it quickly picked up pace. Before long, dozens of shacks were going up each day, and within a couple of months, more than six thousand people were squatting on the field. Today more than twice that number live there. Despite its location across the road from a middle-class "Colored" neighborhood, the occupation is majority "African," although a significant number of "Colored" people live there as well. This makes it a double anomaly: a rare multiracial occupation and a majority "African" settlement in an overwhelmingly "Colored" township. This chapter begins by explaining how these residents, many from townships adjacent to Mitchells Plain, came to participate in the occupation. As in Kapteinsklip, an ANC front group was involved in mobilizing residents, leading them onto the field in solidly DA territory. But unlike that previous occupation, participants were not serialized. Rather, as argued in the second section, the Siqalo occupiers were at least partially organized in advance. This was not simply a case of a party front group leading hundreds of individuals into a mass action, but instead an already constituted collectivity—a fused group—encountering a charismatic leader.

But how did these occupiers come to be constituted as a fused group? And how was this organizational form solidified by their relationship to this leader? A second section charts the self-organization of these residents, who came from an overcrowded informal settlement in the township immediately west of Mitchells Plain. In that area, an informal leadership coalesced around a key figure named Bonginkosi, who was a veteran of the anti-apartheid movement. So too were members of the committee that would be subsequently elected. These figures articulated their project as the self-realization of their rights as postapartheid citizens. They sought to achieve for themselves what the ruling political parties failed to deliver. In other words, they sought to realize the promise of Section 26 of the constitution: the right to adequate

Delivery as Dispossession. Zachary Levenson, Oxford University Press. © Oxford University Press 2022.
DOI: 10.1093/oso/9780197629246.003.0004

housing. This was a presumed completion of the liberation struggle, the autonomous realization of distributive democracy. Rather than seeing the state and its parties as a partner in delivery as in Kapteinsklip, they viewed state agents as their chief antagonists. Accordingly, residents were openly hostile toward all party representatives on the scene, as well as a number of other external organizations—groups like the charities and NGOs that ultimately divided Kapteinsklip. They expelled them from the occupation early on, refusing to admit any external organizations into their encampment.

In a third section, the chapter explains how this articulation of the project of occupation produced a coherent group with shared interests rather than a series. Instead of factionalism, this approach yielded an elected committee. This representative body's origins are developed in a fourth section. As in the previous chapter, it is impossible to detach civil society from political society as a distinct object of analysis.[1] These are two moments in a single process rather than separable spatial or institutional spheres as in liberal political theory. The focus on one as opposed to the other here is, as Gramsci puts it, methodological rather than organic.[2]

The appearance of a fused group in Siqalo captures the dynamics at work in civil society and is the subject of this chapter. The emergence of an elected committee, the articulation of the fused group in political society, will be covered in chapter 6. The fused group was not overdetermined by initial conditions but required the vigilant exclusion of external organizations and the active inclusion of all who wanted to occupy the land. This chapter begins with some of the motivations and rationales advanced by Siqalo occupiers.

Overcrowded and Unaffordable

Before the first wave of occupation, there were a handful of people living on the field along Jakes Gerwel Drive, a major thoroughfare connecting this part of Mitchells Plain to the city center. Faeza told me that they were all "Colored" and that there were only about seven families. "On that field?" I asked, pointing to the Siqalo occupation. We were sitting in my car on the shoulder of Jakes Gerwel, idling between a man selling freshly caught *snoek*[3] from the back his *bakkie*[4] and an older woman selling doghouses she had fashioned from plywood.

"No, in that bush, in that bush—and you couldn't see them," Ebrahiem replied. Living "in the bush" is an idiom that means squatting on an uncleared field, akin to living in the wilderness. The land on which Siqalo was organized was overgrown with all kinds of rough grasses and shrubbery. It was actually two adjacent plots of private land, though there was no obvious border between them. One was held by a property management firm, presumably as a speculative investment. The other was owned by a sand-mining company that used the land for dumping. It was not particularly well maintained, and so initially residents simply lived "in the bush." "In Siqalo, when Siqalo formed, that people was there already," Ebrahiem continued. "They were there for six years."

"Hiding," Faeza added. No one had bothered them as a result of their inconspicuous lifestyle. The fact that this land was private property would prove important. Kapteinsklip was public land, or at least land held by the parastatal railway company, and so the ALIU and police were able to confront occupiers immediately. But in order to act on private land, its owners had to file for an eviction order. As documented in the eventual court case, the city tried for months to get one or both of the landowners to issue a formal demand; once they did so, and it was approved by a judge, the ALIU and police could act to remove them. But both landowners waited many months to bring the case, by which time the occupation was well established, meaning that the occupiers could not legally be evicted until they were offered alternative accommodation. But as the city's lawyers were quick to point out, they could not possibly accommodate the thousands living on the land. Had they brought the case right off the bat, the situation might have played out quite differently. This is a crucial point, as it means that we cannot simply predict the politics that follow from a given property type; rather, how central actors relate to one another powerfully shapes political outcomes.

Ebrahiem continued: "Six years prior to the occupation, people were living there. But they were from the surrounding farms, the majority of the Coloreds that's there." In Philippi, which borders Mitchells Plain to the west, and even in some parts of Mitchells Plain, farmers hire workers but fail to provide them with living quarters—hence the squatting. But this was a very small number.

Then came the first major wave, which primarily comprised "African" isiXhosa-speaking residents from Philippi. Why would a group of "African" residents decide to occupy land in "Colored" territory? They were previously squatting in Philippi, and Siqalo was not far from the border between these townships. Those who participated in this first wave were generally of two types. First, many of them came from a massive informal settlement named for Mozambican liberation hero Samora Machel. This was the case for Khwezi, a bus driver and shop steward for the transport workers' union.[5] As his case makes clear, informal housing is not just for the unemployed or some imagined lumpenproletariat. Here was a unionized worker living in a shack, and he was one of quite a few who was steadily employed but could not afford to rent a formal house, let alone secure a loan for a mortgage. Khwezi was once a militant in uMkhonto we Sizwe (MK), the ANC's armed wing. After spending the 1970s smuggling comrades back and forth across the border with Lesotho from the Eastern Cape, he was redeployed in Cape Town in 1981 under the command of South African Communist Party leader Chris Hani. He moved into a house in Nyanga, an "African" township halfway between Kapteinsklip and the central business district.

I once asked him why he left Nyanga. The late 1990s was the peak of the civil war between residents affiliated to the ANC's anti-apartheid umbrella organization the United Democratic Front (UDF) and a number of more conservative tendencies, including Zulu nationalists and an "African" vigilante group called the *witdoeke* for the strips of white cloth they used to identify themselves.[6] After Khwezi fled this violence, his apolitical cousin took possession of his house, and he was forced to find somewhere else to live. He built himself a shack in Samora Machel and lived there until 2012, when the place grew too overcrowded. Along with a few dozen others, Khwezi and his girlfriend, tired of the conditions in Samora, took part in the first wave of the Siqalo occupation.

The second type of participant came not from informal settlements but from backyards in Philippi. This was the case for Mncedisi, who told me she was renting a space behind a formal house just down the road from Samora and had erected a shack there. She had been out of work for five years by that point, and she had no immediate prospect of finding regular employment in a context in which the recorded unemployment rate is approaching 30 percent, and the real unemployment rate is roughly twice that in her neighborhood. Besides, as Khwezi's example demonstrates, a job hardly meant housing security. Mncedisi's landlord, the owner of the house behind which she was living, raised the rent on her backyard tenancy. She had already been having trouble making the monthly payments, so this was the last straw. After he threatened to have her evicted, she and other backyarders in the area facing a similar predicament joined forces with the Samora contingent—people like Khwezi and his girlfriend—and began to build structures on the land they called Siqalo, a shortened form of the isiXhosa word for "beginning."

Unlike most occupations, Siqalo began slowly. Kapteinsklip began with a thousand participants, and the sports field down the road had four thousand, but Siqalo began with only seven families until another fifty or so joined them in mid-2012, including Khwezi, Mncedisi, and others from Philippi. One of them, Bonginkosi, had organized the residents and acted as their representative. Like others in Samora, he cut his teeth as an activist in the anti-apartheid movement and had become quite politicized. While he had not been particularly active in postapartheid social movements, he had a long history of organizing, which came as second nature to him. He did not particularly like to talk about this period, but others assured me he had been active in the ANC's underground. While he was something of an ANC partisan when I first met him, this did not seem to affect his view of the state. Since the DA rather than the ANC controlled Cape Town, and most struggles were waged on the terrain of the local state,[7] the question of ANC support rarely arose, and only in relation to national elections. This allowed Bonginkosi to treat the occupation almost as if it were a social movement. It was constituted in explicit antagonism with the municipal state, identifying its agents and forces as adversaries. And like a social movement, he wanted to draw in as many participants as possible. This stands in stark contrast to the Kapteinsklip occupation, the politics of which were notably exclusivist. Bonginkosi even led a contingent to Kapteinsklip as it faced its final eviction, convincing dozens of its residents to march with him down the road in Mitchells Plain and set up shop in Siqalo.

Faeza, Ebrahiem, Kayla, and Victor were among them. As eviction day approached, violence flared up on the Kapteinsklip field. "Everyone was running up and down trying to save some of their valuables," Faeza wrote in her diary. "People who belongs to First People First [Marina's faction] . . . started shouting at us, especially me. They were now walking around with sticks and all kind of sharp and dangerous objects, making statements like they don't want us on the field anymore." One of Faeza's allies in TRU, Alex, was so angry that the police were removing his belongings that he set his own couch on fire as it was being dragged away by officers. Now that they had lost most of their things and were receiving threats from other squatters, had lost faith in their legal representatives, and felt constantly undermined by Marina, where would they turn? Why struggle to stay in Kapteinsklip if this was what life was like? "I have tried to be strong for too long," Faeza wrote. "I can't do this anymore. I can't put my husband's life at risk. I can't live without my children anymore. I can't handle people swearing at me, throwing in my windows, every second day running around shouting at me, setting my shack on fire. I just couldn't anymore."

Bonginkosi sympathized with her plight. When he marched with his contingent to Kapteinsklip that October, he asked Faeza if she and Ebrahiem would be interested in moving to Siqalo. Initially she was put off by the idea, convinced that it would constitute a retreat from Marina and their lawyer Marius and thus a tacit admission of defeat. But then she talked to other Siqalo residents who had come to Kapteinsklip to support the evictees, and she realized that she had nothing to lose by leaving. She was already separated from her kids, who were staying with their grandparents for the time being, and the constant violence and squabbling made it an unpleasant place to live.

It was at this moment that she decided to accept Bonginkosi's offer and move to Siqalo. All of her TRU comrades decided to move as well. When this second wave arrived at Siqalo, there were already fifty shacks up—about two hundred people. "But every day—that's *every* day—you could literally see that there's more shacks," Ebrahiem recalled.

"People were building," Faeza agreed. For months afterward, a steady influx of squatters in search of a new start came from Philippi and elsewhere in Mitchells Plain, and soon the place was packed. Within a year, there were upwards of two thousand shacks on the land, an estimated sixty-five hundred people.

Fronting for the Party

It was surprising to see so many "Africans" setting up shop in a solidly "Colored" township like Mitchells Plain. Under apartheid, "Coloreds" were spatially and institutionally segregated from "Africans" and strategically concentrated in Cape Town.[8] The government provided far more substantial funding to "Colored" communities, and as apartheid began to unravel, the National Party (NP) decided to include "Colored" and "Asian" citizens in a new parliamentary system devised in 1983—even as it continued to exclude "Africans" altogether.[9] Even if the NP's strategy ultimately failed, apartheid's carefully regulated ethnoracial hierarchy was internalized by most South Africans. Today, "Colored" neighborhoods are often marked by intense anti-"African" racism, and Colorado, the middle-class "Colored" neighborhood across the road from Siqalo, was no exception. Its residents' association continually mobilized against the occupiers, demanding their immediate

Figure 4.1 Informal housing built by occupiers in Siqalo.
Credit line: Photograph by author.

relocation in starkly racist terms. For this reason, I was surprised to see that many of the Siqalo residents were not themselves "Colored," as moving to a "Colored" area as an "African" was fairly risky.

Moreover, this was not just a majority "African" settlement in a "Colored" area, but a multiracial settlement—incredibly rare for South African land occupations. The initial settlers were "Colored," followed by the "African" wave from Philippi, and then a mostly "Colored" wave from Kapteinsklip, followed by a steady stream of "Africans" from other nearby settlements. When I interviewed one high-ranking DHS official,[10] she described Siqalo as "an orchestrated land invasion. Orchestrated, I'm telling you!" I told her that I found its multiracial character to be remarkable, and she appeared to be in disbelief. "Are you serious?" she exclaimed, as if she had never entertained the possibility. "Where did they come from?" I was not positive myself at the time but told her what I did know: many had come from Talfesig and other parts of Mitchells Plain. She was stunned.

And what of her assertion that the occupation was "orchestrated"? She was not technically incorrect in that all collective actions are orchestrated by definition: there were people attempting to organize the occupation. Certainly the initial round of "Colored" farmworkers squatting on the field predated any coordinated planning, but the first wave from Philippi was actually approached by a party front group—much like the MPHA in the case of Kapteinsklip. In this case, it was a group called the Ses'khona People's Rights Movement (SPRM), which was very involved in the initial stages of the occupation. It began canvassing in Samora Machel prior to the first wave of occupation, before I ever came in contact with Siqalo. A few years later, the SPRM would formally break with the ANC, but at the time, it was an unabashed front group, many of its young organizers aspiring to enter the city's party machine. Unlike the MPHA, however, the SPRM was quite open about its political motives and affiliation. The MPHA never actually admitted its ANC affiliation, though it was quite obvious to anyone who attended its events, whereas the SPRM never tried to mask it.

The SPRM's presumption was that race mapped onto partisan affiliation. Its leaders assumed that "African" residents would be more likely to vote for the ANC, whereas "Colored" Mitchells Plain was solidly DA territory. A major feature of the DA's support base is a continuation of the apartheid-era alliance between white South Africans, of both Afrikaner and British descent, and "Colored" residents. And so the SPRM attempted to move "African" voters into a DA ward. One "Colored" Siqalo resident named Meera told me that SPRM was not the only party front group operating in the settlement. A small Black nationalist party that would later merge with the EFF (in 2013) offered one of its members as the residents' lawyer, free of charge. And there were DA operators in the occupation too. While the DA hardly needed to shore up its support in this section of Mitchells Plain, some of the occupiers tried to organize the settlement as a DA stronghold, hoping to eventually represent the settlement to their ward councilor.[11]

Residents leaving Samora and backyards in Philippi were initially enticed by the SPRM's radical rhetoric. Khwezi told me that they discussed the occupation as if it were a social movement, not too far removed from the way Bonginkosi described it. In any case, it was far from the technocratic articulation of the occupation in Kapteinsklip, in which the MPHA serialized residents as subjects of allocation. In Siqalo, by contrast, residents were addressed as members of a fused group. As a longtime activist and a political independent when we spoke, Khwezi liked what he heard from SPRM speakers who visited his neighborhood. But once he actually moved to his new residence, he became increasingly skeptical of the organization, whose members began to talk more explicitly about aligning Siqalo with the ANC. It was not clear to him exactly what that meant in practice, but the pushiness of the SPRM speakers who visited the occupation made him quite skeptical of party operatives, whom he began to view as potential opportunists.

It was not just the SPRM. The image of multiple party-related organizations jockeying for influence among occupiers, even when only fifty shacks were up, prompted most residents to keep their guard up. Khwezi told me that in the case of the lawyer working for an "African" nationalist party, he offered to represent residents free of charge. "He said we didn't have to actually join the party," Khwezi explained, "but we didn't want all these parties around. It didn't feel right." Another occupier confirmed, telling me that the residents discussed paying the lawyer instead, worried that perceived opportunism would rub the DA-affiliated DHS agents monitoring their occupation the wrong way. Indeed, as in the case of Kapteinsklip, the Anti-Land Invasion Unit showed up as soon as the first wave of Philippi occupiers made their way onto the field. The ALIU had not seemed to mind the seven or so farmworker families squatting on the land before, but once the occupation was obviously growing, the ALIU would constantly monitor it from across the road. In any case, the residents refused all partisan players, ultimately retaining pro bono counsel unaffiliated to any party.[12]

Ntando, who would subsequently be elected to the residents' first representative committee, told me that everyone was skeptical of the party operatives in those first days—and chiefly of the SPRM. Like Khwezi, the radical rhetoric intuitively appealed to him, as he was disillusioned with the failure of the postapartheid project. Here he was, nearly two decades since the end of apartheid, and save for occupying land, he had no options whatsoever. Samora had grown completely overcrowded, and his girlfriend did not want to raise their two small children under such conditions. The notion that dispossessed "African" residents should take what was rightfully theirs really appealed to him. Was this not what the liberation movement had been all about?

A number of the Samora occupiers had roots in the liberation movement, whether in the MK like Khwezi or in the UDF like Ntando. While this explains their affinity to the SPRM's radicalism, it also helps us make sense of their skepticism of the organization. Many UDF militants were disillusioned when the ANC effectively co-opted their movement, as it had in so many prior insurrectionary conjunctures: absorbing Black Consciousness student militants into their Youth League structures after the Soweto Uprising in

1976, taking credit for the Pan Africanist Congress's work on the anti-pass law campaign before and after the Sharpeville massacre in 1960, and elsewhere. And so they kept their guard up. I asked Ntando if he was worried that the SPRM was simply going to enlist new residents as ANC voters. "That's exactly what Ses'khona does!" he exclaimed, excited that I could discern the political dynamics of the occupation.

One did not need to be a conspiracy theorist to allege a coordinated ANC effort to take back Cape Town. The party governed the city until 2006, and while it was in no place to win it back in the near future, it never gave up trying. Six months after the occupation began, then-deputy resident Cyril Ramaphosa[13] spoke at a community center in Mitchells Plain. As he told a community newspaper upon his visit, "We are going to mobilise and form ANC structures in Mitchells Plain and solve these problems. We will take back what is ours and we will win Mitchells Plain."[14] To be sure, the ANC *was* trying to make inroads into DA territory; but that does not mean that occupiers were pawns of the party. In fact, very few of them had any interest in working with ANC representatives, and the majority wanted them out of the settlement.

The Politics of Mutual Aid

Siqalo was not unique in its residents' aversion to working with outside organizations. In Kapteinsklip too, many residents were wary of aligning with such groups, afraid that doing so would implicate them in power struggles beyond their control. But the primary collective voice articulating this position, TRU, only emerged late in the process of occupation. It voiced this concern in opposition to the opportunistic alliances of MPHA members and Marina's faction. But by the time it did so, it was too late: seriality was already well entrenched, and this facilitated the development of factionalism. By contrast, Bonginkosi's leadership militated against any haphazard alliances with exogenous actors, and above all, with political party operatives. He was one of a number of Samora residents with roots in the anti-apartheid struggle. Like Khwezi and some of the other Siqalo occupiers, he had worked with ANC structures, including broad coalitions like the UDF, but the ANC's abandonment of the liberation struggle left him skeptical of all political parties. Above all, he was still bitter about the government's failure to meet its promise of housing delivery, from the Freedom Charter's[15] identification of decent housing and location as an inalienable right, to the 1996 constitution's guarantee, "Everyone has the right to have access to adequate housing." Here they were nearly two decades after the transition, and "decent" (let alone "adequate") housing was nowhere in sight.

Bonginkosi expressed this disillusionment as a general frustration with official state and party politics. If the various parties governing Cape Town since 1994 were not able to help them move out of an overcrowded informal settlement located in an apartheid-era township, they would have to do it themselves. And so the project of land occupation was articulated in these terms as the realization of the national liberation project, the continuation of the anti-apartheid struggle. This progressive content, in other words, was severed from political parties as its necessary bearers. Parties came to be viewed as useless, or even worse than useless: as self-interested organizations parasitic upon people's desires, aspirations, and actually existing struggles.

For this reason, residents were militantly opposed to any organization that tried to openly brand their occupation as a partisan project. This was not just a feeling of opposition but a conscious political strategy. Under Bonginkosi's leadership, residents expelled all parties from the occupation in its earliest days, forcing out the SPRM within the first month (April 2012). While the SPRM would subsequently break with the ANC, moving toward a politics closer to the EFF's, at this point its organizers were resolutely pro-ANC. One might even accuse them of being heavy-handed, attempting to register voters before Siqalo was even fully established. They immediately tried to win over residents to the party, representing it as the vanguard of decolonization, in stark contrast to the conciliatory liberalism of the DA. But this approach backfired. In Kapteinsklip, squatters did not initially view the MPHA as a front group, even if it most certainly was; the MPHA never lectured residents about voting for one party or another, but instead won them over by organizing an occupation. But the SPRM was never essential to the Siqalo occupation in the way that the MPHA was to Kapteinsklip. Siqalo grew in waves, and later in a steady stream; but Kapteinsklip was organized by the MPHA as a once-off incursion. As such, leadership was key; but in the case of the squatters coming from Samora, they already had a leadership in place, and it was not clear to residents what the SPRM added to the mix.

More generally, Bonginkosi's aversion to parties meant that no outside actors were permitted to operate on the field. Some residents maintained known political affiliations, but they were prohibited from identifying themselves as such in meetings. For example, residents were skeptical of Ntando for his open DA affiliation once he was eventually elected to a settlement-wide governing committee—a development that will be described in detail later. But as long as Ntando did not try to convince others to join the party or bring partisan demands into settlement meetings, he was allowed to maintain his position on the committee.

This was not a directed hostility toward any particular party, but instead a generalized disdain for electoral politics. When the Independent Electoral Commission (IEC) set up a tent next to the occupation to register new voters, for example, close to a dozen residents appeared with petrol bombs and set the structure alight, forcing its volunteer staffers to retreat. Other residents stuffed tires with bits of kindling and doused them with gasoline before setting them on fire on Jakes Gerwel, blocking the thoroughfare altogether. Burning tires are a regular feature in the repertoire of service delivery protests,[16] the umbrella term in South Africa for marginalized residents' struggle for access to potable water, electricity, toilets, and housing. A larger number of residents repurposed candidates' campaign posters, scrawling, "No houses, no water, no electricity, no vote"[17] across their blank side and marching with these placards around the burning blockades. The IEC was never able to operate in Siqalo on a sustained basis, and these protests were widely interpreted in local papers as frustration with "empty electioneering promises."[18] The IEC has increasingly become a target of occupiers' (sometimes violent) ire,[19] though as Kapteinsklip shows, this brand of antipolitics is only one of many possible articulations of the politics of land occupation.

In lieu of seeking help from intermediary entities like political parties and NGOs, Bonginkosi articulated a politics of collective self-determination. The only external figure who mattered was a judge, who could regularize their land tenure. And doing this required maintaining unanimity on the field, incorporating as many people as possible into the project of occupation under a unified leadership. This approach to politics was evident to Faeza even before she and Ebrahiem moved to Siqalo. When she first observed the occupation in April 2012, six months before she was evicted from Kapteinsklip, she could not help but contrast Bonginkosi's approach to the factionalism prevalent in her own settlement. "What is different is that they are allowing more and more people to come, [as] opposed to how people are in Kapteinsklip and the boundaries and split groups trying to keep people away and calling the cops. Within days there were a 1000 shacks and serious people and unlike our occupation which is all I have known where ended up there accidentally these people are clear—they need houses and they are taking the land.

This new group with new energy is doing what it has felt impossible to do in Kapteinsklip. And we need them here if we want to cross the racial bound-aries in Mitchells Plain. We need to fight the divide and rule tactics and show that we can be as one."

And why did unity and inclusiveness go hand in hand? Bonginkosi presented the project of occupation as akin to building a social move-ment: unity was essential if the residents were not going to be divided through competitive affiliation to various visitors to the field. When DHS officials, ALIU agents, and police officers would stop by, they would typically try to develop a couple of contacts among residents, which was of course condu-cive to the emergence of factionalism. Even if residents were initially well intentioned, politicians and housing officials are often able to secure housing for a handful of leaders, who subsequently abandon their comrades for this immediate payoff. But in Siqalo, residents fairly consistently referred visitors back to Bonginkosi, or after his rule ended, to the elected committee. Even my own visits, which were purely about information gathering, had to go through these bodies, lest other residents be suspected of aligning with me to secure material benefits—not that I ever provided them to anyone.

Unity required expansion due to the nature of the occupiers' claims. They needed to be recognized by the courts as houseless people in need rather than opportunists jockeying for a quick payoff. If they were to develop a functioning community, one large enough to be observable to DHS officials and judges, they would need to incorporate additional residents into their project. This translated into active recruitment efforts—hence the instance in which Bonginkosi led a faction to Kapteinsklip to recruit its evictees six months after he had moved to Siqalo himself. This was in October 2012, just under a year and a half since the Kapteinsklip occupation began. Faeza recounted the encounter to me: "They came to Kapteinsklip—a taxi full of them. They said, 'Look, we're not going anywhere unless you're going with us. Move with us!' And I said no." She was worried that if she agreed, Marina's faction would read her as giving up. But then her husband convinced her how ridiculous this was, especially since they would likely be happier in Siqalo. Besides, in a worst case, they could always move back to a shack in Faeza's parents' backyard. "I have an option if it don't work out," she told me. And so she decided to try her hand in the new occupation, moving with nearly all of Kapteinsklip's TRU members.

"Bonginkosi was great," Faeza said. "He waited till the very end; he was the last person to leave, and he [rode with us in] the taxi just to make sure that we safe." Kayla, Victor, and the rest of their TRU comrades headed there with them. Their friend Mike, a local NGO employee and community organizer, rented a truck for them to transport their building materials. But I still didn't understand how they got a shack since ALIU and the police had confiscated their building materials.

"Well, when we got there the first day, we just slept," Faeza continued. "We all slept in one shack. It was quite big, where people really looked after us when we got there. They dried clothes for us because it was raining. Children was dressed already, the place was heated up, and there was food. And they was already busy collecting rands for our food for breakfast tomorrow morning! It was stuff like that. And then the next day we sorted. There was empty shacks, and they placed us in the empty shacks. It was only temporary—until we built our own shacks." This was the farthest scenario imaginable from Kapteinsklip's politics of seriality. In Siqalo, residents not only actively encouraged newcomers to join them, but they did so together, as a fused group, collectively facilitating people's moves and sharing services and material resources in the process.

Electing a Committee

Faeza and Ebrahiem only stuck around for five months, eventually deciding to move back to a shack in Faeza's parents' backyard. They left the occupation to participate in an activist workshop in Bloemfontein, more than a thousand kilometers northeast of Cape Town, and when they returned, they found someone living in their shack. As it turned out, these were the residents who initially built the shack into which Bonginkosi had moved them, and so Faeza and Ebrahiem did not really have a claim to the structure. "The people came back and were there to move us from their place," Faeza told me.

"But there was immediately another shack," Ebrahiem added. Bonginkosi and other residents did not want anyone forced out of the settlement. "But we felt like, no, we gonna move our shack" to Faeza's mom's backyard. A friend had recently given them a wendy house, and together they planned to move it. I still did not really understand why they left.

"I got scared," Faeza admitted. "The language: I was bothered that I was placed in the middle of mostly Xhosa-speaking people." Bonginkosi had offered them a place near other "Colored squatters," but "I wasn't going to be placed there because of the division": she was wary of contributing to de facto segregation within the occupation, as there were increasingly "Colored" areas and "African" areas. But there was also an intermediary space, and this is where she wanted to be moved. But when she ended up in an exclusively isiXhosa-speaking area, "I mostly got scared because I didn't understand [the language]."

"She couldn't sleep at night," Ebrahiem added.

"I couldn't sleep at night. I couldn't understand if people would pass and somebody would knock on the door in the middle of the night—stuff like that. And then I was—I'm sorry, I told Ebrahiem. I'm going to get really sick if I stay there because I'm not sleeping." They ended up leaving, but most of their closest friends remained in Siqalo. "We were everyday still in Siqalo," she insisted, almost as if she were embarrassed to have left. "We would still go there every day. We would still pick the kids up for crèche," meaning that she still left her younger children in an informal child-care center in the occupation.

The residents who stuck it out began to assimilate. "Victor's son is speaking Xhosa now," Ebrahiem told me. "All his friends is Xhosa." He seemed a bit nostalgic for their time there. "[If we stayed] we could've had the best parts!" He meant that he was a relatively early settler on the field, which was quickly filling up, and so he could have maintained access to a prime location. "You know the road as you come in? That was empty. Only Bonginkosi's shack was there." I realized I had not heard about Bonginkosi for a while—not since the first few months of the occupation. I asked what became of him, why this figure of whom they had spoken so highly suddenly disappeared from the political scene.

"I don't know," Faeza, replied. "The city." I was not sure what she meant.

"Power. Power changed him," Ebrahiem attempted to clarify, though he remained just as cryptic as his wife. What did Bonginkosi do to fall from their good graces?

A couple of months after bringing the Kapteinsklip evictees to Siqalo, power began to go to Bonginkosi's head. As the specified representative for dealing with DHS, lawyers, police, and other actors beyond the settlement, everything went through him. Eventually, he was offered a deal by a city official: he would oversee a toilet-cleaning operation in this and other nearby settlements in Mitchells Plain and Khayelitsha, enlisting a number of Siqalo squatters to help him. They would all get paid, and Bonginkosi would get a little extra for managing the operation. As one might predict, this immediately caused tension on the field. Were residents not supposed to be militantly opposed to the municipal government? Now they were getting paid by it? And would Bonginkosi's hiring practices not spawn all sorts of gossip about favoritism, perhaps even leading to the development of embryonic factions? By this point, there were nearly six thousand people in Siqalo, and he could not possibly hire representatives from each of its many "neighborhoods."

This was only the beginning of residents' frustration with Bonginkosi. Khwezi, once his staunchest ally, told me that residents would line up around the corner outside his shack waiting to talk to him. It began as a way for residents to access their lawyer—by this point, Faeza and Ebrahiem had put Bonginkosi in touch with their old lawyer Sheldon, who worked on the Kapteinsklip case. As in that occupation, Sheldon only wanted to remain in contact with a single representative of the occupation, which over time had the effect of the concentrating power in Bonginkosi's hands. If anyone wanted information about their case, they had to go through Bonginkosi. And now if anyone needed work, they would have to go through him too. He would also provide community briefings periodically, but these were usually to crowds of hundreds. People often wanted personalized report-backs, or at the very least, assurance that eviction was not immanent. Or else they would speak to Bonginkosi to try to negotiate something from the city. Was the city coming to install more water standpipes or toilets? Would they remove some of the rubble dumped by the sand-mining company that owned the land? Were they going to do something about all of the winter flooding?

There was no shortage of complaints. One resident named Karen told me, "In Siqalo, we have no electricity, and we can't afford paraffin," which residents used to fuel fires for cooking. "There's no work. Then there's the problem of porta portas—we have to put it inside, and that means we have to eat where we shit." She was referring to what city officials termed the "bucket system."[20] People would relieve themselves in buckets, and then the city would pick them up on what was supposed to be a regular basis. But in practice, pickups were irregular and infrequent, and emptied buckets were often redistributed to the wrong shacks without being properly sanitized. "When they tell us to put porta portas outside in front of our shacks [for collection and cleaning], they leak," Karen continued. "Then the children come and touch it, then they come in to eat." The system was so reviled that a number of local ANC dissidents teamed up with more radical elements and organized a series of "poo protests," as they were called at the time.[21] Meanwhile, former DA leader and Western Cape Premier Hellen Zille tweeted, "No one has to use a bucket system in Cape Town." The mayor's chief of staff immediately corrected her, despite being a member of the same party. Throughout the year, protesters on the Cape Flats would fling buckets of human waste at her convoy whenever she would make a public appearance.

Another resident named Lwazi complained about access to water. "Yes, they gave us nine taps, but we have six thousand people," he pointed out. "It's not right." Residents would line up to complain to Bonginkosi, hoping he would relay their collective concerns to the city, either through the medium of their lawyer, or else as the designated representative of Siqalo whenever government officials would visit the occupation.

Eventually, Bonginkosi came to serve as less of an activist. He stopped attending the meetings of a citywide housing movement with which he had been involved called the Housing Assembly,[22] and his community report-backs became less frequent. Once he cashed in his political capital for the gig overseeing toilet cleaning, he lost the trust of residents. Besides, rather than building any sort of organization, it was just Bonginkosi and his perpetually inebriated sidekick calling the shots. No one seemed to take them seriously anymore. Originally some residents had proposed going with his archrival, Ntando, one of the earliest Siqalo residents to openly call him out for concentrating power in his hands. But too many of the residents were skeptical of Ntando's politics, as he was an unabashed DA supporter. How could a sympathizer with the party governing their city lead protests against its offenses? Plus, he had a reputation of maneuvering for speedy recognition from outside organizations—shortcuts, much like the politics that dominated Kapteinsklip. Khwezi told me he had seen Ntando meeting with DHS officials and even ALIU employees behind Bonginkosi's back, trying to form a rival coalition. No coalition materialized, however, largely due to the prevailing politics in Siqalo: residents were too skeptical of what they perceived as factionalism.

But in addition to this political maneuvering, Ntando began to act a bit like the MPHA did at the beginning of the Kapteinsklip occupation, charging for access to land. According to both Khwezi and Karen, both of whom were involved in this first wave of occupation, he was offering plots at Siqalo for up to R10,000.[23] "It's free land! He's selling free land! It's all profit!" Khwezi was livid. But it was hard to simply exclude self-appointed community representatives from governing committees. When Bonginkosi stopped reporting back to residents altogether in early 2013, he was finally deemed a liability. In protest, residents decided to elect a twelve-person representative committee over the winter. Most of those with whom I spoke appeared less concerned about the nature of concentrated power in his hands than they did about his failure to do his job. Besides, fully excluding him—or Ntando for that matter—risked producing an emergent factionalism. Bonginkosi did have his partisans, after all. So a twelve-person committee was elected that included both of them. Elections were held outside in front of Bonginkosi's shack, which had become the equivalent of a town square. This was where he would issue report-backs and legal updates, and it is where residents would line up to meet with him. Nominations were put forward, and residents voted by acclamation. Bonginkosi still had a sufficient support base to remain on the committee, which eased the transition to a more representative body. Residents' demands for this newly democratized committee appeared to have less to do with abstract principles of democracy than with the practical necessity of accessing information about the status of their court case. Bonginkosi simply did not have the capacity to meet with hundreds of residents on a daily basis.

The committee of twelve would represent the entirety of the growing settlement, which was large enough at this point that they decided to create a federated structure. Siqalo was divided into four sections, A, B, C, and D,[24] each with three representatives who sat on the central committee. It included Ntando and Bonginkosi, of course, as well as Karen, the sole "Colored" member of the committee. Then there was Lwazi, the patriarch of sorts. He was the committee's oldest member and therefore commanded a certain amount of authority. He was more soft-spoken than any of the others and spoke less frequently, but his interventions were always given their due. He ran a small informal convenience store called a "tuck shop" on the side of Jakes Gerwel. Then there was Tilde, who, despite her Afrikaans name, identified as "African" and spoke isiXhosa. There was Dumisa, who, like Ntando, was accused of harboring DA sympathies on more than one occasion, but he always managed to keep party politics out of their meetings. There was another woman who never actually spoke in any of the meetings I attended. Indeed, the meetings were completely dominated by the men, who rarely consulted the women representatives. They even sat on opposite sides of the shack used for meetings. Another committee member, Fundani, would regularly show up late to meetings and proceed to exhaust all of the oxygen in the room, rarely engaging others' concerns. Finally, the other four members of the committee rarely attended meetings, and they were therefore replaced. In general, most meetings I attended only had six or seven representatives present.

The function of the committee was twofold.[25] First, it managed the internal affairs of the settlement in a way Bonginkosi alone could not. Lwazi called these "Siqalo issues." In the meetings I was able to attend,[26] domestic violence and interpersonal disputes occupied most of the discussion time. In one meeting I attended, a resident had disappeared for a while, and when he returned, his ex-girlfriend was living in his shack with her child. The committee functioned in this case as an informal small claims court, both adjudicating the dispute and deciding whether damages were owed. In another case, a woman brought her boyfriend before the committee because he was beating her on a regular basis, and she wanted him out of their shared shack. Again, the committee decided how to proceed, with the threat of collective coercion always looming in the background for those who refused to comply with the committee's decisions.

Second and far more importantly for our purposes, the committee mediated between the residents' first lawyer, Sheldon, and residents themselves—much as with Bonginkosi before them. Sometimes they would hold settlement-wide report-backs in a clearing outside of Lwazi's shack on the side of Jakes Gerwel. In stark contrast to the intensely competitive process of accessing lawyers in Kapteinsklip, Siqalo's representative structure enabled their legal team to represent the entire settlement instead of a few haphazardly selected factionalists. It also prevented the strategic hoarding of information for narrow political gain. While this had been the risk with Bonginkosi, the twelve-person committee represented so many different political tendencies that this never emerged as a problem.

Conclusion

This chapter demonstrates the possibility of an alternative to the serialization that developed in Kapteinsklip. By contrast, Siqalo residents formed a fused group. They did not just occupy the field simultaneously but also collectively insofar as they perceived their interests to be shared rather than competing. This was a function of how the occupation was organized, and just as importantly, how it was articulated by its founding leadership. If the MPHA articulated the project of occupation as in partnership with the government, serializing residents in the process, the Samora occupiers who organized the first wave at Siqalo, Bonginkosi among them, articulated the project in opposition to the state. Largely due to their activist backgrounds, these occupiers knew that they would face state repression as soon as they set up shop on the field. Sure enough, they did. But they remained united in the face of their governmental adversary, going so far as to expel all partisan organizations from the occupation.

While we might be tempted to say that they therefore selected civil society over political society—self-organization over formal political institutions—this would fly in the face of Gramsci's theory of the state. For civil society and political society are not self-contained alternatives, but rather two aspects of a singular process of politicization. We can even think of them as two different perspectives or lenses. This chapter has adopted the lens of civil society to narrate the dynamics of representation in a land occupation, detailing how it began, how an initial leadership came into being, and how this leadership was ultimately rejected in favor of an elected committee. But we could just as easily tell the story from the perspective of political society, mapping how activity at the level of civil society necessarily comes into dialogue with government bodies—foremost among them, the courts. As chapter 6 will show, this is precisely what happened: the fused group had its articulation in political society as the unified committee, a far cry from seriality and factionalism. But first, chapter 5 chronicles the solidification of factions as the Kapteinsklip occupiers prepared for their day in court.

5

Political Society I

Kapteinsklip and the Politics of Factionalism

Kapteinsklip and Siqalo followed inverse trajectories. The latter began with a half dozen squatters, who were soon joined by a few dozen more, and it expanded steadily over the course of the next year until it contained over six thousand residents. By contrast, Kapteinsklip began with a burst as a thousand occupiers showed up on the field overnight. But after police bombarded them with rubber bullets, high-powered water hoses, and the threat of arrest, a large number of occupiers relinquished and left the field. Many of those who remained gave up hope as the ALIU repeatedly confiscated their building materials and other belongings, going so far as seizing tarp-covered shopping carts residents used for shelter and filling in underground hovels that desperate residents had dug into the sandy earth. As Siqalo expanded, Kapteinsklip contracted.

Not only did it wither, but as described in chapter 3, Kapteinsklip was marked by intense interpersonal rivalry while the Siqalo occupiers managed to create some sense of unified purpose. In other words, Kapteinsklip's population formed a series, whereas Siqalo's became a fused group. These categories, however, only describe what transpired through the lens of civil society: how the population organized itself without any regard for the formal institutions of the state. This is not to say that these institutions were irrelevant to this process. How residents conceptualized their own relationship with the state impacted their organizing strategies. But the present chapter considers these strategies through a different lens, that of political society. We know that occupiers viewed the state as a partner in realizing their right to housing, and they acted accordingly. But how did their subsequent self-organization affect how government officials saw them? How, in other words, was movement on the terrain of civil society refracted through the lens of political society? How did seriality assume the concrete form of factions?

The first section recounts residents' struggle over legal representation. It explains how skirmishes over access to their lawyer reinforced existing

Delivery as Dispossession. Zachary Levenson, Oxford University Press. © Oxford University Press 2022.
DOI: 10.1093/oso/9780197629246.003.0005

divisions and helped concretize them into formalized factions. A second section continues this discussion in relation to proliferating court dates, which had the effect of disorganizing the occupiers, further exacerbating factionalism. A third section shows how this articulation on the terrain of political society helped shape three different judges' decisions, leading them to adopt state moralism and order the residents' eviction. As we will see in the following chapter, this was not an overdetermined outcome. In the case of Siqalo, the charge of opportunism did not stick, as there was little evidence of controversy or foul play. In forming a unified committee rather than contending factions, this population came to be seen as a population, a fused group, rather than as a fragmented series, as in the case discussed in this chapter.

Scrambling for Legal Representation

After countless delays, the Kapteinsklip occupation finally had a court date. This meant that participants would need to secure legal representation as soon as possible. There were a handful of legal nonprofits in Cape Town, but participants had little experience navigating housing law, let alone choosing among these offerings. Some of them had been arrested before, but this case required a very different sort of lawyer than they were used to. And given the disputes and mutual suspicion that had arisen on the field, it was unclear how they would agree on an advocate. Would they be able suppress infighting long enough to meet collectively with a lawyer? Or if the lawyer wanted to interface with a single representative, who would it be? How could they possibly agree on one person to represent the entire occupation?

In the first days of the occupation, a lawyer actually contacted them, offering his services pro bono. He was affiliated with a party called the Pan Africanist Congress[1] but made no immediate demands on the occupiers. Nevertheless, residents were skeptical of his motives, worried that he was a political opportunist maneuvering for votes in the upcoming municipal elections, set to take place three months after the occupation began. Given that they did not yet need a lawyer—the case was delayed for months—they bided their time, hoping that tensions would sufficiently dissipate to the point where they could agree on a representative.

A couple of months into the occupation, one of the occupiers had an idea. He went by "Biggie" and was one of the very few of them who had a background as an activist, having been an organizer in the anti-apartheid movement of the 1980s. He reached out to an old comrade named Mike from the Housing Assembly—a comrade whom he called "middle class," though he would certainly be categorized as "working class" in a European or American context. Mike also lived in Mitchells Plain, though he had a formal house with a lawn, a full-time job, and a car. His neighborhood was called Colorado, which was viewed by most of the occupiers as fairly wealthy, even if it were not actually so. Ebrahiem once told me that it was all about proximity: Rocklands, Portland, and Westridge—neighborhoods in Mitchells Plain—were all "lower middle class," to use his terms, because they created a buffer between the N2 highway to the city center and the working-class areas to the east, including Lentegeur, Beacon Valley, Eastridge, and of course, Tafelsig. Those areas closer to the central business district, including Colorado, were all wealthier, even if not wealthy by white or international standards. Meanwhile, those proximal to the "African" township of Khayelitsha and toward the beach to the south were considerably poorer and more dangerous.

It was Mike who told Biggie about the Legal Resources Centre (LRC), the largest public interest legal organization in South Africa. The LRC had an office in the central business district, right next to Greenmarket Square, the most popular tourist market in Cape Town. Apartheid may have been over, but to many of the occupiers, this was a white zone, or at the very least, as Ebrahiem once told me, "That's where the bourgeoisie[2] go."

After a long wait, Biggie made contact with Sheldon Magardie, a well-known housing lawyer in Cape Town. He is an advocate,[3] a specialist litigator qualified to represent them in the High Court. Usually advocates work with one or more attorneys on such cases. While Magardie also took on paid cases, he did pro bono work through the LRC. While he could pass as white, his accent and mannerisms were distinctly "Colored." Faeza and Ebrahiem would often laugh when I mistook a "Colored" person for white. "How would I know if I hadn't heard them speak yet?" I would ask. They would giggle, pointing out that his bodily comportment and clothing style were conspicuously "Colored."

Magardie was ultimately unable to win their case, though he was successful in delaying their eviction. He had so many cases on his docket that it was sometimes difficult to reach him, and so Biggie asked Mike for another recommendation. Mike recommended Lawyers for Human Rights (LHR), another legal nonprofit begun by anti-apartheid activists, coincidentally started in the same year as the LRC: 1979. These were the cross-class connections that were essential for securing legal representation. Biggie visited their offices and secured the representation of William Fischer. After Magardie failed to win a stay of eviction, Fischer tried to represent them in the Supreme Court of Appeal. Faeza was particularly fond of Fischer, recalling to me on multiple occasions that he was "Colored" like herself and came from a working-class background. "He used to live on the streets," she wrote in her journal. "He knows. . . . William looks like he is white, but he is actually Colored, and he acts a lot like he is black." As in the case of Magardie, Fischer's "Colored" identity was not immediately apparent to me until Ebrahiem pointed out some of his mannerisms and of course his accent.

"He is the only advocate with a broken cloak," Faeza continued, meaning that his legal costume was in disrepair, "and his firm partner, Marius, the lawyer, has dreads. William would come and throw his bag down, and doesn't care about being up there [in the occupation]. He is right here on the ground with us. His wife and kids say, you can go visit the informal settlements on your own if your heart is there, which is what he says when he drives by where we stay."

After an initial meeting with some of the occupiers, including Faeza, Ebrahiem, and Biggie, as well as Mike, Fischer took their case. Ebrahiem later showed me camcorder footage that Faeza had filmed after their court date. "We went to the Supreme Court of Appeals," Ebrahiem told the camera. He was standing on the field across from the Kapteinsklip train station, with all kinds of commotion behind him. Instead of being thankful that some of the occupiers secured representation, most residents were contemptuous of the small group gathered around their advocate. Of course, in theory he was everyone's advocate; but due to the fragmented nature of organization on the field, opposing factions eyed Biggie's grouping as devious and a potential threat.

In the footage, a large group of occupiers gathered around a man in a suit about a hundred feet away. This was Fischer. Ebrahiem continued: "They did not accept the case. Then it was taken to the Constitutional Court,[4] which they also denied." He switched to Afrikaans. "So it's just a matter of time before they evict us. In our understanding, our lawyer forwarded the papers, but we don't know." He reverted back to English. "We don't have this information due to this woman on the field."

Ebrahiem was referring to Marina, who at this point had consolidated a faction with a number of MPHA leaders. Their rivals in TRU were so disdainful of Marina that they frequently referred to her as "that woman on the field." This was the peak of the struggle between her faction and TRU, though this was more than simple factionalism; it was a struggle over political strategy. And really, it was a struggle over their articulation in political society, that is, how residents wanted to collectively represent themselves to outside observers, not least among them government officials.

TRU's strategy was to include as many residents as possible in a broad coalition, expanding beyond the bounds of the occupation and uniting with residents in the surrounding neighborhood of Tafelsig, the poorest area of Mitchells Plain. By contrast, Marina and the MPHA were exclusivist, a political orientation inherent in a serialized civil society. Even though Marina was not a squatter, by giving out donated materials—primarily blankets and bread—she was granting her allies a certain amount of power over occupation-wide distribution networks. Those aligned with Marina got first crack at the amenities basket; those who were not received the leftovers, if anything at all. This is how it began, rooted in controlling access to donated goods. Soon, however, the stakes increased. As participants in the occupation tried to secure legal representation in order to fight their impending eviction, monopolizing access to their lawyer became the next major axis of contestation among factions.

"I got a call from Mrs. M," Faeza wrote in her journal, again referring to Marina. "She told me William was trying to get ahold of us—our advocate. We were supposed to be at court at 8:30 am to sign papers." For the Kapteinsklip occupiers, court was an oddly formalistic ritual that, despite its excessively bureaucratic strictures, often seemed unpredictable and enigmatic. "I am so sick of everything happening at the last minute," she continued. "Now I have to figure out how to be at court at 8:30 with no money or nothing. It just upsets me that they would call at that time of the morning to say be there at half past eight." For Marina, the journey could easily be made in that amount of time, as she owned a car. Even in the worst traffic—and along Cape Town's N2 highway, traffic was typically at a standstill in the morning—I could make the thirty-kilometer journey to the city center in an hour or so. But by public transport, getting to the High Court took twice that. In theory, one could take the Metrorail. The occupation was across the street from the last stop on the Mitchells Plain line, after all. But the train was too unpredictable. Another line might be more reliable, but not the lines running through the Cape Flats. The line that ran through the white areas in the wealthy southern suburbs, which included Marina's home suburb of Newlands, was fine, even if white people infrequently actually took the train. But the lines sprawling eastward across the Flats would break down incessantly. Or else they were delayed by protests that involved blockading the tracks or even burning the rail cars. Sometimes when there were not even any disturbances, the cars would just stop for a while. Whenever possible, residents would avoid riding the Metrorail.

The other option was catching a taxi, a large white van typically filled with about fifteen passengers, sometimes more. In order to catch a taxi in the mornings, you would walk to the main road and listen for a *gaatjie*—the door operator—to shout "Kaap tyoooooown!" followed by a series of loud whistles. He would be leaning out of the side of the van as it rolled past, holding the sliding door ajar. By raising a finger or even just making eye contact, you could signal to the *gaatjie*, and the minibus would stop. Catching a taxi to the city center involved catching two separate vans, and if the demand was high enough, this sometimes entailed waiting for multiple full taxis to pass by. Or sometimes the problem was the opposite: taxis would not actually depart for the destination until they were filled to capacity, and so they would drive up and down side streets hoping to pick up stray passengers, making the journey worth the gas money. On top of the ride itself, Faeza rarely had disposable cash on hand, and the nearly US$2 round-trip fare had to be scrounged up before she could depart. Sometimes this meant using her last few rands to get to town, but more frequently, she would have to ask everyone in her network if she could borrow a rand or two until she finally cobbled together sufficient funds to get there. Once there, she could ask one of her middle-class activist contacts for return fare, assuming she could track them down.

Frustrated, Faeza borrowed the appropriate fare and walked to a nearby makeshift corner store—a "tuck shop" in South African parlance. She bought a few rands of airtime for her cell phone. It was next to impossible to get someone in Tafelsig to call you back; text messaging was the preferred means of communication. Even texts cost an exorbitant sum by comparison with American providers, and so the most economical way to go about it was to purchase an old Blackberry at a pawnshop. For sixty rand[5] per month one could get unlimited internet access, but this service only existed on Blackberry's network. By using an internet-enabled text-messaging application like WhatsApp, texting became a possibility. The reception was so awful that the internet itself rarely worked in Mitchells Plain, but at least it enabled messaging. In any case, calling was normally off the table. Faeza was going to make an exception. "I phoned William immediately and he confirmed. Ebrahiem, Victor, Kayla, Zaarah, Kathy, and myself went to the train. We scratched money together from everybody." All of the occupiers she named were TRU members. "When we got there [the High Court, in Cape Town's central business district], Natasha and Shanaaz and Mandy"—all MPHA affiliates—"was already there with Mrs. M. They had already signed the papers that was needed to be signed." Faeza and her comrades had traveled all the way to town in vain.

Back on the field, Ebrahiem continued speaking to the camera. He called out to their attorney, Marius, who was working closely with Fischer, their advocate. Even though it was Ebrahiem's close comrade Biggie who had secured the occupiers their legal team, this did not apparently guarantee either of them access. There was an ongoing struggle being waged in the settlement over precisely this question: who would be included in the class represented by their lawyers? Ebrahiem was in for a rude awakening when he asked Marius, "Represent *jy vir ons ook*? [Do you represent us too?]" in a mixture of English and Afrikaans.

"*Wat is jou naam*? [What is your name?]" Marius inquired in response.

"Ebrahiem Fourie and Faeza Meyer," the couple replied in unison.

"*Is jou naam op die lys*? [Is your name on the list?]."

"*Nie*," they replied. "But I have a number on my shack," Ebrahiem insisted. He was referencing the number painted on his front door by a DHS employee. It meant that Ebrahiem's shack was officially counted as one of the structures involved in the occupation. Those without a number were, from the perspective of the government, illegitimate.[6] In most cases, lacking a number suggested that a shack was built after DHS completed enumeration, where de facto addresses were assigned to all new structures.

Marius repeated the question, shaking his fist for emphasis. "Is your name on the list?" Marina was standing behind him, her head visible over his shoulder. About twenty of the MPHA-affiliated occupiers were gathered around them.

"*Nie*!" one of them shouted, shaking her head vigorously. "*Nie*!"

"No," Ebrahiem responded, almost inquisitively, puzzled by the concept of the lawyer representing some of the squatters in his predicament but not all of them.

"Then I don't represent you," Marius told them, brushing off imaginary dirt from the air in front of him.

This was the crux of the issue: the occupiers' serial organization developed into opposing factions, which were intensified when refracted through their legal representative. What began as minor political differences turned into formalized groupings opposing one another. These factions did not simply reflect existing political divisions, but actively constructed them in the process of faction formation. Those who latched onto agents with political capital—figures like Marina or Mike—ended up congealing into camps with a clear line of demarcation between them. There were those represented by the legal team, and there were those excluded from representation. "I don't represent you," Marius told Ebrahiem.

Of course, there were divisions on the field from the outset of the occupation. The struggle over legal representation was not the origin of these rifts. First, there were those organizing on behalf of the MPHA, and there were those duped into occupying the fields. Most of the occupiers thought the occupation was actually legal until the police showed up. Layered on top of this first division, there was a second: those who aligned themselves with Marina and her Cape Care Charity, and those who remained skeptical of her intentions. If aligning with the MPHA was about gaining presumed political capital, linking up with Marina was about obtaining privileged access to a material distribution network. This was not only about accessing bread and blankets, but also about monopolizing the power to distribute these goods to others in the occupation.

Third, there were those represented by the legal team of Fischer and Marius, and there were those who were excluded. This final division maps pretty closely onto the first division refracted through the second, but direct access to lawyers was itself a central source of power on the field. Indeed, when Ebrahiem asserted, "We don't have this information due to this woman on the field," he meant that Marina had reserved access to Marius and Fischer for her allies. Faeza grew increasingly worried that TRU members would be excluded from any sort of legal ruling and wondered how she could contact the lawyers. As she wrote in her journal, "Michael [Mike] advised that I write the advocate a letter explaining my concerns about the few days we have left and about how the application for leave to appeal hasn't even been put through yet."

She continued: "I think that would make sense so I will draft a letter today with others in the community and forward it to William Fischer, our advocate, tomorrow. Marius told me this morning that we should unite on the field because he can't speak to everyone. He says he wants to speak to one person only." Pro bono organizations like LHR and the LRC were overburdened with housing cases, and their lawyers were reluctant to waste time assessing the state of factionalism in each land occupation. They therefore tended to interact with what they perceived to be an organic leadership in each occupation. In some cases, as in the Siqalo occupation, this was a unified body that actually represented the settlement. But in others like Kapteinsklip, the leadership with whom they worked did not represent the entire settlement. Instead, factions used access to the legal team as a means of entrenching their identities *as* factions. In other words, seriality yielded exclusivism, which assumed material form in mutually antagonistic factions. Each factional leadership aligned with exogenous actors for perceived political capital, as well as access to essential supplies.

Factional identities emerged and were ossified in the process. But these articulations, expressed on the terrain of political society, are always unstable, capable of deformation and reformation. These ossifications are never permanent. Stuart Hall[7] describes political articulation as a process of constant reworking in the context of changing material circumstances. As residents faced new rounds of repression, material deprivation, and the incursion of new extra-settlement actors, they would dissolve old linkages while forging new connections—what Hall calls "re-articulations." Rather than a one-to-one correspondence between squatters' material conditions and their respective political worldviews, the appeal of each contending discourse was contingent upon how their leadership articulated the meaning of occupation.[8] In formally attaching each discourse to an organized leadership, faction formation actually entrenched these divisions rather than simply reflecting them. The tentative alliance between the MPHA and Marina's followers was rebranded as a legitimate grouping whose interests were collectively represented by Marius and Fischer. There was an exclusionary exuberance about the group, with members enthusiastically fortifying its boundaries.

This practice of exclusivism, while closely related to seriality, was a consequence of the initial articulation of the occupation by the MPHA as the realization of people's constitutional right to housing through the distribution of mutually exclusive plots, or ersatz private property. Exclusivism was intended as a quick solution to a precarious legal situation. Those with uncertain claims to land and housing relied upon privileged access to their legal team, clutching onto these links with an almost religious fervor, excluding other occupiers in a scramble to the top of the hill. But in so doing, they unwittingly transmitted the appearance of multiple factions on the field, as opposed to a coherent (legible and legitimate) settlement led by a unified representative committee. A judge might then read this incoherence through the lens of moralism, reducing internal dissension to a blanket category of opportunism. This move readies the political terrain for eviction: "opportunists" and "queue jumpers" are viewed as self-interested thieves and thus as "undeserving." The following sections trace this process, which resulted in rulings against the Kapteinsklip occupiers, evicting them from the field not once, but twice.

"They Are Trying to Demobilize Us"

These squabbles over access to their lawyers made the legal process confusing enough. But even without this added element, the process was itself so bewildering that the occupiers rarely understood their status on the field. Court dates seemed to proliferate endlessly for the squatters, with no immediately apparent end in sight. The first ruling came just weeks after the mid-May occupation began, on 1 June, but it was immediately challenged by the squatters' lawyer. It was rescheduled for later in June, but as this date approached, a judge pushed it back to the end of July. The occupiers were given until the end of September to vacate the field, and so they collected their belongings and crossed the cul-de-sac, setting up shop on an adjacent field, this one owned not by the city but by the parastatal railroad company.[9] A new case was initiated, but the decision was postponed first until late November and then again until mid-December, and a third time until the end of January.

At this January court date, the judge ruled that the occupiers had to be off the field by late February 2012, but the police never showed up to enforce the decision. Meanwhile, Fischer appealed the ruling to the Constitutional Court in Johannesburg, delaying the eviction further—first until early August, and then until 29 October, more than seventeen months after the occupation began. The Constitutional Court upheld the eviction interdict, refusing to hear the case, and Kapteinsklip was finally cleared—or almost. A few occupiers quickly returned to an adjacent field, but their encampment was small enough that it was ignored by the city.

If these perpetual delays and consequent indeterminacy are confusing to the reader, this was certainly the case for participants in the occupation, who were continually frustrated and remained uncertain what exactly was happening throughout. As Faeza remarked in her journal, "There are so many eviction dates—they are trying to demobilize us to a point where people are tired of supporting us." All of this confusion only exacerbated contention among factions on the field. "I spoke to Marius our lawyer today," Faeza wrote, a week and a half before the first eviction date. "He had no good news. In fact, he didn't even have bad news. Nothing. We have 12 days left before it's Judgment Day," she continued, referring to the specified eviction date. "No one is doing anything about that. The division on the field doesn't even allow us to do anything. The closer it gets to the eviction the more difficult it is for people on the field to communicate."

One TRU member named Zaarah approached the other side of the field, now physically split into two camps: Marina's faction on the one side, TRU on the other. Zaarah attempted to convince her erstwhile adversaries to come to a meeting so that they could collectively figure out how to strategize around the impending eviction. Not a single MPHA or Marina ally showed up. Meanwhile, internecine acts of violence were increasing. Just before the previous ruling, someone had attempted to burn down Faeza and Ebrahiem's shack, and in mid-February, someone threw a burning cloth through another TRU couple's (Victor and Kayla) open shack window in the middle of the night. While they managed to extinguish the flames without incurring substantial injury, the damage had been done.

Faeza was feeling demoralized and, above all, frustrated. Marius had told her that unless residents united on the field, he was not sure how to represent them collectively. "He says he wants to speak to one person only."

The day before the February 22 eviction, representatives of the city showed up on the field. One DHS employee told the squatters that the number of shacks did not match those that had been officially enumerated. She said she would return after getting official approval to add numbers to these structures—to enumerate them. Faeza explained the discrepancy. Initially residents were told that makeshift housing like overturned shopping carts covered with tarps did not need numbers because they did not qualify as houses. But now the city *was* counting them as such.

Faeza continued, explaining how enumeration exacerbated exclusivist politics on the field: "What worried me was that there were no names put to the numbers on any shacks on the land, not the Anti-Land Invasion Unit or anyone did that. There were numbers but no names to those numbers. For me they put them there to keep us from growing. They basically got that right because they have people phoning the police when someone else puts up a shack." Members of each faction would report their rivals, seeing each grouping as an impediment to their own security. This was exclusivist politics at work. "And people cannot even see that—they cannot see what they are doing—they still call the police. It's just dividing us more and more." This was the irony: many of the occupiers thought that eliminating their rivals would secure their own position, but this had the effect of exacerbating factionalism, increasing the likelihood that they would be viewed as "opportunists."

Faeza desperately wanted information from the legal team. Whenever she phoned Marius, she would either get his voicemail, or else he would tell her to visit Fischer's office. But the two times that week she traveled to Belville[10] to visit Fischer in his office, he was not there, even though his secretary told her he would be. She finally tried calling Marius again. He picked up and told her to call back in half an hour. She waited and then called him back, but he told her he was busy and to try him again tomorrow. This feeling of perpetual court dates and an interminable bureaucratic process was not assuaged by Faeza's inability to get information from her lawyers. This never-ending game of phone tag only exacerbated her anxiety.

Meanwhile, the eviction crew never showed up on the specified date in late February. Had they simply forgotten? Four days later, and still nothing. Faeza phoned the sheriff, who insisted that it was still on. But when she finally got through to Marius—she had been trying for days—he told her that it had been postponed. Was no one going to tell her? How could she comply with these rulings when she could not even ascertain their outcomes? She was certainly relieved that they had a bit more time, but she was also constantly anxious about the growing factionalism on the field. Representatives of Marina's faction were insisting that TRU members were dealing drugs. Meanwhile, TRU members were accusing former MPHA members of smoking *tik* (meth). "Rahim and Natasha and Shaheed, her husband, were walking around with knives and stuff, swearing at us, as usual," Faeza described.

At this point, no one even knew when the next court date would be scheduled. There were no reliable organizers in contact with their lawyers, and everything seemed to be mediated by outside figures. Early one March morning, just over two weeks after the eviction that never happened, Faeza received a call from Marina. Marina told her that Fischer was trying desperately to get in touch with them and needed them at the High Court within the hour to sign papers. Again? How could they possibly make it in time without access to a car? Faeza, Ebrahiem, Victor, Kayla, and other TRU affiliates scraped together enough change and boarded the train to town. But they were too late.

At the court they ran into Natasha and two other members of the opposing faction. Their rivals had already signed papers in the company of Marina. It had happened yet again.

Fischer found the TRU members and told them that the judge's ruling had been "reserved." Faeza asked him what that meant. He told them it meant that the judge needed additional time to reach a decision as to whether he was going to let the occupiers appeal the eviction order. William thought it would take at least a few weeks. It actually lasted quite a bit longer. After countless delays and rescheduled court dates, an eviction was finally scheduled for 6 August.

In the run-up to the eviction, factionalism only escalated. Faeza was getting worried that she would not be able to access information about their case, as Marius and Fischer were becoming harder and harder to reach. She sent Marina an SMS, asking if she could see some of the documents Marius had provided to her. Marina responded with an SMS, telling her, "We decided not to give out documents while working on the case." *Who was this "we"*? Faeza thought to herself. Marina continued: "Info gets leaked out [and] discussed, [which is] not good for any court case, and generally not done."

Faeza was livid. "This is the first time I heard that people don't have access to their own documents. It doesn't even involve her yet she has access. I phoned Marius and asked him 'are you part of the we?' He said he would call me back, but he never did."

For months, TRU members had trouble obtaining information from Marius. In early August, Faeza sent him a "please call me," a way to signal to someone that you want them to call back but without incurring airtime charges. He quickly SMSed her back: "*sal jou so later bel*"—"Will call you later." He never did.

The night before the 6 August eviction, Faeza called the sheriff to confirm that it would actually take place. He told her the crew would arrive at 9:00 a.m. to remove people from the field. But later that afternoon, Marius called her after weeks of remaining incommunicado. He said that he was going to appeal their case to the Constitutional Court in Johannesburg, and that Faeza needed to contact the sheriff to let him know. She could not get through so tried Marius again. He would not pick up either. But the next morning, the eviction crew never showed up.

It was unclear what was going to happen at this point. A number of the occupiers were excited about the prospect of a Constitutional Court victory. Other groups of occupiers had won Constitutional Court cases before, most notoriously the Durban-based social movement Abahlali baseMjondolo,[11] isiZulu for "People of the Shacks." This was the case in which the KwaZulu-Natal Slums Act[12] was ruled unconstitutional in 2009, and it was widely hailed as a landmark for squatter activists across the country. On 29 October, the Constitutional Court's decision was finally handed down. The eviction order was upheld, and the residents' appeal was rejected. Rahim of the MPHA remarked, "We will always be the city's problem and we'll pop up somewhere.[13] The city can evict us wherever we invade, but the problem won't go away. Must I turn sixty or die before I get a house?"

Another occupier, Marcus, told a community newspaper something nearly identical: "We will pop up somewhere and we will remain the city's problem. I don't know how the city managed to convince the court that it doesn't have land when there is so much empty space around."

A third named Benny stated that he had been waiting for a house since he registered with the city's waiting list in 1984. But Tandeka Gqada, the Mayoral Committee (Mayco) member for human settlements, disputed his claim: "Having checked the database, no record of [his] registration exists. He is encouraged to re-register and drop his registration off at the nearest housing office." Benny told me this was erroneous.

The next day, the police cleared everyone from the field, and the Anti-Land Invasion Unit stood by to make sure none of the evictees moved onto adjacent city-owned plots.

"For Their Own Selfish Purposes"

Growing factionalism in the Kapteinsklip occupation inevitably shaped judges' evaluations of the case. This meant that they were more likely to buy into the local government's moralistic narrative of "opportunistic" motives. "Queue jumpers," in this telling, fight each other over a scrap of land; but houseless people in need allegedly work together to realize their goals. While this is of course a caricature, and neither of these ideal types is usually realized in practice, an occupation's articulation in political society can absolutely impact how it is viewed by state actors and, more specifically, judges.

Their struggle for land and housing played out in the courts, echoing the Comaroffs'[14] observation that in postcolonial contexts, struggles tend to shift onto the judicial register. South Africa is no exception. From the vantage point of occupiers, the judicialization of politics is often secondary. Their primary aim, especially when attempting to evade the state's gaze, is to successfully organize the logistics of the occupation and resist police and ALIU incursions into their settlement. But these struggles over self-organization always have an unintended consequence: how residents project themselves to the state. In Kapteinsklip, as in all occupations, residents' struggles played out on the terrain of the integral state, meaning that they simultaneously articulated themselves in both civil and political society. In the case of the former, the residents appeared as a series; and in the case of the latter, they were seen as contending factions. The more occupiers attempted to accrue political capital from outside actors, the more their factionalism intensified; and the more it intensified, the more it shaped judges' visions of their occupation. Appearing deeply factionalized meant that judges would be likely to dismiss occupiers as "opportunists" and uphold their eviction.

In the case of Kapteinsklip, the first such ruling came on 30 August, about three and a half months after the occupation began. Technically speaking, the City of Cape Town was granted an interim court interdict a few days after the occupation began in mid-May, but Marius challenged it, and the case made the docket of the Western Cape High Court. A follow-up hearing was scheduled for 1 June. Asked to comment, the municipal government's spokesperson, Kylie Hatton, told a community newspaper, "We are sympathetic that some people have been waiting for a long time for housing and may be impatient. But the City cannot allow people to illegally occupy vacant land or build informal structures. Illegally invading land may delay or prevent formal housing in areas of invaded land. The Kapteinsklip site has been identified for future housing projects."[15] Hatton was arguing, in effect, that the occupiers were "queue jumpers." She reversed the causal sequence of residents' own argument: squatters explained that they occupied land because they could not obtain housing, whereas Hatton was arguing that they could not obtain housing because they were occupying land.

This should recall the governmental rationale for eviction discussed in chapter 2. Housing officials do not tend to view the self-provisioning of shelter as a last resort. Rather, they imagine autoconstruction[16] as some combination of free-riding and a coordinated assault on the social order, but they rarely associate it with immediate necessity. From their perspective, occupations pose a threat to the order required for a functioning housing delivery system, and more broadly, the realization of distributive democracy. In other words, officials would much prefer ordered houselessness to disorderly survivalism. They attribute the failure of housing delivery to occupations instead of understanding occupations as a consequence of stalled delivery.

The rescheduled court date was again postponed, this time until 27 July. In the meantime, the mayor's office continued to issue statements pointing out that the May interdict prohibited any new structures from being erected. While these delays were simply procedural from the point of view of the city and the courts, the squatters were terrified by the indeterminacy of it all. On the morning of the 27 July hearing, Faeza wrote in her diary, "It has been 75 days. We survived the rain, cold, wind and daily harassment of the police. Our structures and other possessions have been confiscated and many nights we have been forced to sleep in the open. But our spirit of defiance remains strong and we are determined not to be moved."

That day, many of the occupiers headed to the city center to attend the hearing. Faeza felt frustrated that the squatters were not allowed to speak in court. Only their lawyers could participate in the process. She gained some reassurance after the hearing when most of the occupiers marched to the Civic Centre—home to DHS and most other municipal offices—and got to deliver a speech to the mayor. "I really hope things are going to change for us," she wrote. "I hope the Mayor's smile was real."

The next morning, a representative of the Anti-Land Invasion Unit showed up and sought out Faeza. He had heard her speech to the mayor. "He asked me not to allow anyone else onto the field, because according to him, that will only cause problems for us. Our people now have hope again." The idea was to keep the occupation manageable to the city government. This meant both prohibiting newcomers from expanding the occupation and keeping the organization of the existing settlement coherent and structured. But before the High Court ruling was handed down on 30 August, the occupation was far from organized along the lines the city government preferred.

The city presented its arguments, emphasizing the disorganization of the residents. When longtime High Court judge Nathan Erasmus[17] issued his decision,[18] he prefaced his statement: "*Ek doen hierdie opmerkings in Afrikaans, want ek weet die meeste van die betrokke persone in die hof is Afrikaanssprekend.* [I'll give my remarks in Afrikaans since I know most people involved in the court are Afrikaans speakers.]" Rulings are typically issued in English, but he proceeded to release the entire statement, save for the court injunction itself, in Afrikaans.

Erasmus began by contextualizing land occupations. He pointed out that despite the demise of apartheid, Cape Town's housing backlog is entirely

"African" and "Colored," revealing the persistence of apartheid's racialized geography of relegation. Moreover, he insisted, the backlog is actually growing: the government has not successfully housed the dispossessed. Yet it is not the duty of a democracy, he continued, to immediately remedy the situation, but rather to "ensure the basic rights of dignity" in the meantime. This transitional period is key. Those residents who comport themselves as "patients of the state"[19] enable delivery, as they remain compatible with the government's technocratic brand of democratization. Both Erasmus and DHS officials expected residents to meet their needs without sacrificing their legibility and legitimacy in the eyes of the state. In practice, this meant that their political society articulation was key: residents had to represent themselves to the government as a coherent population, or else they would not be included in the project of delivery; they would slip through the cracks. Participating in land occupations was highly inadvisable from the perspective of DHS, whose officials framed participation in an occupation as equivalent to withdrawal from the waiting list, and therefore from the gaze of the delivery apparatus. Judges tended to be more lenient, distinguishing houseless people in need—legitimate populations, really—from opportunists, factionalists, and queue jumpers, whom they viewed as potential threats to functional delivery, and, therefore, to democracy itself, at least in its technocratic conception.

Erasmus referred to members of this latter group as "*die opportuniste* [the opportunists]" who attempt to grab whatever they can from the remedial policies of the municipal government—akin to a concept like "welfare queen" in an American context, but without the obviously gendered qualifier. "Whether it's about their egos or the depth of their pockets and their own self-indulgence is not relevant," he insisted. These people "exploit the community," and this is precisely what happened in the cases of the sports field (Swartklip) and Kapteinsklip, both of which he considered in a single ruling. The MPHA provoked a reaction that exceeded the disdain Erasmus reserved for disorderly residents making immediate demands. These squatters deserved their own category of disgust, as they duped others into participating in the occupation. "I know that they sit here in this court [today]," Erasmus told the audience. He was not pulling any punches. "For their own selfish purposes, they abuse the homeless and the poor."

This abuse, he continued, is rooted in the deceptive project of the front group, though he did not use that specific phrase. In appearing as a legitimate means of housing distribution, complete with earmarked plots and registration fees, a group like the MPHA trafficked in deception. "This is criminal on the face of it," Erasmus declared. "Such elements do not belong in an ordered society, who then abuse their own people who are vulnerable to their schemes. That's what's happened here. . . . It was all a lie." He proceeded to label this sort of opportunism as worse than the situation at the end of apartheid. "It's one thing for someone to say you can't have something, but it's quite another for someone to promise the sun and the moon knowing full well that they can't deliver."

Erasmus explained that he reserved such contempt for this type of deception because it fundamentally undermines the project of democratization. The vast reserves of dispossessed residents returning to cities after apartheid require order if remedial efforts have even a remote chance of success. "The only way democracy will work properly, in my opinion, is in a disciplined and orderly manner in terms of the law." In their noncompliance with the principle of formally rational housing distribution, land occupations threaten the entire system. It remains unfortunate, he reiterated, that people were deceived, but to allow them to access upgrading, municipal services, and the like would be to endorse queue jumping.

Of course, none of the Kapteinsklip occupiers expected the government to provide these amenities. They occupied the land because they had no other spaces in which to build shacks and attempt to fashion homes of their own. Most of them wanted to leave exploitative backyard arrangements, and they certainly did not want to raise their families in their parents' overcrowded, apartheid-era houses. But constitutional guarantees meant that the city had to progressively realize access to housing and services for these residents. Even if this is not what the occupiers were demanding of the city, it is what the city was required to provide; their civil society articulation was read as a political society articulation, their intentions notwithstanding. These occupiers were not trying to jump the queue, but the government's reading of the occupation ended up turning them into "queue jumpers" anyway. And this raised the ire of the judge.

Erasmus's disdain for threatening orderly distribution was expressed when he suddenly deployed sardonic language, insisting that he would implement a process that indiscriminately evicted anyone whom he viewed as jumping queue. "I cannot allow that based on my feelings right now. That piece of land [Kapteinsklip] seems to me to be very nice with the sea air blowing over the hill. I want to stay there, so now I'm going to take me a piece of land so I can just sit there. Then it takes the City Council months to get to me, and since

I built my place and brought my children, even if I'm brought to court, it's now too late to evict me. It does not work like that."

Why did Erasmus see the MPHA as posing such a threat to the delivery order? He dismissed it as a group engaging in "haphazard business" as opposed to "an organization that fights for the rights of backyard dwellers." The names of squatters he received on a list did not quite match those names obtained by DHS officials who visited the site. This was also an issue Faeza described in her journal when she wrote about that day: "They called out the names of the people who should be inside—those on the list of people, which I was on."

Erasmus wrote that the remedy should not be to reward those who have jumped to the front of the line, but rather to help them reinsert themselves onto the waiting list in an orderly fashion. Lawyers, he suggested, should provide guidance in getting them back on the list in such a way as to ensure "that things run smoothly and you do not have this situation." That was his approach to the victims. The perpetrators, however—those who made the occupation appear as the orderly distribution of plots—would face possible charges: "The deceivers must be denounced."

Erasmus finished his statement by telling the occupiers they had until late September to figure something out—just over four months since the occupation began. In the meantime, they could stay on the land, but under no circumstances could additional residents join them. "It cannot grow, and if people think they can let it grow, I'll give the police the right to enter and demolish it and put your things and [building] material in storage, and if it is not claimed within a month, then it is forfeited to the state."

He concluded with an interesting statement, deploying the rhetoric of revolutionary discipline[20] to underscore the importance of order not only to the functioning of democracy, but also to effective activism: "I want you to leave the building in an orderly fashion. There will not be shouting and there will not be *geklappery* [a fracas] when you go outside because there are also other courts in session. Let's start with discipline. As one can see from the history of any revolution where the general population came to rule, the greatest lesson was discipline. So if you want to work to satisfy your rights, it begins with discipline, and this starts with yourself and then your organizations and your community."

He then read the eviction order, giving the occupiers until 26 September to vacate the field.

Conclusion

It was after this order that the occupiers realized that their time on the field was up. They picked up and rebuilt their settlement on a field across the road, this time owned by the parastatal Passenger Rail Agency of South Africa instead of the city. Now PRASA's advocate would have to argue for eviction, and the change in ownership sent the case back to the High Court. Another judge, Judge Saldana, heard the case in late November. He wanted to know if the field was safe for children, or if its proximity to the Metrorail lines posed a danger. He asked if PRASA's advocate had seen the field and could attest to its safety, but the lawyer had never actually been. The judge postponed the case until December, and again until January. When a final ruling was issued on 27 January, it was not authored by Saldana, but by a less compassionate judge who was not particularly focused on the children's safety. There is only a one-line entry in Faeza's journal: "Today the Western Cape High Court granted an eviction order to us to be moved to Blikkiesdorp," the city's most notorious temporary relocation area (TRA). This TRA was the offer of legally mandated "alternative accommodation" described briefly in chapter 2.

By the time of the January hearing, the occupiers had rejected the Blikkiesdorp offer, and so the judge wanted them off the field immediately. Both this judge and Judge Saldana were increasingly bothered by the squatters' failure to organize themselves under a single leadership. When he heard the case again in December, he noticed that some of the occupiers who came to court were not on the list he had received from Fischer, who at that point was working with Marina's faction. "Who is Victor September and is he still on the field?" Saldana asked. Victor was a close friend of Faeza's and a founding member of TRU. I had a number of meals in his shack, and he was definitely on the field since the first day of the occupation. But his name was not on the court record. The judge could not figure out why he had shown up if his name was absent from the ledger. Fischer replied that he was representing both the sixteen people listed officially as respondents and others whose names were not on the list.

"Even that caused division," Faeza described, "because people's names were not on the list. Even my name was not on. Because Rahim [of the MPHA] put only the names of the people he wanted on. I told people not to worry because the document did say 'and others.'" The sheriff returned to the field the next day and added Victor's name to the list. But others, Faeza and Ebrahiem among them, were not home when he stopped by Kapteinsklip.

The sheriff wrote down that those not on the list had refused to give him their names, but I knew that this was not true. I was with the two of them that day when the sheriff arrived, and they really were not at home. By the time of the final hearing in late January, things on the field were as tense as ever. Physical altercations were now a regular occurrence, ranging from fistfights to attempted stabbings and arson. "Everyone is trying to prove that everybody else is doing something wrong," Faeza wrote, "instead of focusing on the real issue and why we really are there. I look at the kids and it makes me sad to think there is a possibility they might be homeless tomorrow. We might get evicted. And I can't even convince their parents to take part in doing something to avoid getting evicted."

This visible tension, frequently manifest as open squabbles in front of the judge, made her sympathetic to the PRASA advocate's argument that the occupiers were "queue jumpers." Indeed, judges are more likely to recognize an occupation as a legitimate settlement and prohibit the government from evicting squatters when their lawyer argues to the court on behalf of all residents. Getting a lawyer to represent all residents is, in turn, dependent upon how residents appear on the register of political society. Because the MPHA initiated the occupation as a project of atomized distribution, civil society on the field exhibited all of the features of seriality. At the level of political society, this was articulated as factionalism, a process described in the present chapter, militating against the election of a unified representative body. As a result, three different judges viewed the Kapteinsklip occupiers as opportunists jockeying for a handout rather than desperate residents squatting out of necessity. The contention from the settlement carried over into the courtroom, and it was quite evident to all involved that there was no unified force on the field. Rather, competing factions actively excluded their neighbors and tried to secure special favors from various external actors—not least of whom were the judges.

If they had been able to form some kind of unified presence, they might have been able to elect a single body to mediate between the occupiers and their lawyer, who would in turn relay their concerns to the judge in an orderly fashion. But persistent factionalism was overdetermined in Kapteinsklip by the way the occupation was articulated in the first place: as the distribution of mutually exclusive plots to each participant. Had the project of occupation been articulated differently, say, as the collective self-realization of access to housing, things might have proceeded differently. This is precisely what happened in the case of Siqalo, in which residents did resolve themselves into a unified settlement committee and were ultimately tolerated by a judge. It is to that story that we now turn.

6

Political Society II

Siqalo and the Politics of Committees

After the initial wave of occupation, Siqalo grew rapidly. An aerial photograph taken from a government satellite in 2011 shows an empty plot of land abutting Jakes Gerwel Drive. An image from the same satellite one year later reveals over twenty-six hundred unique structures on the field containing over six thousand people. Because the occupation was on private property, the police and Anti-Land Invasion Unit could not evict the residents until the owners filed for removal in court. The matter was complicated by the fact that the occupation spanned two adjacent lots with distinct owners, both of whom waited months to file for an eviction order. By that time, the settlement was well established and constantly expanding. Most Siqalo residents actively encouraged newcomers. Bonginkosi and company's offer to the dispossessed Kapteinsklip occupiers was not the exception but the rule.

As it expanded, the occupation grew too large to be governed by a single figure. Once the landowners sought to have the residents evicted, the latter were tied up in court. So many of them wanted personalized report-backs on their legal situation that Bonginkosi was soon overwhelmed. This meant that information was being unevenly disseminated, and allegations of preferential treatment started to fly. But unlike the Kapteinsklip occupiers, Siqalo's residents nipped these embryonic divisions in the bud. They replaced Bonginkosi with an elected body that represented all the various sections of the sprawling occupation. In order to avoid a dual power situation, Bonginkosi was included on the committee, which ensured popular satisfaction. As argued in chapter 4, this drive toward inclusivity was the result of how the occupation was articulated as a necessarily collective project in direct antagonism with the state. The government was not viewed as a partner in delivery, as in Kapteinsklip, but solely as a repressive apparatus. Residents united against their adversary, forming a fused group.

These developments in civil society necessarily produced a political articulation. This chapter, then, views the occupation through the lens of political

Delivery as Dispossession. Zachary Levenson, Oxford University Press. © Oxford University Press 2022.
DOI: 10.1093/oso/9780197629246.003.0006

Figure 6.1 Satellite photographs of Siqalo, December 2011 and December 2012.
Credit line: City Maps, City of Cape Town.

society. It asks how residents' trajectory of self-organization affected how they were seen by government officials. How, in other words, was movement on the terrain of civil society refracted through the lens of political society? How did the fused group produce an elected committee that represented all residents?

The first section below provides an account of how the occupiers maintained unity in practice through their encounters with hostile neighbors and representatives of the municipal government. Faced with openly racist antagonists, they refused to coalesce around an "African" identity, which might have restricted their membership. Instead, they preserved their identity as occupiers, forming a fused group capable of incorporating anyone who wanted to join them. This expansive politics of the fused group, articulated on the terrain of civil society, was represented in political society by an elected committee. The second section provides an account of the committee's emergence, and through a study of its conflict with an outside organization, notes the perpetual instability of political forms. But by working to constantly renew its relations with the wider occupation, the committee was successfully able to represent the occupation as unified to outside observers. The final section reveals the importance of this unity to the legal process. This collective constitution was so vital not because it allowed residents to pressure the state, but because it represented them as "deserving" on a legal register (political society) in which the state's moralizing language set the bounds of acceptable discourse. This ability to determine the conceptual repertoire is precisely what constitutes hegemony.

The Enemy

The residents had secured a pro bono lawyer, Sheldon, and soon court dates began to proliferate. Much as in Kapteinsklip, this sowed confusion among them. The journey to the High Court could take hours, and they typically received relatively short notice. Most of them could not make the excursion in any case, and so they relied entirely upon report-backs. But as discussed in chapter 4, Bonginkosi stopped relaying information to them as frequently as he once did, and no one seemed to know what was going on. This continued for a number of weeks until the elected committee instituted a regular schedule of report-backs.

As soon as the municipal government detected growth on the field in February 2012, it urged the owners of the two contiguous plots to apply for evictions so that the High Court could issue interdicts. The city needed the owners to take this step, as it could not initiate a case by itself. It was in a rush because once the occupation grew beyond a certain point, the city could not practicably provide alternative accommodation, making eviction a tricky undertaking, at least in legal terms. As the city's advocate would subsequently argue in the High Court, at that early stage "the City had the resources to accommodate 100 households under its Emergency Housing Programme."[1] This meant that when there were just over three hundred squatters on the field,[2] Cape Town's DHS could find them alternative accommodation in TRAs or elsewhere. This was feasible. But with the population now roughly twenty times that number, "The demand for housing under the City's Emergency Housing Programme outstrips its supply."[3]

From the government's point of view, it had the capacity to act at the beginning of the occupation, but now it could not possibly house this many residents. And even if it could, this would mean shifting its resources from its housing delivery program to make an exception for these occupiers. It would reward "queue jumping," officials thought. Of course, the occupiers were not asking for housing from the state. They were largely content with their self-built shacks on the field if the city would just install some more standpipes and toilets. But the DHS did not want to condone any occupation for fear that it would inspire subsequent rounds of squatters to seize land. From their point of view, it did not matter if residents were trying to bypass the housing waiting list or not. Given that they did not want anyone "invading" land, intentions were irrelevant; all land occupations were equivalent to "queue jumping."

In late August 2012, more than six months after the city's ALIU began monitoring the occupation, the sand-mining company Robert Ross finally filed for an eviction order. Initially, the company thought the population on the field was under control and did not want to get involved in a protracted legal battle. In April of that year, its private security guards[4] chased a dozen or so occupiers off the land. According to subsequent testimony, by late July, "crowds of unlawful occupiers arrived in *bakkies* [pickup trucks] with building material and invaded the applicant's land."[5] It was at this point that Ross approached the ALIU, which in turn informed the company that it needed to apply for an eviction injunction before ALIU agents could legally act in concert with the police. The occupiers' defense was skeptical of Robert

Ross's suggestion that the occupation did not begin in earnest until July, given that the company's lawyers had previously asserted that there were already two hundred structures on their property by June, "with approximately ten new ones being erected every day."[6]

Meanwhile, Lyton Properties, the owner of the other plot, filed for an eviction interdict just over a week before Robert Ross. As in the case of Ross, Lyton claimed that while there were a handful of squatters on the land since January 2012, the majority "invaded the property"[7] in August of that year—the same month it filed for an injunction. But according to the city's account, not only did the occupation grow substantially in February, but at that time the DHS and ALIU had urged Lyton to bring a case.[8] Lyton rebuffed these repeated requests. The city was able to get permission to remove fifteen existing shacks later that month (in February), as well as another twenty-five structures still under construction. The municipality served Lyton with another notice in late June. Again, it was ignored.

A couple of months into the occupation, as it was really picking up pace, occupiers met with their ward councilor, DA member Natalie Bent, who urged them to leave lest they face charges. The city continued to monitor the occupation closely, and the police met with residents later that month. Throughout April and May, the local government hoped to prevent a number of aspiring squatters from building new structures on the field. But without Lyton and Ross filing for eviction interdicts, there was only so much it could do. "Despite the City's warnings Ross and Lyton allowed the numbers to increase on their properties before bringing an application to court,"[9] the city's lawyers subsequently argued before the High Court.

During all of these behind-the-scenes conflicts among the courts, the landowners, the DHS, and the ALIU, residents maintained some semblance of unity in the face of these threats to their housing security. In Kapteinsklip, residents had initially sustained unity as police and ALIU agents launched repeated incursions into the occupation, producing a series of violent confrontations there and on the nearby sports field. Residents were temporarily united out of necessity. But as soon as these frontal assaults died down, residents decamped into contending alliances, attempting to secure their plots not only against outside invaders, but equally against each other. In Siqalo, however, residents were able to sustain their collective solidarity over time. They remained a fused group. Above all, this was evident in the fact that it was united under a single leadership, whether that was Bonginkosi or the wider elected committee. This leadership changed over time in relation to occupiers' concerns, but it always sought to represent all residents, as opposed to one or another faction. When outside organizations, ranging from party front groups to charities, sought to build support on the field, they were expelled. This unified sense of organization was as useful when legal mediation was required as it was when internal disputes needed to be resolved.

It was through identification with a representative leadership that the occupiers constituted a fused group, united against external threats. Police incursions were not yet the primary threat to the occupiers because they lacked authorization to operate on the field. At this point, they mainly had to worry about middle-class residents across the road. Kapteinsklip's closest neighbors had never organized in any sustained way to demand the occupation's removal, but this was far from the case in Siqalo. Colorado is a "Colored" middle-class enclave in the section of Mitchells Plain closest to Cape Town's city center, located a stone's throw from Siqalo. The neighborhood ratepayers' association wanted the occupiers out immediately. They began to organize mass protests along Jakes Gerwel, waving signs at passing cars with slogans such as "Hoot if you want them relocated," as if community pressure would force the government to act. Sometimes they would directly address the municipal government, as was the case with signs like "Move Siqalo!"

Siqalo residents would organize counterprotests, hoping to demonstrate to passersby that the occupation was not some abstract landscape but a real, human community. But this only galvanized the opposition, who never expressed their indignation in classed terms as we might expect. That is, they never demanded that the squatters be removed because the occupation's proximity to their homes would depreciate their property values. Instead, they articulated their opposition in starkly racialized terms,[10] sometimes as a "quality of life" issue—the smell, the unplanned disorder, and above all, a perceived rise in petty crime, all of which they would often associate with residents' "Africanness"; but more commonly, it assumed the guise of brazen racism, with "Colored" homeowners lobbing the full gamut of racial slurs at the "African" squatters.

Periodically, the ratepayers' association would convene public meetings to discuss the question of Siqalo. At one such meeting, convened in November, about eight months into the occupation, a series of speakers described "the problem" from a podium, insisting upon the incompatibility of so-called "African" culture with their own. A number of speakers dropped the pretense, deploying slurs to demand the removal of people who they insisted did not belong in Mitchells Plain, which they explicitly defined as "Colored" territory, echoing, of course, the apartheid state. Apartheid had ended nearly two decades earlier by this point, but the once heavily policed borders between racialized zones had been internalized by residents to the point where class concerns (and even class hatred) were articulated as naked racism.

Faeza and Ebrahiem rode to the meeting with their friend Mike, the middle-class "Colored" man who worked as a housing researcher for an NGO in town. Mike was quite sympathetic to the plight of Siqalo, and he consistently met with residents to stay up to date on its constantly changing legal status. He was a founding member of an anti-eviction organization in the 1980s that was heavily involved in the anti-apartheid movement,[11] as well as of Cape Town's Anti-Eviction Campaign[12] in 2000. Khwezi, Faeza, and another Siqalo occupier named Sizwe piled into the backseat, and Mike and Ebrahiem sat in front. Mike kept a low profile during the meeting as Cape Town mayor Patricia De Lille met with the disgruntled residents. Her party, the DA, had done little to dissuade residents from framing their grievances in racialized (let alone racist) terms. But as they were leaving, one of the ratepayers started shouting at Mike, pointing at his car. Mike actually lived in that neighborhood—in Colorado—and his allegiance to the occupation rendered him a traitor in his neighbors' eyes. This was not just about property value or even territoriality; they denounced him as a traitor to his race. This was the only time I ever encountered Mike visibly shaken by a protest, and we had attended quite a few together over the years. Even later that afternoon as we were sitting on Mike's couch a few hundred meters away, he had trouble calming down. He clenched his teeth, telling me he was not sure he was going to get out alive. People had started rocking the car with them inside, and Mike was terrified that they would actually turn it over. Thankfully for him and his passengers, however, another confrontation on Jakes Gerwel drew the assailants' attention for a moment. An "African" occupier was arguing loudly with a "Colored" homeowner, and racial slurs were beginning to punctuate their respective insults. Mike sped off.

That was the conflict with their middle-class neighbors. City officials, meanwhile, articulated their disdain not through blatant racism but instead favored the rhetoric of immorality. Mayor De Lille was at this particular meeting, and she spoke from the podium of the community center, ignoring attendees' consistent use of racial slurs and their demands that a wall be built between their houses and Siqalo, obscuring the latter from view. Instead, she went after the ANC for "stoking the fires of racial tension," even though the

ANC was not involved in this struggle in any way. She also blamed the occupiers for opportunism, which, she insisted, threatened the very functioning of democracy.

Not all DA members were so euphemistic, however. The DA ward councilor representing both Colorado and Siqalo, Natalie Bent, told the *Saturday Argus*, "They feel unsafe," referring to her middle-class "Colored" constituents. "Measures like building a wall to separate Siqalo is what they believe will keep them safe."[13] The echoes of apartheid could not be plainer. "There is a similar plan, but with slightly different objectives, to bar access from Samora Machel into Colorado via the R300 highway. Not only is it dangerous to cross the highway, but it is also an attempt to curb break-ins by criminals from Samora." Samora was the informal settlement in Philippi from which Khwezi, Mncedisi, and countless other Siqalo residents had come. There was nothing inherently "criminal" about these residents, nor were they identifiably responsible for any sort of crime wave. But Bent was a DA member, and DA politics were largely predicated upon a white-"Colored" alliance, specifying "Africans" as the enemy, even when this was merely implied, as in her comments.

Bent was not alone. A white DA member of the Mayoral Committee named J. P. Smith publicly aligned himself with the ratepayers' association, identifying Siqalo as responsible for "escalating crime" in the area. Likewise, another white DA member of the Mayoral Committee named Brett Herron defended the proposed wall as a necessary traffic barrier, preventing occupiers from running across Jakes Gerwel for safety reasons.[14] Similar remarks were made by another DA ward councilor for the neighborhood named Eddie Andrews.

Meanwhile, the police actually refused to secure the meeting, boycotting what they perceived to be the meeting of a "fringe, racist group," as cluster commander Jeremy Vearey put it. "To me such phrases create an 'other,'" he said. "They are a clear indication that the group is attempting to aggravate racial divisions and antagonism. This could escalate into crime, intimidation and violence."[15] He proceeded to dismiss the ratepayers' association as "racist and classist." Racist? Absolutely. But fringe? This was the neighborhood's primary residents' association, and here was the mayor meeting with them.

Yet the persistent threat of a wall being built, as well as the unabashedly racist rhetoric, ultimately had the effect of uniting the occupiers. The issue was discussed regularly in community report-backs by the elected committee and by Bonginkosi before he was deposed. The occupiers read this as a frontal assault, and the outlandishness of the rhetoric deployed by the Colorado ratepayers made it fairly easy to convince their neighbors to join with them in the streets. This struggle against racist homeowners, the municipal government, and the owners of the field occurred simultaneously, and they bled into one another, reinforcing feelings of settlement-wide unity. Internal squabbles appeared slight by comparison. Moreover, some residents may have felt ambivalent about occupying land owned by someone else or about challenging a government that claimed to be trying to deliver them housing. But they had no reservations about uniting to challenge the openly racist rhetoric of the ratepayers' association. The fact that major DA figures were associating with these middle-class racists without any apparent reservations allowed residents to rearticulate their occupation as a continuation of the anti-apartheid struggle. This was not about becoming homeowners, property-owning citizens, or the like; it was about completing the postapartheid liberation project, reversing centuries of land dispossession, and regaining access to what was rightfully theirs, at least in their minds. Paradoxically then, while we might expect sustained mobilization by middle-class homeowners to increase the likelihood of eviction, the fact that they regularly deployed such shamelessly racist rhetoric delegitimized their demands among some corners of the state—the police, for example—and actively reinforced whatever embryonic unity was already present in Siqalo.

Maintaining Unity

In addition to this organic unity that developed through conflict, the elected committee also tried to foster settlement-wide consensus. Above all, they did this by limiting the influence of outside organizations trying to operate in Siqalo. Certainly, there were tensions on the committee, above all between those members who supported the DA and those who viewed that party as condoning racism by working with the Colorado ratepayers' association. Khwezi and Lwazi, for example, were openly skeptical of Ntando's and Dumisa's support for the DA, regularly accusing them of opportunism. Sometimes these debates would grow heated. But they never threatened the unity of the committee itself. Ntando and Dumisa knew never to bring party politics into settlement politics. As long as no one did such a thing, the committee functioned along the lines of a sort of agonistic pluralism:[16] there were vigorous debates to be sure, but they never threatened the unity of the whole.

But what did this mean in practice? While all positions were admissible in meetings, committee members had to raise substantive issues instead of parroting partisan or organizational lines. At one meeting I attended in February 2013, just as their legal case was heating up and residents were faced with one rescheduled hearing after another, representatives of the Housing Assembly had come to ask why Siqalo had stopped sending residents to its meetings. Months earlier, Siqalo occupiers had been among the social movement's most enthusiastic participants, regularly taking the hourlong taxi ride to town to meet with residents from across the Cape Flats. The Housing Assembly was a nonpartisan organization that, much like TRU, tried to unite occupiers, backyarders, informal settlers, RDP house recipients, renters, and really any subjects of housing crisis.[17] It was militantly opposed to evictions and shoddy government housing, and it actively worked to defend land occupations, waging its first major campaign around Kapteinsklip and providing support at some of Siqalo's protests—especially those against the Colorado ratepayers' association. But it was not a coherent organization

Figure 6.2 Walking to a makeshift crèche in Siqalo with Mike and the settlement committee members.
Credit line: Photograph by author.

that acted "upon" communities; it was rather an umbrella movement that tried to incorporate new neighborhoods, settlements, and occupations.

I sat with Faeza, Ebrahiem, and Mike, who were there on behalf of the Housing Assembly. Mike was one of its founders, and Faeza and Ebrahiem became politicized from the experience of the Kapteinsklip eviction. Soon thereafter, Faeza was elected the Housing Assembly's chairperson. We sat in a makeshift crèche with seven of the committee members, all perched on tiny plastic chairs clearly designed for toddlers. "You must water the chairs so they can grow," Mike joked. No one laughed. The air was tense.

Ntando broke the silence. He demanded that Faeza explain to him why the committee members were not told about a Housing Assembly workshop on the politics of the Siqalo occupation that it had organized the previous weekend. Were they trying to keep out some residents at the expense of others? He insisted that only certain people were informed of the meeting and that he was not told until the day before. Faeza sat there confused. She had explained to me earlier that day that this was going to be a branch meeting of the Housing Assembly, so to speak. If the committee represented Siqalo, they were going to meet as a Housing Assembly affiliate and discuss relevant issues. But here was Ntando opening by accusing her of political maneuvering. He was not happy. "This is a question of who represents Siqalo," he muttered. "How did you pick people for the workshop? You always say we must be transparent. Well, let's be transparent!"

Faeza was taken aback, as she had not expected to be put on the defensive. She thought this was going to be a straightforward report-back. "It's about who's active," she responded. "There were no elections—I was not conscious. We just called everyone on the rolls, anyone who'd been to a Housing Assembly meeting from Siqalo before."

Dumisa chimed in, challenging her: "Once people see Faeza and Ebrahiem walking around Siqalo, they think the Housing Assembly has come. Now people are getting curious." He was presenting the Housing Assembly as an outside entity descending upon the committee rather than as a group of organizers attempting to facilitate self-organization within the settlement. How unexpected: Faeza and Ebrahiem founded TRU and joined the Housing Assembly precisely to avoid this mode of political engagement, and now they were being accused of it! Meanwhile, the elected committee did not seem interested in grasping the distinction between self-organization and a heavy-handed leadership.

Mike could not hold his tongue any longer. "What's the relation between the Housing Assembly and the Siqalo committee?" he insisted they tell him. "Are you not Housing Assembly members, comrades?" He demanded that they recall the history of the committee, its genesis, and how it related to the Housing Assembly in the process. "What else can we do? How else should we approach Siqalo other than trying to organize and mobilize people here?" It remains difficult, Mike continued, because the Housing Assembly's Siqalo presence was initiated by Bonginkosi, who was now reviled by the other committee members as a one-man show who hoarded information from their lawyer. And he was not present at this meeting despite sitting on the elected body. It was now so awkward between Bonginkosi and Ntando that the former rarely attended meetings anymore. More generally, Mike explained, the dynamic raises real questions about the authoritarian tendencies of representation by a single leader. This was not a problem specific to Siqalo, but one quite typical in areas with small committees that organize on behalf of residents rather than facilitating their self-organization.[18] "They must become actively involved in education and mobilization to overcome this problem. It's not enough to just call meetings; we need grassroots democracy here. The Housing Assembly isn't a welfare organization or something that provides bail money, but something that wants to build a movement!"

Fundani, the least politicized of the committee members but easily the most loquacious, responded immediately: "Before Bonginkosi went alone. But now the committee is different. You say the Housing Assembly is not a welfare organization, Mike, but before, when Bonginkosi brought Faeza, something happened to the community. She gave many beds, and then even six thousand rand [just under US$500], and other things as well. The community sees them as giving. So you can say this, but the community sees something else. This means that the community thinks items are being given to the committee members by the Housing Assembly. It also wasn't organizing before [under Bonginkosi's rule]. Bonginkosi doesn't want to give information from lawyers to the community."

Ntando backed him up: "You must go to the people, Faeza, and not just the committee."

Fundani cut him off: "—and tell people we aren't a political organization, that you're not a political organization." He was distinguishing on-the-ground organizing from simply plugging in to an existing organization like a party. "We just want to fight for decent houses. You must tell them that."

Ebrahiem was not having it. "Fundani, that's *your* job!" he barked. "You've been to so many workshops with the Housing Assembly. Why must *I* come tell people?" Ebrahiem was raising serious questions regarding the politics of representation. How should one communicate with "the community" as such? Was meeting with its elected representative committee not the proper channel?

"Ebrahiem," Fundani responded, "people in the community think there is something behind [your organization, the Housing Assembly]. They think there is money behind [it]." The lines of debate were clear. Faeza, Ebrahiem, and Mike were frustrated because they followed the proper channels and were still meeting resistance. And the committee members were annoyed because their constituents viewed the Housing Assembly as something akin to a political party—or at the very least, as an outside organization, but certainly not something that helped resolve internal struggles. To put it differently, Housing Assembly representatives were preoccupied with questions of political form, whereas the committee members disregarded this entirely in favor of considering content.

Lwazi looked at me and then turned to them. "People ask me why you now bring white people here." He was obviously talking about me, tying my presence in Siqalo to money, and more specifically, to charity. This was not so far-fetched. White people rarely made appearances in Mitchells Plain, especially in informal settlements, and whenever they did, they were either government employees there to enumerate shacks or install basic services, or else they worked for NGOs and charities and were there to distribute money or goods. Lwazi pegged me as the latter.

Faeza was furious. "*You* as the committee need to tell people about the Housing Assembly. That's *your* job, not ours. There needs to be a Housing Assembly presence *within* Siqalo, not just us coming in from outside." She was pointing out the contradiction in the committee's position. On the one hand, they were insisting that the Housing Assembly was a coherent enterprise that should act *upon* the settlement (in lieu of their own branch leadership). On the other, they were accusing the Housing Assembly of precisely this, of acting upon the occupation without consulting all of its residents first. How could they have it both ways?

But Ntando missed her point. "Okay, you must come back and tell the people. But there's a problem: you are being called members of the DA." The irony! Ntando actually was a DA sympathizer. It was also clear that a racialized politics was in play, with residents associating Afrikaans-speaking

"Colored" people with the DA and isiXhosa-speaking "African" people with the ANC. "They think you are like Ses'khona," the ANC front group discussed in chapter 4. "Now it's going all for the ANC even though it said different. They think Faeza is DA. Now they think everyone is DA because she keeps coming." He suddenly switched gears: "Also, I know there are Ses'khona members coming to your workshop from Siqalo. Why? How are they able to come from the ANC and be in both Ses'khona and the Housing Assembly? You must discipline your members!" Ntando concluded his comment by insisting that any Ses'khona members must be expelled from the Housing Assembly, lest Siqalo residents perceive the social movement as an ANC front. He had now accused Faeza of being both DA and ANC in a single tirade.

Faeza was fuming. She tried clarifying the Housing Assembly's strategy again. The group, she explained, would try to access people's frustration with their housing situation and develop it into a systemic critique of housing scarcity in Cape Town. It was about ascending from people's concrete experiences and tying them to broader political explanations—from the concrete to the abstract. The Housing Assembly eschewed the politics of simply presenting an abstract political line to potential members as if it had fallen from the sky.[19] This would constitute a politics of dogmatism. The point, rather, was to make sure that their explanations could actually help people make sense of their everyday lives. If they only knew politics through party affiliation, she explained, then that's where we would need to begin, and ultimately we can convince them otherwise. We cannot win people over by simply telling them what to do. We need to actually do the work of convincing them, of helping them develop their empirical common sense, as Gramsci put it, into theoretical good sense.[20]

Ntando was still not receptive to the point. "Tomorrow they'll wear the T-shirt of another NGO." He continued to represent the Housing Assembly as just another external organization attempting to form a population from on high.

Lwazi interjected and attempted to resolve the conflict. He explained Ntando's point in less abrasive terms, using the example of a civic organization in which he was involved in the 1980s, the key units that made up the anti-apartheid movement. "It was started in 1987, but then later it went into the ANC. It started by speaking from our experience, but then it tried to lead us to the ANC. So now we are skeptical. Who's behind the Housing Assembly? Who is this? Who's behind it? Maybe it's not [a front group], but people think the Housing Assembly is a party, so how can we show the people that the Housing Assembly is [any] different?"

Ntando nodded in agreement, adding, "People are wearing two hats. You need to recognize that and speak to those people."

Mike tried responding by drawing an analogy to union politics. Just because workers are in a union, he argued, does not mean that they cannot also be affiliated to political parties.

Ntando laughed. "But the ANC is capitalist now!"

"Yes," Mike agreed. "It's changed significantly since 1994."

At this point in the meeting, no women other than Faeza had spoken. She would later joke to me that the men on the committee saw themselves as doing committee work and saw the women as doing the actual work of organizing—a division of intellectual and manual labor, so to speak. The recurring theme seemed to be that even if the Housing Assembly were not actually "external," it was still perceived that way by residents. Ntando insisted that the organization was mobilizing one corner of Siqalo rather than the entire settlement, and he attributed it to favoritism. He was wary of the sort of politics that was so prevalent in Kapteinsklip: an outside organization facilitating the formation of a faction by one group of residents to the exclusion of the remainder of the occupation.

Suddenly Karen jumped to Faeza's defense: "But I'm active! They called me, and I mobilized my neighbors!"

Ntando was skeptical: "But why are [they] all active in just one part [of Siqalo]? Why are they only calling people in one corner?"

Fundani agreed with him. "You always call, Auntie Karen, fine, but they are all in just one area. They are all concentrated there. Besides, people are only coming to the meeting because they hear you get R40.[21] If there's no R40, they won't come!"

For the first time, Lwazi challenged his fellow committee members. "No, Fundani, people's hearts were touched at the workshop. We must take the ball forward." He seemed to have been won over by Faeza's passionate pleas.

Ntando attempted a compromise. "We need a workshop *at* Siqalo. We just give people responsibility because they aren't going to take it. People who attend workshops want to stand behind the Housing Assembly, but they aren't actively organizing." He was right. Too many Siqalo residents were attending the meetings without playing any kind of active role.

Dumisa chimed in: "Now people are happy because the whole committee is talking—not just that one man," he smirked, clearly referring to Bonginkosi.

Karen conceded that her neighbors were overrepresented at meetings. "We must phone everyone next time. We'll get everyone to come out. It's really a question of organization—"

Ntando cut her off. "You went around too late last time! Tilde and Auntie Karen did organize and mobilize people, but it was too late. They came the night before, but [by] then we already had plans. They must come four days before!"

Tilde spoke up, insisting that they did call people earlier but that they always had excuses. "People can't say it was because their phones was off. The VM [voicemail] light tells you if you missed a call so that's no excuse!"

The men on the committee seemed a bit sheepish, as if they had been too harsh with Faeza, Ebrahiem, and Mike. Dumisa conceded, "We *are* happy about the lawyer you got us." He was referring to the lawyer that Faeza had secured for him when five Siqalo residents were arrested at a protest.

Mike asked them about the status of the eviction case, the real reason they were all there. He knew it was to be reconvened soon, and he was worried that the eviction might actually be authorized. He pointed out that in the cases of Kapteinsklip and the sports field (Swartklip), the government managed to sow division, facilitating faction formation and pitting residents against one another. He told them that they needed to strategize ways to maintain unity. "You must occupy *together*!" he added for emphasis.

But they had already learned this point well. As this exchange between Housing Assembly organizers and the elected Siqalo leadership demonstrates, the occupation's representatives were completely conscious of the threat factionalism posed to their occupation. They were wary of allowing existing organizations to mobilize in Siqalo, skeptical that this would breed contention and mutually opposing factions. Sometimes this aversion seemed to verge on intransigence, but their caution was advisable. Far too many new occupations are fragmented by external entities working to make inroads not in an entire settlement, but instead gaining influence in a single corner of that settlement—the basis of Ntando's and Fundani's quibble with Karen and Faeza.

Mike asked them again about the status of their eviction case. Fundani mumbled and then told him that they were not really sure. "The case has been postponed, yes, and with no date."

"But the city mentioned that they're looking for land, *ja*?" Faeza asked him. "Did they say anything?"

Dumisa told her that the provincial government laid out what land was available in a document distributed to Siqalo residents, but no one I encountered seemed to have a copy. He then grew antsy, insisting that the meeting was going on too long, and that it was already getting dark. "We can show you the document at the next meeting, maybe next week?" he offered. Faeza, Ebrahiem, and Mike were all visibly excited, but the follow-up meeting never took place. They never got to see the documents.

Moralizing Politics

As the case dragged on, with court dates perpetually rescheduled, Sheldon became less accessible. Siqalo was only one of his many cases, and he did not have sufficient time to give the occupiers special attention. As he stopped returning committee members' calls, they began to seek out alternatives. Faeza secured them a lawyer affiliated to an "African" nationalist organization to represent some of the occupiers arrested during protests, but he refused to represent them pro bono once he learned that they were not receptive to his politics. At this point in 2013, his group was in talks with the various forces that would launch later that year as the Economic Freedom Fighters,[22] and he was eager to recruit some of the Siqalo occupiers to his cause. But they would have none of it.

Instead, two of the committee members reached out to the Legal Resources Centre (LRC), the organization that had helped the Kapteinsklip occupiers connect with Marius. The LRC put them in touch with their advocate, Paul Kennedy, who enlisted Stuart Wilson, the cofounder and executive director of the Socio-Economic Rights Institute (SERI) in Johannesburg. SERI doubles as a think tank, producing well-researched documents on constitutional guarantees, and is among the most knowledgeable legal entities on questions regarding housing and evictions. In practice, Wilson had won major Constitutional Court cases in Durban, Johannesburg, and elsewhere. Indeed, it was he who won the case against the KwaZulu-Natal Slums Act on behalf of the social movement Abahlali baseMjondolo in Durban, and he was certainly helpful to the occupiers' case.[23]

As in Kapteinsklip, moralism was at the heart of the debate in the Siqalo. The city's advocates attempted to represent the squatters as impatient "queue jumpers," whereas the squatters' lawyers portrayed them as homeless people without any other options. The judge in the Kapteinsklip case had focused on opportunism as a threat to democracy, but in this ruling, there was no mention of residents as "matter out of place" or as any sort of obstacle to the realization of the democratic project. Instead, their advocates' argument was accepted at face value: they were without alternatives, and to evict them would simply condemn them to squatting elsewhere. The recognition of this occupation as a deserving community—a group of houseless people in need rather than serialized opportunists—was intimately connected to their ability to represent themselves as a legible, legitimate population: a fused group. Articulated on the terrain of political society, the fused group appeared to the judge as an elected committee with a democratic mandate from all residents involved. Beyond these principles, they appeared orderly. There was no squabbling over lists in court, nor was there a question of whom their lawyer represented. To the outside observer, there was no sign of factions in sight.

In May 2013, the High Court finally heard major arguments from both sides. The city's advocates, Anton Katz and Karrisha Pillay, argued on behalf of the two landowners. The Court expected them to find alternative accommodation if eviction was on the table, and they attempted to explain why this was not a realistic demand. Their argument was structured much like the city's in the Kapteinsklip case. They presented three central arguments for the eviction, only the first of which departed from the Kapteinsklip case. They insisted that the case was "unprecedented"—the word appears repeatedly throughout their appeal—in that they were dealing with six thousand people in one fell swoop, hardly a manageable number in terms of providing alternative accommodation.

"The demand for housing under the City's Emergency Housing Programme outstrips its supply," they maintained, and so "the City is not in a position to immediately provide emergency housing [TRAs] to all persons in need thereof." Besides, the municipal government had already warned both landowners repeatedly. Drawing on precedent, the primary responsibility for protecting their property was theirs alone.

"There is currently no emergency accommodation available at any of the City's emergency housing sites," Katz and Pillay insisted.

> This cannot and is not seriously disputed by any of the parties to the litigation. Indeed, none of the parties contend that the City has accommodation under its Emergency Programme to house the residents. Instead, the residents resort to a bald, unsubstantiated suggestion that the City has

acted in disregard of its responsibility to design and implement a flexible, proactive policy which deals with unlawful occupation of land in an orderly and humane manner. The allegation is unwarranted and unsupported by the facts. So too, is the allegation that the City has failed to plan for or foresee the possibility of the eviction of some 6000 people. We reiterate, this is unprecedented!

There it was again: "unprecedented."

The legal team concluded by explaining the extraordinary nature of the case in terms of supply and demand, though with one notable omission: there was no attempt to explain why nearly twenty years after the fall of apartheid, it was only now that land occupations were proliferating in urban centers. Should this not have been the crux of their argument? "The City has explained that its obligations include addressing the plight of persons living in 223 informal settlements, hostels, backyards and other emergency circumstances, which it is trying to upgrade; this while the recent census results [2011] confirm that over 300,000 people have migrated to the Western Cape from other parts of the country, while the budget has remained the same." The old trope of the squatter as migrant[24] resurfaced, but without any evidence to support the claim. Indeed, Siqalo residents were primarily from Philippi, Khayelitsha, and elsewhere in Mitchells Plain. This was no basis for blaming the growth of land occupations on postapartheid rural-urban migration. If anything, this was *internal* migration.

If the first issue was a pragmatic one of capacity, the second was a moral question. Katz and Pillay represented the squatters as "opportunists," to use their word—just like Erasmus in the Kapteinsklip case. This fit with the city's broader attempt to represent all land occupiers as Machiavellian free-riders attempting to turn a quick profit rather than as houseless people in need. "It is submitted that the legal position is that opportunists should not be enabled to gain preference over those who have been waiting for housing, patiently, according to legally prescribed procedures," they wrote. But where were they to go?

Even the city's advocates acknowledged the situation of many of the Siqalo squatters: "It is apparent from the questionnaires that form part of the record in this litigation that the vast majority of residents have settled on the property either because they could not afford the rental of their previous homes or because they wanted their own homes or because they were forced to move out of their previous homes"—but these same residents are derided as "opportunists." This is despite the fact that "the residents assert in terms that they do not wish to bump anyone off the housing list" and that they "do not assert a claim for formal, permanent housing." So what was the nature of this opportunism?

Ultimately, it boiled down to the abstract logic of land occupations rather than a moral theory developed from a concrete case. When the squatters petitioned the municipal government and demanded that it purchase the plots from Ross and Lyton, the city's advocates rejected this request as impractical and above all, immoral. "Private land is vulnerable to unlawful occupation," they argued. "Accordingly, if this Court were to order that as a result of the unlawful occupation of the properties (which the City has at all times resisted and informed the owners of), the City must purchase or lease this land, this would have the unfortunate consequence of all private land being under threat of occupation by unlawful occupiers; and the City in turn being obliged to purchase or lease such land no matter how inappropriate it may be for its purpose. Indeed, this would actively encourage people to invade private land, and in certain circumstances enable land owners to encourage/permit unlawful occupation with the sure knowledge that the City will be ordered to acquire the land." This is textbook moral hazard, with the city assuming that accommodating the residents would incentivize them to occupy private property everywhere, knowing full well that there were no legal consequences for doing so. Moreover, they insisted, it would entice landowners to tolerate (or even encourage) occupation, since it would force the city to purchase their holdings.

The third issue raised by the city's advocates combined the pragmatics of state capacity with the moral critique of opportunism, representing the squatters as a dire threat to distributive democracy. "Land invasion is inimical to the systematic provision of adequate housing on a planned basis," Katz and Pillay argued. Participants in such an act are "opportunists [who] should not be enabled to gain preference over those who have been waiting for housing, patiently, according to legally prescribed procedures." Opportunism in this model is counterposed to orderly subjects of distributive democracy, "those who have been waiting for housing, patiently."[25] The advocates continued: "For this reason, the residents should not be permitted to claim permanent housing, ahead of anyone else in a queue."

The notion that the Siqalo squatters might be "queue jumpers" in the literal sense of the term is inapposite since they did not occupy land to expedite housing delivery or even access formal housing at all. In fact, the city's advocates recognized this quite explicitly: "The residents do not assert a claim for formal, permanent housing (save for under the UISP [Upgrading of Informal Settlements Programme] programme)," indicating that the occupiers sought service provision and potentially shack upgrading rather than housing delivery. "Indeed, the residents assert in terms that they do not wish to bump anyone off the housing list."

But despite this acknowledgment, the city continued to make the "queue jumper" argument, suggesting not only that the occupiers "sought to short circuit the formal housing allocation process," but also that they "attempt[ed] to obtain some priority for emergency housing," which would be "to the prejudice of other persons desperately in need of emergency housing." This of course is not what the Siqalo squatters were requesting, even implicitly, and as in the case of Kapteinsklip, they remained highly averse to the prospect of relocation to a TRA.

The government's lawyers were unable to comprehend the logic of squatting as a last resort. Instead, they represented them as obstructionists willfully complicating the process of housing allocation. "What the residents, in effect, ask this Court to do is to second guess a legitimate, bona fide and well reasoned decision of an organ of state that is seized with housing delivery." The city's "rational decisions taken in good faith" are counterposed to the irrationality of opportunism, queue jumping, and, to paraphrase Mary Douglas,[26] matter out of place. It was almost an aesthetic critique, reading disorderliness as an inherent affront to the state. Or to draw upon James Scott,[27] the formal, epistemic knowledge embodied in the state apparatus— the way that the state "sees" in his formulation—clashes with local, practical knowledge enacted on the ground. This is not to push for some populist understanding of "planning from below,"[28] but rather to suggest that local governments tend to bifurcate planning knowledge into separable categories, "from above" and "from below," valorizing the former as democratic, orderly, and progressive, and denigrating the latter as authoritarian, disorderly, and unprincipled.[29] They may pay lip service to the participation of residents, but this typically takes the form of hand-selected representatives viewed as nonthreatening.[30]

The residents' lawyers, Kennedy and Wilson, identified the contradictions in the city's argument. First, the very notion that they are opportunists is belied by the government's admission that they are overwhelmingly houseless. "The residents of Siqalo," they argued, "are all desperately poor people who occupy the properties because they have nowhere else to go. They have been evicted from backyard dwellings in Phillipi [*sic*], Khayelitsha and Gugulethu.[31] They were driven to occupy the properties out of necessity." Their eviction "would be nothing short of a humanitarian disaster." In Kapteinsklip the municipality was able to successfully represent the squatters as opportunists vying with one another for plots of land. But in the case of Siqalo it failed to do so. Meanwhile, both Ross and Lyton were willing to sell or lease their properties, or even to be expropriated by the city, but these suggestions were summarily rejected by the city's advocates as "unfeasible." "The City's position is, in short, that it will not assist the residents, that the Siqalo informal settlement is inimical to law and order and that the residents should be evicted without measurable delay." There was their argument in a nutshell. It was not about immediate threats to neighbors or even to the state's capacity to delivery. It was a fundamentally moral argument about the orderliness required for the state to realize distributive democracy. The municipality was arguing that the occupation "can and will compromise the orderly development and effective functioning of the City."

The residents' lawyers' response was to decry the abstract nature of this complaint. "This is, with respect," they declared, "a shocking attitude for an organ of state to take." If the problem were disorder, why would the mass eviction of six thousand squatters do anything to reduce it? As Kennedy and Wilson insisted, "To order otherwise will simply result in the residents occupying property unlawfully elsewhere. They cannot vanish into thin air, and will naturally continue to look for shelter wherever they can get it: on the streets, a park bench, under a bridge, or, most likely, on someone else's land."[32] The majority of the Siqalo squatters either could not afford to live in their previous dwellings, or else they were evicted from backyards and as their advocates insisted, they "would be rendered homeless if evicted from the property."

If the government argued that the spontaneity of land occupations threatened the very functioning of South Africa's distributive democracy, Kennedy and Wilson responded by questioning the inflexibility of the city's plans: "The failure of a municipality to plan for or foresee the possibility of the eviction of a large number of poor people is no excuse for refusing to formulate a rational plan to provide alternative accommodation, once the possibility of an eviction and consequent homelessness is drawn to its attention." It may be frustrating to administrators when unanticipated externalities threaten the functioning of a bureaucracy, but should this not be the entire point of the city's housing policy, that is, to accommodate recipients? If the Siqalo squatters were not in fact opportunists, as the city alleged, but a community of six thousand people living on a roadside field as a last resort, the city's job would be to recalibrate its plan in such a way as to accommodate them, or at the very least tolerate them. The alternative would be to condemn the occupiers to perpetual housing limbo. "Regrettably," they argued, "that is exactly the stance taken by the City in this application."

Nearly two weeks later, on 3 June, Judge Patrick Gamble ruled in favor of the occupiers. Judge Gamble was white and appointed by the DA, and like Judge Erasmus in the Kapteinsklip case, he had a history of ruling both for and against evictions.[33] "The City of Cape Town and the two landowners agree," Gamble wrote, "that the consequences of an eviction at this stage will render the majority of the occupants homeless." He discussed them as a population, never as individual opportunists. Without fail, he identified them as a unified group of "residents"—he always used that word—in stark contrast to Erasmus, who never once called the occupiers "residents." When the latter did refer to them collectively, he called them "defendants," though he usually disaggregated them in various ways—as opportunists versus those who were duped, or else as those who properly registered on the waiting list versus those who did not. But at no point did Gamble divide the occupiers into groups with competing moral content. He continued: "Judging from the expert reports filed, [they] have settled to the extent that there are now some 1800 structures, including crèche's [sic] and spaza[34] shops on the land." He never referred to contending factions or internal strife, as was the case in Kapteinsklip, but always discussed them en bloc as "the residents." In his final ruling, he decided that they "may remain in occupation of their homes . . . pending such further order as may be made by this Honourable Court." The National Department of Human Settlements would subsequently challenge the ruling, but in October, the High Court threw out the objection. For now, the occupiers were safe.

Conclusion

The absence of factionalism made it quite difficult for the judge, let alone the city, to successfully represent the Siqalo occupiers as opportunists; instead, they appeared as houseless people in immediate need. Even if Ntando's attempt to sell parcels of land recalls the MPHA's attempt to charge for plots at Kapteinsklip, he was quickly rebuked by the elected committee, not to mention his neighbors. There was an institutionalized consensus at Siqalo that derived from the initial articulation of the occupation as a collective struggle for liberation. The formation of a single body mediating between them and their lawyer nipped any emergent factions in the bud. When this body addressed the municipal government and the High Court, it was perceived as a legitimate representative of a community in need, and the settlement appeared legible to the judge as a community. They were "residents" rather than "occupiers" or "defendants." This was manifestly not the case in Kapteinsklip.

For the time being, residents received a reprieve. But the ruling was not definitive, and the court could reverse it at any moment. A year after Gamble's decision, police raided Siqalo and broke down doors and windows, brutally beating residents, arresting four elected committee members in the process. One was beaten so badly he could not walk for a few days. While they were ultimately acquitted, they were held in jail for the week. "They [the police] said that Zuma[35] had told them to do this. Did he really tell them that?" one resident asked.[36] While residents feared the worst at the time, it turned out that the police were responding to public violence allegations. The raid had nothing to do with housing law. Residents had protested against political parties campaigning in the settlement, burning tires in the road and even burning a voter registration booth for the second time, tossing the flaming tent into the middle of Jakes Gerwel. The police were there to arrest the ringleaders, though they ended up arresting committee members instead. Even after gaining the right to stay put, residents continued the strategy that had worked well for them thus far: expelling external organizations from the field.

Meanwhile, some residents began to long for the days of Bonginkosi's leadership, even if he were potentially corrupt and even a bit controlling. The democratization of the committee, while obviously well intentioned, was having some unintended consequences. Those of its members aligned with the Democratic Alliance were becoming increasingly vocal about their partisan loyalties. Another member was tentatively working with the Economic Freedom Fighters, and a fourth was interested in collaborating with the municipal government, much as Bonginkosi had. This latter member had secured the installation of nine additional standpipes, using his engagement with the city to shore up his own legitimacy as a representative. The presence of these various external entities—political parties, DHS officials, courts—sowed the seeds for an emergent factionalism, reminiscent of the type observable in Kapteinsklip. Even as some residents continued to guard Siqalo's unity, others began to welcome these organizations into their midst. The irony, of course, is that democratization would seem to undermine the consolidation of a settlement-wide consensus, which appears to require articulation in the form of a strongman to survive. As soon as this united front breaks down and residents begin to explore alternative strategies, factionalism is the most likely outcome. In other words, as consensus crumbles, its articulation on the terrain of political society is likely to undergo transformation.[37] Appeals to outside organizations re-emerged in the absence of any hegemonic force to direct the settlement. And given that Gamble's ruling could be challenged at any time, maintaining unity was essential.

But factionalism was not an overdetermined outcome. Another sort of democratization was possible, one in which committee members did not vie with one another for the right to represent the occupation to outside organizations. Democratization of the committee did not need to mean its own dissolution as a unitary voice, but its unity required that its members stopped trying to align with external actors in the name of the settlement. As long as the elected committee could reach a collective decision and agree that this resolution was binding, they would likely remain united as such. But if different factions began to approach various interested parties, DHS representatives, and charities, these factions would likely be consolidated in the process, entrenched over time, and, ultimately, intrasettlement disputes would begin to escalate. And when this happened, they would be prone to being read as opportunists in any subsequent court hearing. While we can think of Siqalo as a success case in that they were not evicted and provisionally achieved the right to stay put, this decision was just that: provisional. This legal limbo leaves them in a permanently temporary state, with the threat of eviction perpetually looming over them.

7

Four Theses on the Integral State

The Siqalo residents may have beaten their case, but this was not the end of their saga—though that is a tale better left for another book. In such an unstable context, we would do well to heed Stuart Hall's observation that the forging of political links and alliances cannot be understood "as a law or a fact of life, but [actually] requires particular conditions of existence to appear at all."[1] Certain political conditions were necessary for Siqalo to achieve its unified representative committee in the moment that really mattered, even if it were not permanent. Above all, their decision to expel all external organizations from the occupation proved crucial, as it amounted to the purging of factions in embryo. In delegitimizing organizations like Ses'khona right from the outset, residents were able to assert self-organization as a viable alternative. And this worked in Siqalo for two reasons. First, while Ses'khona certainly organized individual squatters into something approximating a collectivity, it never had much legitimacy among its constituents. In Kapteinsklip, the MPHA was able to represent the occupation as its own operation. It even convinced a number of the occupiers to pay the MPHA for plots of land. But Ses'khona never branded the Siqalo occupation in this way, nor did it ever portray itself as essential to the enterprise. Instead, it openly advertised its ANC affiliation, creating hesitancy and ultimately skepticism among residents, who decided that the organization was parasitic upon their project.

In addition to the failed leadership of Ses'khona, we need to consider a second factor: the preexisting organization of the occupiers who came to Siqalo from Samora Machel. As we saw in chapter 4, Bonginkosi began to play a hegemonic role in the process of occupation. He articulated the project as residents' self-realization of their constitutional rights to land and housing, rights that the postapartheid government failed to help them attain. His, Khwezi's, and other participants' backgrounds in the anti-apartheid movement meant that many of them were already familiar with neighborhood-level organizing. They were receptive to this model, as opposed to the way that the MPHA framed the Kapteinsklip occupation: as the distribution of

Delivery as Dispossession. Zachary Levenson, Oxford University Press. © Oxford University Press 2022.
DOI: 10.1093/oso/9780197629246.003.0007

plots of land to homeowners in the making. In Siqalo, by contrast, the occupiers were not aspiring property owners, but participants in a collective project of realizing their constitutional rights. The more the merrier, Bonginkosi
insisted. "Join us!" he implored as the Kapteinsklip occupiers were facing
eviction. If the situation were reversed and Siqalo were evicted just as
Kapteinsklip were picking up pace, it would be inconceivable for someone
from the MPHA to ask Siqalo evictees to join them.

But this does not mean that whenever self-organized residents expel political parties from their settlement, a unified settlement committee is certain
to emerge. And even when it does, its persistence is never guaranteed. The
conditions of its emergence must be actively reproduced; they are "not 'eternal'
but [must] be constantly . . . renewed [and] can under some circumstances
disappear or be overthrown," Hall[2] insists. He calls this process of renewal
"re-articulation": old linkages may be dissolved and new connections forged.
And this is precisely what happened in Siqalo. Shortly after the High Court
decision, conflict re-emerged, with some members of the committee forced
out. But upon these ruins, new connections were forged—and continue to be
forged today. After a decade without reliable access to water and electricity,
residents continue to mobilize and make demands for these basic amenities,
which have reoriented their struggle toward the state. In doing so, they began
to coordinate their protests, which required a base level of settlement-wide
organization. Soon residents resolved their intraoccupation qualms, at least
for the time being, and regrouped under a single committee that directed
their marches. In order to gain the attention of the municipal government,
they had to once again render themselves legible and legitimate. "Everything
we voice out to them is ignored," one longtime resident told a reporter.[3] "It's
like they don't recognise us as South Africans. We are human beings and they
must maintain our rights."

In reuniting under the leadership of a single settlement committee,
residents' linkages have been renewed, though of course these articulations
are never permanent, as Hall points out. As I have argued over the course
of this book, these civil society articulations—the consolidation of alliances
through political leadership—play an absolutely decisive role in the fate of
land occupations as they are translated onto the register of political society.
As much as existing literatures tend to focus on how governments manage
unruly surplus populations from above, the intelligibility of a given occupation *as* a population is never predetermined. Residents' status as members of
a population is the outcome of intraoccupation struggles over who can speak

on their behalf; but these civil society struggles are always already political society struggles, and, intentionally or not, residents project an image to government actors. The inextricability of these two struggles—civil society and political society—means that the articulation of a certain politics in a settlement affects how residents are "seen" by the state. And why does this matter? By way of conclusion, I want to reiterate the theoretical significance of my findings with four theses.

1. The state is not a "thing" but a social relation

This book challenges the idea that "the state" is a coherent institutional entity that simply enacts policies upon passive populations at will. When it comes to analyses of poverty management, we hear about governments regulating, punishing, surveilling, managing, disciplining, containing, and expelling the poor.[4] But here I take a very different approach, challenging the idea that "the state" is an autonomous actor. The government did not simply design urban policies and then implement them upon populations; it was through complex relations with residents that eviction outcomes were determined. Only in this way—that is, by seeing the state as a relation, as the condensation of a relationship of forces[5]—can we begin to understand how it was that squatters were evicted from Kapteinsklip and not from Siqalo.

This is where I break with prevailing accounts of how states govern surplus populations. Many of these theorists, taking inspiration from Foucault and Bourdieu, explicitly disavow[6] autonomist theories of the state, urging us to break with the state's own naturalized self-presentation as a coherent entity that implements policies upon passive populations. Yet their followers retain a certain state-centrism in their work, refusing to think "the state" as an arena of struggle, as in Gramsci's conception of the integral state. For Gramsci, the state encompasses both civil society, the moment of self-organization, and political society, the articulation self-organization assumes in relation to formal government institutions. As we have seen throughout this book, civil and political society articulations are inseparable, and political society articulations are often unintended consequences of struggles within civil society. This is what begins to explain the different outcomes in Kapteinsklip and Siqalo: the internal politics of each occupation were articulated differently, which in turn shaped the development of alliances within each occupation, which ultimately influenced divergent eviction outcomes.

And just as plausibly, we can think about how political society articulations impact lateral civil society struggles within each occupation. It was in seeking to protect their own serialized interests in Kapteinsklip that residents resisted the formation of a single elected committee. By contrast, in Siqalo, a unified political society orientation toward the DHS, the ALIU, and the courts facilitated the development of an accepted representative body in the occupation: first Bonginkosi, and subsequently an elected committee. Of course, this was a fragile hegemony that needed to be constantly reproduced, as the opening to this chapter reveals; but the key point is that these struggles in civil society and political society impact one another, meaning that we cannot think one without the other. They are two dialectical moments in a singular process.

Yet this separation is exactly how followers of Foucault and Bourdieu tend to proceed. Partha Chatterjee, for example, develops concepts of civil and political societies that are mutually exclusive—despite citing Gramsci to justify their use.[7] But unlike Gramsci, he uses "civil society" in the sense in which it was deployed by Hegel, as a collection of rights-bearing individuals or private citizens who access their rights through legally guaranteed channels. But in postcolonial democracies, he argues, society is split between those "who abide by the law" and those who violate it by virtue of necessity.[8] The latter are therefore denied the status of citizens—members of civil society—and are instead treated as component parts of populations, which together make up what he calls "political society." This is his Foucauldian moment: these populations can never impact governmental logics or policies; at best they can address the state, demanding recognition.

What is missing from Chatterjee's account, then, is any substantive treatment of squatters' politics. He is correct that once populations comport themselves as what he calls "moral communities" they may gain toleration from municipal governments. But how do populations become legible and legitimate in the first place? As I have maintained throughout this book, "population-ness" cannot be taken for granted but is rather the outcome of civil society struggles. When governments decide to favor one settlement over another, this is not simply imposed from on high, as in Foucauldian accounts of biopolitics, but is instead the outcome of complex political processes that play out on the terrain of civil society—a space that Chatterjee writes out of squatter's lives altogether. My criticism of his formulation, then, is not that he divorces Gramscian terminology from its intended meaning. Indeed, this is precisely what Gramsci did to the term when he appropriated it from Hegel and Marx.[9] But in returning to a liberal conception of civil society, Chatterjee excludes squatters from civil society struggles altogether. Land occupiers in this telling are inherently tied to amorphous "populations," but their own struggles in civil society do not appear to affect their political society articulations, that is, how (and indeed *whether*) they are recognized as populations by governmental officials.

This is of course backward. While Chatterjee is certainly right that squatters are excluded from standardized legal channels and that they need to become objects of governmental calculation, the notion that associational politics is limited to "elite groups" flies in the face of everything I discovered while researching the politics of land occupations in Cape Town.[10] Most surprising is his awareness of the implications of this expulsion of the poor from civil society, which is the very terrain of representational politics. His separation of political from civil society, he insists, continues the long-standing subaltern studies project of distinguishing "between an organized elite domain and an unorganized subaltern domain."[11] What is surprising about this project is that it echoes a central component of modernization theory: that surplus populations are inherently disorganized and remain external to the sphere of politics. This echoes Chatterjee's fellow subalternists' critique[12] of modernization theory's Marxist[13] iteration in Eric Hobsbawm's assertion that peasants remain "prepolitical." We can also find this distinction in the case of urban marginality theory as taken to task by Janice Perlman, Alejandro Portes, Helen Safa, and others for limiting the space of rationality, organization, and sanctioned politics to those with access to employment and formal housing.[14] The same distinction marked the social disorganization theory of the early Chicago school:[15] "marginal men" were deemed inherently disorganized, fundamentally incapable of articulating their politics and thereby excluded from the space of civil society.[16] Yet here is Partha Chatterjee, one of modernization theory's most vocal critics, reproducing the same distinction!

Another Foucauldian account, that of James Scott,[17] similarly excludes "populations" from the sphere of politics. He argues that statist projects entail rationalization and standardization, which amount to strategies of asserting control over civil society from above. Governments attempt to render society legible so that subjects can be "seen" by the state. In practice, this means comprehensively partitioning the ungovernable space of "society" into calculable, visible, and manipulable units, which ultimately means that governments constitute populations from above. They then act upon these populations, standardizing their language, mapping their land, shaping urban space, measuring their wealth and productivity, and most substantially for our purposes, acting upon them—or as Scott aptly puts it, "finely tun[ing] state interventions."[18]

But what agency do the governed have to shape these interventions? Scott discusses the prospect of withdrawal from the gaze of the state by resisting being measured, worked upon, and governed: becoming "illegible," in his phrasing.[19] There is even less of a possibility of affecting policy outcomes than in Chatterjee; residents' only options are withdrawal or resignation. But much as with contemporary invocations of Polanyi's double movement,[20] this limits our understanding of state intervention to a single, irreducible project: for Polanyi, repairing the fabric of society, and in Scott, rationalizing that society. Of course, state intervention for Polanyi is an inherently good thing, which is a far cry from the antistatist bent of Scott's analysis. But for both authors, the pendulum swings back and forth between more and less state intervention. Scott's subjects may be able to duck behind an obstacle to avoid the swinging weight, but there is no possibility in this account of them affecting *how* they are governed, the very content of state intervention. As the divergent trajectories of Kapteinsklip and Siqalo demonstrate, residents' own politics can impact what are otherwise theorized as one-size-fits-all policies. From the state-centric perspective, we know that the City of Cape Town wanted both occupations cleared. The literature imputes motivations ranging from profitability to governability, but much as in Scott's account, it only describes policies as formulated, which are rarely identical to policies as actually implemented, even in some of the authoritarian contexts he describes, or say, in apartheid South Africa. Urban policy may be devised in a vacuum, but we cannot analyze actually existing policies without seeing how these ideal state visions are refracted through civil society struggles. To restate the point, we need to break with the theoretical tradition that runs from early liberal political theory through the Chicago school, modernization theory, marginality theory, and ultimately permeates certain postcolonial and Foucauldian corners: the age-old separation of a passive subproletariat from an active state that projects policies upon populations. Sociospatially marginalized populations do have politics, and they can represent themselves. The question then is how their own civil society struggles translate onto the terrain of political society, which ultimately affects policy outcomes, ranging from eviction to the upgrading of housing to service provision.

2. Working with existing civil society organizations can be a barrier to the formation of fused groups; autonomously articulating such organization can militate against serialization

As we begin to unravel the processes through which Siqalo came to be tolerated but Kapteinsklip did not, focusing on self-organization—how residents
collectively articulated their project in civil society—gives us an angle typically excluded from the literature on evictions. This book has suggested that
the articulation of Siqalo as a fused group, in stark contrast to Kapteinsklip's
fragmentation into a series, sheds light on a process previously overlooked
in the scholarship. But how was it that Siqalo managed to constitute itself as
a fused group? And why did Kapteinsklip remain serialized? This brings me
to my second point. Civil society articulation works in a surprising way. We
might assume that working with existing civil society organizations would be
the most efficient way for squatters to integrate themselves into civic life and
earn the right to stay put. But as the case of Kapteinsklip illustrates so powerfully, being absorbed into existing civil society organizations can be demobil-
izing. In that case, cliques of occupiers sought out representatives of partisan
front groups like the MPHA, or else party-affiliated charities like Cape Care,
in order to legitimize their claims to the land. But they jealously guarded access to these contacts from their neighbors' advances—what I described in
chapter 3 as an exclusivist orientation. In doing so, the Kapteinsklip occupation appeared to outsiders to be fragmented into factions. Taking the expected route, working with seemingly legitimate civil society organizations,
paradoxically catalyzed division in the group.

In Siqalo, meanwhile, we saw something quite different: residents expelled
all existing civil society organizations from the occupation, including political party organs, front groups, and seemingly nonpartisan political associations. Rather than trying to work with these existing groups, the occupiers
collectively viewed them as a potential source of division. They proceeded to
expel groups like the Pan-Africanist Congress of Azania and the Ses'khona
People's Rights Movement from the occupation. In fact, they remained so
skeptical of the potential fallout from party involvement that they even
attacked nonpartisan workers from the Independent Electoral Commission
when they tried to register new voters in Siqalo. Instead of working with
parties, then, they articulated their project in civil society autonomously,
first delegating authority to Bonginkosi, and subsequently to an elected

representative committee. Accordingly, the Siqalo occupation was more likely to appear to outsiders to be organized into a coherent collectivity, both legible and legitimate.

And why might the Siqalo residents have selected the path of self-organization, whereas the Kapteinsklip squatters did not? As argued in chapter 4, some of the Samora Machel residents who ended up leading the Siqalo occupation had decades of organizing experience, going back to the anti-apartheid movement and both apartheid and postapartheid labor struggles. They were well versed in strategies of mobilizing their community, as opposed to the backyarders who ended up participating in the Kapteinsklip and sports field (Swartklip) occupations. This is not to say that none of them had such a background—I would occasionally meet old anti-apartheid militants in Kapteinsklip—but these were few and far between.

Some of it also likely derives from the respective sociospatial characteristics of their previous living situations. Some Siqalo occupiers also came from backyards, but most of the first wave of the occupation's leadership came from Samora—Bonginkosi, Khwezi, and others. Life in a sprawling, overcrowded informal settlement necessitated that residents make collective decisions about communal governance in that settlement, or in the language of this book, that they develop civil society organization. The Samora residents were well versed in the need for settlement committees when they occupied the field.

We cannot say the same for Kapteinsklip, whose participants were frequently the only tenants in a backyard before they decided to occupy the field. Even in cases where they were not—I encountered numerous instances of four or five shacks in a single backyard, for example—they had no need for formalizing representative leadership. Instead, they typically resolved issues on an individualized basis through the mediation of the homeowner, who functioned as their landlord. But there was no tradition of forming backyard tenants' unions or even informal representative bodies. So when the occupation began, they were only addressed as a collectivity by the MPHA, whose town hall meetings in the lead-up to the occupation were residents' only sites of contact with one another. By contrast, when Ses'khona approached the Samora occupiers, many of the residents had already discussed occupying land, and they certainly did not need some external organization to call their collective association into being; it was already articulated.

But while social and spatial constraints played a role in circumscribing the strategies available to the occupiers in both cases, we should not read their representative bodies as simply reflective of existing social divisions—or lack thereof. Squabbles were a constant in Siqalo, even if they were not reflected in the political leadership. And the entrenched factions that developed in Kapteinsklip did not reflect preexisting social divisions. Most of the occupiers had never encountered indigenist[21] rhetoric before they came into contact with First People First. And while "Colored" anti-"African" racism is fairly common in Cape Town, many of them were not vocal in these terms until they were hailed by ANC- and Cape Party–affiliated actors. These findings resonate with the literature on "political articulation"[22] insofar as it rejects any naturalization of political coalitions. As Cedric De Leon, Manali Desai, and Cihan Tuğal[23] argue so compellingly, the history of political sociology is haunted by the "reflection hypothesis," the notion that political parties (and more broadly, representative bodies) express entrenched relationships, interests, and values. But as these authors point out, parties do not only express existing interests; they often call people's preferences into being in the first place. Certainly people already have social identities and interests, "but parties have the potential to 'make' them at certain historical conjunctures and remake them at others, thereby making power."[24] This "making"—what they call "political articulation"—entails the creation of a stable system of signification, which in turn unites disparate individuals and groups under a shared project.

This is not far off from what transpired in Siqalo. The organic leadership that emerged from Samora sutured together disparate elements into a unified project of occupation: people's need to escape overcrowded shacks and unaffordable backyards; their desire to start households of their own; and perhaps most importantly, the self-realization of the postapartheid project of liberation. Because the postapartheid government could not adequately house people dispossessed under apartheid, they formed a movement to do it themselves. It was not until this leadership organized the squatters into a coherent movement—articulated their interests, we might say—that their politics came into being as such. This was not some straightforward reflection of their objective interests. Many of the Kapteinsklip occupiers had comparable interests, yet the MPHA articulated their political project quite differently. There was nothing about failed housing delivery, but instead the MPHA postured as if it were helping to realize that scheme. It addressed squatters as leaders of individual households—as recipients of distributed plots of land—thereby producing a competitive individualism: the politics of seriality. Just as the Siqalo committee does not reflect some primordial unity, Kapteinsklip's politics does not express some latent desire for private property inherent in the squatters. Instead, it was brought into being by the MPHA.

Yet there is also a major difference between my findings and those of the political articulation camp. For those authors, parties are the major agents of alliance building; it is parties that call collective interests into being. But in the case of land occupations, parties (or at the very least, their front groups) appear to play a consistently divisive role. It was in Siqalo, where residents expelled all party representatives, that the occupation was articulated as a fused group and elected a representative committee. But in Kapteinsklip, parties, charities, and other organizations actually inhibited the formation of such a body.

De Leon and his coauthors[25] are skeptical of this sort of account, noting the persistence of Michelsian arguments in social movement theory, including the idea that parties are self-interested organizations that tend to inhibit radical social transformation. While I am hesitant to universalize my claim, I do think certain characteristics of the postapartheid conjuncture limit the ability of parties to actually articulate unified coalitions in land occupations. Above all, the failure of both of South Africa's major parties to make any progress in closing the housing backlog brands both the ANC and the DA as unlikely candidates for calling occupations into being. Besides, most occupations occur in the run-up to local elections, and this, in combination with heavy-handed partisanship by party advocates, makes occupiers wary of being used and potentially abandoned after they are no longer needed. Their alternative—self-organization—seems more viable on a number of counts. First, a number of nonpartisan housing-related social movements helped organize land occupations in the early 2000s, and these were roundly condemned by most major parties.[26] Second, older participants often resent the ANC's co-optation of some of their previous political organizations from the 1980s, ranging from United Democratic Front affiliates to civic associations, all of which were effectively demobilized by the party in the early 1990s. Third, high-profile cases of occupations led by opposition parties are more likely to be met with increased repression when their competitors are in power.

Finally, parties and their front groups tend to operate in a very specific way in land occupations, and more generally, among urban surplus populations. Ses'khona, the PAC, the MPHA, and Cape Care all offered goods and services to residents instead of simply trying to rearticulate their interests, values, and identities. Whether this was access to a lawyer, plots of land, bags of old bread, blankets, or clothes, they pursued a clientelistic mode of distribution. This does not really qualify as political articulation for De Leon, Desai, and Tuğal, as they define "means of articulation" more narrowly as the deployment of mechanisms that states "*uniquely* possess to politicize social differences that might not otherwise be politically salient";[27] and so this brand of petty clientelism falls beyond the purview of partisan hegemonic projects. Instead, the distribution of these commonly attainable goods and services, hardly unique to parties, tends to divide residents, and it does so in two ways. First, without any kind of unifying values or identities, residents tend to compete over access to these goods. And second, given the size of the occupations considered here, partisan distributors require middlepeople to allot goods, which in turn creates (relatively) powerful gatekeepers who use these distribution networks to accrue political capital. Or in short, clientelism produces factionalism, and partisan clientelism is no exception.

These differences notwithstanding, I still want to highlight the affinity between my argument and that in the political articulation literature: factional divisions are actively constructed; they do not simply reflect primordial political differences or some sort of identitarian logic. But I also want to suggest that especially in the context of urban surplus populations, we might consider agents of political articulation beyond parties. In an aside, De Leon and his coauthors suggest this as a possibility "where political organizations are weak or do not have decisive influence over the state and civil society."[28] While the ANC and DA certainly are not weak, both parties have been riven by internal conflict in recent years, with the ANC hemorrhaging support among urban residents. Most recently, in the November 2021 local elections, the ANC garnered less than 50 percent of the vote for the first time, and the DA had its worst showing in a decade, receiving just over a fifth of the vote. Under such conditions, De Leon and his coauthors suggest, agents beyond parties can "offer . . . integrating logics." Indeed, they even note some of the potential crises that can emerge under such conditions, many of which will be quite familiar from the Siqalo occupation: "perpetual instability," as we have seen with one committee after another; "overbearing charismatic figures" like Bonginkosi; and finally, "turmoil," which they take to mean fascism or civil war, but I might also think about turmoil at a more immediate scale, such as the violence that plagued Siqalo in 2018 following the breakdown of their elected committee, culminating in the displacement of dozens of residents.

3. Every civil society articulation is also a political society articulation

Unified representation is easier to achieve when residents articulate their own civil society organs, expelling mediating organizations like political parties and charities. But why is unified representation so important? This brings me to my third thesis. At this point, the reader might think that my findings are not particularly surprising after all. My comparison appears to reveal an organized occupation successfully pressuring the state where a disorganized occupation could not: a standard narrative of resource mobilization. But there is a problem with this explanation: the occupiers never did try to pressure the state. In fact, they never posed a threat to the state's coercive apparatus, and it was never their intention to pressure the state in this way. This is why the resource mobilization approach to studying social movements only takes us so far. If with McCarthy and Zald[29] we define social movements in relation to their goals, namely "changing some elements of the social structure and/or reward distribution of a society," then neither the elected committee in Siqalo nor the contending factions in Kapteinsklip qualify as such. Even if we leave to the side the question of formalization— how social movements become formally constituted social movement organizations—the very goals of the occupations' representatives do not appear to meet McCarthy and Zald's key criterion of social movements: what is it that they want?

In the case of both occupations—and with a few exceptions,[30] the majority of occupations—residents simply wanted to be officially tolerated by the municipal government. While they would subsequently demand that the city install additional water standpipes, toilets, and electricity, they were not demanding houses, or as much as they would like to see it, an overhaul of the country's housing delivery program. Some of them were openly skeptical of capitalism, and others were even members of anticapitalist organizations, but no one described their participation to me in terms of some broader attempt to decommodify land. These actions were far more routine: they simply wanted a place to erect shacks, and they hoped that the government would leave them alone. Neither Robert Ross nor Lyton moved to have the squatters removed from their respective properties until the city pressured them to file for eviction interdicts. The residents' moments of open struggle only occurred when agents of the city's coercive apparatus, including the police and ALIU, quite literally attacked residents, or else tried to dismantle their housing and repossess their belongings. These confrontations were largely defensive, and we might say the same about the occupiers' noncoercive tactics. When the Siqalo residents marched on Cape Town's Civic Center, or when they rallied outside of the High Court, they were not trying to transform housing policy or even press for some less significant reform. They were trying to get the government to leave them in peace. When they marched on the Civic Center, they wanted the DHS and its Anti-Land Invasion Unit, not to mention the police with whom these offices worked, to leave them alone. And when they chanted outside of the High Court, they hoped the judge would recognize them as having some sort of legitimacy to stay on the field. They wanted their legitimacy recognized, which was much the same as wanting to be left alone—achieving what, to repurpose a term from the sociologist Liza Weinstein,[31] who herself adapted it from Chester Hartman,[32] we might call "the right to stay put."

For Hartman the concept was intimately tied to antigentrification struggles, and for Weinstein, it is a slogan that underpins a Mumbai-based mobilization against eviction that drew in activists and academics from across the globe. But in my use, I want to suggest something slightly different: land occupations are rarely intentionally politically transformative. Certainly they transform the social geography of cities, and the postapartheid period has seen the increasing informalization of neighborhoods since the transition to democracy. But occupations are not typically conscious or coordinated attempts to affect urban policy, let alone challenge the status of land or housing as commodities. This is the danger in reading them as inherently revolutionary, as far too many self-proclaimed radical academics are wont to do. This is particularly an issue in South Africa, where the bulk of the literature on housing struggles involves studies of formalized social movements like Abahlali baseMjondolo, the Anti-Eviction Campaign, and the Landless Peoples Movement. While these organizations have unquestionably been involved in occupations, these are exceptional. The overwhelming majority of cases are not tied to movements or even parties. We need to think through the politics of occupations not as we want them to be, but as they actually are. And this means recognizing the fact that most participants in land occupations are not aiming at anything transformative. Most likely, they just want a place to erect some shelter and be left alone.

In my narrative then, the significance of fused groups does not lie in the combined power they bestow upon occupiers to realize their will through pressure applied on the state, whether through coercive means or the marshaling of symbolic resources. Instead, it lies in the fact that every civil society articulation is also a political society articulation. And in capitalist democracies—especially postcolonial ones—political society articulations tend to be divorced from intentions. When Siqalo residents elected a unified committee, they were simply organizing the logistics of their occupation; but their civil society organization had a political society articulation: residents became legible as part of a coherent population, and they became legitimate as deserving homeless people in need rather than opportunists scrambling for handouts. The key point here is that in these sorts of actions, government actors tend to read political society articulations rather than civil society articulations. Accordingly, fusion is not a way to pressure the state directly; but the political society articulation of a fused group absolutely shapes government responses to an occupation.

Thinking this way about political society articulation as the unintended consequence of self-organization has major implications for our analysis. First and foremost, it posits a concrete mechanism though which bourgeois hegemony is implemented. To return to the Barbara Fields[33] quotation cited in the preface, "Exercising rule means being able to shape the terrain." If the municipal government wants all informally housed people engaged through official legal channels, the right to housing, as appealing as it may be, has precisely that effect. The postapartheid constitution directs all self-organized social struggles into engagement with the courts, which has the effect of judicializing all resistance. The problem with this moment of incorporation is that it does not involve occupiers' own organizations (civil society articulations), but rather their unwitting projection into formal political space (political society articulations). When that space of engagement legitimizes evictions, constitutional prohibition notwithstanding, we need to critically interrogate the role of legal institutions that are typically lionized as progressive. That is, after all, how hegemony works. On the other hand, being conscious of the relationship between civil and political society articulations can help shape occupiers' strategies on the ground.

4. Legal and institutional context is essential to understanding livelihood struggles in the postcolonial world

But why is it that residents can orient their social struggles toward securing toleration from the state instead of having to apply direct pressure, whether symbolic or coercive? What enables a political strategy distinct from the way we typically envision social movement politics? The obvious answer is that the postapartheid constitution guarantees freedom from eviction unless a judge can think of a reason why removal would be warranted. But constitutions have no power of their own; they need to be backed up by a legal system that is both strong and relatively autonomous. In the apartheid period, beginning in the late 1940s, the law functioned as a key means of realizing the national project of separate development. Key political determinations—such as who qualified as members of each racial group, who was allowed to live where, employment decisions—were all made in the courts. And this relative autonomy of the law has continued into the postapartheid period, with legal decision-making as the central terrain of struggle in the government's project of remedying the social inequalities left behind by years of apartheid rule. In other postcolonial contexts, this is the phenomenon the Comaroffs[34] describe as the "judicialization of politics" and that Gautam Bhan[35] refines as the "judicialization of resistance": the shifting of key social and political struggles onto the legal terrain. Nowhere is this truer than in South Africa, where the degree of autonomy afforded to the law is quite distinctive in the global South.

This is not to say that South Africa is entirely unique. Generally speaking, *Delivery as Dispossession* explores how postcolonial democracies tend to balance two needs: the need to regulate the influx of racialized surplus populations to cities on the one hand, and the need to reproduce their own legitimacy as democratic states on the other. We have seen how this plays out in the South African case with its relatively autonomous legal system. The government can no longer simply shift populations indiscriminately, but now requires a mechanism of selection that allows it to represent itself as both objective and just. This is the legal process whereby a court decides whether a population can be justly removed. Even if in reality business is carried out "from case to case," the government represents all cases as "equal before the law."[36] This is what facilitates the state's self-representation as democratic: it can safely relocate populations found to be "opportunists" or "queue jumpers" insofar as their actions can be represented as a threat to the democratic order. If squatters demand housing from the government immediately, but tens of thousands of others are already waiting, then their demands purportedly violate the objectivity of the postapartheid redistributive process—a central component of South Africa's democratization project, as argued in chapter 2. Framed this way, these "threats to democracy" can be safely evicted without undermining the government's own legitimacy as the chief arbiter of democracy. This is why postcolonial democracies tend to abandon the indiscriminate approach to dispossession that marked colonial regimes, opting instead for this mode of selective dispossession: sorting "deserving" recipients from the "undeserving" chaff.

In this sense, South Africa is like other postcolonial democracies attempting to resolve urban and housing crises. While it may be at one end of the continuum in terms of the autonomy of its legal system and the extent to which its constitution renders socioeconomic rights justiciable, we can imagine using a more fully elaborated spectrum to begin to compare South Africa with other postcolonies—some not too far removed from South Africa's legal-institutional context. Brazil, for example, has some version of guaranteed access to urban land built into its 1988 constitution,[37] which was amended in 2000 to make housing a social right.[38] Far from an empty guarantee, it was given teeth with the passage of the 2001 City Statute, which prioritizes social uses of urban housing over its commercial value. Two years, later, as the Workers' Party came to power nationally, it established a new Ministry of Cities and National Council of Cities, both of which worked to build up the capacity of municipalities to actually deliver on their promises of providing low-income housing.[39] While not quite identical to South Africa's constitutional guarantee to housing coupled with freedom from eviction, the Lula regime to its credit did attempt to reduce the frequency of evictions as it expanded housing provision in the early 2000s. Yet in Brazil, real estate developers have been able to engage in more blatant urban land grabs than they have in South African cities. Given the comparable legal-institutional contexts, we need to understand why.

Or take Indian cities, where recent work has shown that mass urban evictions also go through the courts.[40] But they operate according to a completely different logic, with rulings on the basis of how orderly settlements appear—how much they conform to a desired image of the city.[41] Without a constitutional framework comparable to South Africa's and Brazil's, how should we understand this process of judicialization? Subsequent work should treat these cases, and many others, in comparative perspective, thinking through two interrelated sets of questions. First, how does legal-institutional context matter? This is where we might map national cases onto a spectrum, with constitutionally guaranteed housing and eviction protections at one end. Then we would need to interrogate how this context is refracted through residents' civil and political society articulations, and how these articulations have shaped the translation of policy as formulated into policy as actually implemented as in the "integral state" approach deployed in this book. And second, we need to explain the tendency of politics to "judicialize," with housing policies shifting from the exclusive province of the executive and legislative branches to its effective oversight by the courts. And so legal-institutional context becomes not only cause, but consequence. The task then is to think through both simultaneously.

Conclusion

These two domains—the legal-institutional in which political society articulations appear, and the communal-popular in which civil society is articulated—are thus inextricably intertwined. We cannot think about residents' politics without reference to the legal-institutional context, or else we end up ignoring political society articulations and focusing exclusively on the civil society dimension. More often than not, land occupiers wind up in dialogue with the state, even when their occupation was explicitly intended to evade that state. This book explains why. I have argued here that this is how hegemony actually functions. It means that collective actors who are oppositional or even indifferent to the state, however radical, rebellious, and militant they might be, still operate on the state's terrain.

But by the same token, we cannot think about legal-institutional context as some sort of autonomous force or independent variable hovering above civil society. This is the chief limit of autonomist accounts in which governments define populations and then act upon them. As I have argued throughout this book, legible populations do not exist as a feature of some natural landscape but are the outcome of civil society struggles. In other words, populations work to define themselves as such; they do not immediately appear as populations in all instances. This means that any state project predicated upon managing surplus populations turns around how these populations render themselves visible to the state in the first place. But this project of becoming legible is often unintentional: residents experience themselves acting on the terrain of civil society even if it is their political society articulation that is "seen" by government actors. They may not know in advance how certain civil society articulations may translate into political society articulations, and this complicates strategic thinking.

What then to make of this legal-institutional context and the postapartheid constitution more broadly? Delivery and dispossession are linked technologies of population management, and it is through the law that they function. Managing surplus populations is a massive task in postcolonial contexts. Decolonization typically included the relaxation of controls on population mobility, whether in sub-Saharan Africa or on the Indian subcontinent, across the Maghreb or in Southeast Asia. As these legal strictures are lifted, residents who were previously relegated to underdeveloped sections of the country return to cities en masse, eager to find employment and access better schools and living conditions. This precipitates a crisis of sudden urbanization in which demand overwhelms supply to such an extent that governments cannot possibly close the housing backlog. Even in instances where housing delivery does not exist on any scale, democratic governments develop technologies of population management that allow them to manipulate populations in urban space, but they must do so without jeopardizing their democratic legitimacy. This is where housing delivery proves crucial: it is just such a technology of population management, but it also purports to fulfill the postcolonial promise of reversing colonial dispossession.

The postapartheid constitution's promise of housing for all is an instructive example of such a technology. South Africa may be a democracy, but it is a capitalist democracy, and its constitution did not provide the material means through which the state could achieve its goal of decent housing for all. Given its limited resources, this precarious welfare state could hardly keep pace with the Sisyphean demand unleashed by the abrogation of apartheid restrictions on mobility. Against this backdrop of scarcity, demand continues to take the form of land occupations, which are left to vie with one another over access to state resources. It is in this way that the struggle to articulate one's community as a population assumes a competitive form. This is not just a struggle for formal political representation, but as I have demonstrated in this book, struggles over self-organization affect people's very material well-being. Even when occupiers' representative bodies are not intended to hail the government, but instead to bypass it altogether, they still find themselves in dialogue with government actors. This is, after all, how hegemony works: every civil society articulation necessarily has a political society articulation—whether or not residents want this to be the case.

Notes on Data and Method

I did not think much of it at the time. As I made my way down a narrow pathway winding among Siqalo's shacks, perched as they were on rolling dunes, a group of small children began to chant, "*Abelungu, abelungu,*" using the plural form of the isiXhosa term for white people. Faeza, Ebrahiem, and Mike had arranged for me to sit in on a Siqalo committee meeting, and we linked up with Lwazi and began to walk toward the makeshift crèche where they held their meetings. But why were they calling us *abelungu* instead of just targeting me as an *umlungu* in the singular? Did my presence make the rest of the group white?

Three years later, this memory resurfaced as I met with Karen, a former Siqalo committee member who had to flee the settlement. I set up the interview through a mutual acquaintance, but I was not sure she would remember me. I had met her in passing a few times, but I could not have made much of an impression. Either I was sitting in the corner of a shack, frantically scrawling notes during one of the committee's meetings, or else I was on the periphery of a crowd during an occupation-wide report-back, invariably doing the same. But she remembered quite a bit about me: that I was a researcher from the United States, that I was studying land occupations, that I was particularly fascinated by militant protests.

I told her how remarkable her memory was, and she started to giggle. "You know," Karen told me, "the people, they all remember you. Do you see many white people here in Mitchells Plain? *Nie*, man, there's no white people here." She had a point. When I first began fieldwork in the township a decade ago, a group of kids would run after my hulking 1980 Mercedes—"rentamercedes.co.za," it read on the side in 150-point font, just in case I were trying to be discreet. They would chant, "*Polisie, polisie,*" presumably to warn the streets of an impending roundup. It took over a month for them to stop, and even then, they occasionally kept it up, almost as if it were a game. I was being trolled by a pack of first graders. But Karen was right: I had been going regularly to Mitchells Plain for six years by that point, and I had seen two white people during the entire period (excepting police and Anti-Land Invasion Unit agents of course): one was shopping in a nearby mall, and the other was Marina, the white woman from Cape Care who was active in Kapteinsklip.

But it was not the phenotypic novelty of my skin color that made my whiteness so memorable. Karen and the other committee members, much like the kids chanting "*abelungu*" after me, were materialists at heart. They knew that when white people come to Mitchells Plain, and above all, when white people visit informal settlements in Mitchells Plain, they come bearing resources. They did not care how I accounted for my presence, or that I made clear from the outset that I was not prepared to distribute a thing. They of course politely smiled and nodded, but the prospect of a white person constantly visiting the occupation without something to give—blankets, food, jobs, money, privileged access to a lawyer or the state, something!—was entirely alien.

"Everyone thought Faeza was DA for the longest time," Karen continued, referring to Cape Town's ruling party. "So they thought Housing Assembly was DA," which was particularly rich given that the social movement was sharply critical of all political parties. Faeza and the Housing Assembly as DA? How could they possibly think such a thing? I asked her. The group regularly organized protests against the DA, the ANC, and even the self-proclaimed revolutionaries in the EFF. The Housing Assembly's chairperson as DA? It seemed ridiculous on the face of it. Again, Karen laughed. "Because she brought you. They think she's DA, or maybe you're going to bring blankets for the children, or food for the people, or maybe you're helping us get proper toilets, man. But they think you're bringing us something, and that doesn't just happen. So they think Faeza organized it all, but how did she get you here? She must've joined your party. Or something, man. But that doesn't just happen. They think, what did she do for you?"

No matter that I was typically silent during visits to Siqalo or any other land occupation. I was happy to answer any questions, of course, and I would make small talk to retain people's trust, but I also knew this was not a case of proper participant observation. I was certainly an observer, but a participant? Yet apparently my time in occupations made an impression, and so I spent quite a bit of time thinking about ways to minimize my impact.

The Question of Reactivity

Jack Katz[1] warns of one variant of this danger when he describes the problem of reactivity: the very presence of the researcher can "confound substantive findings." Of course, many of the cases he considers involve interview-based research instead of proper ethnography, and many self-identifying instances of ethnographic research are actually closer to the interview model, carrying out one-on-one interrogations in the field. But participant observation fieldwork is necessarily reactive insofar as ethnographic research is an intervention into a field of power relations: "We are automatically implicated in relations of domination"[2] as soon as we enter the field. This being the case, Michael Burawoy[3] advocates for the deliberate violation of Katz's principle of reactivity. "A social order," he writes, "reveals itself in the way it responds to pressure. Even the most passive observer produces ripples worthy of examination." Rereading his essay[4] all these years later, I thought of myself standing in the corner of that makeshift crèche in Siqalo, pretending to be invisible, silent, objective, scientific. But how could a six foot, two inch white man in the corner of a largely "African" settlement in Mitchells Plain comport himself as a fly on the wall? He obviously could not, and my presence in Siqalo, however tactfully I may have thought I pulled it off, attracted attention. I might as well have been wearing an elaborate Halloween costume.

As much as I wished to observe the genesis of political struggles in Kapteinsklip, in Siqalo, and elsewhere, my very presence apparently affected the constitution of my object of analysis. I was there to study the formation of informal representative bodies, yet resource-bearing outsiders were frequently a catalyst for faction formation. As far-fetched as it seems that squatters might constitute a political disagreement around me—those aligned with me and those who were not—I also had no reason to doubt the accuracy of Karen's account. Indeed, what she described was generally how I experienced fieldwork in Cape Town. I cannot recall a single instance in which an adult contact could not remember me in the field, even when we had only met once and the subsequent encounter was years later. And why did they remember who I was, that I was a visiting researcher from the United States, that I tended to spend a lot of time with Faeza and Ebrahiem, that I was often with Mike, or that I used to hang around in Blikkiesdorp and townships in the southern suburbs but was now spending most of my time in Mitchells Plain? They viewed me as a point of access to material resources. Short of being reincarnated as an unemployed backyarder from Tafelsig—and even then—avoiding reactivity was not possible.

Nor was it particularly desirable. Burawoy's point that we should actually embrace reactivity is well founded: I was there to study how residents represented themselves to the government, and the dynamic we might think to guard against—the formation of factions—was already in motion. Whether it was me or any other outsider (and there were many), the notion that my presence might affect an outcome, however unstable, is not problematic from a methodological perspective. The ethnographer as external observer is a positivist fantasy. I was not there to witness some idealized "pure" process of political representation, but to identify this process as it interacted with the social world, and in this case, that social world involved me. We do live in the world we study, after all.

The solution, then, is not to repress one's presence in the field, but to consciously reflect upon it, teasing out all of the various effects it may have on one's object of analysis. And as with the observing sociologist, this object too exists in the social world, not in some sterilized test tube abstracted from it. "This is not a hindrance," Burawoy[5] insists, "but an indispensable support for social research." As long as we are clear about the ways that we as researchers intervene in the field, as long as we reflect upon the effects these interventions may have, and as long as we tie these effects to processes beyond the hyperlocalized scales of our field sites, we can continue to lay claim to the mantle of social science. The residents of Kapteinsklip and Siqalo may have had the misfortune of encountering agents of party front groups and self-interested charities and even a few oblivious lawyers, but they were also unlucky enough to encounter an American sociologist making his way across the Cape Flats.

Two Reactivities

It should be clear, then, that from a methodological and epistemological standpoint, I make no bones about being an active presence in the field. Indeed, it was my presence that illuminated the social dynamics I studied—civil and political society articulations—in the first place. Far from hindering my ability to understand informal politics in land occupations, so long as I was reflexive in my analysis, the effects of my presence provided a clear window into self-organizational dynamics. Karen never would have described faction formation so lucidly to me in relation to other outsiders; but when she did so in relation to my own incursion into the occupation, she felt comfortable describing how my presence affected their internal discussions, and we began to discuss how a similar dynamic was at work in other encounters between residents and outsiders. The same was true in other discussions with occupiers in both Kapteinsklip and Siqalo.

But reactivity in relation to scientific inquiry is only one dimension of the problem, and one relatively far removed from the quotidian concerns of residents themselves. Certainly faulty sociological analysis could adversely impact policy outcomes down the road, but there is little chance that my work will be read by many of the occupiers, a sociologist's fantasy notwithstanding. But there is a second type of reactivity that absolutely impacts residents' lives, and this is where I am hesitant to dismiss reactivity as solely of epistemological significance. In addition to epistemological reactivity, there's what we might call *ethical reactivity*: how does the sociologist's intrusion into a given situation affect the livelihood and well-being of the real people being analyzed?

This takes on particular significance in the land occupations I studied. As the contents of this book hopefully make quite clear, factionalism can have extremely violent consequences. In most cases, this entails tense debates and perhaps a bit of shouting, or as I like to think of it, politics. But these standoffs unfortunately degenerate into violence far more frequently than researchers might like to admit. In the best cases, these were just spontaneous fistfights as a means of settling a disagreement. But in other instances, residents tossed burning rags into rivals' shacks in the middle of the night, or in a few cases, as in Siqalo, they explicitly attempted to murder rivals. But even less explicitly violent effects of factionalism could be disastrous. If the argument of this book is correct, for example, and factionalism shapes eviction outcomes, and the incursion of powerful outsiders into an occupation increases the likelihood of factionalism, then the best thing an ethnographer can do in relation to land occupations is to stay away. But how then to conduct research at all?

The Merits of Bias

My mandate then was, essentially, to stay away—quite odd for someone trying to make a career as a participant observer. Of course, I did not stay away, but I needed to limit my visits to both occupations (as well as to others I studied during this period) to situations in which I would not be associated with one faction or another. That meant that during settlement-wide meetings or elected committee meetings, my attendance would not be seen as particularly partisan, though even this is an overstatement, as Karen's criticism makes quite clear. The very act of showing up in a car with some residents and not others was viewed by residents as my taking sides, and what amounts to much the same thing, as residents successfully using me to access resources. For this reason, I never spent the night in the occupations. Safety concerns aside—a big aside—I also could not be perceived as aligning myself with a single household or even set of residents while staying in the occupation. Instead, I would stay with contacts in a backyard shack in the vicinity, as I did during much of the Siqalo drama, or else I would drive back to the city center, where I rented an apartment during my fieldwork, returning the next day, as I did in Kapteinsklip.

But whose backyard shack did I stay in, and would that not mark me as partisan? Gossip travels quickly in Mitchells Plain, and within weeks, everyone knew I was staying in Faeza and Ebrahiem's shack after they had to leave Siqalo. Word also got around that I was sitting in on Housing Assembly meetings, both in Mitchells Plain and in Salt River, not far from the city center, and so many occupiers assumed I was working for that "party"—which, if you recall (see chapter 6), is how some of Siqalo's leadership perceived the organization, even though it was openly hostile to party politics.

Did this perceived partiality affect my ability to analyze struggles over representation in each respective occupation objectively? Absolutely. And if we were to take a positivistic approach "that reduces social science to the natural science model and suppresses the hermeneutic dimension,"[6] this might be a problem. But as I have already argued, the hypothetical standpoint of the neutral observer is a figment of the positivist imagination. Occupying a particular vantage point is not problematic insofar as we recognize the limits of doing so, as well as the ways in which this standpoint affects our observations and general outlook. And how did this perspective affect my analysis of the situation? I got quite close to Faeza and Ebrahiem, spending months at a time with their family over the course of a decade. All of their children know me well, as do many of their extended family members, spread as they are across the Western Cape. For years after they were evicted from Kapteinsklip, we would stay up late, sitting on the queen mattress in the back of their wendy house. They would regale me with tales of Rahim's *tik*-fueled rants, the time some of Marina's followers tried to beat up a single mother in her early twenties, or the elaborate scheme that the MPHA had devised to skim a few bucks from each of the participants. From their perspective, which actually mirrored the judge's to some extent, the MPHA-led faction was characterized by narrow opportunism.

And they were not wrong. Members of this faction, and indeed, the majority of the occupiers at Kapteinsklip, protected their self-identified plots at any cost; it was a politics of petty proprietorship. But my use of this concept should not be mistaken for political condemnation or moralistic judgment. "Petty" describes the limited nature of the property in question, not the occupiers' interpersonal behavior—think here of the petty bourgeoisie, for example, who are smallholders to be sure but are not necessarily trifling or spiteful. As an outside observer living in a very different context, it would be all too easy for me to pass moralistic judgment, especially if we were to read my story in reductive causal terms: factionalism yields eviction, and so these people are foolishly undermining themselves. Condemning their behavior is akin to decrying their false consciousness, as if (a) we would expect people struggling to survive to think about their situation in relation to some concept of totality, and (b) this sort of strategic view would necessarily yield identical results in every context. As Gramsci teaches us, "Interests are not given but always have to be politically and ideologically constructed."[7] When the occupation began, the MPHA framed it as the distribution of plots to homeowners in the making. We can scoff about a scenario in which people living under overturned shopping carts think of themselves as prospective homeowners, but it was actually a fairly rational position.

Since the transition, discourses of citizenship were very much tied to employment[8] and property ownership. But given the unemployment rate in this section of Mitchells Plain, property was their best bet. The MPHA brilliantly sutured this notion of citizenship to one of personal autonomy, of freedom, that appealed to backyarders who wanted a home of their own. Besides, given the history of South Africa's urban land occupations becoming tolerated informal settlements and subsequently being upgraded by the DHS, it wasn't such a stretch. As Alejandro Portes[9] put it nearly fifty years ago, "Ways of acting in the slum are structurally determined to the extent that individuals continuously look for the most efficient way of improving their positions within the limits and the barriers created by the existing social and economic organization." To his conception of structure, we might add the moment of articulation: the very framing of the occupation and, following Stuart Hall, the way that residents' interests are constructed and presented to them. What is important is not just an abstract conception of structure as such, but the way that residents understand structure as both constituting limits to action and enabling certain strategies—and this is where framing proves crucial.

It was only in identifying with one faction that I was able to gain a full account of its members' politics, as well as their perception of the limits of the politics of rival factions. The alternative, of course, was to simply interview members from all factions. But given their heightened skepticism of all outsiders, this did not appear to be a fruitful route. I gained an intimate and exceedingly personalized account of one faction's experience in the process, and it is crucial that I never generalize this very particular narrative to the entire occupation. But I could have never obtained this level of detail, including interpersonal squabbles, fears, apprehensions, and how the experience impacted their relations with friends and family elsewhere in the township, if I had simply interviewed a cross section of residents. Feasibility issues aside, the information I would obtain would be worthless: many of them would tell me what they thought I wanted to hear, most likely reproducing an image of a valiant social movement struggling for justice. What I learned instead did not always represent the occupiers in an ideal light, but it certainly portrayed them in actually existing terms. If instead I just interviewed a random sample, they would perceive the white American as the bearer of resources and tell me whatever they assumed it would take to gain access.

Triangulation as Method

And so my sample was biased, to be sure, yet this bias is precisely what I was trying to study: how factions emerge and become entrenched (and dissolve again and reform again) in the process of self-organization. And I did all of this while minimizing my impact on faction formation as much as I possibly could, which was primarily by "triangulating" multiple data sources. I gained access to Faeza's diary, which was particularly useful given that she participated in both occupations discussed here. Besides, to my knowledge no other participant kept a detailed written account of the process, and so it is not as if I erroneously relied too heavily upon one account at the expense of others. Certainly unwritten accounts exist for every participant, but again, I did not consider straightforward interviews to be a reliable source in such a fraught context. And as I have argued here, fly-on-the-wall ethnography simply was not an option, at least not in ethical terms.

My next best alternative, then, was to contextualize Faeza's claims as much as possible, which I did by comparing her journal's contents with a number of different sources. I drew on eleven hours of camcorder footage filmed by Ebrahiem, and I discussed the footage with many of the occupiers months and even years after they were evicted. I had the recordings digitalized, and then we watched the videos on my laptop in various backyard shacks. These were informal focus groups, so to speak. In addition, I scoured community newspapers and local radio stations for accounts, constructing an archive with every mention of either occupation, as well as any reference to the politics of land occupation and even housing. I always compared Faeza's accounts to those relayed to local media, as well as any alternative accounts I heard from her rivals. I also consulted other TRU members to make sure that I was not projecting one person's voice onto an entire faction; and I spoke with nonaligned occupiers as well, though this category was fairly small since it was difficult to survive in the occupation without a well-established group of allies. Finally, I interviewed a number of housing officials who worked with one or both occupations and got their account of political maneuvering in the settlement.

I wish I could have done the same with some of TRU's rivals, but of course that is not how politics works. Once the occupiers were evicted, I was able to more openly spend time with Faeza and Ebrahiem, even staying with them for extended periods. Doing so had no bearing on violence they faced in their daily lives, in stark contrast to the situation they experienced in Kapteinsklip. But it did come with a trade-off. On the one hand, I would not be able to obtain sincere accounts from their rivals, as they were convinced that Faeza was using me to gain preferential treatment from the city, or at the very least, to scam a few rands off me. On the other, I would be able to get this sort of account from Faeza, Ebrahiem, and other TRU members. I built rapport with them over a number of years, even after (and *especially* after) the eviction. As a number of them became active in the

Housing Assembly, I offered to drive them to and from meetings, shuttling organizers all over Mitchells Plain. We would watch both American and South African standup comedy together, often with their kids, who were fascinated by Black American comics riffing on race—an entirely alien concept to their own experience of growing up "Colored" after apartheid. We read together, sometimes short texts on political strategy, or else fragments on South African history, discussing the relevance of this writing to their lives in contemporary Cape Town. As we became increasingly familiar, we had to come to trust each other. I entrusted many of them with my own safety, calling before driving to fetch them in order to get the latest report on shootings to make sure it was safe to drive to their respective blocks. I used to think of these as forecasts of sorts. And they entrusted me with extremely personal narratives involving their children, their parents, drug use, gang affiliation, extreme violence, and all sorts of other sensitive material. It was only in building up this sort of rapport that I was able to access this intimate version of politics, a politics inseparable from their everyday lives, which allowed me to understand why this intimacy mattered in the first place.

And why did it matter? As I argue throughout this book, the contrasting ways in which an organic leadership articulated the project of land occupation affected people's self-understandings of their participation. In one case, they occupied a field in order to collectively realize the postapartheid promise of access to land and housing; in another, they wanted to gain the autonomy that comes with property ownership. Their own political sense was inseparable from their life goals, their aspirations for their families, and their understandings of their own opportunities and interests. Politics is not something that we can read off of objective conditions, as if being unemployed and houseless in Mitchells Plain would automatically yield some expected form of collective action. Hall's insistence that interests are constructed politically and ideologically in practice is not only a theoretical point but a methodological one: without a deep understanding of people's common sense, their given understanding of their social situation, we cannot possibly provide a coherent account of how a group of organizers shape their worldview. The MPHA, Bonginkosi, the elected committee in Siqalo, Marina: none of these leaders encountered generic subproletarians, as if we could understand the divergent trajectories of the occupations given their locations and respective positions in socioeconomic space. People had very particular and intensely felt reasons for wanting to build shacks on open fields, and organizers needed to cultivate these feelings through what Gramsci calls intellectual and moral leadership, rearticulating the very project in which they sought to participate. As he writes, "It is not a question of introducing from scratch a scientific form of thought into everyone's individual life, but of renovating and making 'critical' an already existing activity."[10] And reading Faeza's journal, watching 0 videos, and gaining the long-term trust of a faction of squatters were the only way to gain a real sense of how residents' common sense developed over time. The alternative would be to elicit relatively superficial accounts of participation from a more representative cross-section of residents, but doing so would not constitute a meaningful account of popular common sense.

Notes

Preface

1. Liza Weinstein, "Evictions: Reconceptualizing Housing Insecurity from the Global South," *City and Community* 20, no. 1 (2021): 13–23.
2. For an extended discussion of this framework, see Zachary Levenson, "Becoming a Population: Seeing the State, Being Seen by the State, and the Politics of Eviction in Cape Town," *Qualitative Sociology* 44, no. 3 (2021): 367–84; and Sneha Annavarapu and Zachary Levenson, "The Social Life of the State: Political Sociology and Relational Ethnography," *Qualitative Sociology* 44, no. 3 (2021): 337–48.
3. South African Const., ch. II, § 26.
4. Peter Thomas, *The Gramscian Moment: Philosophy, Hegemony and Marxism* (Chicago: Haymarket, 2009), 195. This concept will be further developed in chapter 1 in relation to some of Gramsci's other central concepts, including civil society, political society, and the integral state, all of which are essential to the arguments advanced in this book.
5. Barbara Jeanne Fields, "Slavery, Race, and ideology in the United States of America," *New Left Review* I/181 (1990): 114.
6. John L. Comaroff and Jean Comaroff, "Law and Disorder in the Postcolony: An Introduction," in *Law and Disorder in the Postcolony*, edited by Jean Comaroff and John L. Comaroff (Chicago: University of Chicago Press, 2006), 1–56.
7. Peter Ives, *Language and Hegemony in Gramsci* (London: Pluto, 2004), 72–3, 82–84; Alessandro Carlucci, *Gramsci and Languages: Unification, Diversity, Hegemony* (Chicago: Haymarket, 2013), 16, 173–76. This claim—that hegemony is fundamentally linguistic—is not to adopt a model of discursive determination in the last instance; rather, it is to understand the material foundations of language. As William Roseberry reiterates, "Words signal and express material social, economic, and political relationships and powers. Struggle and resistance concern these powers." Hegemony then constructs "a common material and meaningful framework for living through, talking about, and acting upon social orders characterized by domination." See William Roseberry, "Hegemony and the Language of Contention," in *Everyday Forms of State Formation: Revolution and Negotiation of Rule in Modern Mexico*, edited by Gilbert M. Joseph and Daniel Nugent (Durham, NC: Duke University Press, 1994), 362. For a version of this argument that loses its material bearings, according absolute autonomy to language, see Ernesto Laclau and Chantal Mouffe, *Hegemony and Socialist Strategy: Towards a Radical Democratic Politics* (New York: Verso, 1985); and Ernesto Laclau, *The Rhetorical Foundations of Society* (New York: Verso, 2014).
8. Roseberry, "Hegemony," 363–64.

9. No Sizwe [Neville Alexander], *One Azania, One Nation: The National Question in South Africa* (London: Zed, 1979), 9.

Chapter 1

1. I am grateful to Faeza Meyer for providing me with her journal, which was reconstructed in collaboration with the historian Koni Benson. I am indebted to both of them for allowing me to use this crucial source. The journal will eventually be published in full under the title *Writing Out Loud: Interventions in the History of a Land Occupation*. On their collaborative writing process, see Koni Benson and Faeza Meyer, "'Writing My History Is Keeping Me Alive': Politics and Practices of Collaborative History Writing," in *A Reflexive Inquiry into Gender and Gender-Based Violence: Toward a New Paradigm of Knowledge Production across Multiple Divides*, edited by Samantha van Schalkwyk and Pumla Gobodo-Madikizela (Cambridge: Cambridge Scholars, 2015), 103–27. About thirty pages from the journal have already appeared as Koni Benson and Faeza Meyer, "Reluctantly Loud: Interventions in the History of a Land Occupation," in *African Cities Reader III: Land, Property, and Value*, edited by Ntone Edjabe and Edgar Pieterse (Cape Town: Chimurenga/African Centre for Cities, 2015), 64–95.

2. A. J. Christopher, *The Atlas of Changing South Africa*, 2nd ed. (London: Routledge, 2000); A. J. Christopher, "Urban Segregation in Post-apartheid South Africa," *Urban Studies* 38, no. 3 (2001): 449–66; Kevin Durrheim, Xoliswa Mtose, and Lyndsay Brown, *Race Trouble: Race, Identity, and Inequality in Post-apartheid South Africa* (Lanham, MD: Lexington, 2011); Alan Morris, "Continuity or Rupture: The City, Post-apartheid," *Social Research* 65, no. 4 (1998): 759–75; Jeremy Seekings and Nicoli Nattrass, *Class, Race, and Inequality in South Africa* (Durban: University of KwaZulu-Natal Press, 2006).

3. Philip Harrison and Alison Todes, "Spatial Transformations in a 'Loosening State': South Africa in a Comparative Perspective," *Geoforum* 61 (2015): 148–62.

4. Vivian Bickford-Smith, "South African Urban History, Racial Segregation and the Unique Case of Cape Town?," *Journal of Southern African Studies* 21, no. 1 (2007): 63–78; John Western, "A Divided City: Cape Town," *Political Geography* 21, no. 5 (2002): 711–16; G. P. Cook, "Cape Town," in *Homes Apart: South Africa's Segregated Cities*, edited by Anthony Lemon (Bloomington: Indiana University Press, 1991), 26–42; Charlotte Lemanski, "A New Apartheid? The Spatial Implications of Fear of Crime in Cape Town, South Africa," *Environment and Urbanization* 16, no. 2 (2004): 101–12; Jacobus van Rooyen and Charlotte Lemanski, "Urban Segregation in South Africa: The Evolution of Exclusion in the Cape," in *Handbook of Urban Segregation*, edited by Sako Musterd (Cheltenham, UK: Elgar, 2020), 19–35; Faranak Miraftab, "Colonial Present: Legacies of the Past in Contemporary Urban Practices in Cape Town, South Africa," *Journal of Planning History* 11, no. 4 (2012): 283–307; Sophie Oldfield, "Local State Restructuring and Urban Transformation in Post-apartheid

Cape Town," *GeoJournal* 57 (2002): 29–37; Ivan Turok, "Persistent Polarisation Post-apartheid? Progress towards Urban Integration in Cape Town," *Urban Studies* 38, no. 13 (2001): 2349–77.

5. This was calculated with data obtained from South Africa's Department of Statistics at StatsSA, accessed 3 June 2020, http://www.statssa.gov.za. For illustrative use of this data, see Lungelo Shezi, "The Most Racially Segregated and Integrated Major Cities in SA," *Hypertext*, 23 May 2016, https:// www.htxt.co.za/2016/05/23/map-monday-johannesburg-is-the-most-racially-integrated-city-in-sa/.

6. Suné Payne and Tariro Washinyira, "Metrorail's Own Stats Show How Bad Its Service Is," *GroundUp*, 7 December 2017, https://www.groundup.org.za/article/metrorails-own-stats-show-how-bad-its-service/.

7. John Western, *Outcast Cape Town*, 2nd ed. (Berkeley: University of California Press, 1996), 75; Christian Beyers, "Identity and Forced Displacement: Community and Colouredness in District Six," in *Burdened by Race: Coloured Identities in Southern Africa*, edited by Mohamed Adhikari (Cape Town: University of Cape Town Press, 2009), 79–103; Ciraj Rassool, "Memory and the Politics of History in the District Six Museum," in *Desire Lines: Space, Memory and Identity in the Post-apartheid City*, edited by Noëleen Murray, Nick Shepherd, and Martin Hall (London: Routledge, 2007), 113–27; Henry Trotter, "Trauma and Memory: The Impact of Apartheid-Era Forced Removals on Coloured Identity in Cape Town," in Adhikari, *Burdened by Race*, 49–78.

8. Deborah M. Hart, "Political Manipulation of Urban Space: The Razing of District Six, Cape Town," *Urban Geography* 9, no. 6 (1988): 603–28; Brij Maharaj, "The Group Areas Act and Community Destruction in South Africa: The Struggle for Cato Manor in Durban," *Urban Forum* 5, no. 2 (1994): 1–25; Alan Mabin, "Comprehensive Segregation: The Origins of the Group Areas Act and Its Planning Apparatuses," *Journal of Southern African Studies* 18, no. 2 (1992): 405–29.

9. Throughout this book, I use "Black" in the sense adopted by the Black Consciousness movement in South Africa: subjects of racist discrimination. This encompasses "African," "Colored," *and* "Asian" with a single term. On the part of Black Consciousness's proponents, this was both an analytic and strategic concept. Analytically, it rejected the apartheid state's ability to project artificial divisions of ethnicity, race, and tribe onto the nonwhite population. Strategically, it attempted to join these forces under the banner of a united Black Consciousness, a common "mental attitude" held by all subjects of racist discrimination and oppression by the apartheid state. There are quite a few problematic accounts of the movement, as well as Steve Biko's thought, but there are also some excellent introductions, including Tendayi Sithole, *Steve Biko: Decolonial Meditations of Black Consciousness* (Lanham, MD: Lexington, 2016); Daniel R. Magaziner, *The Law and the Prophets: Black Consciousness in South Africa, 1968–1977* (Athens: Ohio University Press, 2010); and of course, Steve Biko, *I Write What I Like: Selected Writings* (Chicago: University of Chicago Press, 2002).

10. Sophie Oldfield and Saskia Greyling, "Waiting for the State: A politics of Housing in South Africa," *Environment and Planning A* 47, no. 5 (2015): 1100–1112; Zachary Levenson, "'Such Elements Do Not Belong in an Ordered Society': Managing

Rural-Urban Resettlement in Democratic South Africa," *Journal of Agrarian Change* 19, no. 3 (2019): 427–46; Zachary Levenson, "The Road to TRAs Is Paved with Good Intentions: Dispossession through Delivery in Post-apartheid Cape Town," *Urban Studies* 55, no. 14 (2018): 3218–33; Kate Tissington, Naadira Munshi, Gladys Mirugi-Mukundi, and Ebenezer Durojaye, *"Jumping the Queue", Waiting Lists and Other Myths: Perceptions and Practice around Housing Demand and Allocation in South Africa* (Johannesburg: Socio-Economic Rights Institute, 2013).

11. Here I use "African" to cover the group categorized as such by the apartheid state, pointing to the "Colored"-"African" tensions deliberately fostered under apartheid rule. Of course, all South Africans are African insofar as they were born on the continent, or at least live there. Many Black South Africans self-identify not as "Black" or "African," but as members of various ethnolinguistic groups—Xhosa, Zulu, Venda, Pedi, and so forth. But as people have internalized apartheid categories over the course of generations of segregation and apartheid rule, non-"Africans" usually use the term when describing those who are not phenotypically white, "Colored," or "Asian." Even this is fraught with complication, as some "Colored" residents appear darker than their "African" counterparts, whereas other "Coloreds" are as white as Afrikaners. Thus thinking of race solely in terms of phenotype in South Africa is highly problematic; many cases of racial self-identification are based upon performances of certain racialized scripts. On the shift from race to ethnicity and back again, see Michael MacDonald, *Why Race Matters in South Africa* (Cambridge. MA: Harvard University Press, 2012).

12. For more on these party dynamics, see Sam Ashman, Zachary Levenson, and Trevor Ngwane, "South Africa's ANC: The Beginning of the End?," *Catalyst* 1, no. 2 (2017): 75–106. South Africa's 2021 local elections took place after this book was already in press, but briefly, the ANC's share of the vote fell below 50 percent for the first time, with both major parties (ANC and DA) sustaining substantial losses nationwide.

13. Jean-Paul Sartre, *Critique of Dialectical Reason*, vol. 1, translated by Alan Sheridan-Smith (New York: Verso, 2004), 257.

14. I am relying on per capita estimates instead of absolute measures. All demographic information in this paragraph comes from the 2011 census and includes updates from the 2016 General Social Survey where applicable.

15. This is guaranteed by Sections 26(1) and 26(2) of the 1996 constitution's Bill of Rights, still in effect today: 26(1): "Everyone has the right to have access to adequate housing." 26(2): "The state must take reasonable legislative and other measures, within its available resources, to achieve the progressive realisation of this right." In chapter 2, I discuss the implications of this language, including what is meant by "adequate," "reasonable," and "progressive realisation," as well as how these meanings have changed over time. See South African Const., ch. II, § 26.

16. Asef Bayat, *Life as Politics: How Ordinary People Change the Middle East*, 2nd ed. (Stanford, CA: Stanford University Press, 2013), 19–20.

17. Section 26(3) of the 1996 constitution's Bill of Rights prohibits arbitrary evictions in all case: "No one may be evicted from their home, or have their home demolished,

without an order of court made after considering all the relevant circumstances. No legislation may permit arbitrary evictions." See South African Const., ch. II, § 26. In chapter 2, I explain what this means in relation to the frequent evictions I observed on the ground, as well as the evictions that continue to occur across the country and have for the duration of the postapartheid period.

18. Laurine Platzky and Cheryl Walker, *The Surplus People: Forced Removals in South Africa* (Johannesburg: Ravan, 1985). See also Gerhard Maré, *African Population Relocation in South Africa* (Johannesburg: South African Institute of Race Relations, 1980); Cosmas Desmond, *The Discarded People: An Account of African Resettlement in South Africa* (Middlesex: Penguin, 1971).

19. Paul Maylam, *South Africa's Racial Past: The History and Historiography of Racism*, 2nd ed. (London: Routledge, 2016); Saul Dubow, *Racial Segregation and the Origins of Apartheid in South Africa, 1919–36* (New York: Palgrave Macmillan, 1989); Fred Hendricks, Lungisile Ntsebeza, and Kirk Helliker (eds.), *The Promise of Land: Undoing a Century of Dispossession in South Africa* (Johannesburg: Jacana, 2013); Lungisile Ntsebeza and Ruth Hall (eds.), *The Land Question in South Africa: The Challenges of Transformation and Redistribution* (Cape Town: HSRC Press, 2007); Colin Bundy, *The Rise and Fall of the South African Peasantry*, 2nd ed. (Cape Town: David Phillip, 1988); Martin Legassick, *Hidden Histories of Gordonia: Land Dispossession and Resistance in the Northern Cape, 1800–1990* (Johannesburg: Wits University Press, 2016); Martin Legassick, *The Struggle for the Eastern Cape, 1800–1854: Subjugation and the Roots of South African Democracy* (Randburg: KMM Review, 2010).

20. Paul Maylam, "Explaining the Apartheid City: 20 Years of South African Urban Historiography," *Journal of Southern African Studies* 21, no. 1 (1995): 19–38; Mabin, "Comprehensive Segregation."

21. Quoted in Alan Wieder, "Speaking to the Present in South Africa: The Ideas, Writings, and Actions of Ruth First and Joe Slovo," lecture, Institute for Humanities in Africa, University of Cape Town, Cape Town, South Africa, 17 July 2013.

22. Anthony Sampson, *Mandela: The Authorized Biography* (New York: Knopf Doubleday, 1999), 483.

23. Patrick Bond and Greg Ruiters, "The Development Bottleneck," *Southern Africa Report*, April–May 1996.

24. On the tension between technocratic and participatory iterations of democracy in this context, see Zachary Levenson, "South African Evictions Today," *Contexts* 20, no. 1 (2021): 26–31.

25. In fact, the housing backlog has remained roughly constant at the national level and has actually increased in Cape Town since the transition in 1994. For data, see Zachary Levenson, "Precarious Welfare States: Urban Struggles over Housing Delivery in Post-apartheid Cape Town," *International Sociology* 32, no. 4 (2017): 474–92.

26. Barbara Maregele, "Waiting Period on Cape Town's Housing List Is 60 Years, Khayelitsha Meeting Told," *GroundUp*, 2 October 2017, https://www.groundup.org.za/article/waiting-period-cape-towns-housing-list-60-years-khayelitsha-meeting-told/.

27. Interview with Marlize Odendal, 2 October 2013, Civic Centre, Cape Town.

28. For a case study, see Levenson, "Precarious Welfare States."

29. Max Weber, *Economy and Society: A New Translation*, translated by Keith Tribe (Cambridge, MA: Harvard University Press, 2019), 343–44, 353.

30. Asef Bayat calls movements that attempt to fly under the radar in this way "social nonmovements," distinguishing them from social movements, which do, he argues, tend to hail the state. See Bayat, *Life as Politics*. See also Julie-Anne Boudreau, *Global Urban Politics: Informalization of the State* (Cambridge: Polity, 2017).

31. Backyarding is the predominant type of informal housing in Cape Town's "Colored" townships. Many residents simply erect a shack in the backyard of a formal house, favoring the security of this arrangement over that of an informal settlement. Backyarders may be able to obtain access to water, toilets, and electricity; reduce their risk of falling prey to violent crime; and perhaps, most importantly, evade the wrath of the police and the ALIU. See Levenson, "Such Elements"; and Charlotte Lemanski, "Augmented Informality: South Africa's Backyard Dwellings as a By-product of Formal Housing Policies," *Habitat International* 33, no. 4 (2009): 472–84.

32. The term can be traced back to the writings of John Locke, though the sense in which I use it here is often implicit in early modern political theory. See Ted G. Goertzel, "Political Society," in *International Encyclopedia of Civil Society*, edited by Helmut K. Anheier and Stefan Toepler (New York: Springer, 2010), 1248–50. It was Gramsci who developed the concept in opposition to "civil society," a term which occurs far more frequently in the period between the seventeenth and twentieth centuries. When more recent writers like Partha Chatterjee invoke the terms, it is in reference to Gramsci's understanding—though as I will argue in the conclusion, Chatterjee, along with countless others, deploys the concepts in a way that is at odds with Gramsci's formulation. Political society and civil society are not empirical locations in social space, but are, according to Gramsci, two aspects of a singular political struggle.

33. I am of course not referring here to the autonomist Marxism associated with 1970s Italy but rather to the tendency of sociologists and political scientists to view the state as an independent, coherent, and omniscient actor. For example, Theda Skocpol defines state autonomy in terms of "independent goal formulation." See "Bringing the State Back In: Strategies of Analysis in Current Research," in *Bringing the State Back In*, edited by Peter B. Evans, Dietrich Rueschemeyer, and Theda Skocpol (Cambridge: Cambridge University Press, 1985), 9. Likewise, James C. Scott characterizes modern states as having an inherent drive toward simplification and rationalization. See *Seeing Like a State: How Certain Schemes to Improve the Human Condition Have Failed* (New Haven: Yale University Press, 1998). Despite their divergent politics and theoretical approaches, both authors retain an autonomist bias insofar as they understand the state to be a self-enclosed set of institutions that acts willfully and coherently "upon" subject populations. As should now be clear, this view of the state as autonomous is opposed to the relational understanding I develop in this book.

34. John R. Logan and Harvey Molotch, *Urban Fortunes: The Political Economy of Place* (Berkeley: University of California Press, 1987); Harvey Molotch, "The City as a Growth Machine," *American Journal of Sociology* 82 (1976): 309–30.

35. Stephen Gelb, *South Africa's Economic Crisis* (London: Zed, 1991); Sam Ashman, Ben Fine, and Susan Newman, "The Crisis in South Africa: Neoliberalism, Financialization and Uneven and Combined Development," *Socialist Register* 47 (2011): 174–95.

36. David Harvey, *The Urbanization of Capital* (Malden, MA: Blackwell, 1985).

37. Neil Smith, *The New Urban Frontier: Gentrification and the Revanchist City* (London: Routledge, 1996).

38. Western Cape Anti-Eviction Campaign, "St James Street Residents Defend Themselves in Court against Illegal Eviction," press release, 18 March 2009, https://westerncapeantieviction.wordpress.com/2009/03/19/.

39. David A. McDonald, *World City Syndrome: Neoliberalism and Inequality in Cape Town* (London: Routledge, 2008); Tony Roshan Samara, *Cape Town after Apartheid: Crime and Governance in the Divided City* (Minneapolis: University of Minnesota Press, 2011).

40. Marie Huchzermeyer, "The New Instrument for Upgrading Informal Settlements in South Africa: Contributions and Constraints," in *Informal Settlements: A Perpetual Challenge?*, edited by Marie Huchzermeyer and Aly Karam (Cape Town: University of Cape Town Press, 2006), 41–61; Richard Pithouse, "Our Struggle Is Thought, on the Ground, Running: The University of Abahlali baseMjondolo," in *Yonk' Indawo Umzabalazo Uyasivumela: New Work from Durban—Centre for Civil Society Research Reports*, vol. 1, edited by Amanda Alexander and Richard Pithouse (Durban: Centre for Civil Society, University of KwaZulu-Natal, 2006).

41. David Ley, *The New Middle Class and the Remaking of the Central City* (Oxford: Oxford University Press, 1996).

42. Tom Slater, "The Eviction of Critical Perspectives from Gentrification Research," *International Journal of Urban and Regional Research* 30, no. 4 (2006): 749–50.

43. David Harvey, "From Managerialism to Entrepreneurialism: The Transformation in Urban Governance in Late Capitalism," *Geografiska Annaler. Series B, Human Geography* 71, no. 1 (1989): 7.

44. Jason Hackworth, *The Neoliberal City: Governance, Ideology, and Development in American Urbanism* (Ithaca, NY: Cornell University Press, 2007), 170.

45. Neil Smith, "New Globalism, New Urbanism: Gentrification as Global Urban Strategy," *Antipode* 34, no. 3 (2002): 427–50.

46. Rachel Weber, "Extracting Value from the City: Neoliberalism and Urban Redevelopment," *Antipode* 34, no. 3 (2002): 519–40.

47. Hackworth, *The Neoliberal City*, 72–73.

48. Weber, "Extracting Value," 525–26.

49. Don Mitchell, *The Right to the City: Social Justice and the Fight for Public Space* (New York: Guilford, 2003).

50. Smith, "New Globalism, New Urbanism," 442; cf. Jason Hackworth and Neil Smith, "The Changing State of Gentrification," *Tijdschrift voor economische en sociale geografie* 92, no. 4 (2001): 464–77; Loretta Lees, Tom Slater, and Elvin Wyly, *Gentrification* (London: Routledge, 2008), 249; Loïc Wacquant, "Relocating Gentrification: The Working Class, Science and the State in Recent Urban Research," *International Journal of Urban and Regional Research* 32, no. 1 (2008): 198–205;

Loïc Wacquant, *Punishing the Poor: The Neoliberal Government of Social Insecurity* (Durham, NC: Duke University Press, 2009).

51. Hackworth, *The Neoliberal City*; Lees, Slater, and Wyly, *Gentrification*, 39–41.

52. Rowland Atkinson and Gary Bridge (eds.), *Gentrification in a Global Context* (London: Routledge, 2004); Tim Butler, "For Gentrification?," *Environment and Planning A* 39, no. 1 (2007): 162–81; Loretta Lees, Hyun Bang Shin, and Ernesto López-Morales, *Planetary Gentrification* (Cambridge: Polity, 2016) ; Loretta Lees, Hyun Bang Shin, and Ernesto López-Morales (eds.), *Global Gentrifications: Uneven Development and Displacement* (Bristol: Policy Press, 2015); Lees, Slater, and Wyly, *Gentrification*; Tom Slater, "Planetary Rent Gaps," *Antipode* 49, no. S1 (2017): 114–37; Smith, "New Globalism, New Urbanism."

53. James Holston, *Insurgent Citizenship: Disjunctions of Democracy and Modernity in Brazil* (Princeton, NJ: Princeton University Press, 2008); Martin J. Murray, *Taming the Disorderly City: The Spatial Landscape of Johannesburg after Apartheid* (Ithaca, NY: Cornell University Press, 2008); Sarah Nuttall and Achille Mbembe (eds.), *Johannesburg: The Elusive Metropolis* (Durham, NC: Duke University Press, 2008); Janice Perlman, *Favela: Four Decades of Living on the Edge in Rio de Janeiro* (Oxford: Oxford University Press, 2010); Ananya Roy and Nezar AlSayyad (eds.), *Urban Informality: Transnational Perspectives from the Middle East, Latin America, and South Asia* (Lanham, MD: Lexington 2004); Ananya Roy, *City Requiem, Calcutta: Gender and the Politics of Poverty* (Minneapolis: University of Minnesota Press, 2002); Ananya Roy, "Urban Informality: Toward an Epistemology of Planning," *Journal of the American Planning Association* 71, no. 2 (2005): 147–58; AbdouMaliq Simone and Abdelghani Abouhani (eds.), *Urban Africa: Changing Contours of Survival in the City* (London: Zed, 2005); AbdouMaliq Simone, *For the City Yet to Come: Changing African Life in Four Cities* (Durham, NC: Duke University Press, 2004); AbdouMaliq Simone, *City Life from Jakarta to Dakar: Movements at the Crossroads* (London: Routledge, 2009); Li Zhang, *Strangers in the City: Reconfigurations of Space, Power, and Social Networks within China's Floating Population* (Stanford, CA: Stanford University Press, 2002).

54. Michael Watts, "Baudelaire over Berea, Simmel over Sandton?," *Public Culture* 17, no. 1 (2005): 181–92.

55. Mike Davis, *Planet of Slums* (New York: Verso, 2006).

56. Tom Angotti, "Apocalyptic Anti-urbanism: Mike Davis and His Planet of Slums," *International Journal of Urban and Regional Research* 30, no. 4 (2006): 961–67; Alan Gilbert, "Return of the Slum: Does Language Matter?," *International Journal of Urban and Regional Research* 31, no. 4 (2007): 697–713.

57. UN-Habitat, *The Challenge of Slums: Global Report on Human Settlements 2003* (Nairobi: UN-Habitat, 2003).

58. Marie Huchzermeyer, *Cities with "Slums": From Informal Settlement Eradication to a Right to the City in Africa* (Cape Town: University of Cape Town Press, 2011).

59. Javier Auyero and Débora Alejandra Swistun, *Flammable: Environmental Suffering in an Argentine Shantytown* (Oxford: Oxford University Press, 2009); Gautam Bhan, *In the Public's Interest: Evictions, Citizenship, and Inequality in Contemporary Delhi*

(Athens: University of Georgia Press, 2016); Marco Z. Garrido, *The Patchwork City: Class, Space, and Politics in Metro Manila* (Chicago: University of Chicago Press, 2019); D. Asher Ghertner, *Rule by Aesthetics: World-Class City Making in Delhi* (New York: Oxford University Press, 2015); Marie Huchzermeyer, *Unlawful Occupation: Informal Settlements and Urban Policy in South Africa and Brazil* (Trenton: Africa World Press, 2004); Huchzermeyer, *Cities* with *"Slums"*; Jacob Lederman, *Chasing World-Class Urbanism: Global Policy versus Everyday Survival in Buenos Aires* (Minneapolis: University of Minnesota Press, 2020); Xuefei Ren, *Governing the Urban in China and India: Land Grabs, Slum Clearance, and the War on Air Pollution* (Princeton: Princeton University Press, 2020); Ananya Roy and Aihwa Ong (eds.), *Worlding Cities: Asian Experiments and the Art of Being Global* (Malden, MA: Wiley-Blackwell, 2011); Liza Weinstein, *The Durable Slum: Dharavi and the Right to Stay Put in Globalizing Mumbai* (Minneapolis: University of Minnesota Press, 2014).

60. D. Asher Ghertner, "Why Gentrification Theory Fails in 'Much of the World,'" *City* 19, no. 4 (2015): 552–63.

61. Scarlett Cornelissen, "'Our Struggles Are Bigger Than the World Cup': Civic Activism, State-Society Relations and the Socio-political Legacies of the 2010 FIFA World Cup," *British Journal of Sociology* 63, no. 2 (2012): 328–48; Claire Mahon, *Fair Play for Housing Rights: Mega-events, Olympic Games and Housing Rights—Opportunities for the Olympic Movement and Others* (Geneva: Centre on Housing Rights and Evictions, 2007); Udesh Pillay and Orli Bass, "Mega-events as a Response to Poverty Reduction: The 2010 FIFA World Cup and Its Urban Development Implications," *Urban Forum* 19 (2008): 329–46; Bárbara Schausteck de Almeida, Chris Bolsmann, Wanderley Marchi Júnior, and Juliano de Souza, "Rationales, Rhetoric and Realities: FIFA's World Cup in South Africa 2010 and Brazil 2014," *International Review for the Sociology of Sport* 50, no. 3 (2015): 265–82; Dave Zirin, *Brazil's Dance with the Devil: The World Cup, the Olympics, and the Fight for Democracy* (Chicago: Haymarket, 2016).

62. There is a large literature on housing-oriented social movements, including Kerry Ryan Chance, *Living Politics in South Africa's Urban Shacklands* (Chicago: University of Chicago Press, 2017); Nigel C. Gibson (ed.), *Challenging Hegemony: Social Movements and the Quest for a New Humanism in Post-apartheid South Africa* (Trenton, NJ: Africa World Press, 2006); Nigel C. Gibson, *Fanonian Practices in South Africa: From Steve Biko to Abahlali baseMjondolo* (Scottsville: University of KwaZulu-Natal Press, 2011); Zachary Levenson, "Social Movements beyond Incorporation: The Case of the Housing Assembly in Post-apartheid Cape Town," in *Global Resistance in Southern Perspective: The Politics of Protest in South Africa's Contentious Democracy*, edited by Marcel Paret, Carin Runciman, and Luke Sinwell (London: Routledge, 2017), 89–104; Faranak Miraftab, "Feminist Praxis, Citizenship and Informal Politics: Reflections on South Africa's Anti-Eviction Campaign," *International Feminist Journal of Politics* 8, no. 2 (2006): 194–218; Faranak Miraftab and Shana Wills, "Insurgency and Spaces of Active Citizenship: The Story of the Western Cape Anti-Eviction Campaign in South Africa," *Journal of Planning Education and Research* 2 (2005): 200–217; Sophie

Oldfield and Kristian Stokke, "Building Unity in Diversity: Social Movement Activism In the Western Cape Anti-Eviction Campaign," in *Voices of Protest: Social Movements in Post-apartheid South Africa*, edited by Richard Ballard, Adam Habib, and Imraan Valodia (Scottsville: University of KwaZulu-Natal Press, 2006), 111–32; Raj Patel, "A Short Course in Politics at the University of Abahlali baseMjondolo," *Journal of Asian and African Studies* 43, no. 1 (2008): 95–112; Richard Pithouse, "Abahlali baseMjondolo and the Struggle for the city in Durban, South Africa," *Cidades* 6, no. 9 (2008): 241–70; Richard Pithouse, "A Politics of the Poor: Shack Dwellers' Struggles in Durban," *Journal of Asian and African Studies* 43, no. 1 (2008): 63–94; Richard Pithouse, "Struggle Is a School: The Rise of a Shack Dwellers' Movement in Durban, South Africa," *Monthly Review* 57, no. 9 (2006): 30–52; Pithouse, "Our Struggle Is Thought"; Rebecca Pointer, "Questioning the Representation of South Africa's 'New Social Movements': A Case Study of the Mandela Park Anti-Eviction Campaign," *Journal of Asian and African Studies* 39, no. 4 (2004): 271–94.

However, there is very little treatment of less systematically organized struggles over access to housing. A notable exception is the work of geographer Sophie Oldfield, including Claire Bénit-Gbaffou and Sophie Oldfield, "Accessing the State: Everyday Practices and Politics in Cities of the South," *Journal of Asian and African Studies* 46, no. 5 (2011): 445–52; Sophie Oldfield and Kristian Stokke, "Political Polemics and Local Practices of Community Organizing and Neoliberal Politics in South Africa," in *Contesting Neoliberalism: Urban Frontiers*, edited by Helga Leitner, Jamie Peck, and Eric S. Sheppard (New York: Guilford, 2007), 139–56; Jessica Thorn and Sophie Oldfield, "A Politics of Land Occupation: State Practice and Everyday Mobilization in Zille Raine Heights, Cape Town," *Journal of Asian and African Studies* 46, no. 5 (2011): 518–30. See also Trevor Ngwane's recent book *Amakomiti: Grassroots Democracy in South African Shack Settlements* (London: Pluto, 2021) and ethnographic work by Hannah Dawson, "Patronage from Below: Political Unrest in an Informal Settlement in South Africa," *African Affairs* 113, no. 453 (2014): 518–39; Hannah Dawson, "Protests, Party Politics and Patronage: A View from Zandspruit Informal Settlement, Johannesburg," in *Global Resistance in Southern Perspective: The Politics of Protest in South Africa's Contentious Democracy*, edited by Marcel Paret, Carin Runciman, and Luke Sinwell (London: Routledge, 2017), 118–29. But Dawson's, Ngwane's, and Oldfield's work remains the exception, with the bulk of antieviction research focused on flashier (and more institutionally supported) social movements.

63. Huchzermeyer, *Cities* with *"Slums."*
64. Eddie Cottle (ed.), *South Africa's World Cup: A Legacy for Whom?* (Scottsville: University of KwaZulu-Natal Press, 2011); Caroline Newton, "The Reverse Side of the Medal: About the 2010 FIFA World Cup and the Beautification of the N2 in Cape Town," *Urban Forum* 20, no. 1 (2009): 93–108; Udesh Pillay, Richard Tomlinson, and Jacques du Toit (eds.), *Democracy and Delivery: Urban Policy in South Africa* (Cape Town: Human Sciences Research Council, 2007); Gustav Visser and Nico Kotze, "The State And new-Build Gentrification in Central Cape Town, South Africa," *Urban Studies* 45, no. 12 (2008): 2565–93.

65. Sam Ashman, Ben Fine, and Susan Newman, "Amnesty International? The Nature, Scale and Impact of Capital Flight from South Africa," *Journal of Southern African Studies* 37, no. 1 (2011): 7–25; Sam Ashman and Ben Fine, "Neo-liberalism, Varieties of Capitalism, and the Shifting Contours of South Africa's Financial System," *Transformation* 81, no. 1 (2013): 144–78.

66. Huchzermeyer, "New Instrument"; Pithouse, "Our Struggle Is Thought."

67. Scott, *Seeing Like a State.*

68. Bayat, *Life as Politics*, 43. See also Zachary Levenson, "Social Movements beyond Incorporation: The Case of the Housing Assembly in Post-apartheid Cape Town," in Paret, Runciman, and Sinwell, *Southern Resistance.*

69. Perry Anderson, *The Antinomies of Antonio Gramsci* (New York: Verso, 2017 [1976]).

70. Peter D. Thomas, *The Gramscian Moment: Philosophy, Hegemony and Marxism* (Chicago: Haymarket, 2009), 167.

71. Antonio Gramsci, *Selections from the Prison Notebooks*, edited and translated by Quinton Hoare and Geoffrey Nowell Smith (New York: International, 1971), 160.

72. Gramsci, *Prison Notebooks*, 160.

73. Dylan Riley provides a Gramscian account of Fascism, rooting its emergence in strong civil society organizations. See his *The Civic Foundations of Fascism in Europe: Italy, Spain, and Romania, 1870–1945* (Baltimore: Johns Hopkins, 2010).

74. Peter D. Thomas, "Gramsci and the Political: From the State As 'Metaphysical Event' to Hegemony as 'Philosophical Fact,'" *Radical Philosophy* 153 (2009): 31. On the question of the apparent form of the state as opposed to its actual content, Gramsci wrote that his "study also leads to certain definitions of the concept of the State that is usually understood as a political Society (or dictatorship, or coercive apparatus meant to mold the popular mass in accordance with the type of production and economy at a given moment) and not as a balance between the political Society and the civil Society (or the hegemony of a social group over the entire national society, exercised through the so-called private organizations, such as the Church, the unions, the schools, etc.)." As is evident here, the notion that political society is equivalent to the formal institutional space of the state is not only an inaccurate reading of Gramsci, but is precisely the formulation *against* which Gramsci was writing. See Antonio Gramsci, *Letters from Prison*, vol. 2, edited by Frank Rosengarten and translated by Raymond Rosenthal (New York: Columbia University Press, 1994), 67.

75. Karl Marx, *Critique of Hegel's "Philosophy of Right,"* translated by Annette Jolin and Joseph O'Malley, edited by Joseph O'Malley (Cambridge: Cambridge University Press, 1970), 32.

76. Nicos Poulantzas, *State, Power, Socialism*, translated by Patrick Camiller (New York: Verso, 1978).

77. Thomas, "Gramsci and the Political," 31.

78. Panagiotis Sotiris, "The Modern Prince as Laboratory of Political Intellectuality," *International Gramsci Journal* 3, no. 2 (2019): 18.

79. John L. Comaroff and Jean Comaroff, "Law and Disorder in the Postcolony: An Introduction," in *Law and Disorder in the Postcolony*, edited by Jean Comaroff and

John L. Comaroff (Chicago: University of Chicago Press, 2006), 1–56. See also Gautam Bhan's discussion of the "judicialization of resistance" in Bhan, *In the Public's Interest*.

80. Thomas, *The Gramscian Moment*, 194.

81. Sartre, *Critique of Dialectical Reason*.

82. This point is rightly emphasized by Jasper Bernes in an accessible summary of this difficult text. See "Revolutionary Motives," *Endnotes* 5 (2019): 228–31. The literature on Sartre's *Critique* is surprisingly vast. The works I found most useful for navigating the notoriously elusive concepts of seriality and the fused group were not necessarily the most contemporary. See especially Thomas R. Flynn, *Sartre and Marxist Existentialism* (Chicago: University of Chicago Press, 1984) and Wilfrid Desan, *The Marxism of Jean-Paul Sartre* (New York: Doubleday, 1966).

83. Sartre, *Critique of Dialectical Reason*, 259.

84. Sartre, *Critique of Dialectical Reason*, 355.

85. Sartre, *Critique of Dialectical Reason*, 355.

86. This is a reference to Javier Auyero's book *Patients of the State: The Politics of Waiting in Argentina* (Durham, NC: Duke University Press, 2012). While his framing is explicitly Bourdieusian, the atomizing effect of being "hailed" by a state welfare apparatus is remarkably compatible with the Sartrean account I provide here.

87. For additional reflections on methods, refer to the methodological appendix.

88. I am grateful to Koni Benson in the Department of History at the University of the Western Cape, who was then a researcher at Cape Town's International Labour Research and Information Group, for both allowing me to use this document, and for undertaking the labor-intensive project of typing it up. Refer to the first note in this chapter for additional details about the journal.

89. These were the *People's Post* and the *Plainsman*, both owned by larger media conglomerates: News24 in the case of the former and Africa Community Media in the case of the latter.

Chapter 2

1. Jessica Thorn and Sophie Oldfield describe the specter of "queue jumping" as "the state's 'normal' justification against land occupation." See "A Politics of Land Occupation: State Practice and Everyday Mobilization in Zille Raine Heights, Cape Town," *Journal of Asian and African Studies* 46, no. 5 (2011): 522.

2. This is a sorely underresearched aspect of apartheid. There are very few attempts to think through the extent to which racial relegation required an extensive welfare state. More commonly, apartheid is characterized as "racial Fordism": social democracy for "whites," abandonment for everyone else. See, for example, Stephen Gelb, "Making Sense of the Crisis," *Transformation* 5 (1987): 33–50. But apartheid too required much in the way of infrastructural provision, and this goes far beyond shoring up the repressive apparatus. The following texts provide a point of departure for such an analysis: Jennifer Robinson, *The Power of Apartheid: State, Power, and Space in South*

African Cities (Oxford: Butterworth-Heinemann, 1996); Pauline Morris, *A History of Black Housing in South Africa* (Johannesburg: South Africa Foundation, 1981); A. J. Christopher, *The Atlas of Apartheid* (London: Routledge, 1993); John Western, *Outcast Cape Town* (Berkeley: University of California Press, 1996); Ivan Evans, *Bureaucracy and Race: Native Administration in South Africa* (Berkeley: University of California Press, 1997).

3. Laurine Platzky and Cherryl Walker, *The Surplus People: Forced Removals in South Africa* (Johannesburg: Ravan, 1985), 9.

4. Tom Lodge, *Black Politics in South Africa since 1945* (London: Longman, 1983), 212–14; Western, *Outcast Cape Town*, 46.

5. While the passbook system dates back to the late eighteenth century, it was not formalized until a series of laws passed in 1923, 1945, and 1952 extended it to all Black South Africans over the age of sixteen. As of 1952, they could no longer legally reside in a white group area for more than seventy-two hours at a time, unless they had maintained the same job there for a decade, lived there continuously for a decade and a half, or were born there and had never left. See Doug Hindson, *Pass Controls and the Urban African Proletariat* (Johannesburg: Ravan, 1987); Norman Levy, *The Foundations of the South African Cheap Labour System* (London: Routledge and Kegan Paul, 1982).

6. Jennifer Robinson, *The Power of Apartheid: State, Power and Space in South African Cities* (Oxford: Butterworth-Heineman, 1996).

7. On the construction of brick-and-mortar houses (as opposed to site-and-services schemes) for residents relocated to Soweto, see Keith Beavon, *Johannesburg: The Making and Shaping of the City* (Pretoria: University of South Africa Press, 2004), 133–34. While nearly fifty thousand new family homes could be funded if white property owners were taxed by an additional 0.83 percent for a single year, this was still seen as too controversial to implement at the time. Instead, the council borrowed £3 million from various mining companies, including Anglo-American. Minister of Native Affairs Hendrik Verwoerd, however, only allowed the council to accept the loan if the bulk of it was used to build labor hostels for single "African" men. In the end, only fourteen thousand family houses were constructed with this money. See also Noor Nieftagodien and Sally Gaule, *Orlando West, Soweto: An Illustrated History* (Johannesburg: Wits University Press, 2012), 20.

8. J. G. Brand, *Building a New Town: City of Cape Town's Mitchells Plain* (Cape Town: City Engineers Department, 1979), 2; K. A. E. van der Spuy, "Mitchells Plain / New Town: Past, Present, Future—a Summary," *Isilili sam sise Afrika* 2, no. 1 (1978): 9; D. S. Mabin, "Mitchells Plain," *Conference of the Institute of Housing Management* (Durban, September 1977), 1; "Mitchells Plain: A New Era in Mass Housing," *Financial Mail Special Report*, 5 May 1978, 2. For slightly different but still comparable figures, see Richard Le Grange, "Mitchells Plain: A Case Study in the Housing Question of South Africa" (honors thesis, Department of Sociology, University of Cape Town, 1987), 64.

9. The best accounts of these struggles in Crossroads remain Josette Cole, *Crossroads: The Politics of Reform and Repression, 1976–1986* (Johannesburg: Ravan, 1987) and Koni

Benson, "Crossroads Continues: Histories of Women Mobilizing against Forced Removals and for Housing in Cape Town, South Africa, 1975–2005" (PhD dissertation, Department of History, University of Minnesota, 2009). See also the recent graphic adaptation of Benson's thesis, *Crossroads: I Live Where I Like: A Graphic History* (San Francisco: PM Press, 2021).

10. Bill Freund, *The African City: A History* (Cambridge: Cambridge University Press, 2007), 126.

11. Ivan Evans, *Bureaucracy and Race: Native Administration in South Africa* (Berkeley: University of California Press, 1997), 121.

12. Evans, *Bureaucracy and Race*, 128; Saul Dubow, *Apartheid, 1948–1994* (Oxford: Oxford University Press, 2014), 110; Beavon, *Johannesburg*, 121; Eva De Bruyn, "Campus and the City in a South African Context: Reflections on a UWC Satellite Campus in Mitchells Plain, Cape Town" (MA thesis, Department of Architecture and Urban Planning, Ghent University, 2012), 18–19; see also Brenda Bozzoli's discussion of "racial modernism" in *Theatres of Struggle and the End of Apartheid* (Johannesburg: Wits University Press, 2004).

13. Dubow, *Apartheid*, 111; see also Beavon, *Johannesburg*, 121.

14. Platzky and Walker, *The Surplus People*, 341–43.

15. Cosmas Desmond, *The Discarded People: An Account of African Resettlement in South Africa* (Middlesex: Penguin, 1971). Desmond thought that the publication of this account would "penetrate the cloak of secrecy" (6) surrounding removals and that South African whites would be so aghast that they would begin to challenge their government.

16. Platzky and Walker, *The Surplus People*, 131. See also Merle Lipton, *Capitalism and Apartheid: South Africa, 1910–1986* (Aldershot: Wildwood House, 1986), 159.

17. Evans, *Bureaucracy and Race*, 121; see also Deborah Posel, "The Apartheid Project, 1948–1970," in *The Cambridge History of South Africa*, vol. 2, *1855–1994*, edited by Robert Ross, Anne Kelk Mager, and Bill Nasson (Cambridge: Cambridge University Press, 2012), 348.

18. Bill Freund, *Twentieth-Century South Africa: A Developmental History* (Cambridge: Cambridge University Press, 2019), 99. See also Hindson, *Pass Controls*, 84.

19. Dubow, *Apartheid*, 58.

20. Dubow, *Apartheid*, 37.

21. Evans, *Bureaucracy and Race*, 156.

22. Vivian Bickford-Smith, *The Emergence of the South African Metropolis: Cities and Identities in the Twentieth Century* (Cambridge: Cambridge University Press, 2016), 256.

23. Mabin, "Mitchells Plain," 35.

24. Freund, *The African City*, 136–37.

25. Dan O'Meara, *Forty Lost Years: The Apartheid State and the Politics of the National Party, 1948–1994* (Johannesburg: Ravan, 1996), 186. See also Bernard Makhosezwe Magubane, *The Political Economy of Race and Class in South Africa* (New York: Monthly Review Press, 1979), 148.

26. Brand, *Building a New Town*, 24.

27. Brand, *Building a New Town*, 2.

28. Brand, *Building a New Town*, 3.

29. No Sizwe [Neville Alexander], *One Azania, One Nation: The National Question in South Africa* (London: Zed, 1979).

30. Deborah Posel, *The Making of Apartheid, 1948–1961: Conflict and Compromise* (Oxford: Clarendon, 1992).

31. O'Meara, *Forty Lost Years*.

32. Jeremy Seekings, *The UDF: A History of the United Democratic Front in South Africa, 1983–1991* (Athens: Ohio University Press, 2000); Ineke van Kessel, *"Beyond Our Wildest Dreams": The United Democratic Front and the Transformation of South Africa* (Charlottesville: University of Virginia Press, 2000); Tom Lodge and Bill Nasson, *All, Here, and Now: Black Politics in South Africa in the 1980s* (New York: Ford Foundation, 1991).

33. Mark Swilling, Richard Humphries, and Khehla Shubane (eds.), *Apartheid City in Transition* (Oxford: Oxford University Press, 1992); David M. Smith (ed.), *The Apartheid City and Beyond* (London: Routledge, 1992); Owen Crankshaw, "Squatting, Apartheid, and Urbanisation on the Southern Witwatersrand," *African Affairs* 92, no. 366 (1993): 31–51; Owen Crankshaw and Susan Parnell, "Housing Provision and the Need for an Urbanisation Policy in the New South Africa," *Urban Forum* 7, no. 2 (1996): 232–37; Susan Parnell, "Constructing a Developmental Nation: The Challenge of Including the Poor in the Post-Apartheid city," *Transformation* 58 (2005): 20–44; Mitsuo Ogura, "Urbanization and Apartheid in South Africa: Influx Controls and Their Abolition," *Developing Economies* 34, no. 4 (1996): 402–23.

34. Josette Cole, *Crossroads: The Politics of Reform and Repression, 1976–1986* (Johannesburg: Ravan, 1987).

35. Technically speaking, the Freedom Charter was not an ANC program at its adoption but was actually the program of the Congress Alliance. This coalition included the ANC, as well as the South African Indian Congress, the Coloured People's Congress, the South African Congress of Democrats (a euphemism for white participants), and the South African Congress of Trade Unions. In 1959, the ANC would replace its 1949 program with the Freedom Charter, redefining itself as a nonracial organization, thereby absorbing the membership of the other race-based congresses. It was this move that catalyzed the formation of the Pan-Africanist Congress, which rejected this move by the ANC. The full text is available at "Freedom Charter," Wikipedia, accessed 11 June 2020, https://en.wikipedia.org/wiki/Freedom_Charter.

36. Cass R. Sunstein, "Social and Economic Rights? Lessons from South Africa," Public Law Working Paper No. 12, Olin Working Paper no. 124, University of Chicago, 2001.

37. The full text of the 1996 constitution is available at "The Constitution of the Republic of South Africa, 1996," Department of Justice and Constitutional Development, accessed 11 June 2020, https://www.justice.gov.za/legislation/constitution/SAConstitution-web-eng.pdf. Housing rights are enumerated in Section 26 of the Bill of Rights, available on p. 11.

38. Margot Strauss and Sandra Liebenberg, "Contested Spaces: Housing Rights and Evictions Law in Post-Apartheid South Africa," *Planning Theory* 13, no. 4 (2014): 432.

39. On these cases, above all the landmark *Grootboom* case, see Strauss and Liebenberg, "Contested Spaces"; Marie Huchzermeyer, "Housing Rights in South Africa: Invasions, Evictions, the Media, and the Courts in the Cases of Grootboom, Alexandra, and Bredell," *Urban Forum* 14, no. 1 (2003): 80–107; Marie Huchzermeyer, *Cities with "Slums": From Informal Settlement Eradication to a Right to the City in Africa* (Cape Town: University of Cape Town Press, 2011); Pierre de Vos, "*Grootboom*, the Right of Access to Housing and Substantive Equality as Contextual Fairness," *South African Journal on Human Rights* 17, no. 2 (2001): 258–76.

40. Though as we will see in chapter 4, officials often abuse this provision, offering substandard accommodation as cover for removals, knowing full well it will be rejected. Temporary relocation areas (TRAs), government-run relocation camps, are notoriously despised and stigmatized in Cape Town and often play this role. See Zachary Levenson, "The Road to TRAs Is Paved with Good Intentions: Dispossession through Delivery in Post-Apartheid Cape Town," *Urban Studies* 55, no. 14 (2018): 3218–33; and Zachary Levenson, "Precarious Welfare States: Urban Struggles over Housing Delivery in Post-Apartheid Cape Town," *International Sociology* 32, no. 4: 474–92.

41. Zachary Levenson, "'Such Elements Do Not Belong in an Ordered Society': Managing Rural-Urban Resettlement in Democratic South Africa," *Journal of Agrarian Change* 19, no. 3 (2019): 427–46; Levenson, "The Road to TRAs."

42. Philip Harrison, Alison Todes, and Vanessa Watson, *Planning and Transformation: Learning from the Post-apartheid Experience* (London: Routledge, 2008); Mark Hunter and Dorrit Posel, "Here to Work: The Socioeconomic Characteristics of Informal Dwellers in Post-apartheid South Africa," *Environment and Urbanization* 24 (2012): 285–304; Bill Freund, "Is There Such a Thing as a Post-apartheid City?," *Urban Forum* 21, no. 3 (2010): 283–98; Martin J. Murray, *Taming the Disorderly City: The Spatial Landscape of Johannesburg after Apartheid* (Ithaca: Cornell University Press, 2008); Grant Saff, "The Changing Face of the South African City: From Urban Apartheid to the Deracialization of Space," *International Journal of Urban and Regional Research* 18, no. 3 (1994): 371–91; Alison Todes, "Urban Growth and Strategic Spatial Planning in Johannesburg, South Africa," *Cities* 29, no. 3 (2012): 158–65; Ivan Turok, "Persistent Polarisation Post-apartheid? Progress towards Urban Integration in Cape Town," *Urban Studies* 38, no. 13 (2001): 2349–77.

43. These figures come from the Department of Human Settlements, thanks to Steve Topham, at the time the technical team leader for the National Upgrading Support Program.

44. Elise Tempelhoff, "Water: SA hat dalk 20 m. meer mense," Netwerk 24, 6 October 2014, https://www.netwerk24.com/Nuus/Water-SA-het-dalk-20-m-meer-mense-20141006; Kate Wilkinson, "Are There 70 Million People in South Africa? The Claim Is Unsubstantiated," *Africa Check*, 4 December 2014, https://africacheck.org/reports/are-there-70-million-people-in-south-africa-the-claim-is-unsubstantiated.

45. Kate Tissington, *A Resource Guide to Housing in South Africa, 1994–2010: Legislation, Policy, Programmes and Practice* (Johannesburg: Socio-Economic Rights Institute, 2011).

46. Mary Tomlinson, "South Africa's Housing Conundrum," *@Liberty: The Policy Bulletin of the South African Institute of Race Relations* 4, no. 20 (2015): 1–14.

47. Tissington, *A Resource Guide*.

48. Tomlinson, "South Africa's Housing Conundrum."

49. Alan Mabin, "On the Problems and Prospects of Overcoming Segregation and Fragmentation in South African Cities," in *Postmodern Cities and Spaces*, edited by Sophie Watson and Katherine Gibson (Malden: Wiley-Blackwell, 1996), 187–98; Smith, *Apartheid City and Beyond*; Swilling et al., *Apartheid City in Transition*; Ivan Turok, "Urban Planning in the Transition from Apartheid, Part 1: The Legacy of Social Control," *Town Planning Review* 65, no. 3 (1994): 243–58; Ivan Turok, "Urban Planning in the Transition from Apartheid, Part 2: Towards Reconstruction," *Town Planning Review* 65, no. 4 (1994): 355–74.

50. The NHF was the multistakeholder body in charge of devising new housing policies during the transition. On the NHF, see Kecia Rust and Sue Rubenstein (eds.), *A Mandate to Build: Developing Consensus around a National Housing Policy in South Africa* (Johannesburg: Ravan, 1996). Patrick Bond characterizes the NHF's dominant bloc as advocating a "warmed-over neoliberalism," blaming them for limiting postapartheid housing delivery to individually owned sites rather than public rental stock. See Bond, *Elite Transition*, 133–36.

51. The Urban Foundation was founded in 1977 by Harry Oppenheimer, former chairperson of both the Anglo-American Corporation and De Beers and one of the wealthiest individuals in the world until his death in 2000. He was a major funder of an apartheid-era opposition party called the Progressive Federal Party, which would subsequently merge with a number of small opposition parties to form the Democratic Party (DP) soon after the transition. Curiously enough, the DP then incorporated the rump of the postapartheid iteration of the National Party—imaginatively named the New National Party (NNP)—into the Democratic Alliance (DA), which is today the largest opposition party to the ANC. Even if the NNP quickly left the DA, most of its former members remained in the new party, which has governed Cape Town in coalition since 2006 and as a majority since 2009. And while the ANC still retains national power, the DA won most of the largest municipalities in the 2016 local elections, which it now governs either in coalition or outright.

52. To this day, most South Africans continue to refer to state-delivered homes as "RDP houses," despite the closure of the RDP office within two years. After a major housing policy shift in 2006 called Breaking New Ground (BNG), the Department of Human Settlements began officially referring to government-provisioned homes as "BNG houses," but the term never caught on. All of my contacts on the Cape Flats continued to refer to these structures as "RDP houses"—more than twenty years after the demise of the RDP itself.

53. Kate Tissington, Naadira Munshi, Gladys Mirugi-Mukundi, and Ebenezer Durojaye, "Jumping the Queue," *Waiting Lists and Other Myths: Perceptions and Practice around*

Housing Demand and Allocation in South Africa (Johannesburg: Socio-Economic Rights Institute, 2013), 13.

54. Tomlinson, "South Africa's Housing Conundrum."

55. Sisonke Msimang, "Poor-Bashing Is the New Slut-Shaming: Zuma, Sisulu & the Lazy Nation," *Daily Maverick*, 23 October 2014, https://www.dailymaverick.co.za/opinionista/2014-10-23-poor-bashing-is-the-new-slut-shaming-zuma-sisulu-the-lazy-nation/#.WvHk3mbMyCQ.

56. "Free Housing Not Sustainable—Sexwale," *News24*, 26 September 2011, https://www.news24.com/ SouthAfrica/News/%5CNews24%5CFree-housing-not-sustainable-Sexwale-20110926.

57. "We Will Continue to Provide RDP Houses—Sisulu," *IOL*, 10 April 2016, https://www.iol.co.za/ news/politics/we-will-continue-to-provide-rdp-houses-sisulu-2007470.

58. Prior to the de facto 2016 coup that forced out the Workers' Party government in Brazil, the Minha Casa, Minha Vida (MCMV) program was on track to overtake South Africa's housing delivery program by 2018, despite being less than a decade old. But the Temer regime quickly put an end to the program. Brazil makes for some interesting parallels with South Africa. If in the latter, the notion of *house* in "free house" is increasingly being redefined by the courts (allowing serviced sites to meet constitutional requirements for housing provision), in Brazil, emphasis remains on diminishing the *free*. MCMV houses required only a 5 percent recipient contribution from 2009 to 2011, but required 40 percent from 2011 to 2014. The final phase of the program required a 20 percent down payment. Thus it remains unclear whether the MCMV program is really comparable to South Africa's free, formal housing delivery program. These figures are taken from Caroline Gonçalves dos Santos and Flávio A. Miranda de Souza, "My House, My Life: The Reproduction of Socio-spatial Inequalities in Maceió—AL, Brazil," presentation at the International Sociological Association's RC43: Housing and the Built Environment Conference, panel "Institutions and Access to Housing in Brazil," 18 September 2015, University of Illinois–Chicago, Chicago.

59. "ANC Policy Conference to Address Housing Issues," *eNCA*, 3 July 2017, https://www.enca.com/ south-africa/anc-policy-conference-human-settlements-policy-to-address-housing-issues.

60. Gillian Hart, *Disabling Globalization: Places of Power in Post-apartheid South Africa* (Berkeley: University of California Press, 2002), 305; Gillian Hart, "Post-apartheid Developments in Historical and Comparative Perspective," in *The Development Decade? Economic and Social Change in South Africa 1994–2004*, edited by Vishnu Padayachee (Pretoria: HSRC Press, 2006), 305.

61. Stephen Greenberg, "Land Reform and Transition in South Africa," *Transformation* 52 (2003): 42–67; Ruth Hall, "A Political Economy of Land Reform in South Africa," *Review of African Political Economy* 31, no. 100 (2004): 213–27; Richard Levin and Daniel Weiner, "The Politics of Land Reform in South Africa after Apartheid: Perspectives, Problems, Prospects," *Journal of Peasant Studies* 23, nos. 2–3 (1996): 93–119; Cheryl Walker, "Piety in the Sky? Gender Policy and Land Reform in South Africa," *Journal of Agrarian Change* 3, nos. 1–2 (2003): 113–48.

62. Margot Rubin, "Perceptions of Corruption in the South African Housing Allocation and Delivery Programme: What It May Mean for Accessing the State," *Journal of Asian and African Studies* 46, no. 5 (2011): 479–90.

63. Apartheid-era waiting lists were typically consolidated into unified municipal lists. As the Cape Town municipality expanded to incorporate previously independent jurisdictions, these previously autonomous municipalities' waiting lists were amalgamated with Cape Town's to create a master "demand database" for the newly expanded municipality (interview with Brian Shelton, September 2013). So even those on apartheid-era lists were incorporated into the postapartheid system. On the expansion of the Cape Town municipality, see Charlotte Lemanski, "Global Cities in the South: Deepening Social and Spatial Polarisation in Cape Town," *Cities* 24, no. 6 (2007): 448–61; Faranak Miraftab, "Governing Post-apartheid Spatiality: Implementing City Improvement Districts in Cape Town," *Antipode* 39, no. 4 (2007): 602–26; Turok, "Persistent Polarisation Post-apartheid"; Ivan Turok and Vanessa Watson, "Divergent Development in South African Cities: Strategic Challenges Facing Cape Town," *Urban Forum* 12, no. 2 (2001): 119–38.

64. Tissington et al., *Jumping the Queue.*

65. Barbara Maregele, "Waiting Period on Cape Town's Housing List Is 60 Years, Khayelitsha Meeting Told," *GroundUp*, 2 October 2017, https://www.groundup.org.za/article/waiting-period-cape-towns-housing-list-60-years-khayelitsha-meeting-told/.

66. Levenson, "Precarious Welfare States."

67. This is essentially what happened in the case of the occupation described in Jessica Thorn and Sophie Oldfield, "A Politics of Land Occupation: State Practice and Everyday Mobilization in Zille Raine Heights, Cape Town," *Journal of Asian and African Studies* 46, no. 5 (2011): 518–30.

68. Neville Alexander, *An Ordinary Country: Issues in the Transition from Apartheid to Democracy in South Africa* (Scottsville: University of Natal Press, 2002); Sam Ashman, Ben Fine, and Susan Newman, "The Crisis in South Africa: Neoliberalism, Financialization and Uneven and Combined Development," *Socialist Register* 47 (2011): 174–95; Bond, *Elite Transition*; Patrick Bond, *Against Global Apartheid: South Africa Meets the World Bank, IMF and International Finance* (London: Zed, 2003); Gillian Hart, "The Provocations of Neoliberalism: Contesting the Nation and Liberation after Apartheid," *Antipode* 40, no. 4 (2008): 678–705; Hein Marais, *South Africa Pushed to the Limit: The Political Economy of Change* (London: Zed Books, 2011); David A. McDonald, *World City Syndrome: Neoliberalism and Inequality in Cape Town* (London: Routledge, 2008); David A. McDonald and John Pape, *Cost Recovery and the Crisis of Service Delivery in South Africa* (London: Zed, 2002); Faranak Miraftab, "Neoliberalism and the Casualization of Public Sector Services: The Case of Waste Collection Services in Cape Town, South Africa," *International Journal of Urban and Regional Research* 28, no. 4 (2004): 874–92; Sagie Narsiah, "Neoliberalism and Privatisation in South Africa." *GeoJournal* 57, no. 1 (2002): 3–13; Richard Peet, "Ideology, Discourse, and the Geography of Hegemony: From Socialist to Neoliberal Development in Postapartheid South

Africa," *Antipode* 34, no. 1 (2002): 54–84; Vishwas Satgar, "Neoliberalized South Africa," *Labour, Capital and Society* 41, no. 2 (2008): 39–69; John S. Saul and Patrick Bond, *South Africa—the Present as History: From Mrs Ples to Mandela and Marikana* (Suffolk: James Currey, 2014); Sampie Terreblanche, *A History of Inequality in South Africa, 1652–2002* (Scottsville: University of KwaZulu-Natal Press, 2003).

69. This was, after all, the position championed by arch-neoliberal economist Hernando de Soto, who advocated the extension of title deeds to squatters as a means of incorporating them into the "formal" economy. For years, de Soto's position was taken up by the World Bank and other multilateral institutions, as well as Slum/ Shack Dwellers International. See Hernando de Soto, *The Other Path: The Invisible Revolution in the Third World* (New York: HarperCollins, 1989); Hernando de Soto, *The Mystery of Capital: Why Capitalism Triumphs in the West and Fails Everywhere Else* (New York: Basic, 2003).

70. "They conquered the field for capitalist agriculture, incorporated the soil into capital, and created for the urban industries the necessary supplies of free and rightless proletarians." Karl Marx, *Capital*, vol. 1 (New York: Penguin, 1976), 895. See also Michael Perelman, *The Invention of Capitalism* (Durham: Duke University Press, 2000); James Glassman, "Primitive Accumulation, Accumulation by Dispossession, Accumulation by 'Extra-economic' Means," *Progress in Human Geography* 30, no. 5 (2006): 608–25; William Clare Roberts, "What Was Primitive Accumulation? Reconstructing the Origin of a Critical Concept," *European Journal of Political Theory* 19, no. 4 (2020): 532–52.

71. Michael Levien, *Dispossession without Development: Land Grabs in Neoliberal India* (Oxford: Oxford University Press, 2018); Michael Levien, "The Land Question: Special Economic Zones and the Political Economy of Dispossession in India," *Journal of Peasant Studies* 39, nos. 3–4 (2012): 933–69.

72. Saturnino M. Borras Jr., Ruth Hall, Ian Scoones, Ben White, and Wendy Wolford, "Towards a Better Understanding of Global Land Grabbing: An Editorial Introduction," *Journal of Peasant Studies* 38, no. 2 (2011): 209–16; Shepard Daniel, "Situating Private Equity in the Land Grab Debate," *Journal of Peasant Studies* 39, nos. 3–4 (2012): 703–29; Olivier de Schutter, "How Not to Think of Land-Grabbing: Three Critiques of Large-Scale Investments in Farmland," *Journal of Peasant Studies* 38, no. 2 (2011): 249–79; Michael B. Dwyer, "Building the Politics Machine: Tools for 'Resolving' the Global Land Grab," *Development and Change* 44, no. 2 (2013): 309–33; Derek Hall, "Primitive Accumulation, Accumulation by Dispossession, and the Global Land Grab," *Third World Quarterly* 34, no. 9 (2013): 1582–604; Tom Lavers, "'Land Grab' as Development Strategy? The Political Economy of Agricultural Investment in Ethiopia," *Journal of Peasant Studies* 39, no. 1 (2012): 105–32; Tanya Murray Li, "Centering Labor in the Land Grab Debate," *Journal of Peasant Studies* 38, no. 2 (2011): 281–98; Philip McMichael, "The Land Grab and Corporate Food Regime Restructuring," *Journal of Peasant Studies* 39, nos. 3–4 (2012): 681–701; Pauline E. Peters, "Conflicts over Land and Threats to Customary Tenure in Africa," *African Affairs* 112, no. 449 (2013): 543–62. Annelies Zoomers, "Globalisation and

the Foreignisation of Space: Seven Processes Driving the Current Global Land Grab," *Journal of Peasant Studies* 37, no. 2 (2010): 429–47.

73. Peter Alexander, "Rebellion of the Poor: South Africa's Service Delivery Protests—a Preliminary Analysis," *Review of African Political Economy* 37, no. 123 (2010): 25–40; Ashwin Desai, *We Are the Poors: Community Struggles in Post-apartheid South Africa* (New York: Monthly Review Press, 2002); Ashwin Desai and Richard Pithouse, "'But We Were Thousands': Dispossession, Resistance, Repossession, and Repression in Mandela Park," *Journal of Asian and African Studies* 39, no. 4 (2004): 239–69; Nigel C. Gibson, *Fanonian Practices in South Africa: From Steve Biko to Abahlali baseMjondolo* (Scottsville: University of KwaZulu-Natal Press, 2011); Mandisi Majavu, "Making Sense of Municipal Revolts," *Development in Focus* 1, no. 2 (2011): 4–6; Richard Pithouse, "Struggle Is a School: The Rise of a Shack Dwellers' Movement in Durban, South Africa," *Monthly Review* 57, no. 9 (2006): 30–52; Richard Pithouse, "A Politics of the Poor: Shack Dwellers' Struggles in Durban," *Journal of Asian and African Studies* 43, no. 1 (2008): 63–94.

74. Gareth Stedman Jones, *Outcast London: A Study in the Relationship between Classes in Victorian Society* (New York: Pantheon, 1984), 262.

75. Sneha Annavarapu and Zachary Levenson, "The Social Life of the State: Political Sociology and Relational Ethnography," *Qualitative Sociology* 44, no. 3 (2021): 337–48.

76. Nicos Poulantzas, *State, Power, Socialism* (New York: Verso, 1980), 132. In contrast to much of the Poulantzian work appearing in South Africa in the 1970s, my use of Poulantzas remains closer to that of the late Harold Wolpe: "The neo-Poulantzians are pre-occupied merely with the outcome of struggles between the dominant classes, which result in the state giving effect to particular policies favoured by the hegemonic class. How the specific form of the state (for example, the relationship between judiciary, legislature and executive, the dominance over, or subordination of these to the repressive state apparatuses) conditions the struggles and what the consequences are of those struggles for the structure of the state, are not questions addressed in this approach." Harold Wolpe, *Race, Class, and the Apartheid State* (Trenton: Africa World Press, 1988), 39. For an example of the intraclass Poulantzians, see Robert Davies, David Kaplan, Mike Morris, and Dan O'Meara, "Class Struggle and the Periodisation of the State in South Africa," *Review of African Political Economy* 3, no. 7 (1976): 4–30.

77. Poulantzas, *State, Power, Socialism*, 132.

78. John L. Comaroff and Jean Comaroff, "Law and Disorder in the Postcolony: An Introduction," in *Law and Disorder in the Postcolony*, edited by Jean Comaroff and John L. Comaroff (Chicago: University of Chicago Press, 2006), 23, 27.

79. David Bilchitz, "Giving Socio-economic Rights Teeth: The Minimum Core and Its Importance," *South African Law Journal* 119, no. 3 (2002): 484–500; Danie Brand and Christof Heyns (eds.), *Socio-economic Rights in South Africa* (Pretoria: Pretoria University Law Press, 2005); Eric C. Christiansen, "Adjudicating Non-justiciable Rights: Socio-economic Rights and the South African Constitutional Court," *Columbia Human Rights Law Review* 38, no. 2 (2007): 321–86; de Vos, "Grootboom"; Mark S. Kende, "The South African Constitutional Court's Embrace of Socio-economic Rights: A Comparative Perspective," *Chapman Law Review* 6 (2003): 137–60;

Sandra Liebenberg, "The Right to Social Assistance: The Implications of *Grootboom* for Policy reform in South Africa," *South African Journal on Human Rights* 17, no. 2 (2001): 232–57. Sandra Liebenberg and Beth Goldblatt, "The Interrelationship between Equality and Socio-economic Rights under South Africa's Transformative Constitution," *South African Journal on Human Rights* 23, no. 2 (2007): 335–61; John Cantius Mubangizi, "The Constitutional Protection of Socio-economic Rights in Selected African Countries: A Comparative Evaluation," *African Journal of Legal Studies* 2, no. 1 (2006): 1–19; Cass Sunstein, "Social and Economic Rights? Lessons from South Africa," *Constitutional Forum* 11, no. 4 (2001): 123–32; Murray Wesson, "*Grootboom* and Beyond: Reassessing the Socio-economic Jurisprudence of the South African Constitutional Court," *South African Journal on Human Rights* 20, no. 2 (2004): 284–308.

80. This is in line with the Seventeenth Amendment to the constitution, which became law in early 2013: "To amend the Constitution of the Republic of South Africa, 1996, so as to further define the role of the Chief Justice as the head of the judiciary; to provide for a single High Court of South Africa; to provide that the Constitutional Court is the highest court in all matters; to further regulate the jurisdiction of the Constitutional Court and the Supreme Court of Appeal; to provide for the appointment of an Acting Deputy Chief Justice; and to provide for matters connected therewith." See *Government Gazette* 572, no. 36128, 1 February 2013, https://www.justice.gov.za/legislation/acts/const17th_2013gg36128no72.pdf, 2.

81. *Government of the Republic of South Africa and Others v. Grootboom* 2001 (1) SA 46 (CC), 2000 (11) BCLR 1169 (CC).

82. This happens far more frequently than one might imagine in Cape Town. Informal housing is regularly razed in the name of building subsidized formal housing for low-income residents on the recovered land. While at face value this may read as a straightforward project of formalization, this is not the case for two reasons. First, evicted residents are rarely included in subsequent developments, and when they are, typically only a fraction of them find their way into these homes. Second, South Africa's social housing program serves those who make too much to qualify for RDP houses (more than R3,500 per month, just under $300 at the time of research, or just over $200 today), but too little to qualify for a mortgage. This means that the destitute are evicted in the name of provisioning underpaid workers and therefore that this move has both raced and classed implications. Unfortunately, this is a sorely underresearched topic.

83. The full text of the constitution, including the Bill of Rights, is available at https://www.justice.gov.za/legislation/constitution/SAConstitution-web-eng.pdf.

84. The question of "adequacy," as well as what constitutes a "home," has been continuously redefined over the years. To cite but one among countless possible examples, here is an excerpt from *Breede Vallei Munisipaliteit v. Die Inwoners van ERF 18184 and Others* A369/12 (2012) ZAWCHC 390, heard in the Western Cape High Court: "He argued that it was not required of occupiers to persuade the court that the property occupied by them constituted their '*homes*,' in the narrow sense contended for by the appellant, relying on the authority of *Barnett*. Mr Joubert made the additional

submission that, using a purposive approach to constitutional interpretation, the word 'home' in s 23 [sic] of the Constitution, which embodies the fundamental right not to be evicted from one's home or have one's home demolished, must be given a wider meaning than that contended for by the appellant."

85. De Vos, "*Grootboom*"; Marie Huchzermeyer, "Housing Rights in South Africa: Invasions, Evictions, the Media, and the Courts in the Cases of Grootboom, Alexandra, and Bredell," *Urban Forum* 14, no. 1 (2003): 80–107.

86. Marie Huchzermeyer, "Housing for the Poor? Negotiated Housing Policy in South Africa," *Habitat International* 25, no. 3 (2001): 306.

87. Liebenberg, "Right to Social Assistance," 252.

88. The PIE Act explicitly repeals the 1951 Prevention of Illegal Squatting Act, as well as nearly a dozen subsequent amendments and related laws. See Republic of South Africa, "Prevention of Illegal Eviction from and Unlawful Occupation of Land Act" (1998), https://www.gov.za/sites/default/files/gcis_document/201409/a19-98.pdf.

89. Steve Kahanovitz, "An Urban Slice of PIE: The Prevention of Illegal Eviction from and Unlawful Occupation of Land Act in South Africa," Case study prepared for the *Global Report on Human Settlements* (2007), https://unhabitat.org/wp-content/uploads/2008/07/5403_20137_GRHS.2007.CaseStudy.Tenure.SouthAfrica.pdf.

90. Huchzermeyer, "Housing Rights in South Africa," 84.

91. Republic of South Africa, "Prevention of Illegal Eviction from and Unlawful Occupation of Land Act."

92. Republic of South Africa, "PIE Act."

93. Lauren Royston, "South Africa: The Struggle for Access to the City in the Witwatersrand Region," in *Evictions and the Right to Housing: Experience from Canada, Chile, the Dominican Republic, South Africa, and South Korea*, edited by Antonio Azuela, Emilio Duhau, and Enrique Ortiz (Ottawa: International Development Research Centre, 1998).

94. Levenson, "Precarious Welfare States"; Levenson, "Road to TRAs."

95. Mark Hunter, "The Forgotten World of Transit Camps" (2012), http://abahlali.org/node/9231/; Mark Hunter and Dorrit Posel, "Here to Work: The Socioeconomic Characteristics of Informal Dwellers in Post-apartheid South Africa," *Environment and Urbanization* 24 (2012): 285–304.

96. Maano Ramutsindela, "'Second Time Around': Squatter Removals in a Democratic South Africa," *GeoJournal* 57 (2002): 53–60; Duncan Ranslem, "'Temporary' Relocation: Spaces of Contradiction in South African Law," *International Journal of Law in the Built Environment* 7, no. 1 (2015): 55–71.

97. Zachary Levenson, "Permanent Temporariness: Relocation Camps in Post-apartheid Cape Town," *SLUM Lab* 9 (2014): 156–58.

98. Liza Rose Cirolia, "South Africa's Emergency Housing Programme: A Prism of Urban Contest," *Development Southern Africa* 31, no. 3 (2014): 397–411; Levenson, "Road to TRAs."

99. Sarita Pillay, Shaun Russell, Julian Sendin, Martha Sithole, Nick Budlender, and Daneel Knoetze, *I Used to Live There: A Call for Transitional Housing for Evictees in Cape Town* (Cape Town: Ndifuna Ukwazi, 2017).

100. Marie Huchzermeyer, "A Legacy of Control? The Capital Subsidy for Housing and Informal Settlement Intervention in South Africa," *International Journal of Urban and Regional Research* 27, no. 3 (2003): 591–612; Levenson, "Road to TRAs"; Helen Macgregor, Zama Mgwatyu, and Warren Smit, *Living on the Edge: A Study of the Delft Temporary Relocation Area* (Cape Town: Development Action Group, 2007); Turok, "Persistent Polarisation Post-Apartheid."

101. Interview with Disha Govender, 13 July 2017, Ndifuna Ukwazi, Cape Town.

102. Republic of South Africa, "Prevention of Illegal Eviction from and Unlawful Occupation of Land Act."

103. Comaroff and Comaroff, "Law and Disorder."

104. Gautam Bhan, *In the Public's Interest: Evictions, Citizenship, and Inequality in Contemporary Delhi* (Athens: University of Georgia Press, 2016).

105. Bhan, *In the Public's Interest*, 223.

106. Huchzermeyer, *Cities with Slums*; Marie Huchzermeyer, "Invoking Lefebvre's 'Right to the City' in South Africa Today: A Response to Walsh," *City* 18, no. 1 (2014): 41–49.

107. Shannon Walsh, "'We Won't Move': The Suburbs Take Back the Center in Urban Johannesburg," *City* 17, no. 3 (2013): 407; cf. Shannon Walsh, "'Uncomfortable Collaborations': Contesting Constructions of the 'Poor' in South Africa," *Review of African Political Economy* 35, no. 116 (2008): 255–70.

108. Huchzermeyer, "Invoking Lefebvre's Right."

109. Sometimes, however, the line between pressure and recognition is not so well defined. In Melanie Samson's work on waste pickers, for example, she develops the relational concept of "social uses of the law." Following legal outcomes, the letter of the law may be less important than the way these rulings are understood by those affected. Rulings can therefore (inadvertently) shape the collective subjectivities of informal workers and even serve as a call for further mobilization. See Melanie Samson, "The Social Uses of the Law at a Soweto Garbage Dump: Reclaiming the Law and the State in the Informal Economy," *Current Sociology* 65, no. 2 (2017): 222–34.

110. We should read the government's moralizing discourse as the latest iteration of the old Victorian distinction between the deserving and undeserving poor. In the case of mid-nineteenth-century charitable organizations, people were deemed "deserving" insofar as they could reasonably be construed as victims of a social system that necessarily produces a rabble. By contrast, they were considered "undeserving" when they could be blamed for their own predicament, typically through moralistic accusations of idleness. Likewise, "opportunists" and "queue jumpers" in contemporary South Africa are usually represented as free-riders who are responsible for their own houselessness, whereas "homeless people in need" are thought to be the necessary consequence of an economy with an official unemployment rate approaching 30 percent, to say nothing of the legacy of apartheid. As in Victorian England, these distinctions are rarely clear-cut and are more likely to be, as I argue, the outcome of protracted struggles. It is through these struggles that people who are relatively excluded from formal politics project themselves to the state. See Jones, *Outcast London*; Herbert Gans, "Positive Functions of the Undeserving Poor: Uses of the Underclass in America," *Politics and Society* 22, no. 3 (1994): 269–83; Michael B.

Katz, *The Undeserving Poor: America's Enduring Confrontation with Poverty*, 2nd ed. (Oxford: Oxford University Press, 2013).

111. Julie-Anne Boudreau, *Global Urban Politics: Informalization of the State* (Cambridge: Polity, 2017), 60.

112. Julie-Anne Boudreau and Diane E. Davis, "Introduction: A Processual Approach to Informalization," *Current Sociology* 65, no. 2 (2017): 158.

113. Antonio Gramsci, *Selections from the Prison Notebooks*, edited and translated by Quinton Hoare and Geoffrey Nowell Smith (New York: International, 1971), 12.

114. Interview with Alida Koetzee, 23 June 2014, Civic Centre, Cape Town.

115. Interview with Heinrich Lotze and Herman Steyn, 23 June 2013, Civic Centre, Cape Town.

116. Max Weber, Economy and Society: *A New Translation*, translated by Keith Tribe (Cambridge: Harvard University Press, 2019), 343–44, 353.

117. Levenson, "Road to TRAs."

118. Thorn and Oldfield, "Politics of Land Occupation," 521–23.

119. Thorn and Oldfield, "Politics of Land Occupation," 522.

120. Site interviews in Zille Raine Heights, 2 July 2013, Grassy Park, Cape Town.

121. Interview with Alida Koetzee and Michael Goodwin, 23 June 2014, Civic Centre, Cape Town.

122. Interview with Marlize Odendal, 2 October 2013, Civic Centre, Cape Town.

123. The EFF was founded in 2013 as a Marxist-Leninist-Fanonist party by expelled former president of the ANC Youth League Julius Malema. A curiously contradictory figure, Malema led a five-thousand-strong march of the unemployed from Johannesburg to Pretoria in 2011—before boarding a business-class flight to Mauritius that evening for the wedding of property magnate David Mabilu, where he was photographed sipping champagne in a swanky nightclub. Yet despite receiving cars, homes, and dodgy cash payments, he now leads the most radical party seated in Parliament, not to mention the country's third largest. The EFF played a major role in forcing Parliament to debate President Jacob Zuma's misappropriation of millions to upgrade his home at Nkandla and his pay-for-play dealings with the Gupta brothers, as well as keeping the 2012 massacre of dozens of miners at Marikana in the national discussion. Indeed, the miners' primary legal counsel, Dali Mpofu, is (at the time of writing) the EFF's national chairperson. By the end of the first month of Zuma's successor Cyril Ramaphosa's term as president, the EFF had already forced land reform ("expropriation without compensation") onto the political agenda.

124. Making the townships "ungovernable" through mass insurgency is a strategy typically attributed to the ANC, though, as Michael McDonald points out, other organizations ranging from Black Consciousness groups and the Zulu-nationalist Inkatha party to smaller independent formations had adopted this strategic orientation a year before it was ever claimed by the ANC. See Michael McDonald, *Why Race Matters in South Africa* (Cambridge: Harvard University Press, 2006), 77. See also Brenda Bozzoli "From Governability to Ungovernability: Race, Class and Authority in South Africa's Black Cities," seminar paper (1996), Institute of Advanced Social

Research, University of Witwatersrand, Johannesburg; William Sales, "Making South Africa Ungovernable: ANC Strategy for the '80s," *Black Scholar* 15, no. 6 (1984): 2–14; Mark Swilling, "The United Democratic Front and Township Revolt," in *Popular Struggles in South Africa Today*, edited by William Cobbett and Robin Cohen (Trenton: Africa World Press, 1988), 90–113.

125. Weber, *Economy and Society*.

126. Michel Foucault, *Discipline and Punish: The Birth of the Prison*, translated by Alan Sheridan (New York: Vintage, 1995).

127. Pierre Bourdieu, *Pascalian Meditations*, translated by Richard Nice (Stanford: Stanford University Press, 2000), 228.

128. Javier Auyero, *Patients of the State: The Politics of Waiting in Argentina* (Durham: Duke University Press, 2012), 9.

129. For the link between democratization, delivery, and waiting, see Levenson, "Precarious Welfare States."

130. Bourdieu, *Pascalian Meditations*, 228.

131. Michel Foucault, "The Subject and Power," in *Michel Foucault: Beyond Structuralism and Hermeneutics*, edited by Hubert Dreyfus and Paul Rabinow (Chicago: University of Chicago Press, 1982); Michel Foucault, *Security, Territory, Population: Lectures at the Collège de France, 1977–1978* (New York: Picador, 2007).

132. Michel Foucault, *History of Sexuality*, vol. 1, *An Introduction*, translated by Robert Hurley (New York: Vintage, 1990), 95.

133. Sophie Oldfield and Saskia Greyling, "Waiting for the State: A Politics of Housing in South Africa," *Environment and Planning A* 47, no. 5 (2015): 1104.

134. Richard Ballard, "Geographies of Development III: Militancy, Insurgency, Encroachment and Development by the Poor," *Progress in Human Geography* 39, no. 2 (2015): 220.

135. Asef Bayat, *Life as Politics: How Ordinary People Change the Middle East*, 2nd ed. (Stanford: Stanford University Press, 2013), 35; cf. Asef Bayat, "Globalization and the Politics of the Informal in the Global South," in *Urban Informality: Transnational Perspectives from the Middle East, Latin America, and South Asia*, edited by Ananya Roy and Nezar AlSayyad (Lanham, MD: Lexington, 2004).

136. Tatiana Adeline Thieme, "The Hustle Economy: Informality, Uncertainty and the Geographies of Getting By," *Progress in Human Geography* 42, no. 4 (2018): 542; cf. Tatiana Adeline Thieme, "Navigating and Negotiating Ethnographies of Urban Hustle in Nairobi Slums," *City* 21, no. 2 (2017): 219–231.

137. In addition to Gareth Stedman Jones's *Outcast London*, see Roy Porter, *London: A Social History* (Cambridge: Harvard University Press, 1995). Comparable clearances were widespread in nineteenth-century Europe. See, for example, David Harvey, *Paris, Capital of Modernity* (London: Routledge, 2004); David B. Jordan, *Transforming Paris: The Life and Labors of Baron Haussmann* (New York: Free Press, 1995); Carl E. Schorske, *Fin-de-Siècle Vienna: Politics and Culture* (New York: Vintage, 1981).

138. "The ideas of the Free Trade movement are based on a theoretical error whose practical origin is not hard to identify; they are based on a distinction between political society and civil society, which is made into and presented as an organic

one, whereas in fact it is merely methodological." See Gramsci, *Selections from the Prison Notebooks*, 159–60; cf. Carlos Nelson Coutinho, *Gramsci's Political Thought* (Chicago: Haymarket, 2012), 83.

139. Stuart Hall, *Cultural Studies 1983: A Theoretical History* (Durham: Duke University Press, 2016), 170.

140. Peter Thomas has recently argued—correctly in my view—that civil and political societies are not discrete locations in political space, nor are they empirically separable institutional or organizational sites. Rather, they should be understood as two moments in a single process, akin to, say, theory and practice in Marx's "Theses on Feuerbach."

As Thomas writes, "The decisive role of theory in this conjuncture lies not only in the elaboration of the 'raw materials' in 'civil society' (the non-political in an 'official' sense) that could form the foundation for a future self-regulated society. Just as crucially, precisely in order to liberate those 'raw materials' from their subaltern interpellation by the existing political qua principle of speculative organization, it also requires the attempt to elaborate on the terrain of existing 'political society' new practices of proletarian hegemony, conceived as political leadership within the popular classes, capable of challenging its speculative logic; forms in which theory's role will be more that of enabling 'descriptive immanent grammar' of initiatives already under way rather than that of a regulative instance or even externally posed utopian prescription." Peter Thomas, "Gramsci and the Political: From the State as 'Metaphysical Event' to Hegemony as 'Philosophical Fact,'" *Radical Philosophy* 153 (2009): 34–35.

And again: "Hegemony is therefore always-already, even if only implicitly, political; or, in other words, hegemony in civil society is necessarily comprehended in political society and overdetermined by it." Peter Thomas, *The Gramscian Moment: Philosophy, Hegemony, and Marxism* (Chicago: Haymarket, 2009), 194; cf. Karl Marx, "On Feuerbach," in *Early Political Writings*, edited and translated by Joseph O'Malley (Cambridge: Cambridge University Press, 1994). For readings of Gramsci that align with Thomas's, see Wolfgang Fritz Haug, "Rethinking Gramsci's Philosophy of Praxis from One Century to the Next," *boundary2* 26, no. 2 (1999): 101–17; Wolfgang Fritz Haug, "From Marx to Gramsci, from Gramsci to Marx: Historical Materialism and the Philosophy of Praxis," *Rethinking Marxism* 13, no. 1 (2001): 69–82; Panagiotis Sotiris, "The Modern Prince as Laboratory of Political Intellectuality," *International Gramsci Journal* 3, no. 2 (2019): 2–38.

Chapter 3

1. I use "addressed" here in place of the more unwieldy "interpellated" as developed by Althusser. As he famously describes it, someone calls out, and an individual believes that the call is addressed to them, realizing their own subjectivity in the process. In our case, residents were interpellated as occupiers by the MPHA, which had real

political effects. As Althusser argues, "The existence of ideology and the hailing or interpellation of individuals as subjects are one and the same thing." The implications for Kapteinsklip are that in addressing prospective residents, the MPHA unwittingly cultivated a politics of seriality among occupiers. See Louis Althusser, "Ideology and Ideological State Apparatuses: Notes toward an Investigation," in *Lenin and Philosophy and Other Essays* (New York: Monthly Review Press, 2001), 118.

This ideological dimension mirrors quite closely what the young Marx described as "civil society," in which each individual is a "totality of needs" that relates to others instrumentally in order to satisfy these needs, but never collectively or collaboratively. In other words, with the development of capitalism comes the ideology of liberal individualism. Marx is clear that this is an ideology when he emphasizes that civil society is how society "appears to the political economist." But this ideology must not be separated from its real, material effects, namely, the serialization of capitalist society as described by Sartre. As Marx puts it, "*Society*, as it appears to the political economist, is *civil society*, in which every individual is a totality of needs and only exists for the other person, as the other exists for him, insofar as each becomes a means for the other." See Karl Marx, *Economic and Philosophic Manuscripts of 1844* (Amherst: Prometheus, 1988), 128.

2. Jean-Paul Sartre, *Critique of Dialectical Reason*, vol. 1, translated by Alan Sheridan-Smith (New York: Verso, 2004), 251–69.

3. In most accounts of this nature, writers deploy the word "citizens," but I opt for "residents" instead. I never once observed citizenship mattering in land occupation cases, and I do not find any particular utility in using the term to designate all people living under the tutelage of a given government. See, for example, two special issues, both entitled "Cities and Citizenship": the issue of *Public Culture* 8, no. 2 (1996), edited by James Holston, and slightly expanded into James Holston (ed.), *Cities and Citizenship* (Durham: Duke University Press, 1998); and the issue of *Urban Geography* 24, no. 2 (2003), edited by Lynn A. Staeheli.

4. To cite the same Marx passage again, Sartre's series captures Marx's dictum that "every individual ... only exists for the other person, as the other exists for him, insofar as each becomes a means for the other." See Marx, *Economic and Philosophic Manuscripts of 1844*, 128.

5. The term comes from Wendy Darling's playhouse in *Peter Pan*, and in a Euro-American context, it describes a small house for children. But in South Africa, the term is commonly used for prefabricated structures that serve as low-income housing. They look like slightly larger versions of the storage sheds one might find for sale in a hardware store parking lot.

6. There is now an enormous literature on the detrimental effects of water privatization. See, for example, Antina von Schnitzler, "Citizenship Prepaid: Water, Calculability, and Techno-politics in South Africa," *Journal of Southern African Studies* 34, no. 4 (2008): 899–917; Antina von Schnitzler, *Democracy's Infrastructure: Techno-politics and Protest after Apartheid* (Princeton: Princeton University Press, 2017); Alex Loftus, "Reification and the Dictatorship of the Water Meter," *Antipode* 38, no. 5 (2006): 1023–45; David A. McDonald and Greg Ruiters (eds.), *The Age of*

Commodity: Water Privatization in Southern Africa (New York: Earthscan, 2005); Jackie Dugard, "Choice from No Choice; Rights for the Left? The State, Law and the Struggle against Prepayment Water Meters in South Africa," in *Social Movements in the Global South: Dispossession, Development, and Resistance*, edited by Sara C. Motta and Alf Gunvald Nilsen (London: Palgrave Macmillan, 2011), 59–82; Prishani Naidoo, "Struggles around the Commodification of Daily Life in South Africa," *Review of African Political Economy* 34, no. 111 (2007): 57–66.

7. Interview with Alida Koetzee, 23 June 2014, Civic Centre, Cape Town.

8. This was gleaned from 2011 census data, available at StatsSA, "Census 2011," http://www.statssa.gov.za/?page_id=3839.

9. These figures come from Department of Human Settlements data graciously provided by Steve Topham, a former consultant for the National Upgrading Settlements Program.

10. During my fieldwork, this was about US$42. At the time of writing, it is closer to US$29.

11. Anne-Maria Makhulu, *Making Freedom: Apartheid, Squatter Politics, and the Struggle for Home* (Durham: Duke University Press, 2015).

12. Makhulu, *Making Freedom*, 25.

13. Asef Bayat, *Life as Politics: How Ordinary People Change the Middle East*, 2nd ed. (Stanford: Stanford University Press, 2013).

14. When the occupation began, the MPHA was known as the Mitchells Plain Backyard Dwellers' Association (MPBDA). A petty rivalry split the MPBDA in early 2012, with one faction renaming itself the MPHA. By the end of the year, however, the two groups reconciled, reforming as a unified MPHA. In order to avoid needless confusion, I refer to the organization throughout this chapter as the MPHA. This information was gleaned through interviews with MPHA affiliates, attending MPHA meetings, and from a local newspaper called the *Plainsman*.

15. By "front group," I mean an organization that is connected to a political party but disavows or obfuscates this connection.

16. SANCO was formed during the transition in order to consolidate all of the existing local civic movements that came into being during the anti-apartheid struggles of the 1980s. Since its founding, its formal affiliation with the ANC has been a key point of contention, and a number of local branches refused to join SANCO because they were worried that this would compromise civic movements' nonpartisan character. For a good sociological introduction to the organization, see Patrick Heller and Libhongo Ntlokonkulu, "A Civic Movement or a Movement of Civics? The South African National Civic Organisation (SANCO) in the Post-apartheid Period," Johannesburg, Centre for Policy Studies, 2001.

17. 20 October 2013, Beacon Valley Community Center, Mitchells Plain, Cape Town.

18. 22 October 2013, Town Center, Mitchells Plain, Cape Town.

19. This turned out to be Jeremia Thuynsma, whom I was able to interview at length (21 October 2013, Civic Centre, Cape Town).

20. The NDR is the theory underlying the ANC's formal alliance with the South African Communist Party (SACP). Developed by SACP theorists in the 1980s, the NDR is

the pinnacle of orthodox Marxist stageism. Once the ANC has successfully reversed the wrongs of apartheid, it can consolidate a proper bourgeois democracy, or what the SACP calls a National Democratic Society. Only then, the SACP argues, is it time to fight for socialism. Until then, all class militants should line up behind the ANC and back their policy program. For a withering critique, see Gillian Hart, *Rethinking the South African Crisis: Nationalism, Populism, Hegemony* (Scottsville: University of KwaZulu-Natal Press, 2013).

21. The MDM was launched in the same year and saw the consolidation of a formal alliance between the UDF and the Congress of South African Trade Unions. The MDM's campaigns were largely a response to the apartheid government's state of emergency, declared a year earlier.

22. Interview with two Kapteinsklip evictees, 27 October 2013, Mitchells Plain, Cape Town.

23. At the time of my fieldwork, this was approximately eighty-four US cents. It is now just over fifty cents.

24. Interview on 13 November 2013, Mitchells Plain, Cape Town.

25. See Elke Zuern, *The Politics of Necessity: Community Organizing and Democracy in South Africa* (Madison: University of Wisconsin Press, 2011).

26. "Understanding 'determinacy' in terms of setting limits, the establishment of parameters, the defining of the space of operations, the concrete conditions of existence, the 'givenness' of social practices, rather than in terms of the absolute predictability of particular outcomes, is the only basis of a 'marxism without final guarantees.'" Stuart Hall, "The Problem of Ideology: Marxism without Guarantees," in *Stuart Hall: Critical Dialogues in Cultural Studies*, edited by David Morley and Kuan-Hsing Chen (London: Routledge, 1996), 45.

27. "However one may look at it, in the orientation toward the possible extreme case of an actual battle against a real enemy, the political entity is essential, and it is the decisive entity for the friend-or-enemy grouping; and in this (and not in any kind of absolutist sense), it is sovereign. Otherwise the political entity is nonexistent." Carl Schmitt, *The Concept of the Political*, translated by George Schwab (Chicago: University of Chicago Press, 1996), 39.

28. Formerly known simply as the "Pan Africanist Congress," the PAC was formed in 1959 as a split from the ANC. While the party is currently marginal to national electoral politics, it played the key role in organizing opposition to the pass laws in 1960. It was also essential to fomenting the turn to armed struggle after the South African police massacred sixty-nine demonstrators at one such protest in Sharpeville, a city just south of Johannesburg. See Kwandiwe Kondlo, *In the Twilight of the Revolution: The Pan Africanist Congress of Azania (South Africa), 1959–1994* (Basel: Basler Afrika Bibliographien, 2009); Tom Lodge, *Black Politics in South Africa since 1945* (London: Longman, 1983); Tom Lodge, *Sharpeville: A Massacre and Its Consequences* (Oxford: Oxford University Press, 2011); Martin Legassick, *Armed Struggle and Democracy: The Case of South Africa* (Uppsala: Nordiska Afrikainstitutet, 2002). There is, unfortunately, very little of substance written about the PAC's transformation into an electoral party after 1994.

29. This quote is taken from the organization's home page (http://capecarecharity.co.za).

30. SAPA, "Zuma Not Our President: Cape Secessionists," *The Citizen*, 7 May 2009, http://www.citizen.co.za/index/article.aspx?pDesc=95310,1,22).

31. Refer to the party's home page (http://www.capeparty.com).

32. In the postapartheid period, "Colored" Capetonians have increasingly invoked claims to indigeneity, typically under the banner of the Khoisan, a consolidation of Cape Town's two major autochthonous groups prior to colonization in 1652. The political and ethical implications of these claims are quite complex, including some amalgam of both a progressive distancing from the apartheid label "Colored" and a reactionary ethnonationalism complete with territorial claims. For an interrogation of some of these contradictions, see Steven L. Robins, *From Revolution to Rights in South Africa: Social Movements, NGOs & Popular Politics after Apartheid* (Scottsville: University of KwaZulu-Natal Press, 2008); Steven L. Robins, "NGOs, 'Bushmen' and Double Vision: The ≠khomani San Land Claim and the Cultural Politics of 'Community' and 'Development' in the Kalahari," *Journal of Southern African Studies* 27, no. 4 (2001): 833–53; Steven L. Robins, "Land Struggles and the Politics and Ethics of Representing 'Bushman' History and Identity," *Kronos: Journal of Cape History* 26 (2000): 56–75. See also Zachary Levenson and Sean Jacobs, "The Limits of Coloured Nationalism," *Mail & Guardian*, 15 June 2018, 32.

33. Newlands is a wealthy suburb just south of the city center. Whereas the electoral ward containing Kapteinsklip is 96 percent "Colored," Newlands's ward is two-thirds white. The average household income in Newlands is roughly eight times that in Kapteinsklip's section of Mitchells Plain.

34. Land occupations are most common just before municipal elections—the same was true just before the August 2016 elections. For example, see Gertrude Makhafola, "Land Invasions Spiked before Elections—Makhura," IOL News, 16 September 2016, https://www.iol.co.za/news/land-invasions-spiked-before-elections-makhura-2069154. Some of this is attributable to political parties attempting to accumulate political capital, or else to move their supporters into rivals' territory; but these cases are likely exceptional. More generally, occupiers may feel that politicians will be less likely to evict them if they risk alienating a potential voter base.

35. This was the Right2Know Campaign, launched in 2010 to challenge the Secrecy Bill, South Africa's equivalent of the Patriot Act in the US. The activist in question was temporarily on the payroll of R2K, and I regularly observed him scamming that nonprofit out of petty cash. He would frequently claim that he had brought a dozen or so people from the Cape Flats to a march and demand reimbursement, only to pocket the money. Sometimes there really were activists he had brought out, but usually there were not; in both circumstances, he would keep the money. In any case, it takes one to know one: hustlers tend to assume everyone else is equally self-interested. For an overview of Right2Know, see Shauna Mottiar and Tom Lodge, "'Living inside the Movement': The Right2Know Campaign, South Africa," *Transformation* 102 (2020): 95–120.

36. On the politics involved see Zachary Levenson, "Social Movements beyond Incorporation: The Case of the Housing Assembly in Post-apartheid Cape Town," in *Global Resistance in Southern Perspective: The Politics of Protest in South Africa's Contentious Democracy*, edited by Marcel Paret, Carin Runciman, and Luke Sinwell (London: Routledge, 2017), 89–104.

37. Loyiso Mpalantshane, "Squatters Squabble over Eviction Order," *Plainsman*, 7 September 2011, 9.

38. Mpalantshane, "Squatters Squabble over Eviction Order," 10.

39. On this point, see chapter 5 in Peter D. Thomas, *The Gramscian Moment: Philosophy, Hegemony, and Marxism* (Chicago: Haymarket, 2009).

40. Thomas, *The Gramscian Moment*, 194.

Chapter 4

1. "To be sure, Gramsci does distinguish between political society and civil society, but he does so primarily for the purposes of analysis, since the apparatuses of one are quite different from the apparatuses of the other. What Gramsci does not do is separate political society and civil society into state and nonstate; on the contrary, he regards them as the constitutive elements of a single, integral entity—the modern bourgeois-liberal state." Joseph Buttigieg, "Gramsci on Civil Society," *Boundary2* 22, no. 3 (1995): 28.

2. Antonio Gramsci, *Selections from the Prison Notebooks*, translated by Quintin Hoare and Geoffrey Nowell Smith (New York: International, 1971), 160. See also Guido Liguori, *Gramsci's Pathways*, translated by David Broder (Chicago: Haymarket, 2015), 32–35; Giuseppe Cospito, *The Rhythm of Thought in Gramsci: A Diachronic Interpretation of Prison Notebooks*, translated by Arianna Ponzini (Chicago: Haymarket, 2016), 199–206.

3. One of the most common varieties of fish for sale in Cape Town, this is the Afrikaans word for a species of snake mackerel.

4. This Afrikaans diminutive refers to a pickup truck, typically much smaller than the American version.

5. This was the South African Transport and Allied Workers Union.

6. Josette Cole, *Crossroads: The Politics of Reform and Repression, 1976–1986* (Johannesburg: Ravan, 1987). On the broader context of civil war, which is the object of a quite heated debate, see Gerhard Maré and Georgina Hamilton, *An Appetite for Power: Buthelezi's Inkatha and South Africa* (Johannesburg: Ravan, 1987); Stuart J. Kaufman, "South Africa's Civil War, 1985–1995," *South African Journal of International Affairs* 24, no. 4 (2018): 501–21; Anthea Jeffrey, *People's War: New Light on the Struggle for South Africa* (Cape Town: Jonathan Ball, 2009); Stephen Ellis, "The Historical Significance of South Africa's Third Force," *Journal of Southern African Studies* 24, no. 2 (1998): 261–99; Adrian Guelke, "Interpretations of Political Violence during South Africa's Transition," *Politikon* 27, no. 2 (2000): 239–54.

7. For a sustained argument about the local state as the chief site of postapartheid struggles, see Gillian Hart, *Rethinking the South African Crisis: Nationalism, Populism, Hegemony* (Scottsville: University of KwaZulu-Natal Press, 2013). But note that these local forces and relations are always embedded in translocal networks, as she shows in Gillian Hart, *Disabling Globalization: Places of Power in Post-apartheid South Africa* (Berkeley: University of California Press, 2002).

8. The apartheid government defined the entire Western Cape as a so-called Colored Labor Preference Area, meaning that "Colored" job applicants were prioritized over "Africans." This was a pretext for expelling "Africans" from the Cape altogether, relegating them to bantustans, as well as an attempt to build a white-"Colored" alliance against "Africans"—not too far off from the politics of Marina's First People First coalition. On the Colored Labor Preference Policy, see Richard Humphries, "Administrative Politics and the Coloured Labour Preference Policy during the 1960s," in *The Angry Divide: Social and Economic History of the Western Cape*, edited by Wilmot G. James and Mary Simons (Cape Town: David Philip, 1989), 169–79; Ian Goldin, "The Poverty of Coloured Labour Preference: Economics and Ideology in the Western Cape," SALDRU Working Paper no. 59, Cape Town (1984); Mohamed Adhikari, "Between Black and White: The History of Coloured Politics in South Africa," *Canadian Journal of African Studies* 25, no. 1 (1991): 106–10.

9. This system was termed the Tricameral Parliament and was heavily resisted by "Colored" Capetonians, many of whom saw it for what it was: namely, an attempt to grant minor concessions to "Coloreds" and "Asians" as a way of uniting them with the National Party against "Africans." It was against the Tricameral Parliament that the UDF was formed in the first place—in Mitchells Plain of all places. See Jeremy Seekings, *The UDF: A History of the United Democratic Front in South Africa, 1983–1991* (Athens: Ohio University Press, 2000); Rupert Taylor, "Between Apartheid and Democracy: The South African 'Election' of 1989," *Round Table* 79, no. 314 (1990): 56–67.

10. Interview with Marlize Odendal, 2 October 2013, Civic Centre, Cape Town.

11. This is one way in which we see the inextricability of political society from civil society at work. When leaders attempted to organize civil society, they were also creating properly political articulations, hoping to have their informal representative networks formalized (and therefore absorbed) into the government. This would elevate the informal leaders to the status of elected representatives, which, for some opportunists, was actually their stated goal. For others, this might be an unintended consequence—an unintended articulation, we might say—of organizing on the terrain of civil society.

12. This is the subject of chapter 6.

13. At the time of writing, Ramaphosa is South Africa's president. He narrowly defeated the incumbent Jacob Zuma's preferred candidate and ex-wife, Nkosazana Dlamini-Zuma, for ANC president at the party's Fifty-Fourth Elective Conference in December 2017. While normally he would have run for national office in 2019, these are not normal times, and the ANC is currently split between Ramaphosa's faction on the one hand, which emphasizes anticorruption; and Zuma's on the other, which tends

to emphasize Black empowerment and socioeconomic transformation, even if this is largely empty rhetoric. Zuma had accumulated so many corruption allegations in the run-up to the conference—foremost among them, that he sold cabinet appointments to one of South Africa's wealthiest families—that his presidency was not sustainable and risked tearing apart the party. After a seventh(!) vote of no confidence was announced by Parliament in February 2018—this time one that would likely actually pass—Zuma resigned. Ramaphosa was elected unopposed, giving his first State of the Nation address the following day. For more on these dynamics, see Sam Ashman, Zachary Levenson, and Trevor Ngwane, "South Africa's ANC: The Beginning of the End?," *Catalyst* 1, no. 2 (2017): 75–106.

14. Kaylynn Palm, "ANC Moves In for 'Plain," *Plainsman*, 31 July 2013, 3.

15. Drafted in Soweto in 1955, the Freedom Charter was the programmatic statement of the ANC in the moment it officially adopted nonracialism, prompting Africanists to form the PAC. It was actually a broader statement collectively drafted by the ANC, the Colored People's Congress, the South African Indian Congress, and the South African Congress of Democrats (which was of course a euphemism for whites) under the banner of the South African Congress Alliance. Many of its tenets were incorporated into the 1996 constitution, though the original document's emphasis on nationalization and land reform were notably sidelined in the process.

16. There is now an enormous literature on service delivery protests in South Africa, which ranges from valorization to critical interrogation to understanding these actions' roles in the context of the postapartheid state. On these tendencies, respectively, see Peter Alexander, "Rebellion of the Poor: South Africa's Service Delivery Protests—a Preliminary Analysis," *Review of African Political Economy* 37, no. 123: 25–40; Ndodana Nleya, "Linking Service Delivery and Protest in South Africa: An Exploration of Evidence from Khayelitsha," *Africanus* 41, no. 1 (2011): 3–13; Susan Booysen, "With the Ballot and the Brick: The Politics of Attaining Service Delivery," *Progress in Development Studies* 7, no. 1 (2007): 21–32. According to two major reports, services and housing are far and away the most frequent rationales provided for protests. See Peter Alexander, Carin Runciman, and Trevor Ngwane, "Media Briefing: Community Protests," paper presented at Social Change Research Unit, University of Johannesburg, 12 February 2014; D. M. Powell, M. O'Donovan, and J. De Visser, *Civic Protests Barometer, 2007–2014* (Cape Town: Multi-Level Government Initiative, 2014). While I am skeptical of the analytic utility of describing South Africa as the "protest capital of the world"—of quantifying and therefore homogenizing multiple modes of political engagement—it is indisputable that service delivery protests are a regular feature of the country's political landscape. See Peter Alexander, "A Massive Rebellion of the Poor," *Mail & Guardian*, 13 April 2012, https:// mg.co.za/article/2012-04-13-a-massive-rebellion-of-the-poor.

17. Linking a refusal to vote to the failure to deliver has become increasingly standard over the past fifteen years. See, for example, Symphony Way Pavement Dwellers, *No Land! No House! No Vote!* (Oxford: Pambazuka, 2011).

18. Daneel Knoetze, "Fresh Protests Shut Vanguard Drive," *Cape Argus*, 13 February 2014, https:// www.iol.co.za/news/fresh-protests-shut-vanguard-drive-1646676.

19. Lizette Lancaster and Rushdi Nackerdien, "What Does Increasing Political Violence Mean for the Future of South Africa's Democracy?," Institute for Security Studies, 13 May 2014, https://issafrica.org/iss-today/what-does-increasing-political-viole nce-mean-for-the-future-of-south-africas-democracy. See also Marcel Paret, "Violence and Democracy in South Africa's Community Protests," *Review of African Political Economy* 42, no. 143 (2015): 107–23; Karl von Holdt, "South Africa: The Transition to Violent Democracy," *Review of African Political Economy* 40, no. 138 (2013): 598–604.

20. See Colin McFarlane and Jonathan Silver, "The Political City: 'Seeing Sanitation' and Making the Urban Political in Cape Town," *Antipode* 49, no. 1 (2017): 125–48.

21. See Steven L. Robins, "Poo Wars as Matter out of Place: 'Toilets for Africa' in Cape Town," *Anthropology Today* 30, no. 1 (2014): 1–3.

22. Zachary Levenson, "Social Movements beyond Incorporation: The Case of the Housing Assembly in Post-apartheid Cape Town," in *Global Resistance in Southern Perspective: The Politics of Protest in South Africa's Contentious Democracy*, edited by Marcel Paret, Carin Runciman, and Luke Sinwell (London: Routledge, 2017), 89–104; Adrian Thomas Murray, "Contention and Class: Social Movements and Public Services in South Africa" (PhD dissertation, University of Ottawa, 2020); Adrian Murray, "Capitalism, Class, and Collective Identity: Social Movements and Public Services in South Africa," in *Considering Class: Theory, Culture, and the Media in the 21st Century*, edited by Deirdre O'Neill and Mike Wayne (Leiden: Brill, 2018), 149–65; Adrian Murray, "A Decent House, a Decent Job, a Decent Life: Social Reproduction Theory and Working Class Organizing in Cape Town," *Socialist Studies* 14, no. 1 (2020).

23. This was more than US$800 at the time of research but is under US$600 at the time of writing.

24. Dividing townships into sections designated by letter is common practice in a number of "African" townships in Cape Town, most prominently Khayelitsha. "Sites" are often lettered, and then subdivided into lettered "sections." Site C, for example, includes sections A through D, and another site, Khaya, includes sections A through I. Other sites like Makhaya, Makhaza, and Harare include numbered sections, though the same principle obtains. There is no township-wide system however, making navigation quite tricky.

25. On the varieties of settlement committees, see Trevor Ngwane, *Amakomiti: Grassroots Democracy in South African Shack Settlements* (London: Pluto, 2021).

26. As a general rule, these meetings were closed to the public, whether that meant other Siqalo residents or white sociologists visiting from the United States. However, they made exceptions when delegates from a citywide housing social movement called the Housing Assembly visited Siqalo to meet with the committee about coordinating antieviction struggles. When these meetings were held, which also included discussions of regular committee affairs, I was allowed to sit in. In addition, I discussed the function of the committee with Siqalo residents Lwazi, Karen, and Ntando at length, and the other committee members in less depth.

Chapter 5

1. See note 28 in chapter 3.

2. In case the reader is wondering why a houseless South African would use a word like "bourgeoisie," there are two explanations. First, Marxist concepts are in wide circulation in South Africa. Even a president like Thabo Mbeki, South Africa's answer to Margaret Thatcher, regularly deployed marxisant phraseology in his speeches and writing. He was, after all, the son of one of the country's most prominent Communist intellectuals, Govan Mbeki. But this was not particularly exceptional. Marx-adjacent framing is a constant among ANC members, even within its more conservative wing. Second, Biggie's friend Mike was a member of a fairly orthodox, all-Black Trotskyist organization. He patiently led reading groups with some of the occupiers, working through writings by various nineteenth-century Marxists, as well as some South African history.

3. The equivalent in English-law countries is a barrister or a solicitor, though a number of Commonwealth countries, including South Africa, India, and Pakistan, use advocates. This is also the system used in a number of Mediterranean, South American, and Scandinavian countries, as well as in Israel and Poland.

4. The Supreme Court of Appeal (SCA) is the highest appellate court in South Africa, located in the country's judicial capital of Bloemfontein. The Constitutional Court, based in Johannesburg, has superior jurisdiction to the SCA, but it can only hear cases on constitutional matters.

5. At the time of fieldwork, this was about US$5, but at the time of writing it has fallen to US$3.60.

6. Enumeration, therefore, can be understood as yet another technology of moralization, or more precisely, of distinguishing between the deserving and undeserving poor. Of course, the designation is fairly arbitrary, revealing more about when DHS representatives visited the occupation than anything else. Given that the ALIU and police consistently requisitioned building materials, some early occupiers might rebuild structures after those who joined in later.

7. Stuart Hall, "Signification, Representation, Ideology: Althusser and the Post-structuralist Debates," *Critical Studies in Mass Communication* 2, no. 2 (1985): 113–14.

8. The single best argument along these lines remains Ernesto Laclau, "Towards a Theory of Populism," in *Politics and Ideology in Marxist Theory: Capitalism, Fascism, Populism* (New York: Verso, 1977), 143–98.

9. This is Metrorail, which is itself a division of a larger state-owned enterprise called the Passenger Rail Agency of South Africa (PRASA).

10. Belville is a city that was incorporated into the Cape Town municipality in 1996, two years after the transition. It is roughly twenty kilometers due east of the central business district and about twenty-three kilometers north of the Kapteinsklip occupation.

11. The group was founded in 2005 in Durban and has since launched affiliate branches in Cape Town and Pietermaritzburg. For the best analysis of the aforementioned Constitutional Court case, see Marie Huchzermeyer, *Cities with "Slums": From Informal Settlement Eradication to a Right to the City in Africa* (Cape Town: University

of Cape Town Press, 2011), 202–23. See also Anna Selmeczi, "'From Shack to the Constitutional Court': The Litigious Disruption of Governing Global Cities," *Utrecht Law Review* 7, no. 2 (2011): 60–76, as well as the debate between Huchzermeyer and Walsh: Marie Huchzermeyer, "Invoking Lefebvre's 'Right to the City' in South Africa Today: A Response to Walsh," *City* 18, no. 1 (2014): 41–49; Shannon Walsh, "'We Won't Move': The Suburbs Take Back the Center in Urban Johannesburg," *City* 17, no. 3 (2013): 400–408. This is part of a longer-standing and quite heated debate over the uses of Abahlali baseMjondolo by left intellectuals in South Africa. See, for example, Heinrich Böhmke, "Don't Talk about Us Talking about the Poor," *Africa Report*, 19 October 2010, http://www.theafricareport.com/Society-and-Culture/dont-talk-about-us-talking-about-the-poor.html; Heinrich Böhmke, "The Branding of Social Movements," *New Frank Talk*, April 2010, http://heinrichbohmke.com/2013/05/branding/; Ashwin Desai, "Vans, Autos, Kombis, and the Drivers of Social Movements," Harold Wolpe Memorial Lecture, Centre for Civil Society, University of KwaZulu-Natal, Durban, South Africa (28 July 2006), http://wolpetrust.org.za/dialogue2006/DN072006desai_paper.pdf; Nigel C. Gibson, "Upright and Free: Fanon in South Africa, from Biko to the Shackdwellers' Movement (Abahlali baseMjondolo)," *Social Identities* 14, no. 6 (2008): 683–715; Nigel C. Gibson, *Fanonian Practices in South Africa: From Steve Biko to Abahlali baseMjondolo* (Scottsville: University of KwaZulu-Natal Press, 2011); Raj Patel, "A Short Course in Politics at the University of Abahlali baseMjondolo," *Journal of Asian and African Studies* 43, no. 1 (2008): 95–112; Richard Pithouse, "Our Struggle Is Thought, on the Ground, Running: The University of Abahlali baseMjondolo," in *Yonk' Indawo Umzabalazo Uyasivumela: New Work from Durban*, Centre for Civil Society Research Reports, vol. 1, edited by Amanda Alexander and Richard Pithouse (Durban: Centre for Civil Society, University of KwaZulu-Natal, 2008); Richard Pithouse, "Struggle Is a School: The Rise of a Shack Dwellers' Movement in Durban, South Africa," *Monthly Review* 57, no. 9 (2006): 30–52; Richard Pithouse, "A Politics of the Poor: Shack Dwellers' Struggles in Durban," *Journal of Asian and African Studies* 43, no. 1 (2008): 63–94; Shannon Walsh, "'Uncomfortable Collaborations': Contesting Constructions of the 'Poor' in South Africa," *Review of African Political Economy* 35, no. 116 (2008): 255–70; Shannon Walsh, "The Philosopher and His Poor: The Black as Object of Political Desire in South Africa," *Politikon* 42, no. 1 (2015): 123–27. For a book about Abahlali baseMjondolo that manages to sidestep these debates, see Kerry Ryan Chance, *Living Politics in South Africa's Urban Shacklands* (Chicago: University of Chicago Press, 2017).

12. The full name of this law is the KwaZulu-Natal (KZN) Elimination and Prevention of Re-emergence of Slums Act of 2007. It framed new land occupations as a direct threat to housing delivery and authorized the top provincial housing official to require municipal governments and private landowners to evict unlawful squatters. Even after it was ruled unconstitutional in 2009, other provinces tried to emulate the KZN Slums Act, beginning with the passage of the short-lived Mpumalanga Eradication Prevention and Control of Informal Settlements Bill of 2012 in the province immediately northwest of KZN. Indeed, as Marie Huchzermeyer points out, UN-Habitat actually commended the South African government for its commitment

to "slum eradication," reading these policies as a central component of its alignment with the UN's Millennium Development Goals. Delivery and dispossession do not appear so antithetical after all. See Marie Huchzermeyer, "'Slum' Upgrading or 'Slum' Eradication? The Mixed Message of the MDGs," in *The Millennium Development Goals and Human Rights: Past, Present and Future*, edited by Malcolm Langford, Andy Sumner, and Alicia Ely Yamin (Cambridge: Cambridge University Press, 2013), 295–315; Huchzermeyer, *Cities with Slums*, 202–23; UN-Habitat, *The State of the World's Cities Report, 2006/2007: 30 Years of Shaping the Habitat Agenda* (Nairobi: United Nations Human Settlements Programme, 2006).

13. (a) Loyiso Mpalantshane, "Kapteinsklip Residents Finally Go," *Plainsman*, 21 November 2012, 10.

(b) I could not help but recall Engels on the housing question: "This is a striking example of how the bourgeoisie solves the housing question in practice. The breeding places of disease, the infamous holes and cellars in which the capitalist mode of production confines our workers night after night, are not abolished; they are merely shifted elsewhere! The same economic necessity which produced them in the first place, produces them in the next place also." Friedrich Engels, *The Housing Question* (New York: International, n.d. [1872]), 74.

14. John L. Comaroff and Jean Comaroff, "Law and Disorder in the Postcolony: An Introduction," in *Law and Disorder in the Postcolony*, edited by Jean Comaroff and John L. Comaroff (Chicago: University of Chicago Press, 2006), 1–56.

15. Melissa Papier, "Voter Turnout Strong amid Protests," *People's Post Mitchells Plain*, 24 May 2011, 6.

16. Anthropologist James Holston writes of "the 'autoconstructed' peripheries," which he describes as "the kind of impoverished urban periphery in which a majority of Brazilians now live and in which they build, through a process called autoconstruction (*autoconstrução*), their own houses, neighborhoods, and urban life." See *Insurgent Citizenship: Disjunctions of Democracy and Modernity in Brazil* (Princeton: Princeton University Press, 2008), 6.

17. Lest the reader suspect Erasmus of bias, a few remarks are in order. First, one might assume that he is a DA appointee and therefore biased against the ANC, whose front group organized the occupation in the first place, as described in chapter 3. But he was actually appointed by the ANC government, prior to the DA's rule in Cape Town. Moreover, he headed the eponymous Erasmus Commission, created by the then-premier of the Western Cape, Ebrahim Rasool, an ANC politician. The commission was set up to investigate allegations that the DA used taxpayer money to spy on their political rivals in Cape Town. In 2008, the commission was dissolved when the High Court ruled it unconstitutional. In any case, it would be odd to accuse Erasmus of anti-ANC bias. See Dirk Smit, "Cape Town Launches Legal Challenge to Erasmus Commission," *Politicsweb*, 8 April 2008, https://www.politicsweb.co.za/about/cape-town-launches-legal-challenge-to-erasmus-comm. Second, one might assume that Erasmus would be consistently biased against urban informality, but this was not the case. While I could not obtain a complete dossier of Erasmus's rulings on land occupations, I did find examples of him ruling both for toleration and for eviction. And in the same

winter as the Kapteinsklip ruling described here, Erasmus ruled that the city had to build enclosed latrines in an area dominated by shack residents in Khayelitsha. See Cor Dietvorst, "South Africa: Landmark Ruling on Right to Sanitation Ends Cape Town 'Toilet Wars,'" *IRC*, 5 June 2011, https://www.ircwash.org/news/south-africa-landmark-ruling-right-sanitation-ends-cape-town-toilet-wars.

18. *Stad Kaapstad v. Onwettige Okkupeerders van Erf 41078 Mitchells Plain en Anders* (9855/2011) [2011] ZAWCHC 538 (30 August 2011).

19. Javier Auyero, *Patients of the State: The Politics of Waiting in Argentina* (Durham: Duke University Press, 2012).

20. As odd as it might seem for a judge to reference revolution, this is actually pretty standard imagery in South Africa, as it is in many late decolonizers. Countless revolutionaries who participated in the anti-apartheid movement wound up in government and even corporate positions. Watching South African Communist Party members, formally aligned with the ANC, deploy Stalinist phraseology in the service of defending austerity measures is a truly bizarre sight. See Heribert Adam, Frederik van Zyl Slabbert, and Kogila Moodley, *Comrades in Business: Post-liberation Politics in South Africa* (Cape Town: Tafelberg, 1997); Roger Southall, *Liberation Movements in Power: Party and State in Southern Africa* (Scottsville: University of KwaZulu-Natal Press, 2013).

Chapter 6

1. *Lyton Props and Robert Ross v. Occupiers of isiQalo and City of Cape Town* 2013 (1) S.A. 16136/2012 (ZAWCHC) at para 6.4.1. (per Katz A and Pillay K).

2. Throughout this book, I calculate population from number of structures by using the average household size for the Western Cape of 3.2. See StatsSA, *Community Survey 2016 in Brief: Report 03–01–06* (2016), 96.

3. *Lyton Props and Robert Ross v. Occupiers of isiQalo and City of Cape Town* 2013 (1) S.A. 16136/2012 (ZAWCHC) at para 6.4.1. (per Katz A and Pillay K).

4. South Africa has the largest private security industry in the world. Clarno and Murray estimate that there are roughly seven private security officers for every police officer. See Andy Clarno and Martin J. Murray, "Policing in Johannesburg after Apartheid," *Social Dynamics* 39, no. 2 (2013): 210–27; Andy Clarno, *Neoliberal Apartheid: Palestine/Israel and South Africa after 1994* (Chicago: University of Chicago Press, 2017); Tessa G. Diphoorn, *Twilight Policing: Private Security and Violence in Urban South Africa* (Berkeley: University of California Press, 2015); Christine Hentschel, *Security in the Bubble: Navigating Crime in Urban South Africa* (Minneapolis: University of Minnesota Press, 2015).

5. *Lyton Props and Robert Ross v. Occupiers of isiQalo and City of Cape Town* 2013 (1) S.A. 16136/2012 (ZAWCHC) at para 10.5. (per Katz A and Pillay K).

6. *Lyton Props and Robert Ross v. Occupiers of isiQalo and City of Cape Town* 2013 (1) S.A. 16136/2012 (ZAWCHC) at para 10.7. (per Katz A and Pillay K).

7. *Lyton Props and Robert Ross v. Occupiers of isiQalo and City of Cape Town* 2013 (1) S.A. 16136/2012 (ZAWCHC) at para 11.3. (per Katz A and Pillay K).

8. This was confirmed to me in multiple interviews with DHS officials, including the head of the ALIU. Interview with Stephen Hayward, ALIU offices, Belleville, 5 October 2013.

9. *Lyton Props and Robert Ross v. Occupiers of isiQalo and City of Cape Town* 2013 (1) S.A. 16136/2012 (ZAWCHC) at para 10.8. (per Katz A and Pillay K).

10. "The relations of capitalism can be thought of as articulating classes in distinct ways at each of the levels or instances of the social formation—economic, political, ideological. These levels are the 'effects' of the structures of modern capitalist production, with the necessary displacement of relative autonomy operating between them. Each level of the social formation requires its own independent 'means of representation'—the means by which the class-structured mode of production appears, and acquires effectivity at the level of the economic, the political, the ideological class struggle. Race is intrinsic to the manner in which the black laboring classes are complexly constituted at each of these levels. It enters into the way black labor, male and female, is distributed as economic agents at the level of economic practices, and the class struggles which result from it; and into the way the fractions of the black laboring classes are reconstituted, through the means of political representation (parties, organizations, community action centers, publications, and campaigns) as political forces in the 'theatre of politics'—and the political struggles which result.... This gives the matter or dimension of race, and racism, a practical as well as theoretical centrality to all the relations which affect black labor. The constitution of this fraction as a class, and the class relations which ascribe it, function as race relations. Race is thus, also, the modality in which class is 'lived,' the medium through which class relations are experienced, the form in which it is appropriated and 'fought through.'" Stuart Hall, "Race, Articulation, and Societies Structured in Dominance," in *Essential Essays*, vol. 1, edited by David Morley (Durham: Duke University Press, 2019), 215–16.

    "Racial oppression was *the* specific mediation through which this class experienced its material and cultural conditions of life, and hence race formed the central mode through which the self-consciousness of the class stratum could be constructed." Stuart Hall, Chas Critcher, Tony Jefferson, John Clarke, and Brian Roberts, *Policing the Crisis: Mugging, the State, and Law and Order*, 2nd ed. (London: Palgrave, 2013), 379–80.

11. This was the Cape Areas Housing Action Committee, formed in 1980 in response to a city-initiated rent hike in "Colored" areas of the Cape Flats. It expanded across the Flats, with twenty-one civic associations affiliated within five years, and was a major force in the early years of the UDF. Notably, its first secretary was Trevor Manuel, who would subsequently serve as minister of finance from 1996 until 2009. Mike would regularly joke that he, still a militant Trotskyist in his sixties, used to organize with one of the most notorious neoliberals of the postapartheid period, a man celebrated by the World Economic Forum as a "Global Leader for Tomorrow" as early as 1994. See Sipho S. Maseko, "Civic Movement and Non-violent Action: The Case of the Cape Areas Housing Action Committee," *African Affairs* 96, no. 384

(1997): 353–69; Jeremy Seekings, "The Development of Strategic Thought in South Africa's Civic Movements, 1977–90," in *From Comrades to Citizens: The South African Civics Movement and the Transition to Democracy*, edited by Glenn Adler and Jonny Steinberg (New York: St. Martin's, 2000), 52–85; Gail M. Gerhart and Clive L. Glaser (eds.), *From Protest to Challenge: A Documentary History of African Politics in South Africa, 1882–1990*, vol. 6, *Challenge and Victory, 1980–1990* (Bloomington: Indiana University Press, 2010), 47.

12. There is a fairly sizable literature on the AEC, some of it quite critical of the movement's organizational dynamics. See Sarah Chiumbu, "Exploring Mobile Phone Practices in Social Movements in South Africa: The Western Cape Anti-Eviction Campaign," *African Identities* 10, no. 2 (2012): 193–206; Nigel C. Gibson, "Poor People's Movements in South Africa—the Anti-Eviction Campaign in Mandela Park: A Critical Discussion," *Journal of Asian and African Studies* 39, no. 4 (2004): 233–37; Faranak Miraftab, "Feminist Praxis, Citizenship and Informal Politics: Reflections on South Africa's Anti-Eviction Campaign," *International Feminist Journal of Politics* 8, no. 2 (2006): 194–218; Faranak Miraftab and Shana Wills, "Insurgency and Spaces of Active Citizenship: The Story of the Western Cape Anti-Eviction Campaign in South Africa," *Journal of Planning Education and Research* 25 (2005): 200–217; Sophie Oldfield and Kristian Stokke, "Building Unity in Diversity: Social Movement Activism in the Western Cape Anti-Eviction Campaign," in *Voices of Protest: Social Movements in Post-apartheid South Africa*, edited by Richard Ballard, Adam Habib, and Imraan Valodia (Scottsville: University of KwaZulu-Natal Press, 2006), 111–32; Rebecca Pointer, "Questioning the Representation of South Africa's 'New Social Movements': A Case Study of the Mandela Park Anti-Eviction Campaign," *Journal of Asian and African Studies* 39, no. 4 (2004): 271–94. More recently in 2016–17, another founding member of the AEC toured American campuses, promoting the organization as still active. Not only was it effectively defunct by that time, but he remains persona non grata in many of the neighborhoods that he claimed to represent, primarily due to allegations of financial impropriety. Coincidentally, he is from Tafelsig, the section of Mitchells Plain that includes Kapteinsklip.

13. Kowthar Solomons, "Court to Rule on Siqalo," *Saturday Argus*, 8 March 2014, https://www.iol.co.za/news/south-africa/western-cape/court-to-rule-on-siqalo-1658339.

14. Daneel Knoetze, "Fresh Protests Shut Vanguard Drive," *Cape Argus*, 13 February 2014, https://www.iol.co.za/news/fresh-protests-shut-vanguard-drive-1646676).

15. Knoetze, "Fresh Protests Shut Vanguard Drive." Vearey should not be taken as typical of Capetonian police officers. After growing up in a "Colored" township not far from Mitchells Plain, he flirted with Marxism and Black Consciousness before joining uMkhonto weSizwe, the ANC's armed wing and subsequently serving as one of Nelson Mandela's bodyguards. At the time of my research, he led the Western Cape's antigang unit. He was quite critical of routine police work and occasionally gave interviews to left-wing publications such as *Amandla!*

16. "An 'agonistic' approach acknowledges the real nature of its frontiers and the forms of exclusion that they entail, instead of trying to disguise them under the veil of rationality or morality." Chantal Mouffe, *The Democratic Paradox* (New York: Verso,

2000), 105. While I strongly reject Mouffe's contention that "agonistic pluralism" is useful for making sense of the contemporary capitalist state today, I do think it nicely encapsulates the nature of the informal government in Siqalo.

17. For more on this argument, see Zachary Levenson, "Social Movements beyond Incorporation: The Case of the Housing Assembly in Post-apartheid Cape Town," in *Global Resistance in Southern Perspective: The Politics of Protest in South Africa's Contentious Democracy*, edited by Marcel Paret, Carin Runciman, and Luke Sinwell (London: Routledge, 2017), 89–104.

18. I could observe Mike's Trotskyism at work here. In 1904, long before Trotsky joined the Bolsheviks, he denounced Lenin's heavy-handed approach to leadership as effective "substitutionism": acting on behalf of the working class instead of facilitating its self-organization. While he would later, of course, join Lenin's party, he continued to warn of the dangers of ignoring one of Marx's key slogans of the First International: "The emancipation of the working class must be achieved by the working class itself." Karl Marx and Friedrich Engels, "Marx and Engels to Bebel, Liebknecht, Bracke and Others [London, Middle of September, 1879 (Draft)]," in *Selected Correspondence, 1846–1895*, translated by Dona Torr (New York: International, 1942), 376–77. Trotsky's use of the term dates from his 1904 polemic *Our Political Tasks*, which remains untranslated.

19. "Ideas do not fall from heaven, and nothing comes to us in a dream." Antonio Labriola, *Essays on the Materialistic Conception of History*, translated by Charles H. Kerr (New York: Monthly Review Press, 1966), 155. "So here we have arrived once more at the *philosophy of practice*, which is the path of historical materialism. It is the immanent philosophy of things about which people philosophize. The realistic process leads first from life to thought, not from thought to life. It leads from work, from the labor of cognition, to understanding as an abstract theory, not from theory to cognition." Antonio Labriola, *Socialism and Philosophy*, translated by Ernest Untermann (St. Louis: Telos, 1980), 94.

20. Kate Crehan, *Gramsci's Common Sense: Inequality and Its Narratives* (Durham: Duke University Press, 2016).

21. This is just under US$3.25 at the time of fieldwork and US$2.40 at the time of writing. Since the HA meetings were held in Salt River, an upper-working-class "Colored" suburb proximal to the city center, Cape Flats residents had to take a series of taxis to get there. In order to reduce financial barriers to attendance, the HA had funds to reimburse people for travel. Sometimes attendees would figure out ways to scam the system, whether that meant finding a way to get to Salt River for R30 and pocketing the difference, or else claiming to have brought more people than they actually did and keeping the full reimbursement. There was one HA participant who would come from Blikkiesdorp who virtually sustained himself by skimming change from various NGOs and social movements. He would sometimes try to secure reimbursement from two organizations having simultaneous meetings in the same building. Ebrahiem often joked to me that this constituted "*gelukkie* politics," an Afrikaans word that roughly translates to "goodies." He developed an entire typology of *gelukkies*, ranging from free breakfast to ride reimbursement to the ego boost from

participating in politics. He also fleshed out the various types of factionalism that result from this approach to organizing. Much of the analysis advanced in this book has become common sense among the Cape Flats' best organizers—or as Gramsci would put it, this common sense has developed into good sense.

22. See chapter 2, note 123.

23. In the case of waste pickers' legal victory in Johannesburg, Melanie Samson emphasizes the crucial importance of their advocate's celebrity. They enlisted George Bizos, who had represented Nelson Mandela and others at the Rivonia Trial in 1963–64. As Samson argues, "Having Bizos as their advocate helped transform both the way the reclaimers saw themselves and how they were seen in the communities where they lived." See Melanie Samson, "The Social Uses of the Law at a Soweto Garbage Dump: Reclaiming the Law and the State in the Informal Economy," *Current Sociology* 65, no. 2 (2017): 227. While we should not underestimate the importance of residents securing Wilson, his celebrity is not comparable to that of someone like Bizos, whose reputation was not limited to defending the urban poor. In enlisting Bizos, the waste pickers were able to articulate their claims as part of a larger liberation struggle; but Wilson's image did not help them in this respect. His track record in the Constitutional Court may have gained him some additional respect, but most LRC or LHR attorneys involved were highly esteemed. It is unlikely that his reputation made the difference.

24. The trope of the migrant defines "African" Capetonians "as internal immigrants from the Eastern Cape who are coming, not returning, to Cape Town. Under apartheid, they were forcibly expelled to newly created Bantustans in that province. This meant that all Black South Africans were defined as transient workers if they were granted permits, or else as illegal occupants of the city. When they returned years later, both pushed by rural underdevelopment and pulled by urban employment opportunities, they were called 'migrants' by Whites and Coloureds alike, stigmatized as inherently agrarian people." For an extended version of this argument, see the section "Squatters as Undeserving Migrants" in Zachary Levenson, "'Such Elements Do Not Belong in an Ordered Society': Managing Rural-Urban Resettlement in Democratic South Africa," *Journal of Agrarian Change* 19, no. 3 (2019): 437–38.

25. *City of Johannesburg Metro. Municipality v. Blue Moonlight Properties* 2012 (2) S.A. 104 (ZACC) at para 93 (per Van Der Westhuizen J).

26. Mary Douglas, *Purity and Danger: An Analysis of Concepts of Pollution and Taboo* (London: Routledge, 2002).

27. James C. Scott, *Seeing Like a State: How Certain Schemes to Improve the Human Condition Have Failed* (New Haven: Yale University Press, 1998).

28. See, for example, a representative press statement from the Durban-based social movement Abahlali baseMjondolo: "Land occupations are land reform from below. They are urban planning from below." Abahlali baseMjondolo, press statement, 10 September 2015, http://abahlali.org/node/14955/.

29. For an extended version of this argument, see Zachary Levenson, "Precarious Welfare States: Urban Struggles over Housing Delivery in Post-apartheid Cape Town," *International Sociology* 32, no. 4 (2017): 474–92.

30. Establishing "partnerships" with "intermediaries" and "social movements" is above all premised upon "identifying suitable partners" in line with the "participatory approach to urban upgrading." The irony, of course, is that what multilateral institutions now refer to as the "participatory approach" originally derived from a critique of technocratic delivery regimes simply imposing their plans on settlements as passive receptacles. Yet precisely in attempting to codify (and thus formalize) representative leaderships, governments and institutions tend to tokenize the input of hand-selected "partners" to the detriment of broader community sentiment. All of the concepts in quotation marks come from a daylong informal housing conference I observed in October 2013, convened at De Zalze Wineland and Golf Estate in Stellenbosch by the Isandla Institute. A room full of planners, policymakers, and private sector actors talked about participation without anyone mentioning the elephant in the room: there were no residents present. The following day, attendees were taken on an excursion to a small, sanctioned informal settlement nearby, under the guise that this constituted "participation."

31. Like Philippi and Khayelitsha, Gugulethu is another of Cape Town's predominantly "African" townships, its name derived from the isiXhosa word for "our pride." Like most of South Africa's euphemized apartheid-era townships, its name is deceptive. Under apartheid, all "African" people in Cape Town were forced to live in a township called Langa. When this grew too overcrowded, two additional townships, Nyanga and Gugulethu, were built, the former in 1955 and the latter in 1958 (originally simply called "Nyanga West"). Today more than one hundred thousand people live in Gugulethu, with nearly that number next door in Nyanga.

32. Once again, this echoes the same passage from Engels quoted in the previous chapter: "The same economic necessity which produced them in the first place, produces them in the next place also." Friedrich Engels, *The Housing Question* (New York: International, n.d. [1872]), 74.

33. In a recent case, for example, Gamble granted an eviction interdict in another instance of shacks being built on private property. See Kamva Somdyala, "Cape Town Wine Farm Granted Interdict after BLF Land Occupation Fears," *News24*, 17 May 2019, https://www.news24.com/news24/southafrica/news/cape-town-wine-farm-granted-interdict-after-blf-land-occupation-fears-20190517. In another high-profile case, that of Lwandle in 2014, Gamble refused to grant an interdict and likened evictions threatened by the state to "well-documented operations conducted by the apartheid government in the 1980s." See Charlotte Gilliland, "Forced Evictions, Live Ammunition, and Video Documentation in Cape Town," *Witness Media Lab*, n.d.,, https://lab.witness.org/forced-evictions-live-ammunition-and-video-documentation-in-cape-town/. And much like Erasmus, Gamble could hardly be seen as a shill of the DA. Indeed, it was Gamble who upheld Mayor Patricia de Lille's right to remain in office after she broke with the party and it tried to have her removed. See Hlumela Dyantyi, "Patricia de Lille Gets to Keep Her Mayoral Chain, for Now," *Daily Maverick*, 15 May 2018, https://www.dailymaverick.co.za/article/2018-05-15-patricia-de-lille-gets-to-keep-her-mayoral-chain-for-now/#gsc.tab=0.

34. Like a tuck shop, a spaza shop is an informal convenience store.

35. Then-president Jacob Zuma.

36. Daneel Knoetze, "Fresh Protests Shut Vanguard Drive."

37. This is a key point made by Stuart Hall: no political articulation is "'eternal' but has constantly to be renewed, which can under some circumstances disappear or be overthrown, leading to the old linkages being dissolved and new connections— re-articulations—being forged." Stuart Hall, "Signification, Representation, Ideology: Althusser and the Post-structuralist Debates," *Critical Studies in Mass Communication* 2, no. 2 (1985): 113n.2. For a slightly revised version of this formulation, see Stuart Hall, *Cultural Studies, 1983* (Durham: Duke University Press, 2016), 121.

The other important point to make here is that this is another illustration of the inseparability of civil and political societies and another indication that these are not empirically distinct locations but rather two strategic perspectives on a political process that remains in flux. As new articulations emerge on the terrain of civil society, so too do they emerge on the terrain of political society. The disintegration of the fused group likely means the erosion of the collective will that is the basis for the elected committee, or even for Bonginkosi's rule. "The old collective will dissolves into its contradictory elements since the subordinate ones develop socially, etc." Antonio Gramsci, *Selections from the Prison Notebooks*, translated by Quintin Hoare and Geoffrey Nowell Smith (New York: International, 1971), 195. See also the discussion of this passage in Stuart Hall, "The Problem of Ideology: Marxism without Guarantees," in *Stuart Hall: Critical Dialogues in Cultural Studies* (London: Routledge, 1996), 42.

Chapter 7

1. Stuart Hall, "Signification, Representation, Ideology: Althusser and the Post-structuralist Debates," *Critical Studies in Mass Communication* 2, no. 2 (1985): 113 n. 2.

2. Hall, "Signification, Representation, Ideology," 113 n. 3.

3. Suné Payne, "One Dead, 30 Arrested in Violent Clashes between Residents," *Daily Maverick*, 3 May 2018, https://www.dailymaverick.co.za/article/2018-05-03-83011/.

4. Frances Fox Piven and Richard A. Cloward, *Regulating the Poor: The Functions of Public Welfare* (New York: Vintage, 1993 [1971]); Loïc Wacquant, *Punishing the Poor: The Neoliberal Government of Social Insecurity* (Durham: Duke University Press, 2009); John Fiske, "Surveilling the City: Whiteness, the Black Man, and Democratic Totalitarianism," *Theory, Culture & Society* 15, no. 2 (1998): 67–88; Jeff Maskovsky, "'Managing' the Poor: Neoliberalism, Medicaid HMOs and the Triumph of Consumerism among the Poor," *Medical Anthropology* 19, no. 2 (2000): 121–46; Joe Soss, Richard C. Fording, and Sanford F. Schram, *Disciplining the Poor: Neoliberal Paternalism and the Persistent Power of Race* (Chicago: University of Chicago Press, 2011); Silvia Marina Arrom, *Containing the Poor: The Mexico City Poor House, 1774–1871* (Durham: Duke University Press, 2000); Hidetaka Hirota, *Expelling the*

Poor: Atlantic Seaboard States and the 19th-Century Origins of American Immigration Policy (Oxford: Oxford University Press, 2017).

5. This terminology comes from Nicos Poulantzas, *State, Power, Socialism* (New York: Verso, 1978).

6. I am thinking in particular of Foucault's identification of sovereign power as only one of many possible governmental rationalities, as well as Bourdieu's insistence that the concept of "the state" reproduces state thought, and that we should instead think state power through the concept of the bureaucratic field. See Michel Foucault, *Discipline and Punish: The Birth of the Prison*, translated by Alan Sheridan (New York: Vintage, 1995); Michel Foucault, *Security, Territory, Population: Lectures at the Collège de France, 1977—1978* (New York: Picador, 2007); Pierre Bourdieu, "Rethinking the State: Genesis and Structure of the Bureaucratic Field," *Sociological Theory* 12, no. 1 (1994): 1–18. In what follows, I work through two Foucauldian accounts. We might do the same, however, for the Bourdieusian work of Loïc Wacquant on urban marginality in France and the United States, for example, *Urban Outcasts: A Comparative Sociology of Advanced Marginality* (Cambridge: Polity Press, 2008). He insists on understanding the emergence of the (hyper)ghetto through a model of "political overdetermination" (4), "the primacy of the political" (287), and "the pivotal role played by the state" (286). While this is certainly a refreshing antidote to the ahistorical work of urban ecologists, it also takes "the state" as a coherent institutional entity with a predetermined set of interests and motivations. Yet if his French state acts in the interest of the middle classes, but his American state acts in the interest of white supremacy, how then are we to account for these differences? And if following Richard Sennett, Wacquant argues that the institutional form of the ghetto was as much a shield as it was a sword, then clearly civil society struggles in these spaces affect urban policy outcomes. See Sennett's *Flesh and Stone: The Body and the City in Western Civilization* (New York: Norton, 1994). On the one hand, we might think about the creation of the Department of Housing and Urban Development (HUD) and increased housing expenditure as a direct response to the participation of more than five hundred thousand Black Americans in urban riots during the 1960s—not a far cry from my earlier argument that the apartheid government began to deliver formal housing on the Cape Flats in the aftermath of the Soweto Uprising. On the other, we might also consider how the changing class composition of American ghettos precipitated some of these developments, though, of course, Wacquant subsumes these trends under his state-centered explanatory apparatus. Ironically enough, despite his subsequent criticism of David Harvey on precisely this point, he explains the "dualization and desocialization of wage labor" with reference to the retrenchment of the social state. See Wacquant, *Urban Outcasts*, 267; cf. Wacquant, *Punishing the Poor*. My point is that in both cases, Wacquant posits a state that simply acts upon populations in accordance with a set of predetermined motives instead of interacting with them. This is not so different from Scott's omniscient state that projects its visions onto passive canvasses below. See James Scott, *Seeing Like a State: How Certain Schemes to Improve the Human Condition Have Failed* (New Haven: Yale University Press, 1998). On US-based urban riots in the 1960s as "the Great Uprising," see Peter B. Levy, *The Great*

Uprising: Race Riots in Urban America during the 1960s (Cambridge: Cambridge University Press) and Elizabeth Hinton, *America on Fire: The Untold History of Police Violence and Black Rebellion since the 1960s* (New York: Liveright, 2021); and on the relationship between these rebellions and the creation of HUD, see chapters 1 and 2 in Keeanga-Yahmatta Taylor, *Race for Profit: How Banks and the Real Estate Industry Undermined Black Homeownership* (Chapel Hill: University of North Carolina Press, 2019).

7. Partha Chatterjee, *The Politics of the Governed: Reflections on Popular Politics in Most of the World* (New York: Columbia University Press, 2004), 51.

8. Partha Chatterjee, *Lineages of Political Society: Studies in Postcolonial Democracy* (New York: Columbia University Press, 2011), 14.

9. On this point see Norberto Bobbio, "Gramsci and the Conception of Civil Society," in *Which Socialism?*, translated by Roger Griffin and edited by Richard Bellamy (Minneapolis: University of Minnesota Press, 1987 [1976]), 139–61; Carlos Nelson Coutinho, *Gramsci's Political Thought* (Chicago: Haymarket, 2013).

10. Chatterjee, *Politics of the Governed*, 4.

11. Chatterjee, *Politics of the Governed*, 39. See also Ranajit Guha, "On Some Aspects of the Historiography of Colonial India," in *Subaltern Studies No. 1: Writings on South Asian History and Society*, edited by Ranajit Guha (Oxford: Oxford University Press, 1982).

12. Dipesh Chakrabarty, *Provincializing Europe: Postcolonial Thought and Historical Difference* (Princeton: Princeton University Press, 2008); Ranajit Guha, *Elementary Aspects of Peasant Insurgency in Colonial India* (Durham: Duke University Press, 1999).

13. See Eric Hobsbawm, *Primitive Rebels: Studies in Archaic Forms of Social Movement in the 19th and 20th Centuries* (New York: Norton, 1965). This is not only apparent in subsequent stageist versions of Marxism, from Kautsky through Stalin, but also in Marx's own writings. The most obvious examples are his account of the peasantry, a "sack of potatoes," as incapable of self-representation in the *18th Brumaire*, and the highly contested phrase "*dem Idiotismus des Landlebens*" from the *Manifesto*, variably translated as "the idiocy of living on the land" and the "isolation of rural life." While much has been made of the Greek etymology of the German word for idiocy, revealing its emphasis on privacy over stupidity, both translations equally reveal Marx's early skepticism about the possibility of representational politics among the subproletariat and peasantry. See Karl Marx, *The Eighteenth Brumaire of Louis Bonaparte* (New York: International, 1963 [1852]); Karl Marx and Friedrich Engels, "Manifesto of the Communist Party," in *Marx: Later Political Writings*, edited and translated by Terrell Carver (Cambridge: Cambridge University Press, 1996 [1848]), 5; Karl Marx and Friedrich Engels, *The Communist Manifesto: A Road Map to History's Most Important Political Document* (Chicago: Haymarket, 2005 [1848]), 46; Hal Draper, *Karl Marx's Theory of Revolution, Vol. II: The Politics of Social Classes* (New York: Monthly Review, 1978), 344.

14. Janice Perlman, *The Myth of Marginality: Urban Poverty and Politics in Rio de Janeiro* (Berkeley: University of California Press, 1976); Alejandro Portes, "Rationality in the

Slum: An Essay on Interpretive Sociology," *Comparative Studies in Society and History* 14, no. 3 (1972): 268–86; Helen Safa, "The Poor Are Like Everyone Else, Oscar," *Psychology Today* 4, no. 4 (1970): 26–32.

15. Robert E. Park and Ernest W. Burgess, *The City: Suggestions for Investigation of Human Behavior in the Urban Environment* (Chicago: University of Chicago Press, 1984 [1925]); Clifford R. Shaw and Henry D. McKay, *Juvenile Delinquency and Urban Areas* (Chicago: University of Chicago Press, 1969 [1942]); William I. Thomas and Florian Znaniecki, *The Polish Peasant in Europe and America: A Classic in Immigration History* (Urbana: University of Illinois Press, 1984 [1920]).

16. The Chicago School's second generation dismantled these assumptions, though more recent urban ecological work under the guise of "neighborhood effects" appears intent upon reviving them. For the former, see Gerald D. Suttles, *The Social Order of the Slum: Ethnicity and Territory in the Inner City* (Chicago: University of Chicago Press, 1968).

17. Scott, *Seeing Like a State.*

18. Scott, *Seeing Like a State*, 77.

19. Scott, *Seeing Like a State*, 78.

20. Fred Block, "Understanding the Diverging Trajectories of the United States and Western Europe: A Neo-Polanyian Analysis," *Politics & Society* 35, no. 1 (2007): 3–33; Peter Evans, "Is an Alternative Globalisation Possible?," *Politics & Society* 36, no. 2 (2008): 271–305; Peter Evans, "Counterhegemonic Globalization: Transnational Social Movements in the Contemporary Global Political Economy," in *The Handbook of Political Sociology: States, Civil Societies, and Globalization*, edited by Thomas Janoski, Robert Alford, Alexander Hicks, and Mildred A. Schwartz (Cambridge: Cambridge University Press, 2005), 655–70; Richard Sandbrook, "Polanyi and Post-neoliberalism in the Global South: Dilemmas of Re-embedding the Economy," *New Political Economy* 16, no. 4 (2011): 415–43.

21. In May 2018, conflict between mostly "African" Siqalo squatters and the formally housed "Colored" residents across the road erupted again. The latter camp consistently deployed indigenist rhetoric in the service of anti-Blackness. That is, they tied their own ancestry to the Western Cape's indigenous populations—the Khoikhoi and the San—and framed "African" residents as "migrants" because their ancestors traveled southward from the Great Lakes region well over a thousand years ago. These narratives were disseminated through neighborhood-wide WhatsApp chains, often harnessed to a "Colored" nationalism, complete with #proudlycoloured hashtags. Oddly enough, the "African" squatters were simultaneously portrayed as colonizers (they invaded "Colored"/Khoisan space, both the region and the neighborhood) and colonized, akin to the dehumanized occupants living in Fanon's "native town." See Frantz Fanon, *Wretched of the Earth*, translated by Richard Philcox (New York: Grove, 2004 [1961]), 3–5. For more on "Colored" nationalism, see Zachary Levenson and Sean Jacobs, "The Limits of Coloured Nationalism," *Mail & Guardian*, 15 June 2018, 32.

22. Cedric de Leon, Manali Desai, and Cihan Tuğal (eds.), *Building Blocs: How Parties Organize Society* (Stanford: Stanford University Press, 2015); Cedric de Leon,

Manali Desai, and Cihan Tuğal, "Political Articulation: Parties and the Constitution of Cleavages in the United States, India, and Turkey," *Sociological Theory* 27, no. 3 (2009): 193–219; Barry Eidlin, "Why Is There No Labor Party in the United States? Political Articulation and the Canadian Comparison, 1932 to 1948," *American Sociological Review* 81, no. 3 (2016): 488–516.

23. De Leon, Desai, and Tuğal, *Building Blocs*, 7–13.

24. De Leon, Desai, and Tuğal, *Building Blocs*, 21.

25. De Leon, Desai, and Tuğal, *Building Blocs*, 14.

26. See, for example, Mfaniseni Fana Sihlongonyane, "Land Occupations in South Africa," in *Reclaiming the Land: The Resurgence of Rural Movements in Africa, Asia and Latin America*, edited by Sam Moyo and Paris Yeros (London: Zed, 2005), 142–64; Marie Huchzermeyer, "Housing Rights in South Africa: Invasions, Evictions, the Media, and the Courts in the cases of Grootboom, Alexandra, and Bredell," *Urban Forum* 14 (2003): 80–107; Andile Mngxitama, "The Taming of Land Resistance: Lessons from the National Land Committee," *Journal of Asian and African Studies* 41, nos. 1–2 (2006): 39–69; Gillian Hart, *Disabling Globalization: Places of Power in Post-apartheid South Africa* (Berkeley: University of California Press, 2002); Gillian Hart, "Denaturalizing Dispossession: Critical Ethnography in the Age of Resurgent Imperialism," *Antipode* 38, no.5 (2006).

27. De Leon, Desai, and Tuğal, *Building Blocs*, 3.

28. De Leon, Desai, and Tuğal, *Building Blocs*, 31.

29. John D. McCarthy and Mayer N. Zald, "Resource Mobilization and Social Movements: A Partial Theory," *American Journal of Sociology* 82, no. 6 (1977): 1217–18.

30. There have certainly been occupations tied to social movement organizations, as well as more informally organized occupations that sought to transform social structure, or at the very least, the nature of land and housing distribution, but these are exceptional. We can think here of some of the earliest occupations organized by the Landless Peoples Movement near Johannesburg, or even some of the initial Abahlali baseMjondolo occupations in Durban. But most occupations are not about social transformation, however much we as observers may desire such an end; they are far more conservative than that, typically about securing access to a bit of land and ideally, avoiding any confrontation with the state. Classic pieces in resource mobilization theory, then, that focus on the role of coercion—I am thinking here especially of the early work of Charles Tilly—do not do much for us here, as they take social revolutions as a prototypical case of successful movements. Land occupations are usually a far more mundane affair. See Charles Tilly, "Does Modernization Breed Revolution?," *Comparative Politics* 5, no. 3 (1973): 425–47; and Charles Tilly, "Revolution and Collective Violence," in *Handbook of Political Science*, vol. 3, *Macropolitical Theory*, edited by Fred I. Greenstein and Nelson W. Polsby (Boston: Addison-Wesley, 1975), 483–555.

31. Liza Weinstein, *The Durable Slum: Dharavi and the Right to Stay Put in Globalizing Mumbai* (Minneapolis: University of Minnesota Press, 2014).

32. Chester W. Hartman, "The Right to Stay Put," in *Land Reform, American Style*, edited by Charles C. Geisler and Frank J. Popper (Totowa: Rowan & Allanheld, 1984), 302–18.

33. Barbara Jeanne Fields, "Slavery, Race and Ideology in the United States of America," *New Left Review* I/181 (1990): 114.

34. John L. Comaroff and Jean Comaroff, "Law and Disorder in the Postcolony: An Introduction," in *Law and Disorder in the Postcolony*, edited by Jean Comaroff and John L. Comaroff (Chicago: University of Chicago Press, 2006), 1–56.

35. Gautam Bhan, *In the Public's Interest: Evictions, Citizenship, and Inequality in Contemporary Delhi* (Athens: University of Georgia Press, 2016).

36. Max Weber, *Economy and Society: An Outline of Interpretive Sociology* (2 vols.), edited by Guenther Roth and Claus Wittich (Berkeley: University of California Press, 1978), 983.

37. Jessica Budd, "Ensuring the Right to the City: Pro-poor Housing, Urban Development and Tenure Legalization in São Paulo, Brazil," *Environment and Urbanization* 17, no. 1 (2005): 89–113.

38. Márcio Moraes Valença and Mariana Fialho Bonates, "The Trajectory of Social Housing Policy in Brazil: From the National Housing Bank to the Ministry of Cities," *Habitat International* 34, no. 2 (2010): 165–73.

39. Édesio Fernandes, "Implementing the Urban Reform Agenda in Brazil," *Environment and Urbanization* 19, no. 1 (2007): 183.

40. Gautam Bhan, "'This Is No Longer the City I Once Knew': Evictions, the Urban Poor and the Right to the City in Millennial Delhi," *Environment and Urbanization* 21, no. 1 (2009): 127–42; D. Asher Ghertner, "An Analysis of New Legal Discourse behind Delhi's Slum Demolitions," *Economic and Political Weekly* 43, no. 20 (2008): 57–66.

41. D. Asher Ghertner, "Calculating without Numbers: Aesthetic Governmentality in Delhi's Slums," *Economy and Society* 39, no. 2 (2010): 185–217; D. Asher Ghertner, *Rule by Aesthetics: World-Class City Making in Delhi* (New York: Oxford University Press, 2015).

Appendix

1. Jack Katz, "A Theory of Qualitative Methodology: The Social System of Analytic Fieldwork," in *Contemporary Field Research: Perspectives and Formulations*, edited by Robert M. Emerson (Prospect Heights, IL: Waveland, 1983), 137.

2. Michael Burawoy, *The Extended Case Method: Four Countries, Four Decades, Four Great Transformations* (Berkeley: University of California Press, 2009), 56.

3. Burawoy, *The Extended Case Method*, 44.

4. The essay originally appeared as Michael Burawoy, "The Extended Case Method," *Sociological Theory* 16, no. 1 (1998): 4–33.

5. Burawoy, *The Extended Case Method*, 9.

6. Michael Burawoy, "Introduction," in *Ethnography Unbound: Power and Resistance in the Modern Metropolis*, by Michael Burawoy, Alice Burton, Ann Arnett Ferguson, Kathryn J. Fox, Joshua Gamson, Nadine Gartrell, Leslie Hurst, Charles Kurzman, Leslie Salzinger, Josepha Schiffman, and Shiori Ui (Berkeley: University of California Press, 1991), 3.

7. Stuart Hall, "Gramsci and Us," in *The Hard Road to Renewal: Thatcherism and the Crisis of the Left* (New York: Verso, 1988), 167.

8. Franco Barchiesi, *Precarious Liberation: Workers, the State, and Contested Social Citizenship in Postapartheid South Africa* (Albany: SUNY Press, 2011).

9. Alejandro Portes, "Rationality in the Slum: An Essay on Interpretive Sociology," *Comparative Studies in Society and History* 14, no. 3 (1972): 286.

10. Antonio Gramsci, *Selections from the Prison Notebooks*, edited and translated by Quintin Hoare and Geoffrey Nowell Smith (New York: International, 1971), 330–31.

Bibliography

Media Sources Cited

"ANC Policy Conference to Address Housing Issues," *eNCA*, 3 July 2017, https://www.enca.com/south-africa/anc-policy-conference-human-settlements-policy-to-addr ess-housing-issues.

Dietvorst, Cor, "South Africa: Landmark Ruling on Right to Sanitation Ends Cape Town 'Toilet Wars,'" *IRC*, 5 June 2011, https://www.ircwash.org/news/south-africa-landm ark-ruling-right-sanitation-ends-cape-town-toilet-wars.

Dyantyi, Hlumela, "Patricia de Lille Gets to Keep Her Mayoral Chain, for Now," *Daily Maverick*, 15 May 2018, https://www.dailymaverick.co.za/article/2018-05-15-patricia-de-lille-gets-to-keep-her-mayoral-chain-for-now/#gsc.tab=0.

"Free Housing Not Sustainable—Sexwale," *News24*, 26 September 2011, https://www.news24. com/SouthAfrica/News/%5CNews24%5CFree-housing-not-sustainable-Sexwale-20110926.

Gilliland, Charlotte, "Forced Evictions, Live Ammunition, and Video Documentation in Cape Town," *Witness Media Lab*, n.d., https://lab.witness.org/forced-evictions-live-ammunition-and-video-documentation-in-cape-town/.

Knoetze, Daneel, "Fresh Protests Shut Vanguard Drive," *Cape Argus*, February 13, 2014, https://www.iol.co.za/news/fresh-protests-shut-vanguard-drive-1646676.

Makhafola, Gertrude, "Land Invasions Spiked before Elections—Makhura," IOL News, 16 September 2016, https://www.iol.co.za/news/land-invasions-spiked-before-electi ons-makhura-2069154.

Maregele, Barbara, "Waiting Period on Cape Town's Housing List Is 60 years, Khayelitsha Meeting Told," *GroundUp*, 2 October 2017, https://www.groundup.org.za/article/wait ing-period-cape-towns-housing-list-60-years-khayelitsha-meeting-told/.

"Mitchells Plain: A New Era in Mass Housing," *Financial Mail Special Report*, 5 May 1978.

Mpalantshane, Loyiso, "Squatters Squabble over Eviction Order," *Plainsman*, 7 September 2011, 9–10.

Mpalantshane, Loyiso, "Kapteinsklip Residents Finally Go," *Plainsman*, 21 November 2012, 10.

Msimang, Sisonke, "Poor-Bashing Is the New Slut-Shaming: Zuma, Sisulu & the Lazy Nation," *Daily Maverick*, 23 October 2014, https://www.dailymaverick.co. za/opinionista/2014-10-23-poor-bashing-is-the-new-slut-shaming-zuma-sisulu-the-lazy-nation/#.WvHk3mbMyCQ.

Palm, Kaylynn, "ANC Moves in for 'Plain," *Plainsman*, 31 July 2013, 3.

Papier, Melissa, "Voter Turnout Strong amid Protests," *People's Post Mitchells Plain*, 24 May 2011, 6.

Payne, Suné, "One Dead, 30 Arrested in Violent Clashes between Residents," *Daily Maverick*, 3 May 2018, https://www.dailymaverick.co.za/article/2018-05-03-83011/.

Payne, Suné and Tariro Washinyira, "Metrorail's Own Stats Show How Bad Its Service Is," *GroundUp*, 7 December 2017, https://www.groundup.org.za/article/metrorails-own-stats-show-how-bad-its-service-is/.

SAPA, "Zuma Not Our President: Cape Secessionists," *The Citizen*, 7 May 2009, http://www.citizen.co.za/index/article.aspx?pDesc=95310,1,22.

Shezi, Lungelo, "The Most Racially Segregated and Integrated Major Cities in SA," *Hypertext*, 23 May 2016, https://www.htxt.co.za/2016/05/23/map-monday-johannesb urg-is-the-most-racially-integrated-city-in-sa/.

Smit, Dirk, "Cape Town Launches Legal Challenge to Erasmus Commission," *Politicsweb*, 8 April 2008, https://www.politicsweb.co.za/about/cape-town-launches-legal-challe nge-to-erasmus-comm.

Solomons, Kowthar, "Court to Rule on Siqalo," *Saturday Argus*, 8 March 2014, https://www.iol.co.za/news/south-africa/western-cape/court-to-rule-on-siqalo-1658339).

Somdyala, Kamva, "Cape Town Wine Farm Granted Interdict after BLF Land Occupation Fears," *News24*, 17 May 2019, https://www.news24.com/news24/ southafrica/news/cape-town-wine-farm-granted-interdict-after-blf-land-occupation-fears-20190517.

Tempelhoff, Elise, "Water: SA hat dalk 20 m. meer mense," *Netwerk24*, 6 October 2014, https://www.netwerk24.com/Nuus/Water-SA-het-dalk-20-m-meer-mense-20141006.

Western Cape Anti-Eviction Campaign, "St James Street Residents Defend Themselves in Court against Illegal Eviction," press release, 18 March 2009, https://westerncapeantie viction. wordpress.com/2009/03/19/.

"We Will Continue to Provide RDP Houses—Sisulu," *IOL*, 10 April 2016, https://www.iol. co.za/ news/politics/we-will-continue-to-provide-rdp-houses-sisulu-2007470.

Wilkinson, Kate, "Are There 70 Million People in South Africa? The Claim Is Unsubstantiated," *Africa Check*, 4 December 2014, https://africacheck.org/reports/are-there-70-million-people-in-south-africa-the-claim-is-unsubstantiated.

Books and Articles Cited

Adam, Heribert, Frederik van Zyl Slabbert, and Kogila Moodley, *Comrades in Business: Post- liberation Politics in South Africa* (Cape Town: Tafelberg, 1997).

Adhikari, Mohamed, "Between Black and White: The History of Coloured Politics in South Africa," *Canadian Journal of African Studies* 25, no. 1 (1991): 106–10.

Alexander, Neville [No Sizwe], *One Azania, One Nation: The National Question in South Africa* (London: Zed, 1979).

Alexander, Neville, *An Ordinary Country: Issues in the Transition from Apartheid to Democracy in South Africa* (Scottsville: University of Natal Press, 2002).

Alexander, Peter, "A Massive Rebellion of the Poor," *Mail & Guardian*, 13 April 2012, https://mg.co.za/article/2012-04-13-a-massive-rebellion-of-the-poor.

Alexander, Peter, "Rebellion of the Poor: South Africa's Service Delivery Protests—a Preliminary Analysis," *Review of African Political Economy* 37, no. 123 (2010): 25–40.

Alexander, Peter, Carin Runciman, and Trevor Ngwane, "Media Briefing: Community Protests," paper presented at Social Change Research Unit, University of Johannesburg, February 12, 2014.

Althusser, Louis, "Ideology and Ideological State Apparatuses: Notes toward an Investigation," in *Lenin and Philosophy and Other Essays* (New York: Monthly Review Press, 2001), 85–126.

Anderson, Perry, *The Antinomies of Antonio Gramsci* (New York: Verso, 2017 [1976]).

Angotti, Tom, "Apocalyptic Anti-urbanism: Mike Davis and His Planet of Slums," *International Journal of Urban and Regional Research* 30, no. 4 (2006): 961–67.

Annavarapu, Sneha and Zachary Levenson, "The Social Life of the State: Political Sociology and Relational Ethnography," *Qualitative Sociology* 44, no. 3 (2021): 337–48.

Arrom, Silvia Marina, *Containing the Poor: The Mexico City Poor House, 1774–1871* (Durham: Duke University Press, 2000).

Ashman, Sam and Ben Fine, "Neo-liberalism, Varieties of Capitalism, and the Shifting Contours of South Africa's Financial System," *Transformation* 81, no. 1 (2013): 144–78.

Ashman, Sam, Ben Fine, and Susan Newman, "Amnesty International? The Nature, Scale and Impact of Capital Flight from South Africa," *Journal of Southern African Studies* 37, no. 1 (2011): 7–25.

Ashman, Sam, Ben Fine, and Susan Newman, "The Crisis in South Africa: Neoliberalism, Financialization and Uneven and Combined Development, *Socialist Register* 47 (2011): 174–95.

Ashman, Sam, Zachary Levenson, and Trevor Ngwane, "South Africa's ANC: The Beginning of the End?," *Catalyst* 1, no. 2 (2017): 75–106.

Atkinson, Rowland and Gary Bridge (eds.), *Gentrification in a Global Context* (London: Routledge, 2004).

Auyero, Javier, *Patients of the State: The Politics of Waiting in Argentina* (Durham: Duke University Press, 2012).

Auyero, Javier and Débora Alejandra Swistun, *Flammable: Environmental Suffering in an Argentine Shantytown* (Oxford: Oxford University Press, 2009).

Ballard, Richard, "Geographies of Development III: Militancy, Insurgency, Encroachment and Development by the Poor," *Progress in Human Geography* 39, no. 2 (2015): 214–24.

Barchiesi, Franco, *Precarious Liberation: Workers, the State, and Contested Social Citizenship in Postapartheid South Africa* (Albany: SUNY Press, 2011).

Bayat, Asef, "Globalization and the Politics of the Informal in the Global South," in *Urban Informality: Transnational Perspectives from the Middle East, Latin America, and South Asia*, edited by Ananya Roy and Nezar AlSayyad (Lanham, MD: Lexington, 2004), 79–104.

Bayat, Asef, *Life as Politics: How Ordinary People Change the Middle East*, 2nd ed. (Stanford: Stanford University Press, 2013).

Bhan, Gautam, *In the Public's Interest: Evictions, Citizenship, and Inequality in Contemporary Delhi* (Athens: University of Georgia Press, 2016).

Beavon, Keith, *Johannesburg: The Making and Shaping of the City* (Pretoria: University of South Africa Press, 2004).

Bénit-Gbaffou, Claire and Sophie Oldfield, "Accessing the State: Everyday Practices and Politics in Cities of the South," *Journal of Asian and African Studies* 46, no. 5 (2011): 445–52.

Benson, Koni, *Crossroads: I Love Where I Like: A Graphic History* (San Francisco: PM Press, 2021).

Benson, Koni, "Crossroads Continues: Histories of Women Mobilizing against Forced Removals and for Housing in Cape Town, South Africa, 1975–2005" (PhD dissertation, Department of History, University of Minnesota, 2009).

Benson, Koni and Faeza Meyer, "Reluctantly Loud: Interventions in the History of a Land Occupation," in *African Cities Reader III: Land, Property, and Value*, edited by

Ntone Edjabe and Edgar Pieterse (Cape Town: Chimurenga/African Centre for Cities, 2015), 64–95.

Benson, Koni and Faeza Meyer, "'Writing My History Is Keeping Me Alive': Politics and Practices of Collaborative History Writing," in *A Reflexive Inquiry into Gender and Gender-Based Violence: Toward a New Paradigm of Knowledge Production across Multiple Divides*, edited by Samantha van Schalkwyk and Pumla Gobodo-Madikizela (Cambridge: Cambridge Scholars, 2015), 103–27.

Bernes, Jasper, "Revolutionary Motives," *Endnotes* 5 (2019): 228–31.

Beyers, Christian, "Identity and Forced Displacement: Community and Colouredness in District Six," in *Burdened by Race: Coloured Identities in Southern Africa*, edited by Mohamed Adhikari (Cape Town: University of Cape Town Press, 2009), 79–103.

Bhan, Gautam, *In the Public's Interest: Evictions, Citizenship, and Inequality in Contemporary Delhi* (Athens: University of Georgia Press, 2016).

Bhan, Gautam, "'This Is No Longer the City I Once Knew': Evictions, the Urban Poor and the Right to the City in Millennial Delhi," *Environment and Urbanization* 21, no. 1 (2009): 127–42.

Bickford-Smith, Vivian, *The Emergence of the South African Metropolis: Cities and Identities in the Twentieth Century* (Cambridge: Cambridge University Press, 2016).

Bickford-Smith, Vivian, "South African Urban History, Racial Segregation and the Unique Case of Cape Town?," *Journal of Southern African Studies* 21, no. 1 (2007): 63–78.

Biko, Steve, *I Write What I Like: Selected Writings* (Chicago: University of Chicago Press, 2002).

Bilchitz, David, "Giving Socio-economic Rights Teeth: The Minimum Core and Its Importance," *South African Law Journal* 119, no. 3 (2002): 484–500.

Block, Fred, "Understanding the Diverging Trajectories of the United States and Western Europe: A Neo-Polanyian Analysis," *Politics & Society* 35, no. 1 (2007): 3–33.

Bobbio, Norberto, "Gramsci and the Conception of Civil Society," in *Which Socialism?*, translated by Roger Griffin and edited by Richard Bellamy (Minneapolis: University of Minnesota Press, 1987 [1976]).

Böhmke, Heinrich, "The Branding of Social Movements," *New Frank Talk*, April 2010, http://heinrichbohmke.com/2013/05/branding/.

Böhmke, Heinrich, "Don't Talk about Us Talking about the Poor," *Africa Report*, 19 October 2010, http://www.theafricareport.com/Society-and-Culture/dont-talk-about-us-talking-about-the-poor.html.

Bond, Patrick, *Against Global Apartheid: South Africa Meets the World Bank, IMF and International Finance* (London: Zed, 2003).

Bond, Patrick, *Elite Transition: From Apartheid to Neoliberalism in South Africa*, 2nd ed. (London: Pluto, 2014).

Bond, Patrick and Greg Ruiters, "The Development Bottleneck," *Southern Africa Report*, April–May 1996.

Booysen, Susan, "With the Ballot and the Brick: The Politics of Attaining Service Delivery," *Progress in Development Studies* 7, no. 1 (2007): 21–32.

Borras, Saturnino M., Jr., Ruth Hall, Ian Scoones, Ben White, and Wendy Wolford, "Towards a Better Understanding of Global Land Grabbing: An Editorial Introduction," *Journal of Peasant Studies* 38, no. 2 (2011): 209–16.

Boudreau, Julie-Anne, *Global Urban Politics: Informalization of the State* (Cambridge: Polity, 2017).

Boudreau, Julie-Anne and Diane E. Davis, "Introduction: A Processual Approach to Informalization," *Current Sociology* 65, no. 2 (2017): 151–66.

Bourdieu, Pierre, *Pascalian Meditations*, translated by Richard Nice (Stanford: Stanford University Press, 2000).

Bourdieu, Pierre, "Rethinking the State: Genesis and Structure of the Bureaucratic Field," *Sociological Theory* 12, no. 1 (1994): 1–18.

Bozzoli, Brenda, "From Governability to Ungovernability: Race, Class and Authority in South Africa's Black Cities," seminar paper (1996), Institute of Advanced Social Research, University of Witwatersrand, Johannesburg.

Bozzoli, Brenda, *Theatres of Struggle and the End of Apartheid* (Johannesburg: Wits University Press, 2004).

Brand, Danie and Christof Heyns (eds.), *Socio-economic Rights in South Africa* (Pretoria: Pretoria University Law Press, 2005).

Brand, J. G., *Building a New Town: City of Cape Town's Mitchells Plain* (Cape Town: City Engineers Department, 1979).

Budd, Jessica, "Ensuring the Right to the City: Pro-poor Housing, Urban Development and Tenure Legalization in São Paulo, Brazil," *Environment and Urbanization* 17, no. 1 (2005): 89–113.

Bundy, Colin, *The Rise and Fall of the South African Peasantry*, 2nd ed. (Cape Town: David Phillip, 1988).

Burawoy, Michael, "The Extended Case Method," *Sociological Theory* 16, no. 1 (1998): 4–33.

Burawoy, Michael, *The Extended Case Method: Four Countries, Four Decades, Four Great Transformations* (Berkeley: University of California Press, 2009).

Burawoy, Michael, "Introduction," in *Ethnography Unbound: Power and Resistance in the Modern Metropolis* by Michael Burawoy, Alice Burton, Ann Arnett Ferguson, Kathryn J. Fox, Joshua Gamson, Nadine Gartrell, Leslie Hurst, Charles Kurzman, Leslie Salzinger, Josepha Schiffman, and Shiori Ui (Berkeley: University of California Press, 1991), 1–7.

Butler, Tim, "For Gentrification?," *Environment and Planning A* 39, no. 1 (2007): 162–81.

Carlucci, Alessandro, *Gramsci and Languages: Unification, Diversity, Hegemony* (Chicago: Haymarket, 2013).

Chakrabarty, Dipesh, *Provincializing Europe: Postcolonial Thought and Historical Difference* (Princeton: Princeton University Press, 2008).

Chance, Kerry Ryan, *Living Politics in South Africa's Urban Shacklands* (Chicago: University of Chicago Press, 2017).

Chatterjee, Partha, *Lineages of Political Society: Studies in Postcolonial Democracy* (New York: Columbia University Press, 2011).

Chatterjee, Partha, *The Politics of the Governed: Reflections on Popular Politics in Most of the World* (New York: Columbia University Press, 2004).

Chiumbu, Sarah, "Exploring Mobile Phone Practices in Social Movements in South Africa: The Western Cape Anti-Eviction Campaign," *African Identities* 10, no. 2 (2012): 193–206.

Christiansen, Eric C., "Adjudicating Non-justiciable Rights: Socio-economic Rights and the South African Constitutional Court," *Columbia Human Rights Law Review* 38, no. 2 (2007): 321–86.

Christopher, A. J., *The Atlas of Changing South Africa*, 2nd ed. (London: Routledge, 2000).

Christopher, A. J., "Urban Segregation in Post-apartheid South Africa," *Urban Studies* 38, no. 3 (2001): 449–66.

Cirolia, Liza Rose, "South Africa's Emergency Housing Programme: A Prism of Urban Contest," *Development Southern Africa* 31, no. 3 (2014): 397–411.

Clarno, Andy, *Neoliberal Apartheid: Palestine/Israel and South Africa after 1994* (Chicago: University of Chicago Press, 2017).

Clarno, Andy and Martin J. Murray, "Policing in Johannesburg after Apartheid," *Social Dynamics* 39, no. 2 (2013): 210–27.

Cole, Josette, *Crossroads: The Politics of Reform and Repression, 1976–1986* (Johannesburg: Ravan, 1987).

Comaroff, John L. and Jean Comaroff, "Law and Disorder in the Postcolony: An Introduction," in *Law and Disorder in the Postcolony*, edited by Jean Comaroff and John L. Comaroff (Chicago: University of Chicago Press, 2006), 1–56.

Cook, G. P., "Cape Town," in *Homes Apart: South Africa's Segregated Cities*, edited by Anthony Lemon (Bloomington: Indiana University Press, 1991), 26–42.

Cornelissen, Scarlett, "'Our Struggles Are Bigger Than the World Cup': Civic Activism, State-Society Relations and the Socio-political Legacies of the 2010 FIFA World Cup," *British Journal of Sociology* 63, no. 2 (2012): 328–48.

Cospito, Giuseppe, *The Rhythm of Thought in Gramsci: A Diachronic Interpretation of Prison Notebooks*, translated by Arianna Ponzini (Chicago: Haymarket, 2016).

Cottle, Eddie (ed.), *South Africa's World Cup: A Legacy for Whom?* (Scottsville: University of KwaZulu-Natal Press, 2011).

Coutinho, Carlos Nelson, *Gramsci's Political Thought* (Chicago: Haymarket, 2012).

Crankshaw, Owen, "Squatting, Apartheid, and Urbanisation on the Southern Witwatersrand," *African Affairs* 92, no. 366 (1993): 31–51.

Crankshaw, Owen and Susan Parnell, "Housing Provision and the Need for an Urbanisation Policy in the New South Africa," *Urban Forum* 7, no. 2 (1996): 232–37.

Crehan, Kate, *Gramsci's Common Sense: Inequality and Its Narratives* (Durham: Duke University Press, 2016).

Daniel, Shepard, "Situating Private Equity in the Land Grab Debate," *Journal of Peasant Studies* 39, nos. 3–4 (2012): 703–29.

Davies, Robert, David Kaplan, Mike Morris, and Dan O'Meara, "Class Struggle and the Periodisation of the State in South Africa," *Review of African Political Economy* 3, no. 7 (1976): 4–30.

Davis, Mike, *Planet of Slums* (New York: Verso, 2006).

Dawson, Hannah, "Patronage from Below: Political Unrest in an Informal Settlement in South Africa," *African Affairs* 113, no. 453 (2014): 518–39.

Dawson, Hannah, "Protests, Party Politics and Patronage: A View from Zandspruit Informal Settlement, Johannesburg," in *Global Resistance in Southern Perspective: The Politics of Protest in South Africa's Contentious Democracy*, edited by Marcel Paret, Carin Runciman, and Luke Sinwell (London: Routledge, 2017), 118–33.

De Bruyn, Eva, "Campus and the City in a South African Context: Reflections on a UWC Satellite Campus in Mitchells Plain, Cape Town" (MA thesis, Department of Architecture and Urban Planning, Ghent University, 2012).

de Leon, Cedric, Manali Desai, and Cihan Tuğal (eds.), *Building Blocs: How Parties Organize Society* (Stanford: Stanford University Press, 2015).

de Leon, Cedric, Manali Desai, and Cihan Tuğal, "Political Articulation: Parties and the Constitution of Cleavages in the United States, India, and Turkey," *Sociological Theory* 27, no. 3 (2009): 193–219.

Desai, Ashwin, "Vans, Autos, Kombis, and the Drivers of Social Movements," Harold Wolpe Memorial Lecture, Centre for Civil Society, University of KwaZulu-Natal, Durban, South Africa, 28 July 2006, http://wolpetrust.org.za/dialogue2006/DN072006 desai_paper.pdf.

Desai, Ashwin, *We Are the Poors: Community Struggles in Post-apartheid South Africa* (New York: Monthly Review Press, 2002).

Desai, Ashwin and Richard Pithouse, "'But We Were Thousands': Dispossession, Resistance, Repossession, and Repression in Mandela Park," *Journal of Asian and African Studies* 39, no. 4 (2004): 239–69.

Desan, Wilfrid, *The Marxism of Jean-Paul Sartre* (New York: Doubleday, 1966).

de Schutter, Olivier, "How Not to Think of Land-Grabbing: Three Critiques of Large-Scale Investments in Farmland," *Journal of Peasant Studies* 38, no. 2 (2011): 249–79.

de Soto, Hernando, *The Mystery of Capital: Why Capitalism Triumphs in the West and Fails Everywhere Else* (New York: Basic, 2003).

de Soto, Hernando, *The Other Path: The Invisible Revolution in the Third World* (New York: HarperCollins, 1989).

de Vos, Pierre, "*Grootboom*, the Right of Access to Housing and Substantive Equality as Contextual Fairness," *South African Journal on Human Rights* 17, no. 2 (2001): 258–76.

Desmond, Cosmas, *The Discarded People: An Account of African Resettlement in South Africa* (Middlesex: Penguin, 1971).

Diphoorn, Tessa G., *Twilight Policing: Private Security and Violence in Urban South Africa* (Berkeley: University of California Press, 2015).

Douglas, Mary, *Purity and Danger: An Analysis of Concepts of Pollution and Taboo* (London: Routledge, 2002).

Draper, Hal, *Karl Marx's Theory of Revolution, Vol. II: The Politics of Social Classes* (New York: Monthly Review, 1978).

Dubow, Saul, *Apartheid, 1948–1994* (Oxford: Oxford University Press, 2014).

Dubow, Saul, *Racial Segregation and the Origins of Apartheid in South Africa, 1919–36* (New York: Palgrave Macmillan, 1989).

Dugard, Jackie, "Choice from No Choice; Rights for the Left? The State, Law and the Struggle against Prepayment Water Meters in South Africa," in *Social Movements in the Global South: Dispossession, Development, and Resistance*, edited by Sara C. Motta and Alf Gunvald Nilsen (London: Palgrave Macmillan, 2011), 59–82.

Durrheim, Kevin, Xoliswa Mtose, and Lyndsay Brown, *Race Trouble: Race, Identity, and Inequality in Post-apartheid South Africa* (Lanham, MD: Lexington, 2011).

Dwyer, Michael B., "Building the Politics Machine: Tools for 'Resolving' the Global Land Grab," *Development and Change* 44, no. 2 (2013): 309–33.

Eidlin, Barry, "Why Is There No Labor Party in the United States? Political Articulation and the Canadian Comparison, 1932 to 1948," *American Sociological Review* 81, no. 3 (2016): 488–516.

Ellis, Stephen, "The Historical Significance of South Africa's Third Force," *Journal of Southern African Studies* 24, no. 2 (1998): 261–99.

Engels, Friedrich, *The Housing Question* (New York: International, n.d. [1872]).

Evans, Ivan, *Bureaucracy and Race: Native Administration in South Africa* (Berkeley: University of California Press, 1997).

Evans, Peter, "Counterhegemonic Globalization: Transnational Social Movements in the Contemporary Global Political Economy," in *The Handbook of Political Sociology: States, Civil Societies, and Globalization*, edited by Thomas Janoski, Robert Alford, Alexander Hicks, and Mildred A. Schwartz (Cambridge: Cambridge University Press, 2005), 655–70.

Evans, Peter, "Is an Alternative Globalisation Possible?," *Politics & Society* 36, no. 2 (2008): 271–305.

Fanon, Frantz, *Wretched of the Earth*, translated by Richard Philcox (New York: Grove, 2004 [1961]).

Fernandes, Édesio, "Implementing the Urban Reform Agenda in Brazil," *Environment and Urbanization* 19, no. 1 (2007): 183.

Fields, Barbara Jeanne, "Slavery, Race and Ideology in the United States of America," *New Left Review* I/181 (1990): 95–118.

Fiske, John, "Surveilling the City: Whiteness, the Black Man, and Democratic Totalitarianism," *Theory, Culture & Society* 15, no. 2 (1998): 67–88.

Flynn, Thomas R., *Sartre and Marxist Existentialism* (Chicago: University of Chicago Press, 1984).

Foucault, Michel, *Discipline and Punish: The Birth of the Prison*, translated by Alan Sheridan (New York: Vintage, 1995).

Foucault, Michel, *History of Sexuality*, vol. 1, *An Introduction*, translated by Robert Hurley (New York: Vintage, 1990).

Foucault, Michel, *Security, Territory, Population: Lectures at the Collège de France, 1977–1978* (New York: Picador, 2007).

Foucault, Michel, "The Subject and Power," in *Michel Foucault: Beyond Structuralism and Hermeneutics*, by Hubert Dreyfus and Paul Rabinow (Chicago: University of Chicago Press, 1982).

Freund, Bill, *The African City: A History* (Cambridge: Cambridge University Press, 2007).

Freund, Bill, "Is There Such a Thing as a Post-apartheid City?," *Urban Forum* 21, no. 3 (2010): 283–98.

Freund, Bill, *Twentieth-Century South Africa: A Developmental History* (Cambridge: Cambridge University Press, 2019).

Gans, Herbert J., "Positive Functions of the Undeserving Poor: Uses of the Underclass in America," *Politics and Society* 22, no. 3 (1994): 269–83.

Garrido, Marco Z., *The Patchwork City: Class, Space, and Politics in Metro Manila* (Chicago: University of Chicago Press, 2019).

Gelb, Stephen, *South Africa's Economic Crisis* (London: Zed, 1991).

Gerhart, Gail M. and Clive L. Glaser (eds.), *From Protest to Challenge: A Documentary History of African Politics in South Africa, 1882–1990*, vol. 6, *Challenge and Victory, 1980–1990* (Bloomington: Indiana University Press, 2010).

Ghertner, D. Asher, "An Analysis of New Legal Discourse behind Delhi's Slum Demolitions," *Economic and Political Weekly* 43, no. 20 (2008): 57–66.

Ghertner, D. Asher, "Calculating without Numbers: Aesthetic Governmentality in Delhi's Slums," *Economy and Society* 39, no. 2 (2010): 185–217.

Ghertner, D. Asher, *Rule by Aesthetics: World-Class City Making in Delhi* (New York: Oxford University Press, 2015).

Ghertner, D. Asher, "Why Gentrification Theory Fails in 'Much of the World,'" *City* 19, no. 4 (2015): 552–63.

Gibson, Nigel C. (ed.), *Challenging Hegemony: Social Movements and the Quest for a New Humanism in Post-apartheid South Africa* (Trenton: Africa World Press, 2006).

Gibson, Nigel C., *Fanonian Practices in South Africa: From Steve Biko to Abahlali baseMjondolo* (Scottsville: University of KwaZulu-Natal Press, 2011).

Gibson, Nigel C., "Poor People's Movements in South Africa—the Anti-Eviction Campaign in Mandela Park: A Critical Discussion," *Journal of Asian and African Studies* 39, no. 4 (2004): 233–37.

Gibson, Nigel C., "Upright and Free: Fanon in South Africa, from Biko to the Shackdwellers' Movement (Abahlali baseMjondolo)," *Social Identities* 14, no. 6 (2008): 683–715.

Gilbert, Alan, "Return of the Slum: Does Language Matter?," *International Journal of Urban and Regional Research* 31, no. 4 (2007): 697–713.

Glassman, James, "Primitive Accumulation, Accumulation by Dispossession, Accumulation by 'Extra-economic' Means," *Progress in Human Geography* 30, no. 5 (2006): 608–25.

Goertzel, Ted G., "Political Society," in *International Encyclopedia of Civil Society*, edited by Helmut K. Anheier and Stefan Toepler (New York: Springer, 2010), 1248–50.

Goldin, Ian, "The Poverty of Coloured Labour Preference: Economics and Ideology in the Western Cape," SALDRU Working Paper no. 59, Cape Town (1984).

Gonçalves dos Santos, Caroline and Flávio A. Miranda de Souza, "My House, My Life: The Reproduction of Socio-spatial Inequalities in Maceió—AL, Brazil," presentation at the International Sociological Association's RC43: Housing and the Built Environment Conference, panel "Institutions and Access to Housing in Brazil," 18 September 2015, University of Illinois–Chicago, Chicago.

Gramsci, Antonio, *Letters from Prison*, vol. 2, edited by Frank Rosengarten and translated by Raymond Rosenthal (New York: Columbia, 1994).

Gramsci, Antonio, *Selections from the Prison Notebooks*, edited and translated by Quinton Hoare and Geoffrey Nowell Smith (New York: International, 1971).

Greenberg, Stephen, "Land Reform and Transition in South Africa," *Transformation* 52 (2003): 42–67.

Guelke, Adrian, "Interpretations of Political Violence during South Africa's Transition," *Politikon* 27, no. 2 (2000): 239–54.

Guha, Ranajit, *Elementary Aspects of Peasant Insurgency in Colonial India* (Durham: Duke University Press, 1999).

Guha, Ranajit, "On Some Aspects of the Historiography of Colonial India," in *Subaltern Studies No. 1: Writings on South Asian History and Society*, edited by Ranajit Guha (Oxford: Oxford University Press, 1982), 1–8.

Hackworth, Jason, *The Neoliberal City: Governance, Ideology, and Development in American Urbanism* (Ithaca: Cornell University Press, 2007).

Hackworth, Jason and Neil Smith, "The Changing State of Gentrification," *Tijdschrift voor economische en sociale geografie* 92, no. 4 (2001): 464–77.

Hall, Derek, "Primitive Accumulation, Accumulation by Dispossession, and the Global Land Grab," *Third World Quarterly* 34, no. 9 (2013): 1582–604.

Hall, Ruth, "A Political Economy of Land Reform in South Africa," *Review of African Political Economy* 31, no. 100 (2004): 213–27.

Hall, Stuart, *Cultural Studies 1983: A Theoretical History* (Durham: Duke University Press, 2016).

Hall, Stuart, "Gramsci and Us," in *The Hard Road to Renewal: Thatcherism and the Crisis of the Left* (New York: Verso, 1988), 161–73.

Hall, Stuart, "The Problem of Ideology: Marxism without Guarantees," in *Stuart Hall: Critical Dialogues in Cultural Studies*, edited by David Morley and Kuan-Hsing Chen (London: Routledge, 1996), 25–46.

Hall, Stuart, "Race, Articulation, and Societies Structured in Dominance," in *Essential Essays*, vol. 1, edited by David Morley (Durham: Duke University Press, 2019), 172–221.

Hall, Stuart, "Signification, Representation, Ideology: Althusser and the Post-structuralist Debates," *Critical Studies in Mass Communication* 2, no. 2 (1985): 91–114.

Hall, Stuart, Chas Critcher, Tony Jefferson, John Clarke, and Brian Roberts, *Policing the Crisis: Mugging, the State, and Law and Order*, 2nd ed. (London: Palgrave, 2013).

Harrison, Philip and Alison Todes, "Spatial Transformations in a 'Loosening State': South Africa in a Comparative Perspective," *Geoforum* 61 (2015): 148–62.

Harrison, Philip, Alison Todes, and Vanessa Watson, *Planning and Transformation: Learning from the Post-apartheid Experience* (London: Routledge, 2008).

Hart, Deborah M., "Political Manipulation of Urban Space: The Razing of District Six, Cape Town," *Urban Geography* 9, no. 6 (1988): 603–28.

Hart, Gillian, "Denaturalizing Dispossession: Critical Ethnography in the Age of Resurgent Imperialism," *Antipode* 38, no. 5 (2006).

Hart, Gillian, *Disabling Globalization: Places of Power in Post-apartheid South Africa* (Berkeley: University of California Press, 2002).

Hart, Gillian, "Post-apartheid Developments in Historical and Comparative Perspective," in *The Development Decade? Economic and Social Change in South Africa, 1994–2004*, edited by Vishnu Padayachee (Pretoria: HSRC Press, 2006), 13–32.

Hart, Gillian, "The Provocations of Neoliberalism: Contesting the Nation and Liberation after Apartheid," *Antipode* 40, no. 4 (2008): 678–705.

Hart, Gillian, *Rethinking the South African Crisis: Nationalism, Populism, Hegemony* (Scottsville: University of KwaZulu-Natal Press, 2013).

Hartman, Chester W., "The Right to Stay Put," in *Land Reform, American Style*, edited by Charles C. Geisler and Frank J. Popper (Totowa: Rowan & Allanheld, 1984), 302–18.

Harvey, David, "From Managerialism to Entrepreneurialism: The Transformation in Urban Governance in Late Capitalism," *Geografiska Annaler. Series B, Human Geography* 71, no. 1 (1989): 3–17.

Harvey, David, *The Urbanization of Capital* (Malden: Blackwell, 1985).

Harvey, David, *Paris, Capital of Modernity* (London: Routledge, 2004).

Haug, Wolfgang Fritz, "From Marx to Gramsci, from Gramsci to Marx: Historical Materialism and the Philosophy of Praxis," *Rethinking Marxism* 13, no. 1 (2001): 69–82.

Haug, Wolfgang Fritz, "Rethinking Gramsci's Philosophy of Praxis from One Century to the Next," *boundary2* 26, no. 2 (1999): 101–17.

Heller, Patrick and Libhongo Ntlokonkulu, "A Civic Movement or a Movement of Civics? The South African National Civic Organisation (SANCO) in the Post-apartheid Period," Johannesburg, Centre for Policy Studies, 2001.

Hendricks, Fred, Lungisile Ntsebeza, and Kirk Helliker (eds.), *The Promise of Land: Undoing a Century of Dispossession in South Africa* (Johannesburg: Jacana, 2013).

Hentschel, Christine, *Security in the Bubble: Navigating Crime in Urban South Africa* (Minneapolis: University of Minnesota Press, 2015).

Hindson, Doug, *Pass Controls and the Urban African Proletariat* (Johannesburg: Ravan, 1987).

Hinton, Elizabeth, *America on Fire: The Untold History of Police Violence and Black Rebellion since the 1960s* (New York: Liveright, 2021).

Hirota, Hidetaka, *Expelling the Poor: Atlantic Seaboard States and the 19th-Century Origins of American Immigration Policy* (Oxford: Oxford University Press, 2017).

Hobsbawm, Eric, *Primitive Rebels: Studies in Archaic Forms of Social Movement in the 19th and 20th Centuries* (New York: Norton, 1965).

Holston, James (ed.), *Cities and Citizenship* (Durham: Duke University Press, 1998).

Holston, James, *Insurgent Citizenship: Disjunctions of Democracy and Modernity in Brazil* (Princeton: Princeton University Press, 2008).

Huchzermeyer, Marie, *Cities* with *"Slums": From Informal Settlement Eradication to a Right to the City in Africa* (Cape Town: University of Cape Town Press, 2011).

Huchzermeyer, Marie, "Housing for the Poor? Negotiated Housing Policy in South Africa," *Habitat International* 25, no. 3 (2001): 303–31.

Huchzermeyer, Marie, "Housing Rights in South Africa: Invasions, Evictions, the Media, and the Courts in the Cases of Grootboom, Alexandra, and Bredell," *Urban Forum* 14, no. 1 (2003): 80–107.

Huchzermeyer, Marie, "Invoking Lefebvre's 'Right to the City' in South Africa Today: A Response to Walsh," *City* 18, no. 1 (2014): 41–49.

Huchzermeyer, Marie, "A Legacy of Control? The Capital Subsidy for Housing and Informal Settlement Intervention in South Africa," *International Journal of Urban and Regional Research* 27, no. 3 (2003): 591–612.

Huchzermeyer, Marie, "The New Instrument for Upgrading Informal Settlements in South Africa: Contributions and Constraints," in *Informal Settlements: A Perpetual Challenge?*, edited by Marie Huchzermeyer and Aly Karam (Cape Town: University of Cape Town Press, 2006), 41–61.

Huchzermeyer, Marie, "'Slum' Upgrading or 'Slum' Eradication? The Mixed Message of the MDGs," in *The Millennium Development Goals and Human Rights: Past, Present and Future*, edited by Malcolm Langford, Andy Sumner, and Alicia Ely Yamin (Cambridge: Cambridge University Press, 2013), 295–315.

Huchzermeyer, Marie, *Unlawful Occupation: Informal Settlements and Urban Policy in South Africa and Brazil* (Trenton: Africa World Press, 2004).

Humphries, Richard, "Administrative Politics and the Coloured Labour Preference Policy during the 1960s," in *The Angry Divide: Social and Economic History of the Western Cape*, edited by Wilmot G. James and Mary Simons (Cape Town: David Philip, 1989), 169–79.

Hunter, Mark, "The Forgotten World of Transit Camps" (2012), http://abahlali.org/node/9231/.

Hunter, Mark and Dorrit Posel, "Here to Work: The Socioeconomic Characteristics of Informal Dwellers in Post-apartheid South Africa," *Environment and Urbanization* 24 (2012): 285–304.

Ives, Peter, *Language and Hegemony in Gramsci* (London: Pluto, 2004).

Jeffrey, Anthea, *People's War: New Light on the Struggle for South Africa* (Cape Town: Jonathan Ball, 2009).

Jordan, David B., *Transforming Paris: The Life and Labors of Baron Haussmann* (New York: Free Press, 1995).

Kahanovitz, Steve, "An Urban Slice of PIE: The Prevention of Illegal Eviction from and Unlawful Occupation of Land Act in South Africa," case study prepared for the *Global Report on Human Settlements* (2007), https://unhabitat.org/wp-content/uploads/2008/07/5403_20137_GRHS.2007.CaseStudy.Tenure.SouthAfrica.pdf.

Katz, Jack, "A Theory of Qualitative Methodology: The Social System of Analytic Fieldwork," in *Contemporary Field Research: Perspectives and Formulations*, edited by Robert M. Emerson (Prospect Heights, IL: Waveland, 1983), 127–48.

Katz, Michael B., *The Undeserving Poor: America's Enduring Confrontation with Poverty*, 2nd ed. (Oxford: Oxford University Press, 2013).

Kaufman, Stuart J., "South Africa's Civil War, 1985–1995," *South African Journal of International Affairs* 24, no. 4 (2018): 501–21.

Kende, Mark S., "The South African Constitutional Court's Embrace of Socio-economic Rights: A Comparative Perspective," *Chapman Law Review* 6 (2003): 137–60.

Kondlo, Kwandiwe, *In the Twilight of the Revolution: The Pan Africanist Congress of Azania (South Africa), 1959–1994* (Basel: Basler Afrika Bibliographien, 2009).

Labriola, Antonio, *Essays on the Materialistic Conception of History*, translated by Charles H. Kerr (New York: Monthly Review Press, 1966).

Labriola, Antonio, *Socialism and Philosophy*, translated by Ernest Untermann (St. Louis: Telos, 1980).

Laclau, Ernesto, *The Rhetorical Foundations of Society* (New York: Verso, 2014).

Laclau, Ernesto, "Towards a Theory of Populism," in *Politics and Ideology in Marxist Theory: Capitalism, Fascism, Populism* (New York: Verso, 1977), 143–98.

Laclau, Ernesto and Chantal Mouffe, *Hegemony and Socialist Strategy: Towards a Radical Democratic Politics* (New York: Verso, 1985).

Lancaster, Lizette and Rushdi Nackerdien, "What Does Increasing Political Violence Mean for the Future of South Africa's Democracy?," Institute for Security Studies, 13 May 2014, https://issafrica. org/iss-today/what-does-increasing-political-violence-mean-for-the-future-of-south-africas-democracy.

Lavers, Tom, "'Land Grab' as Development Strategy? The Political Economy of Agricultural Investment in Ethiopia," *Journal of Peasant Studies* 39, no. 1 (2012): 105–32.

Le Grange, Richard, "Mitchells Plain: A Case Study in the Housing Question of South Africa" (honors thesis, Department of Sociology, University of Cape Town, 1987).

Lederman, Jacob, *Chasing World-Class Urbanism: Global Policy versus Everyday Survival in Buenos Aires* (Minneapolis: University of Minnesota Press, 2020).

Lees, Loretta, Hyun Bang Shin, and Ernesto López-Morales (eds.), *Global Gentrifications: Uneven Development and Displacement* (Bristol: Policy Press, 2015).

Lees, Loretta, Hyun Bang Shin, and Ernesto López-Morales, *Planetary Gentrification* (Cambridge: Polity, 2016).

Lees, Loretta, Tom Slater, and Elvin Wyly, *Gentrification* (London: Routledge, 2008).

Legassick, Martin, *Armed Struggle and Democracy: The Case of South Africa* (Uppsala: Nordiska Afrikainstitutet, 2002).

Legassick, Martin, *Hidden Histories of Gordonia: Land Dispossession and Resistance in the Northern Cape, 1800–1990* (Johannesburg: Wits University Press, 2016).

Legassick, Martin, *The Struggle for the Eastern Cape, 1800–1854: Subjugation and the Roots of South African Democracy* (Randburg: KMM Review, 2010).

Lemanski, Charlotte, "Augmented Informality: South Africa's Backyard Dwellings as a By-Product of Formal Housing Policies," *Habitat International* 33, no. 4 (2009). 472–84.

Lemanski, Charlotte, "Global Cities in the South: Deepening Social and Spatial Polarisation in Cape Town," *Cities* 24, no. 6 (2007): 448–61.

Lemanski, Charlotte, "A New Apartheid? The Spatial Implications of Fear of Crime in Cape Town, South Africa," *Environment and Urbanization* 16, no. 2 (2004): 101–12.

Levenson, Zachary, "Becoming a Population: Seeing the State, Being Seen by the State, and the Politics of Eviction in Cape Town," *Qualitative Sociology* 44, no. 3 (2021): 367–84.

Levenson, Zachary, "Permanent Temporariness: Relocation Camps in Post-apartheid Cape Town," *SLUM Lab* 9 (2014): 156–58.

Levenson, Zachary, "Precarious Welfare States: Urban Struggles over Housing Delivery in Post-apartheid Cape Town," *International Sociology* 32, no. 4 (2017): 474–92.

Levenson, Zachary, "The Road to TRAs Is Paved with Good Intentions: Dispossession through Delivery in Post-apartheid Cape Town," *Urban Studies* 55, no. 14 (2018): 3218–33.

Levenson, Zachary, "Social Movements beyond Incorporation: The Case of the Housing Assembly in Post-apartheid Cape Town," in *Global Resistance in Southern Perspective: The Politics of Protest in South Africa's Contentious Democracy*, edited by Marcel Paret, Carin Runciman, and Luke Sinwell (London: Routledge, 2017), 89–104.

Levenson, Zachary, "South African Evictions Today," *Contexts* 20, no. 1 (2021): 26–31.

Levenson, Zachary, "'Such Elements Do Not Belong in an Ordered Society': Managing Rural-Urban Resettlement in Democratic South Africa," *Journal of Agrarian Change* 19, no. 3 (2019): 427–46.

Levenson, Zachary and Sean Jacobs, "The Limits of Coloured Nationalism," *Mail & Guardian*, 15 June 2018, 32.

Levien, Michael, *Dispossession without Development: Land Grabs in Neoliberal India* (Oxford: Oxford University Press, 2018).

Levien, Michael, "The Land Question: Special Economic Zones and the Political Economy of Dispossession in India," *Journal of Peasant Studies* 39, no. 3–4 (2012): 933–69.

Levin, Richard and Daniel Weiner, "The Politics of Land Reform in South Africa after Apartheid: Perspectives, Problems, Prospects," *Journal of Peasant Studies* 23, no. 2–3 (1996): 93–119.

Levy, Norman, *The Foundations of the South African Cheap Labour System* (London: Routledge and Kegan Paul, 1982).

Levy, Peter B., *The Great Uprising: Race Riots in Urban America during the 1960s* (Cambridge: Cambridge University Press).

Ley, David, *The New Middle Class and the Remaking of the Central City* (Oxford: Oxford University Press, 1996).

Li, Tania Murray, "Centering Labor in the Land Grab Debate," *Journal of Peasant Studies* 38, no. 2 (2011): 281–98.

Liebenberg, Sandra, "The Right to Social Assistance: The Implications of *Grootboom* for Policy Reform in South Africa," *South African Journal on Human Rights* 17, no. 2 (2001): 232–57.

Liebenberg, Sandra and Beth Goldblatt, "The Interrelationship between Equality and Socio-economic Rights under South Africa's Transformative Constitution," *South African Journal on Human Rights* 23, no. 2 (2007): 335–61.

Liguori, Guido, *Gramsci's Pathways*, translated by David Broder (Chicago: Haymarket, 2015).

Lodge, Tom, *Black Politics in South Africa since 1945* (London: Longman, 1983).

Lodge, Tom, *Sharpeville: A Massacre and Its Consequences* (Oxford: Oxford University Press, 2011).

Lodge, Tom and Bill Nasson, *All, Here, and Now: Black Politics in South Africa in the 1980s* (New York: Ford Foundation, 1991).

Loftus, Alex, "Reification and the Dictatorship of the Water Meter," *Antipode* 38, no. 5 (2006): 1023–45.

Logan, John R. and Harvey Molotch, *Urban Fortunes: The Political Economy of Place* (Berkeley: University of California Press, 1987).

Mabin, Alan, "Comprehensive Segregation: The Origins of the Group Areas Act and Its Planning Apparatuses," *Journal of Southern African Studies* 18, no. 2 (1992): 405–29.

Mabin, Alan, "On the Problems and Prospects of Overcoming Segregation and Fragmentation in South African Cities," in *Postmodern Cities and Spaces*, edited by Sophie Watson and Katherine Gibson (Malden: Wiley-Blackwell, 1996), 187–98.

Mabin, D. S., "Mitchells Plain," in *Conference of the Institute of Housing Management* (Durban, September 1977).

MacDonald, Michael, *Why Race Matters in South Africa* (Cambridge: Harvard University Press, 2012).

Macgregor, Helen, Zama Mgwatyu, and Warren Smit, *Living on the Edge: A Study of the Delft Temporary Relocation Area* (Cape Town: Development Action Group, 2007).

Magaziner, Daniel R., *The Law and the Prophets: Black Consciousness in South Africa, 1968–1977* (Athens: Ohio University Press, 2010).

Magubane, Bernard Makhosezwe, *The Political Economy of Race and Class in South Africa* (New York: Monthly Review, 1979).

Maharaj, Brij, "The Group Areas Act and Community Destruction in South Africa: The Struggle for Cato Manor in Durban," *Urban Forum* 5, no. 2 (1994): 1–25.

Mahon, Claire, *Fair Play for Housing Rights: Mega-events, Olympic Games and Housing Rights—Opportunities for the Olympic Movement and Others* (Geneva: Centre on Housing Rights and Evictions, 2007).

Majavu, Mandisi, "Making Sense of Municipal Revolts," *Development in Focus* 1, no. 2 (2011): 4–6.

Makhulu, Anne-Maria, *Making Freedom: Apartheid, Squatter Politics, and the Struggle for Home* (Durham: Duke University Press, 2015).

Marais, Hein, *South Africa Pushed to the Limit: The Political Economy of Change* (London: Zed Books, 2011).

Maré, Gerhard, *African Population Relocation in South Africa* (Johannesburg: South African Institute of Race Relations, 1980).

Maré, Gerhard and Georgina Hamilton, *An Appetite for Power: Buthelezi's Inkatha and South Africa* (Johannesburg: Ravan, 1987).

Marx, Karl. *Capital*, vol. 1 (New York: Penguin, 1976).

Marx, Karl, *Critique of Hegel's Philosophy of Right* (Cambridge: Cambridge University Press, 1970).

Marx, Karl, *Economic and Philosophic Manuscripts of 1844* (Amherst: Prometheus, 1988).

Marx, Karl, *The Eighteenth Brumaire of Louis Bonaparte* (New York: International, 1963 [1852]).

Marx, Karl, "On Feuerbach," in *Early Political Writings*, edited and translated by Joseph O'Malley (Cambridge: Cambridge University Press, 1994).

Marx, Karl and Friedrich Engels, *The Communist Manifesto: A Road Map to History's Most Important Political Document* (Chicago: Haymarket, 2005 [1848]).

Marx, Karl and Friedrich Engels, "Manifesto of the Communist Party," in *Later Political Writings*, edited and translated by Terrell Carver (Cambridge: Cambridge University Press, 1996 [1848]).

Marx, Karl and Friedrich Engels, "Marx and Engels to Bebel, Liebknecht, Bracke and Others [London, Middle of September, 1879 (Draft)]," in *Selected Correspondence, 1846-1895*, translated by Dona Torr (New York: International, 1942).

Maseko, Sipho S., "Civic Movement and Non-violent Action: The Case of the Cape Areas Housing Action Committee," *African Affairs* 96, no. 384 (1997): 353-69.

Maskovsky, Jeff, "'Managing' the Poor: Neoliberalism, Medicaid HMOs and the Triumph of Consumerism among the Poor," *Medical Anthropology* 19, no. 2 (2000): 121-46.

Maylam, Paul, "Explaining the Apartheid City: 20 Years of South African Urban Historiography," *Journal of Southern African Studies* 21, no. 1 (1995): 19-38.

Maylam, Paul, *South Africa's Racial Past: The History and Historiography of Racism*, 2nd ed. (London: Routledge, 2016).

McCarthy, John D. and Mayer N. Zald, "Resource Mobilization and Social Movements: A Partial Theory," *American Journal of Sociology* 82, no. 6 (1977): 1212-41.

McDonald, David A., *World City Syndrome: Neoliberalism and Inequality in Cape Town* (London: Routledge, 2008).

McDonald, David A. and John Pape, *Cost Recovery and the Crisis of Service Delivery in South Africa* (London: Zed, 2002).

McDonald, David A. and Greg Ruiters (eds.), *The Age of Commodity: Water Privatization in Southern Africa* (New York: Earthscan, 2005).

McFarlane, Colin and Jonathan Silver, "The Poolitical City: 'Seeing Sanitation' and Making the Urban Political in Cape Town," *Antipode* 49, no. 1 (2017): 125-48.

McMichael, Philip, "The Land Grab and Corporate Food Regime Restructuring," *Journal of Peasant Studies* 39, nos. 3-4 (2012): 681-701.

Miraftab, Faranak, "Colonial Present: Legacies of the Past in Contemporary Urban Practices in Cape Town, South Africa," *Journal of Planning History* 11, no. 4 (2012): 283-307.

Miraftab, Faranak, "Feminist Praxis, Citizenship and Informal Politics: Reflections on South Africa's Anti-Eviction Campaign," *International Feminist Journal of Politics* 8, no. 2 (2006): 194-218.

Miraftab, Faranak, "Governing Post-apartheid Spatiality: Implementing City Improvement Districts in Cape Town," *Antipode* 39, no. 4 (2007): 602-26.

Miraftab, Faranak, "Neoliberalism and the Casualization of Public Sector Services: The Case of Waste Collection Services in Cape Town, South Africa," *International Journal of Urban and Regional Research* 28, no. 4 (2004): 874-92.

Miraftab, Faranak and Shana Wills, "Insurgency and Spaces of Active Citizenship: The Story of the Western Cape Anti-Eviction Campaign in South Africa," *Journal of Planning Education and Research* 2 (2005): 200-217.

Mitchell, Don, *The Right to the City: Social Justice and the Fight for Public Space* (New York: Guilford, 2003).

Mngxitama, Andile, "The Taming of Land Resistance: Lessons from the National Land Committee," *Journal of Asian and African Studies* 41, nos. 1-2 (2006): 39-69.

Molotch, Harvey, "The City as a Growth Machine," *American Journal of Sociology* 82 (1976): 309-30.

Morris, Alan, "Continuity or Rupture: The City, Post-apartheid," *Social Research* 65, no. 4 (1998): 759-75.

Morris, Pauline, *A History of Black Housing in South Africa* (Johannesburg: South Africa Foundation, 1981).

Mottiar, Shauna and Tom Lodge, "'Living inside the Movement': The Right2Know Campaign, South Africa," *Transformation* 102 (2020): 95–120.

Mouffe, Chantal, *The Democratic Paradox* (New York: Verso, 2000).

Mubangizi, John Cantius, "The Constitutional Protection of Socio-economic Rights in Selected African Countries: A Comparative Evaluation," *African Journal of Legal Studies* 2, no. 1 (2006): 1–19.

Murray, Adrian, "Capitalism, Class, and Collective Identity: Social Movements and Public Services in South Africa," in *Considering Class: Theory, Culture, and the Media in the 21st Century*, edited by Deirdre O'Neill and Mike Wayne (Leiden: Brill, 2018), 149–65.

Murray, Adrian, "Contention and Class: Social Movements and Public Services in South Africa" (PhD dissertation, University of Ottawa, 2020).

Murray, Adrian, "A Decent House, a Decent Job, a Decent Life: Social Reproduction Theory and Working Class Organizing in Cape Town," *Socialist Studies* 14, no. 1 (2020): 1–19.

Murray, Martin J., *Taming the Disorderly City: The Spatial Landscape of Johannesburg after Apartheid* (Ithaca: Cornell University Press, 2008).

Naidoo, Prishani, "Struggles around the Commodification of Daily Life in South Africa," *Review of African Political Economy* 34, no. 111 (2007): 57–66.

Narsiah, Sagie, "Neoliberalism and Privatisation in South Africa," *GeoJournal* 57, no. 1 (2002): 3–13.

Newton, Caroline, "The Reverse Side of the Medal: About the 2010 FIFA World Cup and the Beautification of the N2 in Cape Town," *Urban Forum* 20, no. 1 (2009): 93–108.

Ngwane, Trevor, *Amakomiti: Grassroots Democracy in South African Shack Settlements* (London: Pluto, 2021).

Nieftagodien, Noor and Sally Gaule, *Orlando West, Soweto: An Illustrated History* (Johannesburg: Wits University Press, 2012).

Nleya, Ndodana, "Linking Service Delivery and Protest in South Africa: An Exploration of Evidence from Khayelitsha," *Africanus* 41, no. 1 (2011): 3–13.

Ntsebeza, Lungisile and Ruth Hall (eds.), *The Land Question in South Africa: The Challenges of Transformation and Redistribution* (Cape Town: HSRC Press, 2007).

Nuttall, Sarah and Achille Mbembe (eds.), *Johannesburg: The Elusive Metropolis* (Durham: Duke University Press, 2008).

Ogura, Mitsuo, "Urbanization and Apartheid in South Africa: Influx Controls and Their Abolition," *Developing Economies* 34, no. 4 (1996): 402–23.

Oldfield, Sophie, "Local State Restructuring and Urban Transformation in Post-apartheid Cape Town," *GeoJournal* 57 (2002): 29–37.

Oldfield, Sophie and Saskia Greyling, "Waiting for the State: A Politics of Housing in South Africa," *Environment and Planning A* 47, no. 5 (2015): 1100–12.

Oldfield, Sophie and Kristian Stokke, "Building Unity in Diversity: Social Movement Activism in the Western Cape Anti-Eviction Campaign," in *Voices of Protest: Social Movements in Post-apartheid South Africa*, edited by Richard Ballard, Adam Habib, and Imraan Valodia (Scottsville: University of KwaZulu-Natal Press, 2006), 111–32.

Oldfield, Sophie and Kristian Stokke, "Political Polemics and Local Practices of Community Organizing and Neoliberal Politics in South Africa," in *Contesting Neoliberalism: Urban Frontiers*, edited by Helga Leitner, Jamie Peck, and Eric S. Sheppard (New York: Guilford, 2007), 139–56.

O'Meara, Dan, *Forty Lost Years: The Apartheid State and the Politics of the National Party, 1948–1994* (Johannesburg: Ravan, 1996).

Paret, Marcel, "Violence and Democracy in South Africa's Community Protests," *Review of African Political Economy* 42, no. 143 (2015): 107–23.

Park, Robert E. and Ernest W. Burgess, *The City: Suggestions for Investigation of Human Behavior in the Urban Environment* (Chicago: University of Chicago Press, 1984 [1925]).

Parnell, Susan, "Constructing a Developmental Nation: The Challenge of Including the Poor in the Post-apartheid City," *Transformation* 58 (2005): 20–44.

Patel, Raj, "A Short Course in Politics at the University of Abahlali baseMjondolo," *Journal of Asian and African Studies* 43, no. 1 (2008): 95–112.

Peet, Richard, "Ideology, Discourse, and the Geography of Hegemony: From Socialist to Neoliberal Development in Postapartheid South Africa," *Antipode* 34, no. 1 (2002): 54–84.

Perelman, Michael, *The Invention of Capitalism* (Durham: Duke University Press, 2000).

Perlman, Janice, *Favela: Four Decades of Living on the Edge in Rio de Janeiro* (Oxford: Oxford University Press, 2010).

Perlman, Janice, *The Myth of Marginality: Urban Poverty and Politics in Rio de Janeiro* (Berkeley: University of California Press, 1976).

Peters, Pauline E., "Conflicts over Land and Threats to Customary Tenure in Africa," *African Affairs* 112, no. 449 (2013): 543–62.

Pillay, Sarita, Shaun Russell, Julian Sendin, Martha Sithole, Nick Budlender, and Daneel Knoetze, *I Used to Live There: A Call for Transitional Housing for Evictees in Cape Town* (Cape Town: Ndifuna Ukwazi, 2017).

Pillay, Udesh and Orli Bass, "Mega-events as a Response to Poverty Reduction: The 2010 FIFA World Cup and Its Urban Development Implications," *Urban Forum* 19 (2008): 329–46.

Pillay, Udesh, Richard Tomlinson, and Jacques du Toit (eds.), *Democracy and Delivery: Urban Policy in South Africa* (Cape Town: Human Sciences Research Council, 2007).

Pithouse, Richard, "Abahlali baseMjondolo and the Struggle for the City in Durban, South Africa,. *Cidades* 6 no. 9 (2008): 241–70.

Pithouse, Richard, "Our Struggle Is Thought, on the Ground, Running: The University of Abahlali baseMjondolo," in *Yonk' Indawo Umzabalazo Uyasivumela: New Work from Durban— Centre for Civil Society Research Reports*, vol. 1, edited by Amanda Alexander and Richard Pithouse (Durban: Centre for Civil Society, University of KwaZulu-Natal, 2006), 5–47.

Pithouse, Richard, "A Politics of the Poor: Shack Dwellers' Struggles in Durban," *Journal of Asian and African Studies* 43, no. 1 (2008): 63–94.

Pithouse, Richard, "Struggle Is a School: The Rise of a Shack Dwellers' Movement in Durban, South Africa," *Monthly Review* 57, no. 9 (2006): 30–52.

Piven, Frances Fox and Richard A. Cloward, *Regulating the Poor: The Functions of Public Welfare* (New York: Vintage, 1993 [1971]).

Platzky, Lauren and Cheryl Walker, *The Surplus People: Forced Removals in South Africa* (Johannesburg: Ravan, 1985).

Pointer, Rebecca, "Questioning the Representation of South Africa's 'New Social Movements': A Case Study of the Mandela Park Anti-Eviction Campaign," *Journal of Asian and African Studies* 39, no. 4 (2004): 271–94.

Porter, Roy, *London: A Social History* (Cambridge: Harvard University Press, 1995).

Posel, Deborah, "The Apartheid Project, 1948–1970," in *The Cambridge History of South Africa*, vol. 2, *1855–1994*, edited by Robert Ross, Anne Kelk Mager, and Bill Nasson (Cambridge: Cambridge University Press, 2012), 319–68.

Posel, Deborah, *The Making of Apartheid, 1948–1961: Conflict and Compromise* (Oxford: Clarendon, 1992).

Poulantzas, Nicos, *State, Power, Socialism*, translated by Patrick Camiller (New York: Verso, 1978).

Powell, D. M., M. O'Donovan, and J. De Visser, *Civic Protests Barometer, 2007–2014* (Cape Town: Multi-Level Government Initiative, 2014).

Ramutsindela, Maano, "'Second Time Around': Squatter Removals in a Democratic South Africa," *GeoJournal* 57 (2002): 53–60.

Ranslem, Duncan, "'Temporary' Relocation: Spaces of Contradiction in South African Law," *International Journal of Law in the Built Environment* 7, no. 1 (2015): 55–71.

Rassool, Ciraj, "Memory and the Politics of History in the District Six Museum," in *Desire Lines: Space, Memory and Identity in the Post-apartheid City*, edited by Noëleen Murray, Nick Shepherd, and Martin Hall (London: Routledge, 2007), 113–27.

Ren, Xuefei, *Governing the Urban in China and India: Land Grabs, Slum Clearance, and the War on Air Pollution* (Princeton: Princeton University Press, 2020).

Riley, Dylan, *The Civic Foundations of Fascism in Europe: Italy, Spain, and Romania, 1870–1945* (Baltimore: Johns Hopkins University Press, 2010).

Roberts, William Clare, "What Was Primitive Accumulation? Reconstructing the Origin of a Critical Concept," *European Journal of Political Theory* 19, no. 4 (2020): 532–52.

Robins, Steven L., "Land Struggles and the Politics and Ethics of Representing 'Bushman' History and Identity," *Kronos: Journal of Cape History* 26 (2000): 56–75.

Robins, Steven L., "NGOs, 'Bushmen' and Double Vision: The ≠khomani San Land Claim and the Cultural Politics of 'Community' and 'Development' in the Kalahari," *Journal of Southern African Studies* 27, no. 4 (2001): 833–53.

Robins, Steven L., *From Revolution to Rights in South Africa: Social Movements, NGOs & Popular Politics after Apartheid* (Scottsville: University of KwaZulu-Natal Press, 2008).

Robins, Steven L., "Poo Wars as Matter out of Place: 'Toilets for Africa' in Cape Town," *Anthropology Today* 30, no. 1 (2014): 1–3.

Robinson, Jennifer, *The Power of Apartheid: State, Power, and Space in South African Cities* (Oxford: Butterworth-Heinemann, 1996).

Roseberry, William, "Hegemony and the Language of Contention," in *Everyday Forms of State Formation: Revolution and Negotiation of Rule in Modern Mexico*, edited by Gilbert M. Joseph and Daniel Nugent (Durham: Duke University Press, 1994), 355–66.

Roy, Ananya, *City Requiem, Calcutta: Gender and the Politics of Poverty* (Minneapolis: University of Minnesota Press, 2002).

Roy, Ananya, "Urban Informality: Toward an Epistemology of Planning," *Journal of the American Planning Association* 71, no. 2 (2005): 147–58.

Roy, Ananya and Nezar AlSayyad (eds.), *Urban Informality: Transnational Perspectives from the Middle East, Latin America, and South Asia* (Lanham, MD: Lexington 2004).

Roy, Ananya and Aihwa Ong (eds.), *Worlding Cities: Asian Experiments and the Art of Being Global* (Malden: Wiley-Blackwell, 2011).

Royston, Lauren, "South Africa: The Struggle for Access to the City in the Witwatersrand Region," in *Evictions and the Right to Housing: Experience from Canada, Chile, the Dominican Republic, South Africa, and South Korea*, edited by Antonio Azuela, Emilio

Duhau, and Enrique Ortiz (Ottawa: International Development Research Centre, 1998), 145–98.

Rubin, Margot, "Perceptions of Corruption in the South African Housing Allocation and Delivery Programme: What It May Mean for Accessing the State," *Journal of Asian and African Studies* 46, no. 5 (2011): 479–90.

Rust, Kecia and Sue Rubenstein (eds.), *A Mandate to Build: Developing Consensus around a National Housing Policy in South Africa* (Johannesburg: Ravan, 1996).

Safa, Helen, "The Poor Are Like Everyone Else, Oscar," *Psychology Today* 4, no. 4 (1970): 26–32.

Saff, Grant, "The Changing Face of the South African City: From Urban Apartheid to the Deracialization of Space," *International Journal of Urban and Regional Research* 18, no. 3 (1994): 371–91.

Sales, William, "Making South Africa Ungovernable: ANC Strategy for the '80s," *Black Scholar* 15, no. 6 (1984): 2–14.

Samara, Tony Roshan, *Cape Town after Apartheid: Crime and Governance in the Divided City* (Minneapolis: University of Minnesota Press, 2011).

Sampson, Anthony, *Mandela: The Authorized Biography* (New York: Knopf Doubleday, 1999).

Samson, Melanie, "The Social Uses of the Law at a Soweto Garbage Dump: Reclaiming the Law and the State in the Informal Economy," *Current Sociology* 65, no. 2 (2017): 222–34.

Sandbrook, Richard, "Polanyi and Post-neoliberalism in the Global South: Dilemmas of Re- embedding the Economy," *New Political Economy* 16, no. 4 (2011): 415–43.

Sartre, Jean-Paul, *Critique of Dialectical Reason*, vol. 1, translated by Alan Sheridan- Smith (New York: Verso, 2004).

Satgar, Vishwas, "Neoliberalized South Africa," *Labour, Capital and Society* 41, no. 2 (2008): 39–69.

Saul, John S. and Patrick Bond, *South Africa—the Present as History: From Mrs Ples to Mandela and Marikana* (Suffolk: James Currey, 2014).

Schausteck de Almeida, Bárbara, Chris Bolsmann, Wanderley Marchi Júnior, and Juliano de Souza, "Rationales, Rhetoric and Realities: FIFA's World Cup in South Africa 2010 and Brazil 2014," *International Review for the Sociology of Sport* 50, no. 3 (2015): 265–82.

Schmitt, Carl, *The Concept of the Political*, translated by George Schwab (Chicago: University of Chicago Press, 1996).

Schorske, Carl E., *Fin-de-Siècle Vienna: Politics and Culture* (New York: Vintage, 1981).

Scott, James C., *Seeing Like a State: How Certain Schemes to Improve the Human Condition Have Failed* (New Haven: Yale University Press, 1998).

Seekings, Jeremy, "The Development of Strategic Thought in South Africa's Civic Movements, 1977–90," in *From Comrades to Citizens: The South African Civics Movement and the Transition to Democracy*, edited by Glenn Adler and Jonny Steinberg (New York: St. Martin's, 2000), 52–85.

Seekings, Jeremy, *The UDF: A History of the United Democratic Front in South Africa, 1983–1991* (Athens: Ohio University Press, 2000).

Seekings, Jeremy and Nicoli Nattrass, *Class, Race, and Inequality in South Africa* (Durban: University of KwaZulu-Natal Press, 2006).

Selmeczi, Anna, "'From Shack to the Constitutional Court': The Litigious Disruption of Governing Global Cities," *Utrecht Law Review* 7, no. 2 (2011): 60–76.

Sennett, Richard, *Flesh and Stone: The Body and the City in Western Civilization* (New York: Norton, 1994).

Shaw, Clifford R. and Henry D. McKay, *Juvenile Delinquency and Urban Areas* (Chicago: University of Chicago Press, 1969 [1942]).

Sihlongonyane, Mfaniseni Fana, "Land Occupations in South Africa," in *Reclaiming the Land: The Resurgence of Rural Movements in Africa, Asia and Latin America*, edited by Sam Moyo and Paris Yeros (London: Zed, 2005), 142–64.

Simone, AbdouMaliq, *City Life from Jakarta to Dakar: Movements at the Crossroads* (London: Routledge, 2009).

Simone, AbdouMaliq, *For the City Yet to Come: Changing African Life in Four Cities* (Durham: Duke University Press, 2004).

Simone, AbdouMaliq and Abdelghani Abouhani (eds.), *Urban Africa: Changing Contours of Survival in the City* (London: Zed, 2005).

Sithole, Tendayi, *Steve Biko: Decolonial Meditations of Black Consciousness* (Lanham, MD: Lexington, 2016).

Skocpol, Theda, "Bringing the State Back In: Strategies of Analysis in Current Research," in *Bringing the State Back In*, edited by Peter B. Evans, Dietrich Rueschemeyer, and Theda Skocpol (Cambridge: Cambridge University Press, 1985), 3–37.

Slater, Tom, "The Eviction of Critical Perspectives from Gentrification Research," *International Journal of Urban and Regional Research* 30, no. 4 (2006): 737–57.

Slater, Tom, "Planetary Rent Gaps," *Antipode* 49, no. S1 (2017): 114–37.

Smith, David M. (ed.), *The Apartheid City and Beyond* (London: Routledge, 1992).

Smith, Neil, "New Globalism, New Urbanism: Gentrification as Global Urban Strategy," *Antipode* 34, no. 3 (2002): 427–50.

Smith, Neil, *The New Urban Frontier: Gentrification and the Revanchist City* (London: Routledge, 1996).

Soss, Joe, Richard C. Fording, and Sanford F. Schram, *Disciplining the Poor: Neoliberal Paternalism and the Persistent Power of Race* (Chicago: University of Chicago Press, 2011).

Sotiris, Panagiotis, "The Modern Prince as Laboratory of Political Intellectuality," *International Gramsci Journal* 3, no. 2 (2019): 2–38.

Southall, Roger, *Liberation Movements in Power: Party and State in Southern Africa* (Scottsville: University of KwaZulu-Natal Press, 2013).

Staeheli, Lynn A. (ed.), "Cities and Citizenship," special issue of *Urban Geography* 24, no. 2 (2003).

Stedman Jones, Gareth, *Outcast London: A Study in the Relationship between Classes in Victorian Society* (New York: Pantheon, 1984).

Strauss, Margot and Sandra Liebenberg, "Contested Spaces: Housing Rights and Evictions Law in Post-apartheid South Africa," *Planning Theory* 13, no. 4 (2014): 428–48.

Sunstein, Cass R., "Social and Economic Rights? Lessons from South Africa," Public Law Working Paper no. 12, Olin Working Paper no. 124, University of Chicago, 2001.

Suttles, Gerald D., *The Social Order of the Slum: Ethnicity and Territory in the Inner City* (Chicago: University of Chicago Press, 1968).

Swilling, Mark, "The United Democratic Front and Township Revolt," in *Popular Struggles in South Africa Today*, edited by William Cobbett and Robin Cohen (Trenton: Africa World Press, 1988), 90–113.

Swilling, Mark, Richard Humphries, and Khehla Shubane (eds.), *Apartheid City in Transition* (Oxford: Oxford University Press, 1992).

Symphony Way Pavement Dwellers, *No Land! No House! No Vote!* (Oxford: Pambazuka, 2011).

Taylor, Keeanga-Yahmatta, *Race for Profit: How Banks and the Real Estate Industry Undermined Black Homeownership* (Chapel Hill: University of North Carolina Press, 2019).

Taylor, Rupert, "Between Apartheid and Democracy: The South African 'Election' of 1989," *Round Table* 79, no. 314 (1990): 56–67.

Terreblanche, Sampie, *A History of Inequality in South Africa, 1652–2002* (Scottsville: University of KwaZulu-Natal Press, 2003).

Thieme, Tatiana Adeline, "Navigating and Negotiating Ethnographies of Urban Hustle in Nairobi Slums," *City* 21, no. 2 (2017): 219–31.

Thieme, Tatiana Adeline, "The Hustle Economy: Informality, Uncertainty and the Geographies of Getting By," *Progress in Human Geography* 42, no. 4 (2018): 529–48.

Thomas, Peter D., "Gramsci and the Political: From the State as 'Metaphysical Event' to Hegemony as 'Philosophical Fact,'" *Radical Philosophy* 153 (2009): 27–36.

Thomas, Peter D., *The Gramscian Moment: Philosophy, Hegemony and Marxism* (Chicago: Haymarket, 2009).

Thomas, William I. and Florian Znaniecki, *The Polish Peasant in Europe and America: A Classic in Immigration History* (Urbana: University of Illinois Press, 1984 [1920]).

Thorn, Jessica and Sophie Oldfield, "A Politics of Land Occupation: State Practice and Everyday Mobilization in Zille Raine Heights, Cape Town," *Journal of Asian and African Studies* 46, no. 5 (2011): 518–30.

Tilly, Charles, "Does Modernization Breed Revolution?," *Comparative Politics* 5, no. 3 (1973): 425–47.

Tilly, Charles, "Revolution and Collective Violence," in *Handbook of Political Science*, vol. 3, *Macropolitical Theory*, edited by Fred I. Greenstein and Nelson W. Polsby (Boston: Addison-Wesley, 1975), 483–555.

Tissington, Kate, *A Resource Guide to Housing in South Africa, 1994–2010: Legislation, Policy, Programmes and Practice* (Johannesburg: Socio-Economic Rights Institute, 2011).

Tissington, Kate, Naadira Munshi, Gladys Mirugi-Mukundi, and Ebenezer Durojaye. *"Jumping the Queue," Waiting Lists and Other Myths: Perceptions and Practice around Housing Demand and Allocation in South Africa* (Johannesburg: Socio-Economic Rights Institute, 2013).

Todes, Alison, "Urban Growth and Strategic Spatial Planning in Johannesburg, South Africa," *Cities* 29, no. 3 (2012): 158–65.

Tomlinson, Mary, "South Africa's Housing Conundrum," *@Liberty: The Policy Bulletin of the South African Institute of Race Relations* 4, no. 20 (2015): 1–14.

Trotter, Henry, "Trauma and Memory: The Impact of Apartheid-Era Forced Removals on Coloured Identity in Cape Town," in *Burdened by Race: Coloured Identities in Southern Africa*, edited by Mohamed Adhikari (Cape Town: University of Cape Town Press, 2009), 49–78.

Turok, Ivan, "Persistent Polarisation Post-apartheid? Progress towards Urban Integration in Cape Town," *Urban Studies* 38, no. 13 (2001): 2349–77.

Turok, Ivan, "Urban Planning in the Transition from Apartheid, Part 1: The Legacy of Social Control," *Town Planning Review* 65, no. 3 (1994): 243–58.

Turok, Ivan, "Urban Planning in the Transition from Apartheid, Part 2: Towards Reconstruction," *Town Planning Review* 65, no. 4 (1994): 355–74.

UN-Habitat, *The Challenge of Slums: Global Report on Human Settlements 2003* (Nairobi: UN- Habitat, 2003).

UN-Habitat, *The State of the World's Cities Report 2006/2007: 30 Years of Shaping the Habitat Agenda* (Nairobi: United Nations Human Settlements Programme, 2006).

Valença, Márcio Moraes and Mariana Fialho Bonates, "The Trajectory of Social Housing Policy in Brazil: From the National Housing Bank to the Ministry of Cities," *Habitat International* 34, no. 2 (2010): 165–73.

van der Spuy, K. A. E., "Mitchells Plain / New Town: Past, Present, Future—a Summary," *Isilili sam sise Afrika* 2, no. 1 (1978): 58–66.

van Kessel, Ineke, *"Beyond Our Wildest Dreams": The United Democratic Front and the Transformation of South Africa* (Charlottesville: University of Virginia Press, 2000).

van Rooyen, Jacobus and Charlotte Lemanski, "Urban Segregation in South Africa: The Evolution of Exclusion in the Cape," in *Handbook of Urban Segregation*, edited by Sako Musterd (Cheltenham, UK: Elgar, 2020), 19–35.

Visser, Gustav and Nico Kotze, "The State and New-Build Gentrification in Central Cape Town, South Africa," *Urban Studies* 45, no. 12 (2008): 2565–93.

von Holdt, Karl, "South Africa: The Transition to Violent Democracy," *Review of African Political Economy* 40, no. 138 (2013): 598–604.

von Schnitzler, Antina, "Citizenship Prepaid: Water, Calculability, and Techno-politics in South Africa," *Journal of Southern African Studies* 34, no. 4 (2008): 899–917.

von Schnitzler, Antina, *Democracy's Infrastructure: Techno-politics and Protest after Apartheid* (Princeton: Princeton University Press, 2017).

Wacquant, Loïc, *Punishing the Poor: The Neoliberal Government of Social Insecurity* (Durham: Duke University Press, 2009).

Wacquant, Loïc, "Relocating Gentrification: The Working Class, Science and the State in Recent Urban Research," *International Journal of Urban and Regional Research* 32, no. 1 (2008): 198–205.

Wacquant, Loïc, *Urban Outcasts: A Comparative Sociology of Advanced Marginality* (Cambridge: Polity Press, 2008).

Walker, Cheryl, "Piety in the Sky? Gender Policy and Land Reform in South Africa," *Journal of Agrarian Change* 3, nos. 1–2 (2003): 113–48.

Walsh, Shannon, "The Philosopher and His Poor: The Black as Object of Political Desire in South Africa," *Politikon* 42, no. 1 (2015): 123–27.

Walsh, Shannon, "'Uncomfortable Collaborations': Contesting Constructions of the 'Poor' in South Africa," *Review of African Political Economy* 35, no. 116 (2008): 255–70.

Walsh, Shannon, "'We Won't Move': The Suburbs Take Back the Center in Urban Johannesburg," *City* 17, no. 3 (2013): 400–408.

Watts, Michael, "Baudelaire over Berea, Simmel over Sandton?," *Public Culture* 17, no. 1 (2005): 181–92.

Weber, Max, *Economy and Society: A New Translation*, translated by Keith Tribe (Cambridge: Harvard University Press, 2019).

Weber, Max, *Economy and Society: An Outline of Interpretive Sociology* (2 vols.), edited by Guenther Roth and Claus Wittich (Berkeley: University of California Press, 1978).

Weber, Rachel, "Extracting Value from the City: Neoliberalism and Urban Redevelopment," *Antipode* 34, no. 3 (2002): 519–40.

Weinstein, Liza, *The Durable Slum: Dharavi and the Right to Stay Put in Globalizing Mumbai* (Minneapolis: University of Minnesota Press, 2014).

Weinstein, Liza, "Evictions: Reconceptualizing Housing Insecurity from the Global South," *City and Community* 20, no. 1 (2021): 13–23.

Wesson, Murray, "*Grootboom* and Beyond: Reassessing the Socio-economic Jurisprudence of the South African Constitutional Court," *South African Journal on Human Rights* 20, no. 2 (2004): 284–308.

Western, John, "A Divided City: Cape Town," *Political Geography* 21, no. 5 (2002): 711–16.

Western, John, *Outcast Cape Town*, 2nd ed. (Berkeley: University of California Press, 1996).

Wieder, Alan, "Speaking to the Present in South Africa: The Ideas, Writings, and Actions of Ruth First and Joe Slovo" (lecture, Institute for Humanities in Africa, University of Cape Town, Cape Town, South Africa, 17 July 2013).

Wolpe, Harold, *Race, Class, and the Apartheid State* (Trenton: Africa World Press, 1988).

Zhang, Li, *Strangers in the City: Reconfigurations of Space, Power, and Social Networks within China's Floating Population* (Stanford: Stanford University Press, 2002).

Zirin, Dave, *Brazil's Dance with the Devil: The World Cup, the Olympics, and the Fight for Democracy* (Chicago: Haymarket, 2016).

Zoomers, Annelies, "Globalisation and the Foreignisation of Space: Seven Processes Driving the Current Global Land Grab," *Journal of Peasant Studies* 37, no. 2 (2010): 429–47.

Zuern, Elke, *The Politics of Necessity: Community Organizing and Democracy in South Africa* (Madison: University of Wisconsin Press, 2011).

Index